GOTHIC POLITICS
IN THE DEEP SOUTH

By Robert Sherrill
GOTHIC POLITICS IN THE DEEP SOUTH
THE ACCIDENTAL PRESIDENT

Robert Sherrill

GOTHIC POLITICS IN THE DEEP SOUTH

Stars of the New Confederacy

Grossman Publishers
New York
1968

Acknowledgments

By rights, at least a co-authorship should be assigned to Mary Sherrill, who did much of the research and most of the editing, and supplied the kind of critical backdrop essential for focus. But Southern women, after all, are accustomed to being cheated of credit. Several lengthy sections of this book appeared first in *The Nation* magazine; Carey McWilliams assigned them and Robert Hatch polished them, just as they have done for most of my work in the past four years. Some other, briefer parts appeared first in *The New York Times Magazine,* where I benefited from the editing of Harvey Shapiro and Gerald Walker and the other robust and amiable field hands in that office. In writing any sort of political history of a whole region covering nearly two decades, one has to rely on, lean on, and borrow from many great reporters. I certainly did, and I name some of them here with the most grateful deference: Martin Waldron, Pat Watters, Frank Trippett, Charlie Pou, Claude Sitton, Allen Morris, John Popham. Research funds were furnished by The Rabinowitz Foundation.

Contents

For T. V. Smith and Peter

GOTHIC POLITICS
IN THE DEEP SOUTH

The Unbroken Mold

During one of the 1960 civil rights filibusters, Senator Russell Long of Louisiana, with the assistance of Senator John McClellan of Arkansas, was holding the floor in an almost empty chamber by reading from the Bible. Prodding the absent northern senators for rebuking the South when racial conditions in the North were also bad, Long chose as his text that portion of the Sermon on the Mount in which the multitude was counseled, "Judge not that ye be not judged." At that point the filibuster deteriorated, as filibusters commonly do, into tasteless trivialities.

> Long: ". . . 'but considered not the beam that is in thine own eye?'
>
> "Mr. President, some folks may not be Bible readers and may not know what a mote is. A mote is a teeny, teeny speck of dust. 'Teeny' means it is almost impossible to see with the naked eye. If a person can see it at all, he is lucky.
>
> "On the other hand, the beam, the other Biblical term referred to, is a fairly good-sized piece of wood, I suppose about the size of a splinter. Jesus said to the people, in his Sermon on the Mount: 'And why beholdest thou the mote'—this little speck of dust—'that is in thy brother's eye, but considerest not the beam that is in thine own eye? Or how wilt thou say to thy brother—' "
>
> McClellan: "Mr. President, I think it quite unfortunate that the senators from the state of New York are not in the chamber to hear this able discussion. Does not the Senator agree with me? . . . Even when the Senator quotes from the Bible, they do not come to listen."
>
> Long: "Not even to the word of Jesus." (Laughter)

The cynicism and the laughter are still characteristics of the Deep South's politicians, even though in the intervening years they have, on paper, lost the civil rights fight. Of course it may be (and there is already much evidence in that direction) that the Deep South's defeats in the courts and in Congress may prove no more permanent—in altering its attitude toward race, for example—than were its defeats on the battlefields a century ago, defeats which left southerners broken and dispirited, but still slaveowners in every practical sense. Even so, its manner of conducting its latest resistance has left the region thoroughly discredited. In social matters, in humanistic affairs of the nation, its motives are properly suspect and its word is generally viewed as worthless; and this is some loss. The end might have been otherwise if the people of the region had been willing for their leaders to take a less primitive route to escape integration.

"These people," said William Faulkner, "would fight another civil war, knowing they would lose." But there are many ways to fight. No one, of course, can say today that a reasonable, flexible leadership would have led the region around the pitfalls (as the segregationists judge them) of 1964 and 1965; all we do know is that the conduct of the South's leaders brought on those seemingly total legislative defeats. To a great extent, of course, the nation was stirred to make a final assault on the South because of the barbarisms that the politicians did little to prevent and which many non-Southerners will never be persuaded were not actually choreographed by the politicians. What *was* the relationship of Governor Orval Faubus to the riots in Little Rock and of Governor Allan Shivers to the school riots in Mansfield, Texas; of Governor John Patterson to the brutalities committed against the Freedom Riders in Alabama; of Governor George Wallace to the neo-Nazi movement of Alabama; of Governors Ross Barnett and Paul Johnson to the frenzy of Ole Miss and to the triple murder in Philadelphia, Mississippi; of Governor Farris Bryant to the uncontrolled Klansmanship in St. Augustine, Florida? Not even the most elastic conspiratorial theory of history could stretch this narrow band around such enormous events; in this sense only, they are disappointing as villains.

But equally responsible for the second defeat of the South was the steady droning of stupidities—economic as well as racial—that came out of the statehouses, the governors' mansions, and the rebel caucuses in Washington; blundering, illogical, antiquated advice that left an entire region dazed and vulnerable as a nation's coaxing turned to bitterly angry demands for change. The "mote" that was in the South's eye blinded it to the defects of many of its leaders; occupied with racism, that "teeny, teeny speck of dust," it did not observe the residual betrayal of its politicians' devastating incompetence and cheap trickery.

This book is a look into the careers of some of these politicians, marking the major episodes that led to the Deep South's latest embarrassment. In a sense it is a tribute to this region, the noblest slice of America, in that it not only survived but materially prospered despite the men it elected. Very likely this can be attributed to the South's noted sense of humor, and we suspect that it will not be too many generations—ten or twelve, perhaps— before southerners, blacks and whites together, will be able to look back to this post-World War II period with a mote-less eye and, nicely assigning its cruelty to forgetfulness, come to see the ribald humor in the lives of these political generals who led them into a trap in what might be called the Second Battle of Pea Ridge.

At the same time, I intend this book as a tribute to the politicians, too, men who could have been personally mean as well as wrong, but generally were not. History will not forgive them for encouraging the bullies and the cheap aristocrats to set the tone of an entire region for another generation, but as individuals these politicians were often easy-going, even kindhearted, fellows. I think of George Wallace and Lester Maddox, who dreaded to sign the death certificates of condemned murderers (including black murderers); and Ross Barnett, a peat-bog mentality, who was confounded when a prison trusty ran away while on an errand for the governor ("If you can't trust a trusty, who can you trust?"); and blustering Marvin Griffin, whose willingness to sacrifice himself to defend a way of life had an appealingly human limitation ("Bein' in jail kind of crimps a governor's style").

Perhaps, after all, it is best to proceed on the assumption that their encyclopedic mistakes can produce redirection without moralisms, since the best as well as the worst my subjects can be charged with is that they were in politics, something that can be changed in shape but never in character. Of this certainty nothing more appropriate has ever been said than was said on the floor of the Alabama state senate one day as I sat enthralled—in much the same degree that the students at the Lyceum must have been enthralled by *their* philosophers—to hear some red-faced, sweating lawmaker from the Black Belt observe with incontrovertible logic: "Some folks talk about takin' politics outta politics. I like to know how you goin' to take politics outta somethin' where politics is so deeply imbedded."

I have not tried to "take politics outta politics"; I have, in fact, tried to put politics back into Deep South politics, which for most of the nation has been for too long boiled and rendered down to the sludge of racism. Southern politics is far more interesting and complex than that, and if one wants to really understand and appreciate the racist portion, he must also take time to discover that racism is what it is in the Deep South because there are other determinants of government, such as who pays for the campaigns and who pays the taxes, and who does not.

I have gone into some details in the government careers of my men because only details can show that the phenomenon of George Wallace, for example, is actually an accumulation and repetition of tricks and cranks that are rather common to other notable Dixie freebooters. Herman Talmadge, Marvin Griffin, Ross Barnett, James Eastland, George Smathers, Strom Thurmond, Orval Faubus, Leander Perez—each learned from the other. They are rare fellows, but the mold has not been broken.

2

Leander Perez: The Swamp's Gift to Dixie

Perez: . . . I have devoted a good deal of time to this question of communist infiltration. I remember when the Supreme Court handed down that decision in March 1954, I could smell it. . . . Then I came up here and with certain other help we dug into the question of the communist background of the authorities cited by the Court, especially Gunnar Myrdal's book, and so on.

I have done a great deal of work on that and I am not going to be fooled. I know the result of this thing. I know how it will fit in with the Black Belt conspiracy. . . .

Senator Hart: It just strikes me as absolutely nuts to suggest that—

Perez: Absolutely what?

Senator Hart: Nuts.

Perez: N-u-t-s?

Senator Hart: Nuts. . . .

Perez: Yes, sir.

> *Exchange at the Senate Judiciary Committee's hearing on the Voting Rights Bill, 1965*

Believe it or not, I'm a reformer at heart.

> *Leander Perez, 1949*

5

Grassroots totalitarianism that is balanced with insolent precision on the will of one man, or one man and his kin, is rather common in the rural South, but nowhere is it found more melodramatically exercised than in Plaquemines Parish, that strange demi-swamp spreading down more than a hundred miles from New Orleans to the mouth of the Mississippi River, a ragged effluvial tit, where the past is marked not by the fluttering of Old South fans and lace but by the hoofprint of the dinosaur. This is the region which is sometimes known, though it is hard to see why, as "the happy land."

Forty percent of the parish is under water; until recent decades one of the major industries was muskrat trapping, and it still goes on. It used to be that many homes (and it is still true of some) could only be reached by boat; and even now, when bands of concrete give the mocking illusion that Plaquemines is tied to the outside world and united within, isolation is still the basic characteristic of life in this parish.

But whereas Plaquemines used to be isolated and needy, today it is isolated and rich, thanks to the world's second largest sulphur cone of its kind and to the lushest oil deposits in Louisiana.

Growing richer right along with the parish—and, in fact, often accused of winding up with the money that was first the parish's and should have been the state's—is the cold-eyed dandy Leander Henry Perez: "Little" Perez, as he was known in college, when he was a contemporary and chum of Louisiana Senator Allen Ellender; Judge Perez, as he has been known for the past forty-seven years to the world at large, although he hasn't been a judge for forty-three years; and "Mr. Leelee" as he is known with both fear and intimacy by his water-logged neighbors.

Proud, arrogant, boastful, a crafty publicist of his often-imagined deeds of anarchy, Judge Perez looks the part of the backwater tyrant that he is. He has a blockish body, a boomish voice, a sweeping pompadour, a cast-iron mouth, a ready but humorless laugh, a limitless capacity to harangue, a bottomless fund of spite and grudge,* and a view of the world that one shocked congressman, Emanuel Celler, told him is "beyond the bounds of reason." This is a judgment many have had of Perez' actions over the years, although until recently not many would, in public, call him

---

* Many are the events that could be cited to illustrate this aspect of Perez' character, but none makes it clearer than the time he had two men put in jail without bond for tearing his picture off a ferryboat's wall; it took the signatures of four Supreme Court judges to free them.

more than "too wild," since power and money (Perez' wealth has been estimated as high as $100 million by some Louisiana politicians) are generally accepted as their own certification of sanity.

To consider Perez as a man possessed by demons is, however, to abuse him; actually his fault is in being a living caricature of Deep South officialdom, the prototype of which is not insane but merely, in turn, a caricature of sanity. Like the Mississippi River gathering together all the upstream torrents into a muddy flood, Perez has gathered into one spirit all the money lust, moon-spawned hatred for the black man and Jew and foreigner, and painful paranoiac reaction to federalism, that have marked the Deep South for many years; he has gathered them from many sources, and then slopped them back upon the land.

He is only one of many men who brought the Dixiecrat movement into being, but he became its unchallenged paterfamilias and remained in love with that narrow-gauge political track long after the farce of the Thurmond & Wright States' Rights ticket had left the road, long after the majority of southern conservatives wanted to wash that discredited term out of their banner—not because they no longer believed in it but because it *was* discredited.

It is believed that Perez was the die-hard who persuaded Senator Harry Byrd to speak for the "massive resistance" idea, and it is known that Perez was behind countless of the blood-lusting White Citizens Council meetings across the South. None stands ahead of Perez in the ventures of excess. Moreover, Perez, more than any of the Dixiecrat leaders, was unabashed to admit that the real reason he was upset with the federal government had relatively little to do with lusty pickaninnies but a great deal to do with money, with oil, with fortunes in oil lying out there in the tidelands. In Perez more than in any other leader of the South in this generation or the last, we find the interdependency of racism and profiteering brought to such a blaring perfection that it is sometimes embarrassing to those who, in principle, heartily agree with him.

When it comes to campaign politics, Perez keeps an eye on the dollar, which is to say on a probable winner, and principle must await those flaming between-campaign speeches. Perez can look back with some satisfaction to one such harangue he delivered to a 6,000-man gathering of Citizens Councilers, at which he suggested that before "these Congolese rape your daughters" the CCers should take action, "now!" The mob slept on that advice and decided it was good; the next day they went about beating Negroes in the streets, stoning automobiles and homes owned by Negroes, and in general doing what they could to prevent the raping of their daughters by Congolese.

But that sort of rally is something Perez usually conducts as an avocation. In campaign politics he sticks to business. When his fellow racist-rightwinger William Rainach was on the ballot for governor in 1959, he didn't get the votes Perez controlled; those went to dull Jimmy Davis, who was more likely to, and did, win. Nor did he switch his votes in the general election to that great states'-righter Kent Courtney, running in the States' Rights Party; Perez stayed with Democrat Davis. When upstate segregation leaders and the Louisiana Citizens Council threw their support to a weak candidate in 1963, Perez let his friends make that mistake by themselves; *he* went for ex-Governor Robert Kennon, a good man for the oil interests, and, when Kennon failed, Perez went with the best bet, McKeithen, whom he had previously denounced as "a Kennedy candidate." Perez is not altogether as uncontrolled as he sounds.

And even when he embarrasses his more timid philosophical peers, he serves them well; none better, in fact, for after Perez has done his work, the more plodding political bigots can pretend almost to a kind of humanity. Not long ago on the floor of Congress a California congressman said of Perez that "by comparison with him, Governor George Wallace of Alabama seems an angel of reason and moderation and ex-Governor Ross W. Barnett of Mississippi a towering intellect." Though that seems hardly possible, it is true. There is something about Perez, perhaps best described as the gargoyles of his mind, that is not unkin to the misshapen, magical, evil creatures of medieval mythology. One is constantly expecting him to resume the shape of a toad.

He is still revered as a rabble-rouser emeritus by deep ranks of last-ditchers throughout the South. But in Louisiana his influence, when it existed, was less symbolic, more practical and much, much shadier. In Plaquemines itself, where Perez still has the power of a potentate, he is representative of a phenomenon that is quite common in Dixie. There is nothing mystic about it. The owner of the fabric mill in a company town in Georgia or South Carolina, the oldest banker in a little town in north Florida or Mississippi who has carried so many notes that now he carries most of the citizens' loyalties, the biggest landowner with the largest number of sharecroppers in south Alabama—Perez is nothing that they are not, except much, much richer and more domineering and above the law.

But in addition to being an example of a hyper-massa, Perez has promoted the legend of himself as a statewide political power. He has done this by being a consistent hanger-on of important coattails and by outliving many who could correct his stories of self-aggrandizement.

Journalists usually credit Perez with saving the Huey Long dynasty from dying almost before it was well founded, but this is such an exaggerated conception of his role in Huey's salvation as to be almost funny. Perez is also sometimes called the "mastermind" of Earl Long's rise to power. If one believes that Earl came to power through the help of the clique which included Perez, oilman William Feazel (who reputedly kicked in $300,000 for that campaign and was well rewarded), Robert S. Maestri, for a previous decade mayor of New Orleans in a very crooked administration, and Dudley LeBlanc, best known to the nation as the promoter of Hadacol—if one can believe *that* spotty crew brought Earl Long to the governor's mansion, then it is, looking them over, easy to go on and say Perez was the "mastermind." The vote margins for Earl in Perez-controlled parishes were not even impressive; true, he received five times as many votes in Plaquemines and three times as many in St. Bernard as his nearest opponent, but that, considering what Perez had done for some other politicians in the past, was almost a repudiation; and it was hardly more than the margin of victory Earl received in many north Louisiana counties that had never heard of Perez. At no time, either in the primary or the runoff of 1948, did an opponent come closer than 2 to 1; it was Earl's victory alone.

Russell Long admits he received several thousand votes stolen for him by Perez in 1948, the year of Russell's first U.S. Senate election. But he would have won anyway.

In a few other important, successful Louisiana campaigns Perez' mark can be found, but not to the extent that he pretends. If the phony legends ever die, Perez' place in history will still be well established as Dixie's loudest racial hawk, screeching from the damp, impregnable thickets of Plaquemines.

Plaquemines, one of the richest, is also one of the modestly populated parishes, having only about 25,000 residents (about forty percent Negro or mulatto). Conceiving a direct relationship between, on the one hand, his power and wealth, and on the other, this scanty and scattered brood, Perez has done all he could to keep the population down. In neighboring St. Bernard Parish, where his rule used to be almost as absolute, the shadow of Perez casts no fears these days; industry moved in, bringing outsiders who were not willing to buttress the legend, and eventually St. Bernard became an independent member of the Perez empire, willing at times to go through the ritual without actually giving obedience. Perez learned from this. Thus when the president of National Lead Co. approached him to talk of locating a plant in Plaquemines, he expected the usual groveling reception given industrialists by southern politicians and was met instead with an arm-waving, shouted scat: "Sir, you are wasting your time! I don't want you down here! Now, with the Freeport Sulphur crowd, we've got to know them and like having them around, but we don't want any more!" That was said in the 1950's. In recent years he has become a little more hospitable to newcomers bringing cash.

When Governor Fielding Wright of Mississippi called together one of the preliminary pep rallies of the Dixiecrats in Jackson in 1948, those true white Jeffersonian Democrats passed a number of resolutions, one of the more important ones being a condemnation of the federal government's efforts "to confiscate the tidelands as manifesting a strong tendency towards the destruction of state rights"—not to mention the tremendous financial loss to some promoters. From the way the Dixiecrats interpreted this threat to the oil industry, some editorial writers got the impression that perhaps there was oil money behind the movement, an impression which subsequent events hardly disproved. Former Secretary of the Interior Harold L. Ickes, on hearing the Dixiecrat war whoops in 1948, paid no attention to the racial chatter and cut straight to the heart of their complaint: "It's not a matter of states' rights, but the issue of the rights of certain oil companies to take oil from the states because it's easier. Those who are backing bills to continue state ownership are raising the cry of 'Stop thief' in order to let the oil companies get away with murder."

The Dixiecrat movement got rolling one year after the U.S. Supreme Court, ruling in a California case, said that not only were the offshore lands federal but the natural resources in those lands were federal also. The government was also suing Texas and Louisiana over the rights to the oil in marginal seas. Great wealth was at issue. It has been estimated that the continental shelf contains more oil than the land area of the

United States and the Near East combined. Other estimates put the oil reserves along the shores of Louisiana and Texas alone at between four billion and ten billion barrels.

Like Texas, Louisiana claimed that her state land stretched into the Gulf three Spanish leagues (ten and a half miles), rather than three miles as the federal government contended. In fact, Louisiana claimed her land sometimes stretched twenty-seven miles into the Gulf. Feelings in the matter reached such a pitch that at various times some of the more imaginative officials of Texas and Louisiana suggested secession as the solution. The Submerged Lands Act of 1953—sponsored by Eisenhower as a payoff to his financial patron, Sid Richardson of Dallas, and other big oilmen who helped him get elected—laid out the boundaries of the states as they were at the time they joined the union, up to three Spanish leagues, and in 1960 the Supreme Court ruled that for Florida and Texas the states had jurisdiction ten and a half miles into the Gulf, but Alabama, Louisiana, and Mississippi had jurisdiction of three miles. While the matter was being fought in court, the states' possible share of the oil income was held in escrow. Since Louisiana is still fighting with the United States of America in court, the money is still there—now totalling about one billion dollars, a sum of sufficient size to make most important Louisiana politicians both highly diplomatic and highly aggressive in dealing with Washington.

Oil had entered Perez' political life twenty years before the Dixiecrat movement. Wanting to personally control the oil that he had found in Plaquemines in 1928, Perez knew that he first must win a cronyship with the governor. The next year, when the Louisiana legislature attempted to impeach and oust Huey Long from office, Perez had his chance.

His assistance in persuading a sufficient portion of the legislature on this occasion was no sensational feat, the Louisiana legislature being what it was, "the best legislature money can buy," according to Huey.* When *New Orleans Item* editor Clayton Fritchey on a later occasion said the legislature was made up of "trained seals and lackeys," he was threatened with a contempt citation, though the reason for the legislators' unhappiness became unclear when one state senator acknowledged, "I'd rather be a trained seal than an untrained polecat," this apparently being in many legislators' minds the only choice.

* Only eight years ago *Look* magazine reported that a quarter million dollars was scattered around the legislature on a right-to-work bill.

It is true that Perez was one of Huey's attorneys in the impeachment fight and that he helped arrange some of the "rewards" to loyal legislators, but that was the extent of Perez' role. He was not the most effective lawyer in the half dozen attending Huey, and Huey himself arranged for most of the rewards.

However, Perez has always given himself a central heroic position.

By his account, he sped to Baton Rouge when he heard that his Huey was in trouble, found him face down on a bed in the Heidelberg Hotel, weeping into a pillow. Immediately Perez (according to Perez) seized a lawbook and pieced together a winning stratagem: friendly legislators in the house of representatives, where the impeachment had to be voted, would delay things so much that only one charge would be voted on within the special session. Whatever was voted *after* the session expired could be argued down as being unconstitutional.

When the trial began in the senate, the one "legally-voted" accusation was voted down, and then fifteen senators announced that they would not vote conviction under any circumstances, because the other charges had been arrived at by the House after its legal expiration.

Perez claims he did it all. He says the delaying tactics in the house were his idea, and that the Round Robin was his idea.

Congressman Hale Boggs of Louisiana, whip of the U.S. House, says it is all "a lie, a myth." Of course, Boggs hates Perez, so he might be expected to play down Perez' part. But Louisiana Senator Allen Ellender does not hate Perez. He likes him. They are friends, and have been all their lives, ever since they were fraternity brothers (Pi Kappa Alpha). Ellender considers Perez a good lawyer and a worthy member of Huey's defense team. But that's all.

Ellender, too, was one of Huey's defense attorneys. More than that, he was speaker of the Louisiana house at that time. The delaying tactics, he said, were not planned by Perez at all but were, in fact, one of those fortunate accidents of history. As for the Round Robin plan, Ellender remembers that very well: "I put it together while Leander and some of the other attorneys were out to lunch. Then I took it to Huey and he changed a few words, and that's the way it was."

Perez had served the Kingfish sufficiently, however, to hold him in his debt, and within three years practically all of the oil in Plaquemines wound up in Perez' hands, through the skillful manipulation of old laws and new alliances. It happened like this:

Back in the late part of the nineteenth century, the state turned over to Plaquemines great swatches of land, thousands of acres, which the parish could lease and tax and thus draw an income with which to build levees. The U.S. Corps of Engineers does most of the flood fighting these days, but back then—in that region—inundation was the number one civic worry, and the locals would have gone broke meeting the problem without this help from the state.

With the finding of oil, the state discovered that it had given away the potential for a great deal of income. But too late. Perez says, with unattempted wryness, "I saw the potential."

Still, the oil was not in Perez' control. It was in control of the levee boards, which means that the governor controlled it, since he controlled the levee boards through appointments. But Huey was big about it and pushed through the legislature a law that gave the parish police jury the right to take over the assets and revenues of any levee board within the parish that was in debt. After that, it was simple, for Perez controlled the police juries. The levee boards went into debt, and the police juries took over their assets—meaning oil revenue.

Getting the oil money actually into his pocket took a little more maneuvering, but nothing to tax the ingenuity of such a man as Perez. First he set up a handful of corporations—some of them incorporated by relatives, some by people who worked for him—and then the police jury leased the oil lands to these corporations, which then hired Perez as their attorney at fees which drained off the profits as fast as the pumps could operate. One company, incorporated by three Perez kinfolk and a Perez employe, paid out one-third of its income to Perez in attorney fees for three years.

The finding of one of the world's largest sulphur cones in Plaquemines had the same profitable results for the Judge.

And why would the levee board have given this all away? Well, why not?—Perez was the board's legal counsel.

While A. J. Liebling has preserved for us Earl Long's snappy challenge, "Whatcha gonna do now, Leander? The Feds have got the atom bomb," we are not told what Perez responded, but it surely must have been something incorrigible and, preferably, vulgar. He would retreat before the A-bomb as he has always retreated before any strong opposition, but not before he had at least tried a bluff. This is another aspect of his career which makes him so much the perfect Dixiecrat: he is a great bluffer. A dozen years ago the U.S. Department of Justice, intimidated by Perez, would not respond to the complaints of citizens in Plaquemines Parish who were refused registration: These were *white* citizens. The Department of Justice would invariably reply that such complaints were a matter for the Louisiana Attorney General to take care of, and the Louisiana Attorney General would invariably reply that it was a local problem. Perez achieved this, as Dixie achieved its victories until recently, solely by bluff.

He has fought two declared wars, and lost both. The first one was in the 1920's and is in the record books as The Trappers War. Just as Perez was to be so effective in filling his pockets by serving in the dual capacity of advisor to the levee boards and attorney for the companies to which the levee boards turned over the rich oil deposits, so also in this case Perez was busy working both sides of the street—as attorney for the St. Bernard Trappers' Association and (so it was generally assumed at the time, and never contradicted) also attorney for the buyers who tried to outwit the trappers.

The Trappers' Association had exclusive trapping rights to 100,000 acres. On Perez' advice, and with Perez handling the transaction, the association sold these rights to somebody whose name the trappers never did learn. The mysterious buyer—many suspected it was Perez himself—immediately tripled the fees charged the trappers. Well, they weren't going to stand for that and they tried to get the sale rescinded; failing to get quick justice, they went for their guns, swarmed over the trapping area, posted sentries and dared the new owner to try to stop them. At this point Perez quit pretending to be the trappers' attorney and began revealing his self-interest; he imported a squadron of tough Texas trappers to go in and take over. Retaliating, the Plaquemines boys went for the throat; they set out to gun down Perez himself, but he found out about it and hustled himself and his family into a rowboat and fled across the Mississippi. Meanwhile, back in the swamp, the imported Texan and Plaquemines toughs met, muskets blazing, and when the owls had quit howling and the mist had cleared, one of Perez' trappers was face-down dead and five others were flopping around in the muck, wounded and wishing they had never crossed the Sabine. The Plaquemines warriors counted three bullet holes in their own ranks, but none too serious. Perez understood superior firepower, and soon thereafter he admitted he was whipped and sold the land back to the trappers.

His second declared war came in the early 1940's, during Governor Sam Jones' reform administration (what else could any administration be called, coming after Perez-supported Governor Richard W. Leche, who said, "When I took the oath as governor, I didn't take any vows of poverty," and proved it in such a way that his administration caved in under fifty indictments; he resigned as governor and later went to prison for mail fraud). Earl Long had fun, in his usual fashion, ridiculing Jones as a nonrube, which is supposed to be a fatal identification in Louisiana; he was, to Earl, "high hat Sam, the high society kid, the high-kickin', high and mighty snide Sam," but as a matter of fact Jones turned out to be, despite the failure of local politicians to help him carry out his efforts, a true reformer, and although he certainly does not deserve such a grandiose title as "The Liberator of Louisiana," conferred upon him by one historian, he did at least show his constituents something they were beginning to doubt: that looting need not be an automatic ingredient of state administration.

Jones set up a Crime Commission, which was supposed to put the political rascals out of business. Naturally, its first project was Perez. Before the commission was declared unconstitutional on a budgetary technicality, it had set out to prove (what everyone suspected) that Perez "diverted to his own private gain, through subterfuge (involving dummy corporations), all of the mineral wealth of the various public levee boards and the school boards of Plaquemines and St. Bernard parishes" and ". . . corrupted the office of district attorney by setting himself up as a political tycoon and by the use of fraudulent registrations and poll taxes, had built up a dynasty saturated with crime and corruption." The commission charged that in one recent election "5,361 votes were cast for certain constitutional amendments, with only 3 against. At this time not over 3,000 voters were existent in Plaquemines parish." He was charged with using his office to play favorites, and with failing to prosecute in murder cases, election frauds, and fish and game violations; he was also accused of paying salaries to officials who were no longer working.

But the commission did not get very far in its investigation, because Perez simply refused to hand over the dummy companies' books and, while waiting for his friends in Baton Rouge to kill the commission, tied it up with an astounding number of counter-lawsuits.

While that was going on, Perez and Governor Jones clashed over who was to become Plaquemines's sheriff, the old one having died. It was only an interim question, of course, because as soon as a new election was held a Perez-picked man would get the post; but in the meanwhile, Perez didn't want someone in that office who might take his work seriously—especially in view of the fact that the sheriff also held the office of tax collector. When the man Governor Jones named interim sheriff went by to pick up the tax books, Perez told him to get out.

Jones began warming up the state guard, and Perez (whom the New Orleans newspapers promptly dubbed General Pipsqueak) organized a weird, patchy outfit called the Plaquemines Parish Patrol. This was during World War II, and he pretended this was a home guard to protect Plaquemines's many miles of coastline from Japs and Germans, but after a while he dropped that pretense and admitted he was ready to repulse Governor Jones who "has been kidding himself into thinking he could conquer this province. If the governor or anyone else should send any band of men, state guards or gestapo, into Plaquemines Parish to attempt to take the sheriff's office by force, they would be the aggressors and would be held criminally responsible for the consequences."

However, despite this apparent warning to Jones that he could wind up in a Plaquemines jail, and despite the ramparts built around the Plaquemines courthouse, behind which stood a hundred citizens and a couple dozen sheriff's deputies armed with gas grenades, pistols and rifles— the governor nevertheless decided to risk it, and down the road into Perezland rolled 500 state guardsmen armed with machineguns, grenades, sideguns.

Quickly Perez convened a grand jury and filed charges against Governor Jones for conspiracy to incite a riot. Jones responded by declaring martial law in Plaquemines. Perez blocked the road in front of his plantation ("Promised Land") with an overturned truck; elsewhere there were roadblocks of oil piping and oyster shells soaked in gasoline which were to be set afire when the state guard approached.

It looked like the makings of a good encounter, but as the guard approached, Perez' army melted. Perez himself retreated to his navy, fled back across the river. When the state guard got to the courthouse, where the pitched battle had been promised, nobody was there to greet them but some seagulls perched on the ramparts, a couple of tobacco-stained deputies, and the Perez-sheriff-pretender. Perez had not been so panicky, however, as to forget to destroy all records that might have embarrassed him; all drawers and filing cabinets had been cleaned out, and their contents were never again seen.

Governor Jones did win the war, but his sheriff was removed by a court order and Perez had his own man in the office as of the next election. Then the crime commission was laid to rest, and everything returned to normal in Plaquemines.

It was a petty, almost a ribald, episode that was blown out of all proportion by a citizenry tired of the global war going on at that time and only too eager to turn their attention to a fuss of a size they could comprehend, and laugh about. There was nothing brave or nobly defiant about Perez' role in it; he was acting like a wardheel rogue, no more, and a governor of stature with the legislature and the people could have used the excuse to push Perez into the Gulf. Unfortunately, while Jones was admired for his honesty, that was the limit of his appeal.

In his personal religious war Perez has shown more stubbornness. Indeed he has, Catholics feel, laid his immortal soul on the line by opposing integration so violently that the late Archbishop Rummel excommunicated him in 1962 for "provoking the devoted people of this venerable archdiocese to disobedience and rebellion." In this state of gracelessness he remains today, proudly, likening himself to Joan of Arc and so convinced of his own superiority to the church fathers that he thinks Archbishop Rummel was only perpetrating a "monumental fraud and a bluff," because he had sold out to President Kennedy for a $3 million housing grant. For excommunicating him Perez feels "the archbishop has earned the punishment of hell."

If good Catholics elsewhere feel that Perez says such things daringly, despite fears of eternal damnation, they are probably forgetting that Perez is *of* Plaquemines, a land where the Creoles and Cajuns and Tockos blend witchcraft and a weedy, proud, tribal lawlessness with religious orthodoxy.* If Perez is like the majority of Plaquemines's old residents, the Pope is not nearly such a mystic influence in his life as is the memory of St. Huey. Trying to imitate the Kingfish, Perez has put together a

---

* As Etienne Barrois, who knows this land so well, wrote in *Commonweal*: "Magic and superstition are dying, they say, but many is the Cadillac and many the fine folks who seek out Tante Belle, Nanaan Titi and Uncle Cacoos for cures and for taboos to ward off hexes and curses. With the black candles, nail parings, and blessed water go the inevitable three Credos, three Paters, and the *trois* Aves."

pathetic formula of "benevolence," which has given him neither more power (that was already total) over his parishioners nor hardly an increase of affection from them. He claims that all of the people in his parish love him, except just a "little group we call soreheads," but the affection is not so widespread as he supposes. What, after all, is so great about a $50,000 college scholarship fund, from a man who has made millions of dollars in coercive deals with Texas, Shell, Humble, Tidewater, Gulf and California oil companies, plus Freeport Sulphur? It's true, he helped get some good highways built through the muck, but the oil companies needed those for their trucks more than did the peasants.

Balanced against that paternalism is a subjugation that has kept the residents of Plaquemines, and sometimes of St. Bernard, so afraid and secretly rebellious that when gas vapors accumulated and blew up Perez' motor yacht everyone, including Perez, just naturally assumed at first that it had been bombed by one of his numerous enemies. The sources of his unpopularity are not difficult to hunt out. He has sometimes been accused of using Louisiana's miscegenation law as a cleaver; some families in this parish, where the color line has often been lost in the bog, live in dread that the true state of their blood will be discovered and the parents separated. He is ruthless in all things. When a Catholic school in the parish set out to integrate, Perez used every weapon. He had Negro fathers fired if they even let it be known that they contemplated sending their children to the school; he pressured oil companies into influencing their employes not to participate; he held public rallies at which he predicted that if his white people became violent in their opposition to the integration of "the filthy little niggers," they could be sure that Plaquemines police would not interfere. Not surprisingly after that, the school was bombed and the school bus was sabotaged. The priests kept the school open, but the Negroes were afraid to come. All of this, said Perez retrospectively, "might be expected in the ordinary course of human events."

And he was correct in putting it that way, because this was the ordinary course of human events in Plaquemines. In 1960 Perez ordered library service stopped to Negroes, and barred from the parish library all books even mentioning the United Nations or Eleanor Roosevelt or FDR or Dean Acheson; any book "showing a liberal viewpoint," or that spoke favorably of the Negro race, or that was printed by Unesco. "Wipe that filth from the shelves," thundered Perez, and it was wiped. In World War

II, California Nisei brought into Plaquemines to work on the farms were greeted with a loud nay. Perez would not have it, for "No matter in what kennel you may buy the highest pedigreed dog, he's still a son of a bitch, and no matter where a yellow Jap is born, he's still a yellow s.o.b." Negroes, of course, are similarly identified: "There's only two kinds, bad ones are niggers and good ones are darkies."

His cataloging of bloodlines does not end there. Until recently schools were not just segregated black and white; there was also a segregation among the blacks as to depth of blackness. Schools for whites, schools for blacks, schools for mulattoes; that's the order, and that, Perez insists, is the way the nonwhites want it: "The mulattoes and the Negroes would not even sit in the same pews in church. There is a caste among them." He may be right, but when a new movie house showed two signs over the stairs leading to the gallery—"For Dark Colored" and "For Light Colored" —the mulattoes would not patronize the theater.

The uniformity of political thought in Plaquemines Parish would be unique if it were lawful, but of course it isn't. Perez likes to pretend that it is all a matter of persuasion and intelligent analysis, as between Eisenhower and Adlai ("Oh my God, anybody who heard Adlai Stevenson make that speech in the Mormon Tabernacle, great scott alive. I went all out against him, of course, and all of our people went along with us"). They went, in fact, 98 percent for Eisenhower in 1952, which was the most enthusiastic response of any county in the nation, about the same in 1956 (after, Perez boasts, he had put into Eisenhower's speech the statement on the tidelands), roughly the same for States' Rights in 1960, and "by a landslide" (a cliché which in Plaquemines means 99.9 percent) for Goldwater in 1964. And how does this uniformity happen? Are the votes bought or coerced? Not at all, says Perez, "We just tell our voters, wherever you see Dave Dubinsky and his liberal party go, wherever you see Walter Reuther go, go on the other side and you are safe." That's all. "We don't play belly politics in Plaquemines, we use reason."

But from earliest times in Perez' career there have been doubters. For one thing, they point to the fact that in local elections, Dubinsky and Reuther could hardly be considered a potent influence, and yet in recent years the offices of sheriff and clerk of the court and state representatives have gone via margins of 12 to 1. That, however, could be considered a reform margin.

There was the year when St. Bernard Parish split its vote 3,080 to 15 in a U.S. Senate race—a demonstration of fervent political consciousness, especially in light of the fact that there were only 2,500 registered voters in the parish. In Huey Long's day, the cooperation was more than that. Earl Long, who frequently feuded with his brother, testified before a Senate investigating committee that he was in the Roosevelt Hotel in New Orleans with Huey in 1932 on the day *after* the election, and that Huey was lying up in bed talking on the phone to "somebody from Plaquemines Parish" and deciding how many votes should be given to James O'Connor in a First Congressional District race with "Bathtub Joe" Fernandes. ("They agreed to let O'Connor have 250 votes," said Earl.) Up to that point O'Connor had won the race by 3,500 votes. But then the Plaquemines-St. Bernard votes came in, and he was loser by 1,500 votes. This sort of thing became known as a "plaquemines count."

It may be that the "somebody from Plaquemines Parish" plotting with Huey on this occasion was not Perez, but on the other hand nobody in Plaquemines but Perez has ever been known to make an important political decision in the last half century. As he said on another occasion, after ordering his registrars to keep their books closed to FBI agents, "It was my idea. *Who the hell else has any ideas in Plaquemines?*" There has been a little trouble now and then. Frank Giordano, Perez' nephew and also Plaquemines registrar of voters, was indicted by a federal grand jury for vote fraud but the case was *nol-prossed*.

Five Plaquemines election commissioners were convicted of vote fraud but given suspended sentences, which was consideration they heartily deserved, said Perez, because there was nothing criminal about what they did. "Some of our people," Perez said, "don't have any way of getting to the polls, so they used to ask their friends to cast their votes for them. That's all that happened."

Well, it wasn't quite all that happened. There were some other irregularities, though not likely traceable to Perez, who has almost no sense of humor. From time to time the registration rolls carried the names of Jack Dempsey, Charlie Chaplin, Clara Bow, Zasu Pitts, Babe Ruth, and Charlie McCarthy, none of whom have been known to live in Plaquemines for any length of time. Sometimes, as an extra dash of humor, the "voters" in some precincts were all voted alphabetically. But Perez hotly denies that this sort of thing should be called, as Senator Hugh Scott of Pennsylvania has put it, "the current Louisiana purchase."

Local residents who attempted to buck the Perez regime found all sorts of difficulties just getting on the ballot. For one thing, the parish Democratic committee says who is qualified to run, and if you aren't a Perez man, you aren't qualified. That's just common sense, but if you want to get petty about it and try to get on the ballot anyway, go right ahead and sue—by the time the court speaks, the election will be over.

Sometimes would-be opponents were sent the wrong filing forms, which, on their return, were of course disqualified.

The latest political plaything for Perez is home rule. Plaquemines has had it since 1964. The charter gives the five-man commission—of which Perez is president—the right to meet secretly and, if there is a balky member of the group, to take away his powers.

But one must not credit Perez with bringing boss rule to Plaquemines and St. Bernard parishes, for indeed that was the routine form of government in that area for more than two generations before he arrived on the scene. His only singularity is to live in an era when strong-arm political bosses get more publicity. His first venture into politics was to run, ironically enough, as a "reform" candidate against "the bosses" (there were three in the parish then), and he received for his efforts the same treatment he was later to give reform candidates who ran against him—12 votes. He was introduced to the second part of the pattern when, on the death of the district judge, he was appointed by the governor to take the bench for the rest of the term. When Leander, then twenty-seven, showed up at the courthouses in Plaquemines and St. Bernard, he found the doors locked by the bosses, so he was sworn in on the lawn. Perez was later a fast man with the lock himself.

During his interim service on the bench, he managed somehow to coax the grand jury to his side, and by doing so, kept the next election relatively honest; Perez was elected to a full term—by 3 votes.* Then, using the friendly grand jury as a snow plow, he moved in on the gamblers and rum runners, or at least those who were his political enemies.

The opposition fought back by filing suit to have him removed from office; twenty-three charges were made against him, including the accusation that he had a pearl-handled pistol lying on the bench beside him

* He kept the judgeship one term, then shifted to District Attorney, an office he kept until 1960, when he bequeathed it to his son. In December 1967, Leander also retired as president of the Plaquemines Parish Commission-Council, bequeathing this to his son Chalin O. Perez. Thus for the first time in 48 years he was without a formal political office. But he was politically active as ever.

within easy reach when he presided in court, and the accusation that he had protected a participator in the Violet Bridge Murder Case, which in its day was the most publicized rum-running assassination in that sanguinary region.

As for the pistol charge, that was not enough to impress many Louisianans, grown accustomed to violent and well-armed leaders. Julius Long, for example, used to say that he could taunt Earl with complete immunity from Earl's well-known temper and physical impetuosity (he once bit another politician on the cheek) because Earl knew that Julius habitually kept a pistol in his briefcase. But more to the point, not long before this charge was brought against Perez, a Louisiana judge had blasted away at an enemy on the streets of Natchitoches, and, as Perez' attorney pointed out when his impeachment trial reached the Supreme Court, "If this court holds that a man who has carried a pistol and shot down another on the streets is not subject to removal, then it cannot consistently remove Judge Perez for the *frivolous* charges made here." No effort was made to prove Perez did not carry a gun, because it was well known then and throughout much of his career that he frequently carried guns, and that his henchmen frequently carried both guns and billy clubs. The defense was based on the argument that it really didn't matter.

Perez' part in the Violet Bridge Murder Case is more significant as showing the way the man works. This was back in the 1920's, during prohibition, when the watery accesses of Plaquemines seemed very hospitable to the rum-filled ships wallowing in the offshore Gulf waters. Rum-running was accepted as a legitimate and very important industry to Plaquemines and St. Bernard. But there was, from time to time, trouble. There were killings. And in one of these slayings one Claude Meraux, a well-known valiant, was indicted. Fortunately for Claude, he was the brother of Sheriff L. A. Meraux, political boss of St. Bernard at that time and also a chum of Perez. L. A. Meraux was very much a realist; on one occasion he said, sighing: "You have to have money to be sheriff of St. Bernard, or you have to rob a whole lot." So, despite the fact that Claude fled to Europe, the indictment against him was dropped and, so good was his fortune, in less than a year after he had been indicted and faced the possibility of execution, he was sitting on the bench as a district judge, having been hand-picked by Perez for the job because Perez wanted to move over to the district attorney's post instead; and there Claude remained, handing out justice, until 1940, when he had a falling out with the man who made him, and was removed. Strangely enough, this removal opened Claude's eyes, and he began to recount all sorts of evil aspects of Perez' career, but everyone wondered why it had taken him sixteen years to open his mouth.

The impeachment trial of Perez came to nothing. Like many other events in Perez' life, its ending was mysterious. In the midst of everything and for no apparent reason, the prosecution and the defense attorneys began shaking hands, patting each other on the back, smiling, complimenting each other, and walking out. If Leander had erred, one of the judges remarked benignly as he got ready to follow the lawyers, what son of man had not?

A second impeachment effort was aimed at Perez fifteen years later, when Judge Meraux split with him, and once again that amazing luck followed Perez into court. For six months the grand jury met, sometimes for seven hours a day, and listened to involved tales of Perez' mischief, of how he jiggered the voter registration books, of how he burned incriminating county records, of much naughtiness. And when everyone had been heard, the grand jury ignored every and all charges against Perez and brought in a finding instead that the courthouse paint was peeling and the lawn needed cutting. It was as though the jury had never sat. For his troubles Meraux wound up himself being impeached for operating a divorce mill.

Partly as a result of these rigged escapes, Perez' large group of admirers through the South—among whom are few who actually live with and under him—have pieced together the legend of him as a great constitutional lawyer, and Perez has come to believe it of himself.

When the U.S. Senate Judiciary Committee was considering the bill to safeguard the Negro's voting rights, he bubbled with wrath because the senators did not know the U.S. Constitution any better than to entertain such a venture. "You are violating the Constitution . . . and nobody is *dumb* enough *not* to understand that." Word got out that there was a wild man engaged in a four-hour talkathon in the judiciary hearing, and eleven senators turned out and sat ball-eyed as he rolled on through his racist catechism. (The previous day, when a prominent constitutional lawyer testified, only three senators were there; the day after Perez appeared, another prominent constitutional lawyer came, but only one senator was present.) To protect Negro voters, he told Senator Dirksen, "is un-American." When he went on to say that it was "communistic," the spell was broken. "That," said Dirksen, "is as stupid a statement as has ever been uttered in this hearing." With Dirksen insisting that he do so, Perez had it stricken from the record, but when he got back in Plaquemines he went on television to deny that he had taken back "a damn thing," boasted that he had "rubbed the smell of communism in their nostrils," and, lifting his fist and shouting in the general northeasterly direction of Washington, demanded to know, "Who's stupid now?"

The framers of the Voter Registration Act tried to slip one over on the American people, but the great constitutionalist was too clever for them. "Nowhere is the word 'citizen' used. Isn't that odd?" When none of the eleven senators staring down at him seemed to catch the point, he moved into his accustomed sub-bellow rumble. "Is that accidental? I say NO. This bill provides no person, *no person,* NO PERSON—I counted them— seventeen times the word 'person' or 'persons' is used. *Not one time is the word 'citizen' used in this bill.* Why?"

The dumb senators still didn't appear to catch on, so he spelled it out: it meant that the communists in the federal government meant to import Cubans, Yugoslavians, Chinese, *any*body who would vote the communist line and be willing to overthrow Dixie—"and they would be led to the polling places right from the gang planks." It meant opening the door of political participation to "convicted felons . . . perverts, the unmoral people, aliens—*persons.*" But what else could the South expect from "all the queers and everything in government positions, thousands and thousands of them."

Probably the high, or low, point in Perez' career as a self-proclaimed constitutional giant, came in 1951, when he tried to get Hale Boggs scratched from the ballot as a gubernatorial candidate. Actually the chal- lenge to Boggs came from another candidate, Lucille May Grace, but Perez was her attorney and in fact the real moving force.

Perez took Boggs to court on two counts. He said that because Boggs was in Congress and had not resigned from that office, he had no right to run for governor. But most important, he charged Boggs with being a communist. There was a law against communists being on the ballot in Louisiana.

Louisiana newspapers were damning him as a "poor man's McCarthy" (which misses the mark, since Perez has hobnobbed with rich men far more than McCarthy ever did) and as the pirate captain of a "smelly scow armed with mud guns." Since most of this abuse came from New

Orleans, which Perez was already convinced was run by "the most dangerous people in this country today—the Zionist Jews," this editorial comment hardly bothered him, and he plowed ahead to his priceless courtroom summation of proof of Boggs' guilt:

"Alger Hiss denied having communist connections.

"Congressman Boggs has denied communist connections.

"Therefore, Congressman Boggs is as dangerous as Alger Hiss." That was the extent of his evidence against Boggs; Perez did not call a single witness. Boggs, on the other hand, had so many top politicians taking the stand that it turned into a veritable pro-Boggs testimonial occasion. But the damage was done anyway. Many thousands of ignorant Louisianans couldn't understand the niceties of what went on in the courtroom, but they understood Perez' original accusations. It knocked Boggs out of the run-off (he ran a strong third) and very likely out of the governorship; Boggs has always felt so, at least, and most of the evidence seems to support his wistfulness.

Weird pronouncements such as that are apt to disguise the fact that Perez is an able tactician, in a blitzkrieg way. Those who oppose him can look forward to being buried under a veritable hail of injunctions and writs, from which only the most astute shoveler will ever emerge. His deft snubbing of the spirit of the law, however, is another thing. When he encountered a couple of labor leaders in federal court seeking protection for picketing in Plaquemines, he grabbed his sheriff by the elbow and hustled him over to look at the union men. "If you ever see them in Plaquemines," Perez instructed, "put them in jail." So much for constitutional guarantees of assembly and the right to protest. His answer to the civil rights activists who threatened to move into Plaquemines to exercise the same constitutional rights was to prepare 200-year-old Fort St. Phillip, sixty miles south of New Orleans, as a prison. The fort, whose tomblike rooms stink with sweating decay, is surrounded by water. Let CORE come. He would arrest them all, stuff them in two boats equipped with cattle pens, and transport them to the prison island. CORE and other outside civil rights workers decided to bypass Plaquemines, one of them explaining, "I don't fear the prison so much but I'm scared of the man who made it." Homegrown Negroes, having lived for so long with the demons of the swamp, are more forward, and in the late 1950's they staged their own voter registration drive. It ended abruptly when the wife of the drive leader, involved in a personal feud, went down to the Negro school and whipped the teacher with a stick. It was only a minor fracas, but inasmuch as Perez was the district attorney and inasmuch as he owned the sheriff and the judge, the Negro woman was faced with a prison term on a felony assault charge. However, Perez was understanding: if the rights leaders would end their drive, he would see if he couldn't talk the judge into being lenient with the woman. And that was the end of efforts to get civil rights in Plaquemines until the federal registrars set up their desks in the back of the Buras' post office and invited the Negroes to come in, in 1965.

From such episodes has grown up Perez' reputation as the grand inquisitor of the black man, but this he angrily denounces as "nefarious, willful, malicious, lying propaganda." Even before the Voter Registration Act, any Negro who wanted to register in Plaquemines was free to do so, he said, but because they had "so little intelligence and urge, so little character," only 96 of the 2,897 Negroes in the parish had registered before the federal registrars arrived. "I will admit that we do not go out and beat the bushes to register the Negroes," he conceded, but that was only because he didn't want crooked voters contaminating the county, and Negro voters were all crooked. "You have got to bribe them. You have got to pay the preachers. Now, that is the story, and that is why we do not try to register them." On the other hand, he is only too happy to get white folks registered because the whites of Plaquemines are all morally upstanding, fine, decent people. "Oh, there may be a few exceptions, of course," Perez allowed. "Some of them are romantic, I would say."

Perez talks so much that sometimes he exposes what he means, and this was one of those occasions. After saying that some white voters of Louisiana charge $10 for their vote, and others charge $5, while Negroes and the poorest whites will settle for $2, he went on to explain: "People of low character are a little cheaper. Really it is funny. As a matter of fact, it was so well established that they knew each other, the $5 and $10 voters would not ride in the same automobile with the $2 voter when they are being brought to the polls. It was beneath their dignity. A $10 vote would not ride in the same car with a $2 vote."

Asked directly, "You segregated the voters according to how much you paid them," he replied, "Yes, sir."

Perez came to riches through Huey and to national infamy through the Dixiecrats, but he did not implant the full effect of his bigotry in Louisiana until the second coming of Jimmy Davis, the Singing Governor, in 1960. Davis was Perez' *tabula rasa,* on which he could scribble all sorts of insults for the federal government and the Negroes to read.

In other administrations Perez has thought he had well-trained haters in the governor's mansion, only to have them rebel finally against his grating obsession with tomfoolery. His vain estimation of what his support meant to a candidate left him with the mistaken notion that Earl Long was an ally, but even if that were briefly true, the "last of the red-hot poppas" not only turned on him but turned on him so completely that on at least one occasion, amidst the usual shouts and shovings, they came close to blows in the legislative chambers (where each was habitually presumptuous, Perez taking over the seats of some of "his" law-makers, sprawling around, talking loud, acting very much the legislator he never was; Earl grabbing the microphone away from legislators and in other boisterous ways ignoring the separation of powers). It is indica-tive of Perez' basic inability to judge other men that he entertained the idea he could maintain a steady alliance with Earl, this instinctively great madman who fell out with his brother Huey ("you big-bellied coward"), and his nephew Russell ("Louisiana's leading deadwood"), and his wife, and many, many former allies. And when it came time for Earl to boot Leander, he had ready a fine description for him, too, that of a primitive headhunter who is "still in the jungle and wants to stay where they eat berries and scratch for lice." It was a new experience for Perez and one that he did not know how to take. Earl to him thereafter was "that maniac in Baton Rouge." There were many Louisianans who would have agreed with both. In any event the money Perez put into Earl's campaigns and the votes he programmed for him were, for Perez, highly unprofitable. For one thing, while Perez did prevent Harry Truman from appearing on the 1948 ballot under the traditional Democratic emblem, Earl at least prevented Perez' removing the President altogether. (Louisiana went for Thurmond.) And not only did Earl put through the legislature laws to reduce Perez' totalitarian powers, The Maniac in Baton Rouge also squealed on Perez' business tactics: "As the chief executive of this state, I thought I had a right to look at income taxes. . . . I found several astounding revelations. I found a certain district attorney in a certain parish had gone, I think, from $24,000, $25,000, or $26,000 to $200,000 [income a year]* . . . I'm informed that the levee boards in Plaquemines

---

* Perez' salary as a public official was never over $7,000 and for most of his career it was under $5,000.

Parish, and some companies that a certain man is interested in, are receiving royalties from the Freeport Sulphur Company. I'm informed that that's not necessarily a voluntary contribution. . . . If you want to do well, you've got to stay with the King. I had a man the other day to tell me—he's a millionaire—that he swore he would not give an overriding royalty, I think of one-sixteenth. He stood out and stood out and finally his partners came to him and said, "Listen, we've got great investments. Everybody else in that part of the country has done it. Go ahead and do it and let's recover something on our investment.' "

Earl was, in short, accusing Perez of blackmail. But the pronouncement lacked much shock effect because most of Louisiana was already quite familiar with Perez' tactics.

Of special hurt to Perez, though, was Earl's steadfast and often violent opposition to the Rainach-Perez racism. While proclaiming himself "one million percent" for segregation, Earl confounded the Rainachers by snarling at their leader: "I'm sick and tired of you yellin' nigger, nigger, nigger! People aren't with you, they're just scared of you!" And, on another occasion, "You can't kick the Supreme Court in the slats on one hand and expect a square deal on the other." So long as wild Earl was governor, there was still a chance to fight off Rainach's anti-integration bills (no mixed racial meetings, no use of public facilities by both races at the same time, no mixed entertainment, etc.), but when Earl went out in 1960 and Jimmy Davis came in, supported by rural right-wingers and the New Orleans shady ring politicians and the oil companies—the strange sight of "the cows, the polecats, the poodle dogs and the other dogs lyin' down together in the Davis campaign," as Earl ridiculed it, although he had some odd combinations in his own camp—Louisiana entered its worst era of black–white enmity.

While Perez was *totally* disappointed in Earl, he was later—jumping Davis' regime and coming down to post-1964—somewhat disappointed in what he got for the money he spent on John ("Won't You He'p Me?") McKeithen, who rode into office by adopting many of Earl's campaigning routines and defeating the perpetual hard-luck candidate deLesseps S. Morrison, New Orleans' reform mayor, by accusing him of wearing a "toopee" and of putting perfume in his bath water and wearing $400 suits —the same devastating line used by Earl in 1956—but also accusing him of sneaking off to NAACP headquarters back east to get help and advice.*

Although Perez had not supported him in the primary, McKeithen won his support in the 1963-1964 run-off by sounding like a splendid nigger-hater; he didn't turn out to be quite as emphatic as he sounded. The governor did appoint segregationists to the top anti-poverty jobs and refused to let the FBI investigate the beating of a Negro prisoner with a baseball bat, but on the other hand he refused to let the rednecks do unrestricted violence to the Negroes of Bogalusa. And Perez was able to have McKeithen send him to Washington as his emissary only by trickery. First he went by and got McKeithen to promise that if he sent *anybody*, he would send him; next he got McKeithen to promise that if anybody on the Senate Judiciary Committee *asked* him to send a witness for Louisiana against the voter registration bill, he would. McKeithen didn't think they would ask. But Perez promptly got on the phone and arranged with Senator Eastland to make the request, and Perez was on his way. (McKeithen repudiated most of Perez' testimony.)

No, looking back on it, the one real ace of a bigot that Perez can claim some major credit for getting in the mansion was Jimmy Davis, best known as the composer of that fine honky-tonk tune, "You Are My Sunshine" as well as other less well-known bawdy songs like "Bearcat Mama from Horner's Corners" and "High-Powered Mama, Get Yourself in Gear." Putting it like that is not quite accurate either; Davis was not so much a bigot—because he was really not much of anything—but merely a conduit of bigotry. He had no heart for it, as he had no heart for anything. His ambitions were modest. "He only wanted to get in office and steal," as one old-time New Orleans reporter sympathetically summarized it. He set up his own bank and channeled state funds into it. He built a bridge, happily designated as "The Sunshine Bridge," which at the time had roads leading neither to nor away from it; it was just a bridge for favored contractors to play with. Under oath an officer in the Mississippi Pilots Association has told of dropping by the governor's office and paying big money to have a bill vetoed. To get at these sources of profit, Davis was quite willing to be anything. If he was capable, at least figuratively, of "singing Nearer My God to Thee in north Louisiana on Sunday

* Roy Wilkins of the NAACP tells me that even as McKeithen went on TV to unload this accusation his lieutenants were meeting secretly with Louisiana NAACP leaders to solicit their help in his campaign.

morning and ending with a chorus of Bedbug Blues in south Louisiana Sunday night," as Earl accused, this did not point to hypocrisy but to the notorious instability of his standards. *The Nation* magazine called Davis "the meanest man in high public office" in 1960 for pushing through the legislature a retaliatory package bill to evade public school integration and to show the Negroes how puritanically tough whites can be. Negro women were being forced into prostitution while their children (23,000 children affected) were being sent out to search through garbage dumps for food, because the Davis legislation cut off funds (mostly federal money) to any woman who had a bastard while on relief. Davis merits the blame, all right, simply because he was governor and spineless, but the legislation was the handiwork of Perez and his henchman Rainach (who, after running third in the 1959 primary, threw his support to Davis, and this did help). Davis was capable of bluster; after some patient coaching by Perez he was able to correctly recite the watchword of all segregationist governors across the South, that he would "rather go to jail" etc., but neither Perez nor Rainach ever felt sure of Davis and for good reason, because when all the bluster was blustered he remained, what Churchill once called a political opponent, "a sheep in sheep's clothing."

There were many in the state who, for good reason, felt that Davis was a political mortician, come not to lead the state but to bury it, and Davis' statements did nothing to discourage their view. Campaigning, he had indeed described himself and all Louisiana in dying terms, describing politics as nothing but a preparation for The Judgment: "I look beyond this election. I look beyond all elections. I look to the time when they're going to take me, just like they're going to take you, to some silent city on the hill. And that's the last ride because we're not coming back. They'll take us to a place where there are no big men and no small men; no big shots and no little shots; no rich men and no poor men; where six feet of earth makes us all the same size. And when they take me there, I want people to say that I was decent and honorable and respectable and . . ."

But he also found time in his speeches to squeeze in a few remarks about segregation being "the most noble cause that has ever arised [sic] during the lifetime of any man living in the world today." And many felt that in the final analysis Davis defeated Morrison only on the strength of a whispering campaign, based not on segregation but on the religious question, picturing Morrison, a Catholic, as a tool of the church. It is true that Morrison got 53 percent of the vote in southern Louisiana, where the population is heavily Catholic; he carried every parish that was predominantly Catholic, which, if it signified anything, surely must have meant that he controlled the church as much as it controlled him. In any event, the loss of the Catholic areas was something that Davis could afford and knew from the long experience of Louisiana politics that he could afford; in the Protestant north he carried some parishes by margins of 8 and 9 to 1. (Morrison encountered the same frustration in his next race, against McKeithen. While Morrison carried some Negro areas 100 to 1, he didn't carry a single parish in north Louisiana.)

Jimmy Davis was almost as much a caricature of failure as was the Dixiecrat movement. Everything about him sagged: his eyes, his voice, his spirit, his careers as governor, for indeed he had two, the first beginning in 1944, a spartan year in which the homefolks were, obviously, desperate for amusement. Fred Hand, once speaker of the Georgia house, has observed that any governor can make a fine record and develop no enemies if he doesn't have to hire all his supporters' kinfolks and if he doesn't have to build roads or anything else. That was one reason Ellis Arnall made such a good record in Georgia (governor 1942-1946). Davis, coming to power at the tail end of the war, at first was not required to hire or build, since the kinfolk were overseas fighting and there was no building material. He ran that time as a "happiness" candidate, the "peace and harmony" candidate, meaning that he would disturb the state with neither scandals nor reforms, but hew to a line of cheerful and quiet skulduggery; he felt sure that Louisiana was tired of bickering and just wanted to go through life humming and aiming for that meritorious tombstone. His first session with the legislature came to a happy-do-nothing close with Jimmy leading the legislators in a round of "You Are My Sunshine," while two doves fluttered around the chamber, one marked Peace and the other Harmony. They might have gone on flapping for the next three years but unfortunately the war ended before his term was up, and suddenly the state wanted to do things. Decisions. How fluffy-headed Jimmy hated to make them. When there was a labor strike that needed his attention, or there was a rough conflict over the awarding of contracts, or a budgetary adjustment to be faced, the governor became sick with anxiety. Louisiana writer Harnett T. Kane tells a well-circulated anecdote of the day: "When Jimmy was a young boy his father installed a new Chic Sale facility out back. Asked by workmen if it should be a one or two-holer, Daddy replied: 'One. Otherwise that boy would stand there all day, just a-spoiling before he could decide which to use.' "

At length it came to him, the perfect solution: he would simply leave Louisiana. This may not sound like a very sensible solution for the governor of the state to make, but Davis' life was unmarked by subtleties or logic or intellectuality. He was far better at yodeling (which he had once taught for a living) than headwork. He did get through a Baptist college, excelling at glee club, but he was never known thereafter to open a book or to read to its conclusion an article in either magazine or newspaper; he even avoided reading the headlines, because they left too much to his imagination, of which he had little. Thus, if Louisiana's problems got under his skin, he simply departed the state, compiling the all-time record for absenteeism: 220 days in three years. One outing was to make a film of his life story in Hollywood.

This was the same back-eddy politician who returned to lead Louisiana in 1960. His character was unchanged, but now he had two friends to help him make decisions on racial matters, Rainach and Perez, and countless friends, as always, to assist him in making decisions in economic matters. In some quarters he was better known as "Perez' Putty."

When Perez stepped down as district attorney in 1960, 900 persons crowded into the Roosevelt Hotel to cheer him on his way. Governor Davis made him a colonel and gave him a card permitting him to exceed the speed limit on trips to Baton Rouge; another speaker likened him to Washington, Jefferson, Lincoln, Wilson, and the two Roosevelts; and somebody else called him "the noblest Roman of them all" and the "father of Plaquemines Parish."

The only threatening note was struck in the compliment given by Congressman F. Edward Hebert, whose district embraces Plaquemines: "He's like Tennyson's brook. 'Men may come and men may go, but I go on forever.' "

That, as it turned out, was all too true. Perez, who was probably at the height of his influence nationally in the 1948-56 period, had gradually declined as an arouser. He was in a temporary lull at the time of the Roosevelt Hotel blowout. But the next year he started up again, and by the time Goldwater came around, Perez was again in a good position to help him whoop it up. To nobody's surprise, it was less than a year before Perez was back in the news and in such a way as to make the North gnash its teeth. He had been caught hoking up a movie of "mixed" school children misbehaving on Washington playgrounds. School officials said the shots were faked, that the children told them the cameraman asked them to fight and throw rocks through a car windshield. The pictures were arranged through Congressman Hebert's office, and although Perez denied the faking, he did say he was interested in getting something White Citizens Council members would enjoy watching.

With the beginning of the civil rights sit-ins of 1960, Perez was ready for another Puff-Ball Putsch, and ever since then his voice has periodically thundered across the South to rally the troops.

Amazingly enough for Louisiana, where liberal statements are not unknown among the politicians, Perez has not been subjected to over-whelming denunciation for his social stupidities. McKeithen, who is trying to fabricate a "new image" for Louisiana, recently told a press confer-ence on the West Coast, "Perez isn't all bad." That, at a non-southern news conference, was received as indeed news, but McKeithen did not talk himself into a corner by attempting to name a non-bad characteristic. Congressman Boggs has said privately that Perez "is entirely evil," but he has never said so publicly. The nearest thing to a denunciation of The Perez System (which is much more crucial to the fate of the South than is Perez alone) made publicly by a Louisiana politician was enunciated by Congressman T. Ashton Thompson shortly before his death: "Were it not for people of his ilk—protected by the vast sums of money he has accumulated—Louisiana could solve its problems in peace and harmony, and the people would be allowed to work their will as they should." This is far too naïve a reliance on the virtues of "the people" of Louisiana, most of whom have a concept of fair play as reflected in the Louisiana Manual of Procedure for Registrars of Voters (circa 1957), which noted that "We are in a life and death struggle with the Communists and the NAACP to maintain segregation and to preserve the liberties of our people. *The impartial enforcement* of our laws is the *key to victory* in this struggle." The impartial gutting of the NAACP is something that Louisi-ana would have stood for, Perez or no Perez, but there has been an added drag to progress from his cash-protected arrogance that not many Louisi-ana politicians have wanted to mention, money having long ago assumed a blameless and almost sacred role in their lives.

So eager is the outside world to believe that Perez' position is de-teriorating that it reads too much into those little fusses that are the blood of Louisiana politics. In a quarrel with Perez over the evolvement of party relationships, for example, Senator Russell Long stormed at him: "People are getting tired of being called a communist just because they don't agree with you. . . . It's getting so it will be respectable to be called a communist."

Bravos were heard throughout the land, but what most people didn't realize was that Long had no basic disagreement with Perez' technique; what he did not like was Perez' overusing the technique and thereby discrediting it to the point that it was becoming useless to other politicians. Russell Long himself is no slouch at suggesting senators who disagree with him on foreign policy just might be cohabitating with the communists, but he saves this kind of attack for special occasions. (For example, his vicious innuendos of this sort in response to Senator Gruening's "dove" stance on Vietnam.)

Congressman Boggs once accused Perez of committing "the most un-American smear in the history of American politics"—but Boggs, of course, was referring to the job that had been done on himself, not the continual smear job that Perez was doing on the Negro, the North, and the federal government. *That* smear didn't upset Boggs quite so much.

For the most part when Perez has been scolded at home, it has been in the style of Earl Long, as an almost flippant rejoinder. The cause of this toleration is that Perez' neighbors know the old boy has taken upon himself all their sins, not for their salvation but his own. He is the South's Word made flesh: *I am not obsessed with the Negro question. . . . It was the Stalin conspiracy to stir up revolution in the Black Belt in this country, among the Negroes and the sharecroppers. It was the Stalin plan then to recognize this Black Belt as an independent state, or nation, and back it up with aggressive military force. Failing in that, naturally, the communists turned to infiltration. And my God! They . . . Yes, the Negro is inherently immoral! . . . Yes, I think it's the brain capacity. . . . You make a Negro believe he is equal to the white people and the first thing he wants is . . . A WHITE WOMAN . . .*

Southerners who hear Perez say these things, as he has said them countless times, know they are hearing the inner convictions of Dixie, the scrotum sociology of the Deep South. They are not the statements of a politician. Very few important politicians in the Deep South are that open. And this is another thing that saves Perez from being rebuked for making a spectacle of himself: his people realize that he is not a politician but a kind of hyperthyroid lobbyist–evangelist.

Perez has admitted as much. "Control and influence," he once observed, "are two different things." He has controlled that trivial piece of half-floating real estate, but outside its murky borders he has never had control. And while a great deal of his influence has been political, the part he is proudest of is not; it is spiritual. When Perez was proposing that Johnson's name be kept off the ballot in 1964, and came close to achieving it, he swaggered, "This will force Mr. Lyndon B. Johnson to come to Louisiana and tell the voters what he has been doing to them—and then the voters will give him a kick in the pants." That is the statement of a spiritual, not a political leader; politicians talk only of giving their peers a kick in the pants, while spiritual leaders, grown accustomed to bruising the dark unfathomables, shrink not from a direct assault on the mightiest. Perez would proudly nail his ninety-five theses to the White House front door, and it is this attitude—not uncommon in the Deep South—that has made Perez the natural leader of the Dixiecrats, who are not a political movement at all.

Connoisseurs of the tirade were not disappointed when the federal registrars moved into Plaquemines Parish in 1965. Perez was furious. He went on television and urged unregistered whites to sign up "to avoid the curse of a second Reconstruction"—and out of the bog they came, once ending the day with eight times as many whites registered as Negroes. Perez, like the rest of the South, was needlessly perturbed. If every Negro in Plaquemines registered, and every white, Perez' forces would outnumber the enemy three to one—not counting the votes he has always been able to pull from his pocket.

Registering under federal protection, and voting under the sheriff's protection, are decidedly different things in Plaquemines, but the Negroes are a hardy lot and they insist that they will vote, at least for the practice. When they take that step they will begin, in the most primordial way, in the same tentative way early life emerged from the nearby Gulf shoreline, to move into the techniques of influence (if not control) that were set by the likes of Perez. And the farther they go, the more frustrated they will become, even as Perez, even as the Dixiecrats.

Not long ago the aging Judge spoke to the Port Sulphur School civics class on politics, which, he told them, "is the curse of the country"; the nearest likeness he could think of was "the old Tanglefoot fly-catching paper. Like flies, we go for nourishment and get caught and die. I hate politics." It was a pathetic summation of his half century in Louisiana and southern politics, but he meant it all. "Politics," he told the kids as they gawked up at the roaring legend, "is the sinful game of fooling people!"

There were no Negroes in that classroom, of course, but what he said there is something that they, of all voters, would be most likely to agree with. What he didn't tell the youngsters, but what the new Negro voters will soon discover, is that it's no more sinful to play than to watch.

3

Herman Talmadge: How a Demagogue Adapts

God forbid, Mr. President, that our rights and freedoms are in such jeopardy that they must be preserved
under the heels of storm troopers. . . .

Senator Talmadge, 1964
Opposing Enforcement of Civil Rights Act

Old Gene was dead, and the redfaced crackers packed the capitol galleries;
some in overalls, some from as far away as Bainbridge, old folks too,
who had started on the road before the previous midnight to get here in
time to see justice done to his memory, coming with food in paper sacks
to last the day, cold and now shriveled corn on the cob, cold biscuits
stuffed with fried salt meat. Old Gene had never done anything for them,
but he made them feel like people, fit for laughter, supreme over the black
man at least, and sharing with him the sly knowledge that since only the
rich could profit from government, the poor man was foolish to take
government seriously. *Sure I stole, but I stole for you! Sure I took those*
beefs off the prison farm, and they're all in the freezer up at the mansion
and I want y'all to come by and help me eat 'em! Old Gene was a case.
I don't hate the nigger. I like the nigger, but I like him in his place, and his
place is at the back door with his hat in his hand! Old Gene might be a
clown but there was a lot of truth in what he said. *You folks only got*
three friends who never let you down—God! Sears Roebuck! and Ol'
Gene!

37

Eugene Talmadge had personified the politics of protest for these depressed country people, and they still had plenty to protest. The war had brought money to Georgia, but somehow very little of it had spread out to them. They were still riding in broken-down flatbed trucks and they were still proud to head them out to a Talmadge rally. This was a new kind of rally for them, sad, but mawkish and corrupt, so they knew they had come to the right place for the changing of the kings.

Ol' Gene was dead, goddammit, but there was always Hummon.

Herman Eugene Talmadge, then thirty-three, was being hoisted into a cockpit for which he was only partially trained. Up to this point in his life, despite some fringe participation in his father's political activities, Herman was most adept as a playboy; once married unsuccessfully to a model who discarded him because, she said, he smoked smelly cigars, he was trying marriage again; but, just back from the war and still edgy and boozing around, he wasn't sure he was ready to settle down just yet to the role of heir-in-fact. Those men and women in the gallery with perspiration circles on their denim shirts and dresses had other ideas about that, however, and so, more importantly, did a very powerful band of palace politicians.

They had known Gene was dying. But their first notice of the need for crash strategy had come from, of all places, one Gibson Ezell, manager of the Five and Ten Cent Store in Monticello. Ezell had been reading the new constitution concocted under Governor Ellis Arnall, a document so sloppily redone that even a five and dime manager could smell trouble. "Somebody up there better get busy," Ezell warned Talmadge headquarters by phone, "because if anything happened to Eugene, you may have a Republican governor of Georgia." The Gene crowd read the constitution again. Sure enough, there was nothing in it to direct matters if a winning candidate died before he was certified the winner. But they decided, taking heart from another section of the constitution, that the legislature could elect the governor from the top two runners-up if no person "still in life" had a majority. This was something to work with. D. Talmadge Bowers, a Republican, would have some write-in votes. So would James Carmichael, whom Talmadge had beaten in the primary.

But Herman was going to have more than either. The word went out: Scratch Eugene, write in Herman. That done, there shouldn't be any trouble, for the Talmadge faction controlled the legislature.

The schemers were so sure they had covered all loopholes that they even leaked their success to the press before the official count: Herman would have well over 1,000 write-in votes and Carmichael would have around 600; Republican Bowers was supposed to get some trifling amount.

The night before the legislature convened to elect its governor, the great strategists first got a shock, and then witnessed one of those miracles that have so often marked Talmadge politics. The special legislative committee convened to count and certify the votes; in came the sergeant at arms and his Negro helpers carrying two laundry baskets and two big cardboard boxes containing the county returns. The write-in tally: Carmichael 669, Bowers, 637, Herman 617!

Then, glory be, somebody found that other parcel. Good old Telfair County, the Talmadges' home, had come through after all with a surprise SECOND batch of votes—58 of them to be exact, pushing Herman safely first by 6 votes. Well, well. It was a bit unusual, but of course it wouldn't have been courteous to challenge the 58 as unauthentic, so the burden was swiftly passed along to the legislature to make the final choice.

A hoked-up mess, vintage Talmadgism. Many of the votes were fraudulent. The Atlanta *Journal* discovered it, later, and won a Pulitzer for the discovery. There was no finesse, no effort even to save Georgia's face by delicate cheating. The last thirty-four names on the Helena voters' list except two were written by the same man; other evidence indicates that Herman received 10 legitimate write-in votes instead of the 48 certified in that precinct. At least 2 of those listed were dead, 5 had moved away, 5 said they did not vote. Another dozen could not be found. In the A's, the first 3 voters could not be found, the next 2 were found living in Macon, the sixth said he didn't vote, the seventh (listed as his wife) could not have voted since he had no wife. Following two missing, two others said they had not voted, another died before election, another did not exist. "I guess the boys just got tired of explaining why the write-ins were needed and took the easy way out," said a key Talmadge man* later, much later.

The shuffling, shouting, drinking, spitting crowd in the gallery, coupled with the shuffling, spitting mob of legislators on the floor—where the only whispers were those that dealt with rumors of wild and plentiful bribe offers

---

* Roy Harris, of whom more later.

for thusly cast votes*—made the scene somewhat unique even among southern legislative sessions. But the outcome, after all, was never in doubt, what with 100 of the 205 house members known to be Talmadge supporters and twenty-five of the fifty-three senators deeply branded as old-line Talmadge men, and a comfortable portion of the other house and senate members willing to go along with the inevitable. They had been softened up with whiskey, cigars, threats and promises the night before in Roy Harris' room on the 14th floor of the Henry Grady Hotel.

So Herman was elected, the people cheered and went home, their inferiors came in and swept out the corncobs and chickenbones and empty bottles, and Georgia had a governor.

In fact, it would soon have two. Operating under *another* section of the grab-bag constitution, Governor Arnall was about to resign and let Lieutenant Governor M. E. Thompson be sworn in to serve until the next election, in 1948.

Now begins the celebrated battle of the two governors, a crass battle in which the intemperate and sometimes brutal high jinks of Herman made him appear to be, outwardly at any rate, a true son of Gene. Action:

> Herman marches into governor's office, flanked by cronies: I am here to take over.
> Arnall: I consider you a pretender. Get out.
> Herman sets up quarters in the outer offices of the governor's executive suite. Siege conditions are acknowledged by both sides. Arnall refuses to leave for lunch for fear Herman will move all the way in. That night, with Arnall gone, all locks are changed in both the governor's offices and at the mansion. Next morning at 7, preceded by Roy Harris and surrounded by uniformed military men, Herman marches into the governor's chambers, turns to his followers and proclaims, "I am in control." Crowd whoops it up. State guardsmen and highway patrolmen are everywhere in the capitol and guarding the mansion. Arnall arrives, is repulsed at governor's office, retreats and sets up new bastion in information booth on first floor, charging "military *coup d'etat* by thugs" and "infiltration of storm troopers." Tear gas employed at one juncture in governor's office. Half-drunk and totally drunk Talmadge gangs roam capitol area. Talmadge crowd overwhelms and breaks jaw of highway patrolman loyal to Arnall. Hysteria mounts. Next morning Arnall finds himself blocked even from his rotunda desk. Blocking

---

* Among rumors: $60,000 for blocs of 6 votes. One legislator told of receiving a $100,000 offer.

is done by Representative Jimmy Dykes, a mountain of a man. Dykes had arrived at 8 a.m., Arnall shows up at 10. Cold stare meets sneer.

Dykes: Would you like an appointment with the governor?

Arnall: Jimmy, I am the governor. (Crowd cheers.)

Dykes: (looks very angry now) Ellis, you remind me of a hog in the slops. You've got your head in the trough and you just can't stop. (Crowd boos.) You have no more right to sit here than I do. It's my day to play governor. (More boos. He peels off coat and offers to fight all comers.)

Herman hears of routing of Arnall and jeers, "I understand he's holding down the bathroom in the basement now." Arnall resigns and leave fight to Thompson, who is sworn in. Asked what he intends to do, Thompson replies: "Just yet I do not have a strong military force at my back so I am not in a position to answer." One side claims National Guard, the other the state guard. Clash of troops is feared. Thompson says he will not hesitate to call federal troop reinforcements if necessary. Public sentiment in favor of Thompson appears to be growing.

Two thousand students march on capitol singing, "Open the doooor Herman," yelling, "Who stole my vote"; they hang the effigy of Herman where a few years earlier they had hung his daddy's effigy—from the strong arm of Tom Watson's statue. Herman goes on radio to denounce "present revolt" against his leadership as "crusade of radicals, and its ugly roots are fixed in soil outside Georgia, its purposes determined to destroy the dominance of the white race in the South." Two circuit judges rule for Herman; a third calls him "jackass." Finally, after two-month drag, state supreme court by 5-to-2 margin rules Herman holding his share of the office illegally, but, nevertheless, feels compelled to apologize for ruling, saying that one reason it ruled against him was that if he could get into office on that constitutional provision, then at sometime in the future the legislature, swayed by un-Georgian sentiments, might in like manner elect as governor "some person wholly undesirable because of his communistic or other alien philosophies of government." Legislature, peeved at being over-ruled by courts, goes on strike. Herman calls the justices a bunch of lackies, vows to take his "appeal" to "the court of last resort, the People," and moves out of offices and mansion within thirty minutes, indicating by his light baggage that he never had felt too secure in the post. End of war.

Herman's departure only inflamed the spirits of Talmadgism through-out the state. The legislature would not pass either appropriations or revenue bills for Governor Thompson, hoping to leave him $30 to $40 million short. "I'll get along," he said, and did, building hospitals in rural areas, increasing old-age benefits, building farm-to-market roads, increasing teacher pay 50 percent—and leaving a $26-million surplus.

Herman, sulking at the failure of his friends in the legislature to ruin the Thompson regime, threatened to stump the South with Gerald L. K. Smith, speaking against communism and for white supremacy. Roy Harris told him to shut up and lay low until the election of 1948, since the Klan, which was to endorse him, already knew how he felt.

Talmadgism, meanwhile, was making violent appearances. Bombers struck at the home of C. E. Gregory, one of the *Journal's* unflattering reporters. Governor Thompson thought the same bombers were scared away from the mansion. In Telfair County things got even messier. A CIO organizer and his wife were beaten. There were political floggings. A minister who upbraided his congregation because they put the "name of Talmadge before God," was told to get out and stay out.

One of the main differences between Herman and Gene was the relationship of each to that mystic force, "Talmadgism." Gene's power had an inner source; it began with himself, the man—in his showmanship and recalcitrant fury (as when he used a blowtorch to cut a hole in the state treasury safe because he didn't like the treasurer's delay in meeting his demands) and earthy joustings with all sorts of elaborate straw men. Herman's influence was borrowed. It was drawn from the vast and unmanageable, and therefore more easily abused, symbol of Talmadgism which he had inherited. What were creations with his father, and therefore modifiable by his father, were passed on to him as institutionalized clan actions and mottoes, and the most melancholy feature of Herman's career is that he kept acting on these clichés and re-voicing them until the day was past when he could with credit modify them, for they had been outdated by law.

It was not so much a defect of will as it was a mistake in calling. Herman looked somewhat like his daddy, though handsomer, and he had picked up his daddy's mannerisms. But whereas Gene had courage, Herman had only insolence; whereas Gene had a hard pride and initiative, Herman had only ego; at least this was true in the beginning, back when he was nicknamed "Three-fourths Talmadge" because of suspected, and real, deficiencies as a politician.

Apparently Herman had some insight into those deficiencies. He has given this account of how he moved into the shadow of his father: "When I was in the Pacific (in World War II), I thought it was foolish to be in politics, and I thought I would never be active in that way again. But when I got back and my father launched his fourth campaign, I found it necessary to help him. After his death, circumstances forced me into the fight. Then when I was elected by the legislature and kicked out, of course I felt I had to be vindicated. Too, there was the pleasure of winning, and it's a great honor to be governor. Politics is a rough, hard, mean, vicious life."

The note of deference here perfectly counterbalances, while it leaves unexplained except as a genealogical achievement, Herman's success. He did not hanker after a political career, but tried to avoid it; he did not help his father from political instincts but because it was "necessary"; he fought for election as his father's substitute not because he enjoyed a political fight but because "circumstances forced me." Nor was it by accident that he listed last the incentives any natural politician would have placed first: spoils, power, honor, and the "pleasure of winning."

For a young man motivated as he was, yet giving himself to the motions as dutifully as a loyal mercenary, it is not surprising that the regimen impressed him as a "rough, hard, mean, vicious life."

There were those at hand, however, who not only were willing to give young Herman guidance but who in fact had sought him out as the continuation of Talmadgism, through which they could carry out a few private dealings, including revenge.

To a great extent Herman the successful neophyte was the creation of Roy V. Harris, now president of the Citizens Councils of America, the lobbyist–lawyer who still carries his book of incantations back and forth between law offices in Augusta and the Henry Grady Hotel in Atlanta.

There is some dispute, but not much, over Harris' powers—or former powers, since he has stumbled in recent efforts and, with the passing of the county-unit system, will never be the same man again. Former acting Governor M. E. Thompson, who had no reason to admire Harris, during the Talmadge administration once asked: "Is he really The Boss? Will the records of the telephone calls from Atlanta to Augusta and vice versa substantiate his claim that Herman Talmadge asks his permission to powder his nose? Or is The Boss the creation of a clever press agent, a vain, pompous myth, without substance, moving here and there in an aura of cigar smoke and laughter?" There was no doubt how Thompson would have answered the questions. But he was, and is, in the minority. Most Georgians have viewed Harris as a cross between Svengali and Merlin, a magical maker and breaker. Although Thompson snorts at the idea, most Georgia politicians would agree that Harris had something important to do with the victories of Ed Rivers in 1936 and 1938, of Ellis Arnall in 1942, of Eugene Talmadge in 1946, of Herman's abortive palace take-over, and of his election in 1948 and 1950. He was also among those in 1956 responsible for dumping poor Walter George (whom he had helped elect in '26) so that Herman could have that Senate seat. The multiplicity of these successes has not always been interpreted as virtue. "Mr. Harris has been on so many sides of the different political fences in Georgia during his long career that he has practically made a gate for himself," the *Macon News* once observed. "But make no mistake. He is a good man to have on your side—so long as the money holds out." Another commentator on this fickleness was political writer Charles Pou, who once noted that because Harris has been in so many camps and loyal to none, "some politicians would rather have Mack the Knife behind them than Roy V. Harris."

In his defense it must be said, however, that Harris' fickleness was, at this crucial juncture in Georgia's political life,* the result of his having been betrayed by two men whom he with much justification believed owed *him* a chance at the governorship. Harris was then, and for some time had been, the smartest organization man in Georgia politics; he certainly had had a great deal to do with the two elections of Rivers and the election of Arnall, and he had reason to think that they were in his debt. Confident that he would get their support, he started building up his candidacy for the 1946 race. But Rivers was not through with politics; he was determined to win the governorship once more and prove that the scandalous reputation of his last term was not his fault. On top of this Arnall told Harris that he, too, wanted to run for another four-year term, and he asked Harris' support in pushing through a constitutional amendment to allow him to do it. Harris felt completely betrayed. He had not much minded that Rivers was blowing around on the edge of the clearing; after

---

* V. O. Key, Jr., was perceptive in noting, as early as 1948, that the 1946 campaign was setting up the Talmadge dynasty for a seemingly unending run, just as it appeared to be dying. If a non-Talmadgite had held the capitol for the next four years, this would have meant that the gang would have been out of power for an eight-year stretch, and it is unlikely that after such a lapse it ever could have recaptured the state machinery in the way that it subsequently did.

all, Rivers' endorsement might have done him more harm than good. But he had really been anticipating Arnall's endorsement, and now Arnall —fawned over as a "fresh, new, non-Talmadge politician" by outside observers (who did not know that Arnall, when in the legislature, was such an admirer of Gene that he even took to wearing red suspenders like his idol)—began to think that Georgia couldn't do without him and that he must find some way to change the constitution and give himself to the state for another four years. Harris claims today that Arnall told him privately he wanted the governorship so that he would be in a position to receive a vice-presidential offer in 1948.

Harris' revenge took two normal routes: he set out to kill the Arnall constitutional amendment and—with the help of lobbyists representing railroads, bus and truck lines, public utilities, and certain manufacturers— he did that easily enough; secondly, he renewed his alliances with the Gene Talmadge gang.

Despite the ingratitude of Rivers and Arnall, he still thought he had a chance for the governorship. In Richmond County (Augusta) his "Cracker Party" had for several years run the political show, often in a ruthless way. Opponents said that if they spoke out against Harris or the Cracker Party, they were likely to wind up in jail or with their taxes tripled. Harris was a little king. Now, in 1946, he advanced the primary in Richmond County and ran solely on the issue of creating a white primary; having been re-elected to the state legislature, as he had been without much trouble since the early 1930's, he thought he would get the endorsement of Gene for the governorship, since Gene was very keen on the idea of a white primary, too.

The only soft spot in this scheme was that enough Georgia boys had come back from the war by then, tired of dictators at home or abroad, to vote Harris out of office; this they proceeded to do.

This crushed Harris' hopes for a chance at the mansion. Still, there was an opportunity for revenge. Arnall had thrown his endorsement to Carmichael, a decent man but a corporation conservative; Rivers was still in the race; Harris talked Gene, already visibly sick, into running again. Rivers had no chance, and knew it, carrying only ten out of 159 counties, but he pulled enough votes in thirty other counties to take them from Carmichael and give them to Talmadge.

Meanwhile Harris was on the telephone, orchestrating his courthouse gangs. No one has ever doubted that it was Harris who put Talmadge back in. A Georgia slowly shaking off the scales of deep parochialism would likely have gone for Carmichael, despite the rube fascination of Gene, if it had not been for Harris' masterful work on the telephone. And as the final, expert touch, wise to the times, Harris even forced Talmadge to loosen up and run on a few semi-progressive economic planks. This was not mere strategy with Harris, however, it was his own bent. As speaker of the house from 1937 to 1940, he had helped pass laws enacting homestead exemptions, free school books, aid for the aged needy, better buildings for state institutions, and a longer school term. It was the most progressive legislation Georgia had had up to that time. And although Arnall is credited, rightly, with the progressive legislation of his term, this also was accomplished only with the help of Harris, still in the speaker's chair. If Harris had not wanted it passed, it would not have been passed.

Harris even today calls himself an economic liberal. By Deep South standards, perhaps he is. At the same time, he is a racial Neanderthaler; and it was this side of his character that was so disastrously creative in the administration of Herman.

In racial matters, as in other political activities requiring the show of strong feelings, Herman borrowed his heat from others. Marvin Griffin once said of Gene, "When he took sides, he *took* 'em." And Georgia's senior senator, Richard Russell, said at the height of one of the civil rights battles, "If they overwhelm us, you will find me in the last ditch." Not so, Herman. He is philosophically not a last-ditcher, and when the last ditch seemed the popular place for southern politicians to be, he had to ask men like Harris to show him how to get into it. He asked the right man.

"Some people think the nigger is beneath their dignity," Harris told me cheerfully, around a cheap, black Tampa cigar. "They *talk* Constitution but they look at the nigger question. They *talk* states' rights but they mean nigger. This never will be a dead issue. Some issues never die."

So long as Harris' influence was strong upon Herman, that's how he felt, too. But it never took the firm root in his spirit that Harris desired, and it is in this more than in anything else that Talmadge has been a disappointment to little Roy and his county-courthouse phalanx.

"I have looked upon it [the segregation question] as a political issue and not as a legal issue," Harris said. "I have believed that public sentiment will control. I sold Herman on the idea in 1948 and in 1950, and we went all out in a crusade to the people. As a result, sentiment became so unified in Georgia that there was no real effort made over five years to integrate the schools in Georgia. So far as I am concerned, I propose never to surrender. I may be hung. I may be shot. But regardless of what happens, there will be no surrender on my part." No, not even any retreat; not even any retrenchment under new battle conditions. "If one little nigra is entitled to go to Henry Grady High School in Atlanta, then all nigras are entitled to go to some high school with the whites."

It is a monumentally absurd position for a man so politically canny, otherwise, to take; segregation is a side issue, like the income tax and immigration and redistricting, something to use and play with and demagogue over, but not worth risking a career for. Despite his previous oaths, even the unflinching Senator Russell has shown his awareness that the day is past when he can get by with advocating, as he once did, that southern Negroes be shipped North. If Herman Talmadge does not feel anything very strongly, if he is "straw inside," as some say, even that weakness is more compatible to winning politics than is Harris' cast-iron attitude, which Herman had to drift away from to survive. Harris is an adrenalin segregationist. Intemperance marks everything he says and does. He tried to break up a bus strike with a shotgun. He beat up an editor in court. As Regent of the University of Georgia (once under Herman and a second time under Ernie Vandiver, at Herman's insistence), Harris tried to suppress the university newspaper, run by a "little handful of sissy, misguided squirts," and announced that it was "time to clean out all of these institutions of communist influences and the crazy idea of mixing and mingling of the races which was sponsored by the commie party," a cleaning out which was justified because "if the state is willing to spend this money it has the right to control what is taught and what is done at the university." In the Vandiver term, when the first Negroes were admitted to the University of Georgia, and rioting resulted, Regent Harris praised the rioters. "They had the courage and the nerve to stand up in the face of federal court decrees and to defy the police and the army of deans and get Negroes out of the university. These students are entitled to your encouragement." On another occasion he got so mad at some officials he thought were advocating integration he tried to organize a campaign of harassment. "Call them on the phone," he counseled. "Call them forty times a day. Call them all hours of the night." The legislature, no longer under his thumb, promptly passed a law making such harassment a misdemeanor. When Harris got sick of criticism in the newspapers, he suggested that what Georgia needed was a state-owned press.

Herman Talmadge once said of his father, "If he made up his mind that a certain thing was right, the whole world and all the family could try to persuade him to the contrary and it was like trying to push Stone Mountain over. Once he had made a decision, nothing could deter him. That was his greatest asset and also his greatest weakness."

Herman could have said the same for his mentor, Harris. Not long ago Harris said it for himself: "Sometimes a fellow can be so impolitic as to destroy his own usefulness. I might be a livin' example of that."

The election that made Herman Talmadge governor in 1948—youngest governor in the nation at thirty-five—held clues of what was to come. In the first place, the people of Georgia were barely sure they wanted him. Thompson, an able but rather colorless governor, received 300,000 votes while Talmadge was getting only 40,000 more than that, and Thompson had all sorts of handicaps. He did not get the support of the Atlanta newspapers, which had always been anti-Gene but now refused to take a positive position for a candidate who might have beaten down the resurgence of Talmadgism. Too, he was having to drag along behind him undeserved ties with national candidates who were in almost total disrepute in Georgia. Arnall had backed Henry Wallace for Vice President in 1944, and Thompson had been Arnall's executive secretary, so it was quite plain to many Georgians that Thompson was just as pink as Wallace and his Progressives. Happily Herman pointed out the "egg and tomato" reception Wallace had received in the South, with the implication that that was what true southerners thought of Thompson, too. Truman delivered his civil rights message to Congress that year, and Thompson, while he did not support the program, was loyal to HST. And when Dr. Samuel Green, Atlanta physician and the Imperial Grand Dragon of the Georgia Klan announced, "We are going to support the man who will put Georgia back in the white man's column," there was no confusion about whom he meant (if there had been, it would have been dispelled after Herman took office and made Dr. Green a member of his staff). Herman, of course, was running on a white-supremacy platform, not just vaguely theoretical but with practical applications. He had passed a "white primary" law during his two months as pretender, a law (nullified when he was nullified as governor) which wiped the Negro out of Democratic politics, and he vowed to pass it again. Thompson kept insisting that civil rights was no issue at all, kept trying to get the campaign back to a debate on his record in office, but Talmadge had only the one issue—civil rights—and he said that Thompson had Communist and Progressive Party support.

Not the least burden for Thompson was the fact that, after an earlier dispute, Arnall and Rivers were in open alliance again and supporting him. To many, Rivers' name was still a synonym for questionable conduct, and Arnall, in the two years since he had left office, had become more publicly linked to the racial moderates. His lecturing in the North had certainly deepened many Georgians' suspicions. He was even sniffed at by Ralph McGill and the Atlanta *Constitution* for accepting an award from the Southern Conference for Human Welfare, which McGill, like Talmadge, considered a communist-front organization. However good the intent of Arnall and Rivers, there was more than a little truth in Herman's observation, "They think two dead mules can carry more than one dead mule."

Because of their progressive reputation today, the role of the Atlanta *Constitution* and of Ralph McGill in that race is difficult to understand. While the paper did not endorse either candidate, the fact that it withheld endorsement from Thompson in itself was a victory for Herman. Further, it editorially judged both candidates' platforms to be the same, which of course was an absurd judgment. "My platform has one plank which overshadows all the rest of the planks in mine and all the rest of the other platforms," said Herman. "This plank is my unalterable opposition to all forms of the 'civil rights' program." Thompson did not make one utterance of this nature. And after the race was done and Talmadgism had set itself up again for a disastrous hold on the state during the crucial civil rights years, the *Constitution* lamely excused its share in the Talmadge victory by saying that Thompson, after all, had allowed some mismanagement of road contracts and had made one bad appointment to the revenue commission. McGill came in with his own he-deserved-it appraisal of Thompson as a defeated candidate by remarking that since less than half the registered Negroes went to the polls, "they couldn't have been too excited about Thompson." (Far less than half the white Georgia adults voted for Herman, which McGill did not mention.) And he spoke with high hopes of Herman the great emancipator who "promised more to the Negro—though separate—than ever promised before."

First it must be remembered that editor McGill was never more than one step, at best, ahead of the community, not three steps. And sometimes he sounded right in step. In that era, at least, he believed the FEPC, the anti-lynching bill and the anti-poll tax bill to be unconstitutional, and said so.

Also, there was bad blood between McGill and Thompson that was not exactly purified when McGill made an out-of-state speech in which he said, or at least Thompson was told that he said, that Georgia should thank God for Dr. Green, the top Klansman. "Now, Dr. Sam Green had married my cousin, I knew him before Ralph did, and I knew he wasn't the type of fellow you should get on your knees and thank God for," said Thompson, who came out blasting McGill's "hypocrisy." McGill responded in kind, explaining he meant Dr. Green was such a boob that Georgia should be grateful the Klan wasn't run by someone more able. It was years before feelings between them dropped to normal.

There were other factors that resulted in surprisingly good press for Talmadge. For one thing, lawyer Hughes Spalding, father of Atlanta *Journal* editor Jack Spalding, was at that time one of the most important behind-the-scenes men in Georgia politics, and he liked Talmadge. He was almost a political godfather to him. The Spalding firm, aside from representing the pillar Trust Company of Georgia and Coca Cola and numerous other fraternities of economic power, represented more important out-of-state business (and that's where some of the big political money came from in those days) than any other law firm in Georgia. The Spalding–big-business–newspaper tie-in was to mean a lot to Talmadge, especially when suspect dealings were not mentioned or were brushed aside in the press. When a college friend of Herman's made a couple million dollars extra building a bridge, it was played routinely in the Atlanta papers.

At first Herman's flirtation with the Atlanta press was covert and spasmodic. Today, of course, they could hardly be chummier, since the papers and Herman share a warm awareness that their prosperity depends on keeping the Atlanta establishment happy; but back in the county unit days, when the country boys had enough votes that they could make lewd signs at the city's wealthy elite, Herman, the country boy, could show more independence, could embarrass the *Constitution* with his outbursts of hillbilly hysteria, and make Atlanta's rulers content to get economic conservatism out of him. But in his bobtailed term, and for a time thereafter, he still ragged the papers because they criticized him, especially the *Journal*.

Three years after his election he was trying to get the legislature to pass extremely inhibitory legislation aimed specifically at the *Constitution* and the *Journal*, including a law that would have allowed them to be sued in every county. It did not pass because he did not press it, preferring to let it lie fallow as a threat. He was gauche with his intimidation of the press but he was equally gauche in his efforts to reward newsmen who supported him. Shortly after taking office he put on the state payroll seven editors and three former editors of papers that supported him, at salaries ranging from $50 to $500 a month, under the guise of writing for *The Statesman,* a shrieking political tabloid started by Gene Talmadge. A majority of the newspapers in Georgia, both daily and weekly, had opposed his election in 1948; these opponents he punished with a law repealing the apology provision in the state libel law which had enabled papers to correct honest mistakes. It was later ruled unconstitutional.

In the last couple of years of his second term as governor, Talmadge worked up a fine backscratching relationship with the Atlanta newspapers, especially with McGill, whose now-and-then opposition to the Talmadges had never fully covered his underlying admiration for them. Gene had even asked McGill to write his biography. In 1954, when Talmadge forced Stevenson to come to Georgia to make peace with the southern Democratic hotheads (Stevenson had never been at war with them, but they had been soured on his racial liberalism and had given only party—not personal—allegiance in the 1952 campaign), McGill was critical of the Atlanta liberals ("grim liberals," he called them) who, "with their stiff-necked demands for conformity, will not wish the Stevenson southern visit to be a happy one. They will try to enmesh him in the dialectics of civil rights and associated issues."

What had these "grim liberals" done to offend Talmadge, and, seemingly, therefore McGill? Well, in the presidential race two years earlier Talmadge had refused to spend any of the state Democratic money on a Stevenson–Sparkman headquarters. Instead he used the money to circulate anti-Negro literature in support of the amendment he was then trying to pass, which would have put the county-unit system into the state constitution with the aim of permanently cutting Georgia away from the one-man, one-vote concept. The amendment failed, and now Talmadge, trying to salvage something with the national organization, was buttering up to Adlai and didn't want the liberals (who had spent their *own* money to set up and operate a Stevenson headquarters) getting in the way with their "stiff-necked demands" to "enmesh him in the dialectics of civil rights," as his friend McGill put it so well.

Had the enmeshment come about, it presumably would have included questions about why Talmadge, only a week before Stevenson's visit, had asked his legislature to clear the way for abolishing the public-school system and subsidizing private instruction if the U.S. Supreme Court should actually go through with the feared desegregation. This came close to destroying the "new Herman" image being developed by the Atlanta press, but the *Constitution* did its best to repair the damage by editorially hailing the move as "sensible, calming," and went right on with this deadpan reaction by joining in "a salute to the Governor who, for all his extreme feelings on the subject, has risen to the challenge of it and come forward with the *only two proposals possible for a civilized people dedicated to Christian ethics.*"

Georgia's scattered band of embattled liberals read this with numbed incomprehension, only the more sophisticated realizing that the procedure of signal-calling in the Atlanta establishment is so cumbersome that sometimes the newspaper spokesmen, for all their good intentions, find themselves stepping on their own editorial heels.

After Herman packed off to Washington, the Atlanta papers went all out for him, finding virtue in the most shadowed alcoves of his life. In January of 1959, for example, Talmadge had taken the Senate floor to ask support for constitutional amendments that would return control of the schools to local authority, arguing that such an amendment was necessary because the Supreme Court decision of 1954 "is an accomplished fact which will remain so until it either is reversed by the Court itself or is nullified or modified by the Congress or the people."

Most liberals saw the move as, at best, bunkum, and, at worst, an attempt to deprive the nation's children of their share of federal court protection. The *Constitution,* however, interpreted it all much differently. The newspaper picked up the phrase "an accomplished fact" and made it seem that Talmadge was in the forefront of those who were calling for moderation and acceptance of the law. Talmadge was hailed as a politician of "courage and character," since "seeking a constitutional amendment to return control of schools to local authority did a necessary service for his state and region." What was the service? "He became the first Deep South Senator or Representative publicly to state that the Supreme Court decision 'is an accomplished fact.' " Of such slender hairs have the *Constitution* and the *Journal* helped Herman weave his rope to respectability. Of course, Herman has sometimes made it hard for them. Just three months after those editorial hurrahs, Herman was back in Atlanta, still talking about the Supreme Court's "accomplished fact," but now going on to say that he would prefer to see the public schools closed than to "surrender" to the Court's accomplished fact, and he knew the South shared his feeling of rebellion. "Whether one likes it or not, the overwhelming majority of the people of the South will neither accept nor submit to the forced implementation of that decision and there is no prospect of any change in that position within the foreseeable future."

The Atlanta papers weren't able to clean that up, editorially, and the publishers were ever so grateful when the Atlanta money establishment told Talmadge to shut up about closing the schools. That was his last outburst, the reason coming out later when Roy Harris released a letter he received in January 1960 from James S. Peters of Manchester, a banker and long-time power in state politics (he was one of the big seven from Gene's camp who ramrodded the move to seat Herman in 1946), as well as chairman at that time of the state Board of Education. Peters was urging Harris also to shut up about closing the schools, reminding him that Arnall had said that if the schools were closed, he would run for re-election. Wrote Peters: "Given twelve months with our schools closed to register 600,000 Negroes and to convince the mothers and fathers the only way to re-open is with him as governor, Ellis will be difficult indeed to defeat and Herman could very easily go down with him. *Thus we would lose control of the government and entrench Ellis Arnall and the integrationists in the control of the government for decades to come.* I do not agree with you as to the public sentiments. In fact, it is changing and will change much faster between now and September 1962 [when Talmadge was up for re-election] unless Herman Talmadge and his friends find a better answer to this problem than the closing down of the public school system. . . . If the leaders in our camp would get together and talk this problem over, maybe we could arrive at some kind of solution. *Otherwise, we are headed towards defeat and the loss of our power and influence in the government of this state.*" This was the message of big business, and Herman heard it very clearly.

Herman had a hard time taking hold as governor. Except that they

served as a period of semi-alert apprenticeship, most of his first two years
in office was wasted time. The Talmadge gang—especially road boss Jim
Gillis, comptroller Zack Cravey, speaker Fred Hand, and, of course,
Harris—ran the government while he played. A number of the bills put
through the legislature in this period, one reporter noted at the time,
"could make a dictator out of Talmadge," but he added, "the young man
doesn't look nor act like a dynamic dictator pulling legislative strings. He
has been criticized for not furnishing administrative leadership in the governor's office. He doesn't show too much interest in another term." Another reporter recalls Herman as a "lost sheep" during the first two years.
Lost wolf might be another appropriate description. He spent part of the
'48 campaign on crutches because of an auto. crackup with his blonde
secretary. (As Big Jim Folsom of Alabama once noted, apropos of the
flirtations of another southern governor: "I guess women is just a professional handicap of us leaders.") Herman had only five speeches—a
women's club speech, a civic club speech, a Glorious South speech, a
loyalty speech, and what he called his "bull" speech for farm groups.
Sometimes, being tipsy, he would mistakenly give his bull speech to a
women's club. Hand recalls that Herman would sometimes carouse for
four or five days "and finally they would send me to hunt him up to get
some of the bills signed." Eventually evangelist Billy Graham got Herman
to quit, and this led one Talmadge enemy to note coldly and with some
disappointment, "Well, it looks like Hummon isn't going to be a sot
after all."

The people of Georgia were not able to detect any great signs of
leadership from Herman in his bobtailed term, and when Thompson came
back in 1950 to challenge him again, Georgia was almost of a mind to
take Thompson this time. Some still wonder if a majority of Georgians
didn't vote that way.

Charlie Pou remembers the 1950 election as "the longest count since
the Dempsey–Tunney fight," the main difference being that in the prize-
fight the counting was done out in the open. At 11 p.m. of election night,
Thompson was far ahead in popular vote and slightly ahead in county-unit
votes. But strangely, reports of the counting stopped coming in at that
point, and it was two hours later before any new tabulations were given.
Rumors were strong that the Talmadge strategists used those two hours
to keep the telephones rattling into counties where the vote was still
undecided, gaining assurance, in the accepted way, that the count would

come out all right. Thompson said he later reproached Harris "for stealing the election from me. And he said, 'M. E., we didn't steal as many counties as you think.' I said, 'How many did you steal?' He said, 'Only about thirty-five.' It's hard to tell when Roy's kidding or not." Several counties first reported Thompson winner, later saying this was an error and that Herman actually had won. When the fox was gone and all the feathers had fallen to earth and were counted, Herman not only had the county-unit vote, he also had the slightest of edges—around 6,000 votes— as the popular hero. "Nobody in Georgia today thinks, I believe," says Thompson, "that he got most of the popular vote honestly."

But that—as Coke Stevenson discovered in his 1948 Senate race with Lyndon B. Johnson—is not finally of much importance. The rules seem to have a rather negligible place in a career, such as Talmadge's, that was begun with several dozen questionable votes and perpetuated with a late and highly suspect count—when, whether or not such judgments are accurate, the result is to establish a man in a highly powerful position and keep him there indefinitely. Thompson may have been victimized, but so far as Georgia politics is concerned he is just a loser, getting increasingly faint sympathy as the state's memory of the backroom balloting grows dimmer.

Low though the clouds may have hung over his second election, Herman was willing to accept any margin as a mandate to get tough, step out of the shadows, send the palace gang on lowly errands and stop letting them make the laws. Picture the man. He tacked a scoreboard up in his office and let it be known that he would keep precise watch on the voting records of each and every member of the legislature; those who voted non-Talmadge could expect their constituents to travel over dirt roads from then on, for all he would help. Gene, who once said he didn't know if Herman would ever amount to much in politics because he said nigra, would have been proud of him. Now he was regularly saying nigger. His newspaper, *The Statesman,* was also turning out fine copy and photos, with one of Talmadge's hired snoopers going around to interracial meetings with a tape recorder and camera, taking pictures of Herman's political enemies.

As for those damned niggers soaking up the welfare money which honest people and corporations were having to pay for, at least he could parade their shame; he instructed state and county welfare officials to make relief rolls public.

Things were going along pretty well for those who counted. As soon as old minimum-price laws were declared unconstitutional, new ones were cranked through the legislature. Herman was luring industry by going around the country boasting, "our workers are satisfied and we have no delays and anticipate none," a subtlety the industrialists understood without translation. Just to put the fear of decent folks in those commie labor organizers, a law with a twenty-year penalty for "subversion" went through the legislature. Wiley Moore, the big mule lobbyist of Georgia, gave a fancy party for the legislature and said, "I'm doing this because I love you, not because I want anything." And why not? He had all he wanted. This was the session Herman gave Moore's crowd the sales tax.

Herman always found it a little hard to keep his word when it came to taxation. Not only did he vow never, never to bring upon the people of Georgia a sales tax; he promised he would institute no tax program whatsoever without the people's approval. So he put a $46 million tax referendum to them, to improve schools, roads, health and other services —it would have increased taxes 42 percent, mostly from the consumer— and the people slushed through the mud and rain to vote 3 to 1 against the corporations' boy being so generous with their money. That was in April. Less than three months later he went back on his promise and pushed through $20 million in new taxes anyway, without a referendum, and again all but the smallest fraction of the money was to come from the consumer. Again in 1950 he campaigned on the promise that he would not pass a sales tax. But with his approval a different kind of campaign was being pushed covertly for him, largely by his lobbyist-advisor Harris, who recalls, "I told Herman to wait until I had made it popular and then for him to pick it up. Well, long before the '50 campaign I started putting out speakers through the P-TA's. We got teachers to talk up the sales tax—teachers will sell out to anybody for a pay raise—then I went down to my hotel in Atlanta and set up school during the session. I would call in ten or twelve legislators each night and say, "Now, fellows, your job doesn't really amount to a shit, does it? And they would agree. And I would say, "Even if you were defeated, it wouldn't hurt anything but your pride, would it?' And they would agree. So, I said, 'There comes a time when you've just got to sacrifice your career for your state, and that time is now.' But you know, we only lost one legislator in the next election. and I'm not sure he got defeated for that reason."

Sure enough, the 1951 legislative session saw Herman's gang pushing through the most all-inclusive sales tax in the nation. There was a record budget that year, but a tremendous slice of it would come right out of the pocket of the poorest people in Georgia with that sales tax. To some extent it was sold to the taxpayers with the theme that teachers were underpaid, which they were, but inasmuch as the highest paid teacher in Georgia in that day made only a little over $2,000—the lowest maximum in the nation—it was evident the people didn't give much of a damn about keeping their teachers in luxury. So Herman gave them a much more appealing pitch, to wit, that the money would help equalize Negro and white school facilities and thereby keep the federal government off the South's back. It was the same sales talk Governor James Byrnes used to pass the sales tax in South Carolina and other politicians used elsewhere. Wasn't it, after all, worth just an extra three measly pennies on top of each dollar to keep the nigger boys from going to school with your daughters and taking them into the bushes at recess?

Out of this successful ploy evolved Herman's reputation as a progressive governor. *Harper's* magazine, for just one example, went into a spasm of praise. "Talmadge—the Best Southern Governor?" the magazine asked, and then answered with an emphatic *yes*, well supported with data about how Talmadge had spent more on public schools than all other Georgia governors put together: teachers' salaries had been raised 125 percent, the state mental hospital appropriation doubled* and staff salaries also doubled, and maximum drawable under state pension doubled.

All very good, but there has probably never been a modern southern governor of whatever degree of reaction who would not have been perfectly happy to spend money on the people, if the people—not corporations—would put it up. Power is drawn from favors, and if the people will pay for the favors, any politician will accept the resulting power without much protest. For the corporations of Georgia, Talmadge removed all but a token property tax. For the people of Georgia, he passed the 3 percent sales tax, giving himself a budget three times larger than any previous governor had had to play with.

---

* In states like the Georgia Herman was ruling, it does not take much to achieve quite a reputation for progress. In the Georgia insane asylums the patients were dying and dead for three days before found; rats ate them. Herman did give the patients a ratless place to sleep and to die.

George Wallace, the South's most notorious loser, must have consciously imitated the career of Herman Talmadge, and Wallace would have had good reason for doing so, because Herman, ten years before the coming of Wallace, had proved very ingenious in building a successful political career on a broad foundation of demagogic failures. It was not a matter of snatching victory from defeat but of making defeat a prerequisite for victory.

He tried to protect the Klan, then realized that the Georgia public, however reactionary, didn't care to have their trashy brothers protected, so Herman turned on his old hooded supporters.

He tried to get the Negroes disenfranchised by wiping the registration roles clean and requiring that everyone re-register—only to discover that the Negroes were re-registering but the poor whites weren't—so he had the law repealed.

He tried to get the state to go on the private-school system rather than integrate the public schools, but only managed to get everything so botched up that his banker friends in Atlanta, six years after he left office, were still trying to "work things out" for the legislature in a face-saving way.

He talked about leading a nationwide crusade (picked up by Wallace later), but that fell through, just as his willingness to tout for Gerald L. K. Smith had fallen through earlier.

Again and again he called for total resistance to the Supreme Court's edicts, but almost as frequently he would state publicly that there wasn't a chance of outwitting the Court.

Herman was always a bungler as an anti-communist, perhaps because Georgia has never exactly been a hotbed of communism. When in 1954 his legislature created a new, involved questionnaire for state employes to sign—although they already had to sign another loyalty oath—and when the state workers found that one of the demands of the new questionnaire was that they tattle-tale on any of their relatives whom they considered a little too liberal, complaints reached such a peak that within three days Herman had backed down on the most obnoxious portions.*

Of all these failures and reversals, none was more elaborate and pro-

* But remaining was the threat of a twenty-year prison sentence for anyone caught trying to "overthrow or *alter*" the governments of the United States, Georgia, or any political subdivision, including, presumably, trying to throw out the court-house rascals.

tracted than the private-school concept. This gripped him like rigor mortis. And, as one in rigor mortis, he never could seem to get moving. Right after he was re-elected in 1950, the new-tough Talmadge rammed through a bill to enable the state to close down the public schools if the courts ordered even one Negro admitted. Two years later he was grumbling threateningly that the state could transfer public schools to private schools in just a few days if necessary to prevent "strife and bloodshed." Five years later, now in the U.S. Senate, he joined with Senator Russell in pleading for state leaders to carry on with the private-school plan. Two years later, in 1960, knowing they were confronted with an impossible mess if the private-school plan took effect, the money kings of Atlanta stepped in to quietly wipe out Herman's nonsense but in such a way as to save both Herman's and the legislature's face. Appropriately, considering how much money his group had sunk in Herman, the job was supervised by John A. Sibley, law partner of Hughes Spalding. After a series of hearings at which the public could express its opinion, the men who owned the legislature went ahead and ordered what they had in mind to begin with: public schools, permanently, and no funny business. Herman's great threat was dead without ever having really been alive.

Tall in the saddle and seemingly half-crocked, Herman went charging about the countryside lusting for a tilt with federalism, and pudgy Roy Harris, a faithful Sancho Panza, went clippity-clopping along behind, shouting encouragement and advice. The fact that, like Don Quixote, Ol' Hummon generally wound up in a ditch, did not diminish the romantic Georgians' love for him.

However, it is too much to say, as one newspaper did recently: "Whatever Senator Herman Talmadge has been depicted as, one thing is for sure: you can't find anything in the record to show where he has tried to hurt Negroes EXCEPT TALK." (Their capitals.) This is not true. He has taken numerous legislative steps to hurt the Negro, but they all failed, except for demoralizing effect on the Negro and exciting effect on the redneck. And of course, although it is correct to say that the upshot of all his efforts was so much talk, no one but a fool would suppose that just talk, in the South, when fused by racism, cannot be as dangerous as the airy shock waves from a dynamite explosion.

Like his father, Herman has a very limited concept of the proper separation and balance of the three branches of government, especially in regard to the judiciary's place, and there are times when he seems to have no idea at all of what due process means. The best way to circumvent the court is simply, in the best anarchist fashion, to deny its jurisdiction. He sneers at "court-made law," but he also sneers at constitutional law —when it gets in his way. As governor, Talmadge's greatest achievement was in circumventing the state constitutional prohibition against any bonded indebtedness. He did it by setting up "authorities" to take the debt responsibility. It wasn't the state that sold all those school bonds, no, it was the School Building Authority; and the same dodge was employed by Herman and his hand-picked successors in the Stone Mountain Authority, the Jekyll Island Authority, the Office Building Authority. By the time Herman left office the state was strapped with more long-term debt ($250 million) than the framers of the state constitution had ever dreamed possible even when they wrote the precautionary prohibition against that very thing. So much for the sanctity of constitutional law.

It was a disdain he extended in all directions, down as well as up. In the last year of his bobtail term, Talmadge's cop-driven limousine was stopped in Adrian, Georgia, by Police Chief E. W. Avery and charged with speeding through town at 65 and 70 miles an hour in a 25-mile zone, and going through a red light. Talmadge told Chief Avery he had no right to arrest him. Avery said he had the powers given to him by the city charter. To that Herman responded typically: "That charter isn't worth the paper it was written on." When he was sworn in as U.S. senator, six years later, he was ready to step that isn't-worth-the-paper appraisal up to take in the U.S. Constitution; asked about his attitude to the oath to support the Constitution, he replied: "I've got as much right to interpret the Constitution as anyone else in this country. *I'll be bound by what Herman Talmadge thinks it means.*"

The same year he was asked if he thought it would be possible to overthrow the Supreme Court ruling on segregation, and he said yes, he thought it would be possible, simply by ignoring the Court. "The court of last resort in a republican form of government is the people" (this not terribly profound concept he had picked up, almost word for word, from Roy Harris ten years earlier and had been repeating to the point of almost total nausea). *"As long as the people resist on the local level in a determined manner there is little that the federal government can do to enforce its desegregation decision."* On another occasion he said, "I think the court of last resort is the people, and if the people don't comply, there's little the courts can do about it."

He went on to say that no decision of the Supreme Court or any other court "is entitled any greater moral weight than its context merits. If a decision of the federal Supreme Court is doctrinally correct and in accord with the fundamental law of the Constitution, it carries great moral force. If on the other hand, it undertakes to announce a rule contrary to the federal Constitution, contrary to the dual system which is the foundation of the national government, and clearly indicates that the law and the facts have been ignored, the Supreme Court is teaching error and its ruling should be sternly disapproved by both officials and general public. Such a decision is not the law. It simply is a theoretically enforceable pronouncement of the court."

This throwback to the ancient query of how many *ad hoc's* can be put on the point of a pin really comes down to mean, of course, every man for himself. If you don't like a decision, if you think the court is "teaching error," why, ignore the judge. Is that what Herman means? Well, yes, that's what he meant back then, before the civil righters got to trespassing on private property and breaking "bad" municipal laws; that's what he meant back when most of the law-breaking fun was being had by state and municipal officials in relation to the federal laws. *Then* obedience to the law was strictly an *ad hoc* thing that came equipped with nullification and interposition gadgets that permitted all sorts of patriotic-rebellious games to be played. "We're not going to secede from the union but the people of Georgia will not comply with the decision of the Court. It would take several divisions of troops down here to police every school building and then they wouldn't be able to enforce it." That sort of thing was being said by Herman in 1954 and 1956 and even 1958.

But in recent years, with the civil righters outploying the segregationists in the game of anarchy, Herman has suddenly become very law-abiding. Speaking at the annual Law Day at the University of Georgia, Herman stated with massive indignation that the reason "all of the rules of civilized and orderly conduct seem to have been forgotten" is that the demonstrators have been listening to "the ill-advised philosophy that whenever anyone does not agree with authority, he may scorn it, whenever the law is not to your liking you may disobey it."

It so happened that by the irony of programming, Lindsey Cowen, Dean of the University of Georgia law school, had some words to say on the same occasion on the same subject, but his conclusions were quite different. (The *Constitution* diplomatically printed the stories three pages apart.) The Selma trouble was going on at the time and Dean Cowen, likening the Negro protestants to the signers of the Declaration of Independence, said that Americans have always taken the position that "we are entitled to use all effective means to achieve our fundamental rights, and if this suggests disregard of parade permit laws or other local ordinances, then this is justified."

Herman was furious. Weeks later he was still privately damning Cowen's cheek in disagreeing right there out in the open. At one meeting with several cronies in state politics he brought it up and they offered to do what they could to get Cowen's budget whittled down at the next legislature.

Walter George went to the U.S. Senate, replacing the lately dead Tom Watson, with the support of the Ku Klux Klan and trailing the (they thought) unbreakable reins of Georgia business and utility interests. That was 1922, and for a time he lived up to the hopes of the monied men and rubes who sent him to the Senate, by denouncing all foreign entanglements but especially denouncing the League of Nations. He proposed liberalization of immigration laws, so the mill owners could be sure of a steady supply of cheap foreign labor. The soldier bonus, he said, was typically the idea of those who want something for nothing, at the expense of the business community. Not only was he in favor of the Volstead Act, he wanted stiffer laws against illegal booze, so that businessmen and factory owners could anticipate steadier and more sober work from their employes, to say nothing of keeping down the cost of welfare.

However, George was not a man to stay tied. He remained conservative, but he became magnanimous. Within the next decade George had voted for the World Court, had supported Al Smith (the nation's foremost foe of prohibition) for president, and was himself scorning the Volstead Act as federal intrusion into "a private citizen's habits and wishes." Later he opposed the wage-hour law, the Wagner Housing Act, and enlargement of the Supreme Court. But he voted for all those alphabetical torments to the capitalist, the NRA, AAA, SEC, and TVA. He backed social security.

Georgia Power & Light got some return for its money when George fought regulation of utility holding companies, and the country-club cardiacs loved him when he fought FDR's tax on the undistributed profits of corporations. As Chairman of the Senate Finance Committee, he had been during the war, some critics thought, markedly solicitous of the tax problems of rich people and corporations.

But since World War II he had distressed this set with what appeared to them a treacherous mellowness. When Congress proposed to chip away tax exemptions benefiting lower and middle-income groups, George raised hell in his stately manner, countering with the proposal that exemptions for these groups be expanded. His conservative followers viewed this as madness.

He had in other ways drifted from the static right—and from Georgia. There were some counties he had not visited in two decades. There had been a time when he was against loans and other aides to foreign countries, but his boy had been killed in the war and now he was ready to support anything, even what Herman was to call "global WPA," if there was a chance that it would postpone the next war. George did not realize that the predominant creed in his home state held that the only virtuous spending was military spending, because it kept those war dollars coming into Georgia. Russell knew this and catered to it; Herman knew it and was willing to cater if he ever got to the Senate.

So concerned for the welfare of the world did George become that he switched over from the chairmanship of the Finance Committee to head the Foreign Relations Committee—the last thing needed, if more were in fact needed, to prove to his financial supporters that he was no longer trustworthy and could even be dangerous.

(Things had reached this point by the time Herman left office. Coca-Cola liked him, he liked Coca-Cola. He had nowhere to go, if he didn't go to the Senate, and neither he nor the business cadre wanted to waste the county-unit machine he had developed so expertly. Dumping George would give him special delight, anyway, since Gene Talmadge had always believed George's group had stolen the election from him in 1938.)

When, in 1955, Germany was criticized for resuming diplomatic relations with Russia, the German ambassador flew off to Georgia to offer excuses to Senator George. Such was the power of this old man (seventy-eight) with the gee-gaw eyes and the voice of Gideon. On economic matters he was still far more conservative than the mainstream of America, but even such a liberal magazine as *The Nation* recognized old George as "the indispensable man in Washington" on international affairs. "It has been his influence and initiative rather than President Eisenhower's or Mr. Dulles'," *The Nation* editorialized, "which has given a new affirmative emphasis to American policy."

But what was this to the ranks of Georgians? Praise from outsiders only made George appear all the more suspicious in their eyes. He must, by damn, be going Yankee, or global, or one-worldly. Better listen to Talmadge, who was not mentioning George by name—except when with Mark Antony-like deference he called him "venerable and distinguished" —but was striking at his defects. Talmadge suggested (and Wallace was to parrot him, almost word for word, ten years later when he prepared for his second and more earnest Presidential campaign) that he had done all he could on the state level and now needed to follow the foe onto the broad fields of the world, striking distant blows for Dixie. "It has been impressed upon me that these forces seeking to undermine our state and local governments and our southern way of life," he growled, "are operating on a nationwide scale and are well organized, deeply entrenched and lavishly financed from the national level. CONSEQUENTLY, the battle for survival of Georgia and the South must likewise be waged on the national level." He would volunteer for the fight.

Senator George, meanwhile, knew he was in trouble, not from his enemies but from his friends; he and Talmadge would have to tap the same campaign-fund sources, and already there were indications that the affections of some old George supporters were weakening. Gently he had been felt out about retiring. He had responded with a firm refusal. After Herman had announced his own candidacy, George was still firm: "My health is good and I will run and expect to be re-elected."

Then the heat increased. A close friend of George's tells of going by the senator's office about this time. "He said he wanted to show me something. It was an editorial on his desk from the Savannah *Morning News*. It said he had had a long and distinguished career but now he should retire. Then he gave me a folder of about fifty letters in it, from people like the president of Johnson & Johnson, Monsanto, and people like that. They also would begin by saying 'You have had a wonderful record as a Senator. I think, however, the time has come for you to make an honorable retirement.' They were so much alike it almost looked like the same person had dictated all of them. Senator George said, 'Somebody inspired these letters. I know these people personally, and they have no reason to have ever met Herman Talmadge.' He then straightened up in his chair and said,

'————————, there was one time I said I would make this race if my health permitted it. Now I assure you I'll make this race if I'm living.' "

It takes more than courage or determination to see a man of George's age through a campaign, however. It takes easily obtained money. He was too old to go to the people and conduct the only kind of exhausting race that can be conducted if one has no money, and he was too old to exert the kind of brutal pressures that are sometimes required to get money from reluctant sources. Either he got his financial support easily and generously, or he was finished. Game though he was to take on Talmadge in what had been by that time billed as one of the great political battles of the century, he could not do it without funds.

He thought he had them. He ordered his campaign to begin at full steam. Then, almost overnight, he discovered there was no steam. A major source who had furnished the funds to get the campaign briefly underway and told him there would be plenty more shortly, now told him there would be no more from him or from any other major source in the state. The same people whom George had befriended over so many years in the Senate now withdrew; he was too old and too politically mystic, and there was a much younger man at hand who better understood their practical needs.

President Eisenhower was visiting in Thomasville. Robert Woodruff of Coca-Cola and some of the other Top People of Atlanta went by to see him and work things out. And in a matter of hours George had received the telephone call.

On May 9, 1956, bitterly bringing to an end a Senate career of thirty-three years, longer than any other member, last of an era that had included such men as Borah, Lodge, Norris, and La Follette, George called a press conference to announce that "for good and sufficient reasons which I will not elaborate on at this time," he was dropping out of the race.

The television lights were hot and George was sweating. At times his voice could not be heard at the back of the room. As he started to read a letter from the President, offering him the new post of ambassador to NATO, he choked up for a moment and his wife, Miss Lucy, patted him on the shoulder. No, he told reporters, he did not want to leave the Senate. No, his health was not that bad. And once again he muttered something about "good and sufficient reasons."

There was more than one price George would not or could not pay. "If he had just made one speech giving the Supreme Court hell," said Roy

Harris, "nobody could have beat him." But George had come too far from the days of KKK support for that. He had, in fact, come too far from Georgia in general.

And that's the end of the Talmadge success story. Having arrived in the Senate—the mountain from which he had intended to dispense the loaves and fishes of his segregationist-isolationist wisdom, a promontory which his father had twice tried and failed to reach—Herman watched everything dissolve and fade away.

The machine at home was still safe; his admirers now included Atlanta's flashiest; he could undoubtedly have the post for life, or at least until Coca-Cola decided that things would go better without him. Yet everything was suddenly blah. Partly it was circumstances, partly it was his own doing.

One of the tales told about Herman's departure for Washington has it that when he went to see his mamma down on the old plantation at Sugar Creek she got him aside and asked seriously, "Hummon, what you want to go up to Washington for with all them old fogies? You know you can't do nothing with 'em, or change their ways of thinkin'." To which Herman is said to have answered, "I know, Mamma, but I'll sure have a lot of fun working 'em over."

Like old cheese giving off mold, such legends of aggressiveness keep developing around the memory of Gene, and then, without any basis, spreading to Herman. Actually the last thing Herman intended to do in Washington was to "work over" the old fogies. Doubtless the purse holders of Atlanta had given him his instructions: Be nice, don't embarrass us, we sent you and we can bring you back; for the power structure of the South, being utterly unterrified of the obvious, accepts stereotypes with much greater alacrity than most people, and thereafter assumes that the stereotype, having been accepted by its omnipotence, will never change. Talmadge did not need the advice. He was and is smarter than the purse holders. He knew what the country as a whole thought of his election. Thomas L. Stokes reported Democratic Party leaders "disturbed at the prospect of having Herman Talmadge, white supremacy crusader," in the Senate. "Among some Democrats, the looming figure of Herman Talmadge caused almost a shudder." His potential was seen as equal to that of James Eastland as "a real bugaboo for Republican campaign purposes."

One important northern newspaper (*Baltimore Sun*) had said of

Herman's election to the Senate that "he is not fit to polish Senator George's shoes, much less fill them." It was not an uncommon judgment, as Herman was well aware. A more accurate anticipation was that of Douglass Cater, that Talmadge's entry onto the national scene would not mean "a return to old-fashoned demagogy" but rather "would mean a rebuke to a conservative, constructive brand of southern statesmanship, particularly in foreign policy"; such expectations of a mere change of philosophy, however, were rather rare.

Herman came to Washington as the foremost contemporary spokesman for white supremacy. This was his reputation and it was deserved. To most of the nation this made it a perfect certainty that he would dribble on his chin, he would talk of making Eleanor Roosevelt queen of an African colony, he would assert his deathless preference for being a yaller dog baying at the southern moon than making one concession that might defile the blood of the white race. Everybody just *knew* it.

And of course Herman played it the other way. He was quiet. He was reasonably sober. He declined an invitation to speak before the women's press corps on segregation. He deferred to one and all of his colleagues. He stood in line for assignments. And after waiting two months before opening his mouth on the floor, did he choose segregation, the Supreme Court, or any variation of the expected theme for his maiden speech? No, he put on his glasses and stood at his desk at the back row and he read in a very genteel voice seven legal-size pages disagreeing with Eisenhower's policy in the Middle East.

Furthermore, to give the speech he passed up a conflicting appointment to present his views on the Administration's civil rights program before the Judiciary Committee.

The reaction was more than Herman had hoped and planned for. Washington hostesses and Washington columnists clucked around him delightedly. He did not, after all, have blood on his cuff. What a sweet, sane, dignified young demagogue he was! Not at all like that cancerous Bilbo! It was almost the first thing said—"not at all like Bilbo"—and the refrain was never ended. Suddenly it became one of his great accomplishments, not being Bilbo. He had discovered a new way into the heart of America: being a disappointment. Two years later, Speaker Sam Rayburn still thought it was worth commenting on: "Herman Talmadge has fooled a lot of people by turning out to be . . . not a hell-raiser as some of his critics had billed him." Turning out not to be something had verily such

a traumatic effect on Washington's anticipations that the automatic con-
versational reaction to the mention of his name is still, "Talmadge? Well,
at least he didn't turn out . . ." Herman had blotted himself out. What
started as a transient ploy, a procedural gimmick for getting good freshman marks, has ground on grimly to become a career of not being somebody else.

And the main reason that this is about all one can say of his senatorial
career to date is that he *is* so unlike Bilbo in one aspect usually not considered by the hostesses and the columnists: foulmouthed, unfair, bullying and unprincipled though he was, Bilbo loved the Senate.

And Herman does not.

He is bored by the homework necessary for committee work. He is
glum and short-tempered as he is forced to stand in the deep shadow of
Richard Russell, and pretend for the sake of harmony that he does not care.

Twelve years ago when Herman went up to the Senate, Paul Mayhew
wrote of him that "he has a tighter rein on his impulses and has a better
mind [than Gene]. A better mind, but not cultivated nor truly civilized.
What Herman does possess is a shrewd intelligence, which he uses as a
compleat materialist. To him, as to Peter Bell, a primrose by the river's
brim is a yellow flower, and nothing else. He moves passively and porten-
tously within the range of his narrow outlook. . . . He is immune to the
stir and fret of a world in transition. Like his father again, he stands for
a particular kind of chauvinism, which would make the dark, brooding
intolerance of the Georgia backwoods the yardstick of national and international conduct."

Mayhew had only Herman's time as governor from which to draw
his conclusion; his Senate years have more than confirmed it. Where he
was once exuberantly parochial as a governor, he is now sullenly petty
as a senator. He is on George's old committee, Finance, but he has made
no mark there. If Herman has any specialty in the Senate, it is attacking
foreign aid, which he does with monotonous hyperbole and myth (it is too
clumsily done to be lies). He complains of U.S. money being spent to
build highways to gambling hotels in Portugal—highways which, in fact,
were in operation six months before counterpart funds were released.
When he is corrected in such errors, he responds by repeating the original
accusation, perhaps adding something even more far-fetched. "We have
used foreign aid dollars to send iceboxes to the Eskimos, ultra-violet-ray
lamps to India, dress suits to Grecian undertakers, and collapsible tooth-

paste tubes to Cambodia." Pure imagination.

He attempts to maintain some agreement between his real life and the image of the "new" Talmadge, but, relaxing in private conversation, he still slips easily into the nigger–coon vocabulary of race relations, and in the Senate he cannot refrain from sideswiping the Negro occasionally by insisting, for instance, on an investigation to see if federal welfare payments might not be encouraging illegitimacy—all good southerners knowing who those bastards belong to.

He has time to perfect trivial skills. He is known among newsmen as a genius of weaseling. There is hardly a serious topic, even including segregation, on which they can get a hard and fast answer from him.

Q. Are you against foreign aid?

Talmadge: If it costs you one dollar to make a friend, you'd better keep the dollar. If it costs you a friend to make a dollar, you had better keep the friend.

He has time, too, to tinker with Cotton Mather bills that would allow states to establish their own anti-pornography standards, unaffected by federal court rulings.

His abuse of the Supreme Court, of course, continues, but without much notice. When Potter Stewart was up for confirmation by the Senate, even Eastland treated his name with dignity, although he opposed the appointment. Of the entire southern delegation, only Talmadge played dirty pool, clearly suggesting that there was one case in Stewart's past which pointed to a possibly invidious strain of sympathy for Negro men who rape white women. The facts of the case, briefly, were these: James Henderson, a Michigan Negro, was accused of raping a white barmaid. The investigation into the case and the preparation of his defense were not extensive; in fact, *two and a half hours* after his arrest, he had been brought to trial and convicted on a plea of guilty and sentenced to life in prison.

The law of the land today, founded on the famous *Gideon* v. *Wainright* decision of 1963, is that every man tried in a felony case must have an attorney. Henderson's case, preceding this decision, was processed without its protection and therefore at every appeals level Henderson was turned down. Between the trial judge and the U.S. Supreme Court, only Potter Stewart, then on the U.S. Court of Appeals, believed that Henderson deserved a new trial, noting that not only had the Negro been denied an attorney, he had not even been asked if he wanted one. Said Stewart, in his dissent: "Swift justice demands more than just swiftness."

Ah, said Talmadge, doesn't it seem a "strange thing" that "among all that vast array of legal talent, state and federal, Associate Justice Potter Stewart is the only one who dissented and took the position that the criminal *should be freed after he had committed that atrocious crime?*"

So long as he watches over the special interests of those who sent him to Washington, he is perfectly free, in this way, to empty his chamber pot on society. Seldom is he questioned at home, seldom challenged. When, not long ago, Talmadge started chewing again on his old theme of "people" cranking out "a large number of illegitimate children" so they could "draw several hundred dollars a month in welfare payments," the chairman of the Georgia State Board of Family and Children Services denounced his statement as "damaging" and "misleading," pointing out that in Georgia it didn't matter how many dependent children a woman had, illegitimate or otherwise, she could not receive more than $134 a month. The mere fact that someone in public life would dare to take issue with Herman left the Atlanta press quivering with amazement and grudging admiration. The *Constitution,* only half humorously, called it "sheer political boldness," adding with what appeared to be a wry awareness of its own meek record in controlling Talmadgism, that "as everybody in Georgia political life knows, [upbraiding Talmadge] is such a flagrant violation of unwritten political law that few would even dare contemplate it. It just *isn't* done." And the newspaper's editor, Eugene Patterson, noted in his own column, "Nearly a generation has grown up since it was considered imprudent to cross Senator Herman Talmadge." The fact that so much stir was created from one trivial disagreement illustrates better than anything the protection that has been given to Herman by those who know how to dilute opposition. It may be he will need this assistance of the press and the purse handlers of Atlanta, for he has never run for office against measurable opposition except under the old county-unit system, by which a rural voter had approximately eleven times more to say about the outcome of an election than a city voter could say.

But not until 1966 did Herman discover that, despite the freedoms allowed him by his keepers, he is far from being a free man.

The circumstances under which he made the discovery were indeed ironic. Two years before the last campaign for governor opened formally, it was plain that the real contest for the Democratic nomination would be between two ex-governors—Ernest Vandiver, sweetheart of the railroads, and Ellis Arnall, now a well-padded corporation attorney who would certainly do the monied establishment no harm if elected but who defined himself as a "loyal, national Democrat" and thereby irritated many. Only, the contest never came off. Vandiver had a heart attack in 1966 and withdrew.

Great lamentations were heard from many Democrats who did not want to leave the field to "liberal" (northerners should read that "moderate-conservative") Arnall. Who, at that late hour, would come to their rescue and snatch the Democratic standard?

Talmadge, pining in Washington, heard their cries and responded. *He* would return to Georgia and run again for governor. So excited was he at the thought of going home that he announced his intentions without checking with the kingmakers of Atlanta. That was an embarrassing mistake. They had to correct him privately: *No, Herman, we put you in Washington and we will tell you when to come home. Use your seniority like we tell you, and hush up.* When he made his Faustian pact to crush George, the Top People meant for him to carry out his part of the bargain. Watching from his Capitol prison, Herman must have felt he was seeing fragments of something he had gone through himself twenty years before. There on one side was his old enemy Arnall; coming from Lester Maddox was an earthy racial pitch that sounded much like his daddy, Gene's; and there were other familiar faces, Bo Callaway, for instance, a remnant of the old Talmadge ring who had switched parties if not alliances; and there was the whole uproar ending, just as it had twenty years ago, in the Georgia legislature. Quaint, but highly frustrating to Hummon, for he knew that if he *had* gone back he could have won easily. But he was stuck.

For the first decade of his political life he was like Pancho Villa; it did not matter who was head of state, *he* was the wild and romantic one whom the people watched. Now his personality is buried under many more assertive personalities and he is just one of a mob of 100.* Away from the old political gang, those Falstaffian roisterers and gentle grafters who kept the courthouses of Georgia safe for him, he is, more than anything else —lonely.

A Georgia congressman who has watched Herman since he entered

* Georgia Comptroller James L. Bentley, whose wife's father baptized Herman's father (that's the way close friendships are started in the South), says Talmadge sees Washington as "an exercise in futility. It comes down to how many times do we vote no this week. Talmadge is the kind of man who likes to go bang bang and get things done. He likes the decisive aspect" of the governor's office that is missing in the U.S. Senate.

politics says, "He's a miserable creature right now. Of course he never relished politics like his pa. He just felt he *had* to carry on the dynasty. I think he would be happier down on the farm. National politics are oceanic, and a person will get seasick and lost unless he knows how to get his bearings. Most politicians work up a constellation of values. Herman hasn't. He doesn't know what he believes in. The other day he dedicated a Hill-Burton hospital and damned the federal government. He'll praise the United Nations and condemn all those foreigners in it. His most used speech these days is how to love your country a little bit less. He's tired of the Washington routine, but still efficient. At a cocktail party, he'll be there right on time, shake everybody's hand, and then go home."

The next morning he is up at farm hours, 3:30 or 4; then he'll sit alone listening to music on his tape recorder, take a mile walk, and be off to another day of Washington routine. "I don't know anybody," said the congressman, "who is buddy-buddy with Herman."

And so we leave him restlessly and clumsily preparing for his first campaign as a big-city boy. Old habits are, for him, difficult to break, especially since, having had no stomach for the game, they were so difficult to establish in the first place. What in his shiny new role can he run on? Why, race, of course. Only now it comes partially disguised as something else. "If the present trend continues unabated and unless steps are taken to halt lawlessness in the streets . . ." "Mobs take over the public streets, with total disregard for the rights and property of others . . ." "Let nothing, not the mob in the streets nor . . ." "The mob has become master . . ." "The mob then is virtually in control in many areas of our great nation. The mob was in control in Selma . . ." "Those who have put themselves above the law, who resort to mob action instead of employing legal and civilized methods . . ." "Here in our own country, mob action is a relatively recent matter . . ." "We have seen so-called civil disobedience reach such proportions that entire communities are placed under mob rule . . ." "Mobs take the law into their own hands, and declare open war on entire cities, counties, and states. . . ."

Each of these quotes is from a different speech, a different newsletter. The man who has made a career of advocating disobedience to the U.S. Supreme Court recently told the Georgia Association of Student Councils of his anguish in viewing "the rash of campus demonstrations and street marches which indicate a growing rebelliousness against authority and disrespect for law and order." He sees mobs everywhere, taking over the campuses, the city halls, the shops and homes of America. The man who of all contemporary southern leaders used a mob to ride to power now will use The Mob as his theme to stay in power. Rebellious young people, many of them black, are saying ugly things about our foreign policy. Their peace marches, Talmadge warns dourly, are "organized and fostered to a very large degree by known communists." With increasing frequency he has sounded this warning since Julian Bond—the young Negro who pried his way into the Georgia legislature only with the help of the U.S. Supreme Court—and Atlanta-based Dr. Martin Luther King have become leaders in the Negro wing of the peace movement. Well, it's worth a try; it's the kind of patriotic racism that even the sophisticates of Atlanta may go for.

4

Orval Faubus: How to Create a Successful Disaster

If the Confederacy had won the battle of Pea Ridge we would now be living in the Confederate States of America rather than as subjects of the United States Supreme Court.

Orval Faubus, 1964

Just because I said it doesn't make it so.

Orval Faubus, 1957

Early in 1958, at a time when most of the world was fuming over the crude triggering of racial violence in Little Rock, Governor Orval Faubus of Arkansas, the man who pulled the trigger, attended a $100-a-plate Democratic Party dinner honoring Harry Truman. It was the usual peach melba affair and of no historical significance except that at one point in his speech Truman began to scold both Eisenhower and Faubus, one as a bungler and the other as a bully.

"I think," he said, "that firm and foresighted leadership might accomplish [the protection of liberties] without calling on the army for help. Indeed, I know that patient and persistent action, coupled with firmness, can work wonders in the field of civil rights. But unless a President works at it, day and night, and shows the people where he stands [here Truman began giving Trumanesque chops with his hands], *you can expect the demagogue to move in and make trouble.*"

74

A great deal of applause came at this point, and people turned to stare at Faubus to see how he was taking it; they found that he was smiling, nodding, and clapping as enthusiastically as anyone in the banquet hall. Asked later by newsmen how he felt about that passage, Faubus said, "I think all Democrats can pretty well agree with that, yes sir," and without waiting to be prompted by further questions he went on, "I don't think there's anyone anywhere who wants to deprive any citizens of their civil rights."

Nobody corners Orval Faubus. After periods of almost cowering indecision, he has made disastrous decisions, followed by inept recoveries and silly defenses; he has been caught *in flagrante delicto* so many times he hardly bothers to pull up his political pants anymore; Averell Harriman, voicing a judgment that was rather mild compared to the feelings of many northern Democrats, once remarked that Faubus "will go down in history with Quisling," and at the height of the Little Rock trouble, the foreign press became so incensed with him that one Paris newspaper was even moved to suggest that Faubus was actually trained by the Kremlin for the assignment and planted in the governorship to ruin America. At home he has also had his troubles. Far from relying solely and comfortably on the love of his constituents, Faubus has required the assistance from time to time of Arkansas's picturesque voting frauds. His availability to carry the bucket for special interests is notorious.

And yet, despite what appear to be wide weaknesses, one will find in southern political history few fit comparisons to Faubus as the possessor of almost absolute control over his own future. Only one other governor in the nation's history has matched his record of re-elections. His machine was almost flawless and its flawlessness and success were something that did not escape the notice of other southern leaders. From all appearances, George Wallace patterned much of his career on Faubus' previous successes.

He was the first to violate a federal court school desegregation order and, by doing so, demonstrate the political profit to be gained from it. The state did not profit but he did. Arkansas lost 7 percent of its population between 1950 and 1960, most of this loss occurring after the school war. Little Rock was gaining population in the first half of the decade, but it fell off again after the event. Little Rock was showing fine progress industrially until 1957; not one major industry moved in during the next three years. And just when the nation was beginning to forget that "Arky," dating back to the depression days, was a term meaning unclean wanderer, Faubus again made the state a symbol of contempt.

At the time there was widespread speculation about what the gamble had done to Faubus' career—ruin it, or merely mash it out of alignment? The *Arkansas Gazette,* the foremost voice of sanity in the state, wondered: "He has defied the government of the United States—and has gotten away with it so far. He is a hero to the mob and behind his barricade of bayonets he is untouched by the shame he has brought to his more responsible fellow citizens. But time passes and passions die and reason somehow is restored. Summer will come again, and a new campaign—and Mr. Faubus will have to count what he has lost against what he has gained. It is too early to strike the political balance."

Every summer that has come again and gone, and every campaign, since that editorial was written, left him better off than he was before.

The London *Economist* had predicted from afar that "like the Roman general [Fabian] whose name so closely resembles his own, Mr. Faubus may one day be commemorated by a reference in a military lexicon: Faubian tactics, or the techniques of fighting a losing battle in such a way as to cause the greatest loss to all concerned." It was a bad prediction. The costs of Faubus' action in 1957 were heavy indeed, but he was not the one who paid. Despite the contempt lobbed into his state from the North and despite the business slump, the bad days at Little Rock—other southern leaders noted enviously and with a willingness to imitate—were the real beginning of his power.

The employes used to joke around the office of Governor Sid McMath about what a hick he had hired as his administrative assistant. Orval Faubus always chewed a matchstick, and although that was an era when wide ties were in style, his ties were much wider. He slicked his black hair back flat and he grinned and laughed like a happy peasant, and those sophisticates around Little Rock wondered what McMath saw in the little fellow.

In a different way, McMath today wonders the same thing. "I brought Orval down out of the hills," he said in 1966, "and every night I ask forgiveness."

At the time it had seemed a good thing to do. McMath, a brilliant, hard-driving politician and something of a progressive, recognized Faubus' potential from a distance. For one thing, Faubus has the kind of stubbornness that serves impoverished, untutored hillbillies as the extra evolutionary gene needed to pull them out of the mud and onto the sunlit shore of civilization. He just wouldn't stay down. He had no education to speak of —he finished grade school at eighteen and taught his way through high school—and his folks had done little better than scratch out a living on Greasy Creek, in northwest Arkansas. For a while after they were married, Orval and Alta were seasonal migrants—fruit tramps—when he wasn't teaching country school. Those were the depression years. The choice they faced was not an uncommon one for rural people of the early thirties: stay at home and starve, or hit the road. They hit the road, wandering with the berry and vegetable crops into Texas, Louisiana, Missouri, Michigan, swinging out to Washington, where Faubus also worked in logging camps and, incidentally, where he heard the arguments of the Wobblies, who were thick in that area, and was not offended by what he heard. It fitted in rather well with what he had heard around the cabin at home from his pappy, Sam, who was a great admirer of Eugene Debs (and who, right up to his recent death, was still writing liberal letters to the editor but signing them with an assumed name so as not to embarrass Orval). He differed from most country school teachers in that he knew he was ignorant and cared. Three years after he was married, and at an age when most people have been out of college a year or two, Faubus decided it was time to try for a better education. He read an advertisement about a college at Mena—Commonwealth College—where he could work his way through, and he made one brief pass at it before deciding it wasn't the place for him. (This foray was to give him trouble later, but the trouble, in turn, was going to elect him governor.) Then, being pretty much at the end of his row, he decided to enter politics.

Madison County was traditionally a Republican county, but it didn't believe in holding an ambitious son down even if he was a Democrat, just so long as he wasn't uppity about it, and Faubus lost his first race only because he forgot about that qualification. But the second campaign he went out attired in dungarees, the apparel of most of those who would be voting, and was elected clerk of the circuit court. Not much, but it was better than picking fruit. That was 1939. Three years' blackout. Four years of war. Now he had a Bronze Star, a nickname ("Ernie Pyle of the Ozarks," for stories he had sent home—"I don't think I really deserved to be called that, but it didn't hurt"), and a down payment on the local newspaper. Also, still burning under his shirt was the one-gallus lust for politics.

He wrote his way out of the hills. McMath read his editorials extolling the liberal virtues of St. Paul and Lincoln, and was enchanted. Faubus can talk either way, but at the moment he was talking pine-cone liberal. McMath brought him down to be his assistant, his highway commissioner, his state highway director. The beauty of a state like Arkansas is that a little man can still move fast, with luck, and Faubus went up with one lucky spring from country editor to become a controller of the cornucopia most important to any southern state: highways.

Though he owed it all to McMath, over the years he would not return in kind.

McMath was an enlightened governor, which, in Arkansas as elsewhere in the South, meant a governor who believed in allowing Negroes to have at least .01 percent of the privileges of citizenship. Negroes have never been considered a problem in most of Arkansas. Over in the east they're thick, but there are parts of western Arkansas where people have grown to adulthood without seeing a Negro. Faubus is reputed to have had just such a Negro-less upbringing. The big political campaigns were carried on with scarcely a reference to the subject during the period we are dealing with now. The question was always out there, hanging on the hatrack, of course, but Arkansas politicians just didn't bother to wear it. McMath went out of office on economic issues, and partly because of a mild scandal in the highway department. Mild scandals are normal flora on southern highways. There is always some official who will help out a friendly contractor for a kickback, or merely for fun. This was right after the war and McMath was building rural roads with abandon, trying to get Arkansas out of the mud; and he succeeded rather well, for a start, but he and his underlings manipulated the highway department a little too wildly. Strangely, although Faubus was in the highway hierarchy and although he later admitted there had been some wrongdoing, he himself was never smudged by it.

In 1952 along came Francis Cherry, a professional Mr. Clean, backed by the most powerful financial force in the state at the time, the Arkansas Power and Light Company (owned by Middle South Utilities, with headquarters in New York), and that was the end of McMath. Hamilton Moses of Arkansas Power and Light had enough power in those days that he could have come in and taken the spittoons out of the capitol and nobody would have tried to stop him.

The fanciest part of the assault on McMath had been arranged by the power company-dominated legislature when it set up the Highway Audit

Commission (one member was a director of Arkansas Power and Light; another was campaign manager in the later gubernatorial campaign of Pratt Remmel, son-in-law of the power company's founder). The audit commission was a good thing, but in this case it was being used quite openly as a political knife. A grand jury—one member was treasurer of A.P. and L. and two others were employes of a bank whose president was a director of the power company—indicted two highway department employes, but the cases were so flimsy that the trial judge threw out the charges against one of the workers and the other was acquitted by a jury that stayed out only four minutes.

If there was gross and widespread fraud in McMath's highway department, the most eager inquisitors in the state had failed to find it. Doubts about the righteousness of the outfit had been raised, however, and McMath was hurt badly.

McMath was also done in by his friend Faubus. Assigned the campaign job of bringing in the hill votes, he spent more time pushing his own name for the future than he did in pushing McMath. At least the hill ballots, which now respond so magically to Faubus' need for a last-minute count that puts him over the line, did not so respond to McMath's needs.

Back to Greasy Creek went Faubus, to become postmaster and bide his time. He had to wait only two years. Cherry, botching it from the beginning, had no conception of public relations. He was cold; he couldn't, or wouldn't, communicate. Basically he did not like people. He was moody and despondent, probably because of his health. He didn't care what the public thought; with his waiting room full of people come miles to see him, he would knock off work early in the day and walk over their feet in leaving, without an explanation. His heart was weak and he didn't want to tax it, but the pople felt insulted and remembered the brushoff. He antagonized the county judges this way, and they ganged up on him. Too, Cherry was not proving to be the Mr. Clean he had represented himself. The manipulations of the highway department continued, but with the added drawback that the loot was not being spread as far as it had been spread under the McMath administration. And as the final crusher, the people who owned him drove him too far at the wrong time. Because it wanted higher rates in effect before the Dixon-Yates contract was completed, Arkansas Power and Light forced Cherry to push the increase through his utilities commission not long before the 1954 election, and that, coming after Cherry's veto of a bill to exempt feed, seed and fertilizer from the sales tax (in Arkansas!), would have been enough to defeat him even if he hadn't worked hard to defeat himself.

But he did that too. In Perryville, for example, while Orval Faubus was hunkering down in the sun outside the courthouse, a blade of grass in his mouth, making jokes with the one-gallus and two-gallus boys, where was Cherry? Oh, it was too, too hot for that kind of campaigning. Cherry was sitting in his air-conditioned Oldsmobile, in full view of the crowd, listening to a ball game. A distinguished-looking judge from northeast Arkansas, Cherry had never had any conception of how to campaign. If much had depended on his campaigning style the victory in 1952 would have been pure fluke. He had made the run-off with a radio talkathon, and Arkansas Power and Light money pushed him the rest of the way in. The same political hucksters who sold the talkathon to Brailey Odham in Florida, and did very well with it there, came swinging into Arkansas next and sold the idea to Cherry. Get on the radio and stay there until you wear out; let people phone in with questions about your politics, and you sit there answering them day and night. It has the same appeal flagpole sitting had in the 1930's. It drew attention to a drab man. But he did not learn anything by it. In the 1952 campaign, he had *one* telephone in his campaign headquarters, and that was a pay phone.

Faubus, who was himself one of the South's authentic "natural" politicians, had the services of two veterans behind the scenes: his old boss, McMath, and McMath's alter ego and former campaign manager, Henry Woods. But the thing that really put Faubus into the governor's office, ironically, was the state's sense of fair play, something he manipulated masterfully to help himself on this occasion, but three years later, when the Negroes had nothing else to rely on, he cancelled out in a racial frenzy.

Cherry tried to get smart, and, for Cherry, that was always disastrous. Senator Joe McCarthy was pulling it successfully on the national scene, so why couldn't he pull the same thing in Arkansas? He called Faubus a communist. No, worse than that, a Godless Communist, a Free-Loving Communist.

It went back to that Commonwealth College period. The rumors started in a sleazy Little Rock weekly, but three days later Cherry was including them in a television speech, and before the campaign was over he had planted them by radio, leaflet, daily newspaper and word of mouth. Faubus called it a "whispering campaign," but it was much louder than that. Commonwealth College was, they said, a wicked place, the home of students who believed in free love, atheism, and Marxism; and Orval Faubus had gone there! This had supposedly transpired in the early depression years when there had been a lot of uninhibited campuses around the country; the only difference to Arkansans was, this one was in Arkansas.

The descriptions of Commonwealth College that went around were distorted, but the part about Faubus was not untrue; he had gone there, briefly, as we have said, when he was trying to get out of the fruit-picking cycle. He wanted a college education, and he didn't have any money. Commonwealth College gave him a scholarship and promised to help him work his way. For some reason—it has never been explained consistently by Faubus—he left the school shortly after he got there. Thirty years after the event, he said he left because "I soon found that there was a strong communist factor—one-third of the faculty and students were card-carrying communists." (A discerning young man.) But on an earlier occasion, when such open admission of the school's "communistic" leanings might have been fatal politically, he said he left when he found that the school was not accredited. Faubus' immediate response to the Cherry telecast had been to threaten to sue anyone who accused him again of— of attending Commonwealth College? no—of "subversion," something Cherry had never accused him of. Then candidate Faubus cancelled all speaking engagements for a day to concentrate on working up a better refutation. When he came out of his closet again, he began a series of conflicting statements about how long he had stayed at Commonwealth College. Panicking, he said everything from two days to two weeks. Since he was elected class president, two days would seem a rather hasty visit; but to most Arkansans, removed as they were from the main stream of McCarthyism, the true answer was not something that seemed terribly necessary to arrive at in 1954—nearly a decade after the school had shut and two decades since Faubus had walked across the campus—and they generally responded to Cherry's smear with a loud raspberry, especially after Faubus finally settled down to a forthright explanation (in a speech reportedly prepared by none other than his most severe critic of later years, the *Arkansas Gazette's* Harry Ashmore).

Cherry could have done Faubus no greater service. If there was anything the little man from Madison County needed it was a cause. Up to this point he really had nothing to give his campaign a positive tone; he had been running against Cherry but not for anything in particular. Now he could, and did, recast himself as a naïve but honest hillbilly fighting a sophisticated smear, a war hero going up against makeshift skeletons from his past. If Cherry had not tried to be so creatively mischievous, he would undoubtedly have won. There had been defects in his administration, to be sure, but on the other hand his appointments had been fairly sensible, he had wisely fostered property assessment reform, and his fiscal control system was a progressive step; but above all, working in his favor, was the Arkansas tradition of giving the governor a second term. This gift was considered almost automatic. In losing his bid for it, Cherry was the first governor in a generation to be so rebuffed. A clumsy, sick man, captive of economic powers better-equipped men could not have coped with, he is classically a more-to-be-pitied-than-censured politician, yet his ending was a just one; for giving Faubus to Arkansas and to the nation, which he did with his foolish accusations, Cherry was properly condemned by the gods to end his career, and his life, chasing other petty communist shadows as chairman of the Subversive Activities Control Board in Washington. When he died in 1965, he had as yet not run one authentic communist to earth and made him confess.

Faubus the victor approached his work warily. The legislature was not his legislature. He controlled neither house. He was the first governor in Arkansas's history who had no "honeymoon" legislative session. His credentials were from an administration whose liberalism carried a faintly corrupt smell. As for his personal philosophy and bent, these had escaped slander but not suspicion; he had been carried into office by sympathy rather than respect. It was, he felt, a time for waiting, and so he waited. Arkansas needed new revenue as it had not needed new revenue for decades, but Faubus' only response to need was to ask one tax cut, an economic wiggle aimed at satisfying a campaign promise. Then slowly, as he moved with lessening humility and more control into the second legislature, Orval the dreadnaught manipulator began to emerge.

And so we come to the reason Orval Faubus helped to destroy the South in 1957. As everyone in Arkansas knows very well, it had nothing to do with his personal feelings toward the Negro, which were rather friendly feelings at that time, just as they had been all his life; Faubus liked the black man and in fact carried his vote more conclusively than he carried the white man's. Later on, the cynical hammering of 1957 having apparently done permanent damage to his conscience, he would blandly sign a law requiring hospitals to label all blood as to race to safeguard whites from "Negro-type" diseases. But for the first thirteen months he was in office he made no statements about segregation. Most of the buildings erected in his first two administrations had only one rest-room for whites and blacks to share. During the segregation crisis at Hoxie in 1955, he remained quiet, just as he was quiet during the desegre-gation of half a dozen other school systems during 1954-56. He had no protests to make about the presence of Negroes at the University of Ar-kansas, where they had been at the graduate level for several years before the U.S. Supreme Court spoke, and at six of the seven state colleges. Faubus himself publicly boasted that during his administration all trans-portation systems had been integrated . . . that he was the first Demo-cratic governor in the South to put Negroes on a Democratic state com-mittee . . . that he had recommended to the Democratic state convention that the white primary be abolished . . . that Negroes had been appointed to boards and commissions where no Negro had ever sat before . . . that Arkansas's law school had been integrated since 1947, its medical school had Negro graduates . . . and that his son was attending an integrated state-supported school. With his encouragement, the State Department of Education's ratio of Negro employees was the highest in the South. Fur-thermore, early in his career he killed a bill requiring the legislature and certain elected officials to oppose integration, his reason being that to require opposition "regardless of federal laws or court decisions" would only bring on "needless litigation," and that since "it makes no provision for working within the framework of the federal laws in defending state rights" it would probably be declared unconstitutional anyway.

In his first campaign he once and only once brought up the topic of race, and then dropped it. The one occasion was an advertisement that opened ominously:

Let's Face It
The Great Issue In This
Gubernatorial Campaign Is
DE-SEGREGATION!

But then he went on immediately to say that it should be achieved "in peace and harmony, with fairness to all and injury to none," and that it was "no time for Rabble-Rousers." It's true, the advertisement contains a bit of flim-flam about "communist agitators" trying to exploit the race issue, but with real foresight he warned that "unless we meet this issue as it should be met, without fear or favor, it can divide this state and eventually divide this nation." He went on:

> The truth is—that you should beware of anyone, candidate for governor included, who spreads prejudice and hatred in this time of great national peril, because prejudice and hatred cannot solve the problem, and struck between our white and Negro population can destroy both races economically and socially.

His 1956 campaign was just about as free of race-baiting. He was running against two loudmouthed segregationists, but he was not yet panicking. He said race was not an issue. He said, "Those who preach hate today do an injury to the cause for which we fought and many of our comrades died. Whatever our differences are, we can solve them through the democratic processes—not through hate and scorn."

Faubus' most worrisome opponent was Jim Johnson, a weird caricature of a politician (later on the Arkansas Supreme Court and in '66 the Democratic nominee for governor) whose trademarks were a brown homburg and a blue tie with white stripes. A former state senator who was a tooth-grinder on the stump, Johnson made his first statewide race in 1954, the year Faubus won the governorship. Although the U.S. Supreme Court had already handed down its school desegregation order, Johnson did not think to use this as an issue in '54. That year he was a cheerful candidate for attorney general, known as the " 'Mockingbird Hill' candidate" because of the tune he was wont to hum, whistle and sing on any occasion, with or without accompaniment. He didn't become a professional segregationist until the Supreme Court handed down its implementation order in 1955 and he, meanwhile, had discovered that if he were going to do any good in his race for governor the next year, he would need a passionate issue. Immediately Johnson started pawing the dirt and became not only the state's loudest voice among the segregationists, but also the chief organizer of the Arkansas White Citizens Council; that organization returned the favor by plugging his gubernatorial candidacy in every issue of its magazine, oddly named *Arkansas Faith*. By the time the campaign really got going in '56, Johnson was thumping away with that old southern theme, "A vote for —————— is a vote for race-mixing," filling in the blank with Faubus.

There is in Faubus' makeup a weakness that, in moments of pressure, makes him act seldom from logic, often from fear, and even more often from whatever the last stress happens to be before action is demanded of him. It is said that in the 1956 Democratic convention, although the Arkansas delegation had caucused and agreed to support Senator Albert Gore of Tennessee for Vice President and then, when Gore stepped out of contention, switched its support to Hubert Humphrey, and even as Arkansas's junior Senator J. W. Fulbright was at the podium nominating Humphrey, Arkansas's senior Senator John McClellan, the encrusted spokesman for big business, slipped over beside Faubus and went to work on him. When Faubus cast Arkansas's vote for Vice President, it went—surprise!—to John F. Kennedy.

The same kind of galvanic groping was being evidenced by Faubus the same year in his domestic strategy. Although he had defeated Johnson by a better than 2 to 1 margin—whipping him even in Hoxie, where, as the result of an integration split, Johnson had got his start as a segregationist—Johnson's allusions to his racial "softness" were beginning to get to him. Faubus' response was aggravated by his conviction that racial attitudes were changing in the state, a conviction that resulted from a poll in January of 1956. This was about the dozenth poll on various subjects Faubus had had taken since he became governor, and he relied heavily on what they told him.

This poll, coupled with the fact that he needed the support of several key east Arkansas legislators to swing a sales tax increase in the next session, prompted Faubus to build a backstop for himself in racial matters. By May of 1956 he was circulating an interposition resolution for signatures and pushing for a pupil placement act. The interposition resolution only called for Arkansas "to join with other states in *expressing opposition*" to integration decisions of the court, and this was so mild a protest that it was viewed with complete tolerance and often with approval by the state's moderates, who said that the crackpot interposition theory was just a stalling procedure and not nearly so good as the threat of nullification proclaimed by Alabama—the first state in modern times to stand behind the rebellious doctrine. Too, liberals and moderates pointed out in the governor's defense that he was only saying he was against *"sudden and complete* integration," something that nobody was then demanding anyway. Faubus saw his position in the same low-keyed way, assuring a crowd in east Arkansas that segregation was a sociological problem, not a political issue, and that "under my interposition plan, we can maintain segregation in Arkansas. I don't have to jump up and down and stomp on my hat to tell you that."

When Faubus became a wild man in 1957, there was a reason for it. No dull demagogue like Ross Barnett, just demagoguing it for the frivolous hell of it, Faubus steered his rickety craft of state down the rapids and over the falls—willingly, knowingly, even though it meant helping to "divide this state and eventually divide the nation," as he had predicted it could do—because he became convinced that this was the only way to assure himself of a third term and because only by winning that third term could he begin to distribute the favors that mark a man of power.

Two terms had not allowed him to appoint a majority to state regulatory boards; a third term would give him the majority appointment, with a resulting advantage, obviously, for those supporters who operate under the boards' jurisdiction.

His greatest assistance so far had been of a negative kind: he had ignored campaign promises of reform. When Faubus ran for governor the first time, he said he considered the Public Service Commission too friendly to the utility companies and too eager to give rate increases— a slap at Cherry, of course, who had rushed through a rate increase— and he vowed to seek legislation requiring an exhaustive study before any utilities rate increase could be made. That promise was promptly forgotten.

In his first race he had stormed up and down the state crying out against the sinfulness of Hot Springs, with its flagrant violations of state law against gambling. "I would use the state police to prohibit any violations that come to my attention," he shouted, "and the Hot Springs situation is big enough that it would come to my attention!" In this he was taking a different position from either McMath or Cherry, both of whom said the state should keep its hands off Hot Springs unless its gambling spread and became a statewide problem. But not Faubus. He was going to reform that town. Two years later something had changed his mind. Now he was saying he didn't know of any gambling in Hot Springs, and that if there was some going on, it was strictly a local matter, a position he took for most of the rest of his career. In 1962 he was still saying, "Hot Springs has judges, police officials, and means of enforcement. If Hot Springs has a problem they have plenty of authority to solve it. If I did something about it, they'd call me a dictator."

So Faubus was doing the best he could by his friends, but this was not nearly good enough. For one thing, he did not have control of the highway department. A law had been passed—passed under McMath, in fact, and with Faubus' approval—that kept any one governor from appointing a majority to the highway commission, assuming—assuming as was normal to do, since nobody had been elected to a third term in fifty years—that he wouldn't be re-elected but once. This galled Faubus. No, no, he gave assurance after he had been in office a couple of years, he had no intention of exactly seizing control of the highway department, but he felt the department should "cooperate" with his office. If he got elected a third term, he wouldn't have to ask it; he could appoint enough men to the commission to do it automatically.

The same comforting thought applied to other regulatory bodies, such as the Public Service Commission, although it is hard to imagine what more Faubus could have wanted from that agency he was not already getting. Faubus' best political friend is W. R. Stephens, who in 1954 borrowed $20 million and gained control of Ark-La Gas Company, the state's major supplier of natural gas. It began getting a yearly rate increase, averaging $3.2 million each of the first three years; but this was no great feat, seeing as how two of the PSC commissioners and several top employees owned stock in Ark-La. Beginning with the 1956 campaign and thereafter, Stephens has been the biggest contributor to Faubus' ambitions. The friendship has been very profitable for both the governor and Ark-La; the corporation's officers are often found on the boards of the biggest banks of the state; these banks are given state funds to hold (up until 1966 no interest was required of the banks; now there is a law that will allow a special commission, under the governor, to set an interest rate; so far, none has been set). As McMath pointed out in his 1962 campaign against Faubus, banks thus tied to Ark-La sometimes have as much interest-free state money on deposit as they have capital and surplus.

The future of big business and industry in Arkansas would be much advanced if Faubus got to drive deeper these special-interest pegs in a third term, and so, in mid-August of 1957, he called his staff together and announced that he was determined to run again and he was also determined to grease the way by calling out the troops when Central High School rang its first bell.

(The idea for this great mischief, as Faubus has hinted at one time or another, was given to him by an episode that occurred in Texas the previous year, a landmark incident which has strangely not been given the proper catalytic credit for helping to ruin the post-war Deep South. This was the occasion when Governor Allan Shivers—out of meanness rather

than philosophy; his own children were going to an integrated Catholic
school—challenged the Supreme Court, and got by with it. It received
comparatively little notice at the time—except among southern politicians
—and today it is the rare southerner who remembers it at all, the greater
tragedy of Little Rock having blanked it out entirely. Mansfield, about
seventeen miles southeast of Fort Worth, was a town of about 1,450 in
those days. The school district was made up of 688 white and fifty-eight
Negro students; the latter were bussed seventeen miles into Fort Worth
to school. With a U.S. Circuit Court of Appeals ruling behind them, three
Negro boys announced their intention to enter the Mansfield school in
1956. For three days before school opened a mob controlled the town.
On the morning the Negro youngsters started off to school, about 200
men gathered at 7:30 to head them off; the mob later doubled in size.
Free knives were offered to white students who would use them. A Negro
was hung in effigy from the school flagpole. The school superintendent
assured the segregationists: "Now you guys know I'm with you . . ." and
advised them on the best way to barricade the school. An assistant district
attorney who showed up was hit, kicked and cursed. TV cameras were
broken. Newsmen's cars were forced to the curb. At this point, the Negroes' attorney wired Governor Shivers for protection; Shivers replied
that he was "certainly not inclined to move state officers into Mansfield
at the call of a lawyer affiliated with the NAACP, whose premature and
unwise efforts have created this situation at Mansfield." But he did call
out the Texas Rangers with instructions to protect the white people of
the town. He said he would not use state troops to "intimidate Texas citizens who are making orderly protest against a situation instigated and
agitated by the NAACP. . . . *If this course is not satisfactory under the
circumstances to the federal government, I respectfully suggest further
that the Supreme Court, which is responsible for the desegregation order,
be given the task of enforcing it"*—the old Andrew Jackson cliché which
the South so loves to refer to. He advised the Mansfield school board to
transfer any Negroes out of the district whose attempts to attend Mansfield "would reasonably be calculated to incite violence"—basing the
action on the "general welfare" decision in the Autherine Lucy case
arising from the mob action at the University of Alabama. But it was a
slender excuse and, as every southern governor knew, Shivers was striking
into new and untried legal areas: the public peace was not at issue in
Mansfield, for the sheriff had shown himself capable of controlling the
mob at its inception and two rangers, properly instructed, could have

kept the larger mob under control; Mansfield was not about to become a
Tuscaloosa in violence, and Shivers could not pretend that it was. His
act was defiance of the federal government through the *encouragement*
of violence. And he got by with it. Thus was the pattern established for
whatever other southern governor wanted to try it next. As it turned out,
this was Faubus.)

Although Faubus surely could not have realized all the side effects
that step would bring about, he was nevertheless troubled at the thought
of going against his habit of handling racial matters in an easy-going
fashion. Some of his saner friends, like McMath and Winthrop Rockefeller, were flabbergasted to learn of his plans for Central High. When
they begged him to back away, he did not attempt to argue with them on
logical grounds. He was, in fact, quite honest about why he was doing it.
Rockefeller later said that when he made his plea with Faubus, the little
governor replied, "I'm sorry, but I'm already committed. I'm going to run
for a third term, and if I don't do this, Jim Johnson and Bruce Bennett
[the two segregationists who were still lusting for the governorship] will
tear me to shreds." Faubus denies he said any such thing. But McMath
claims Faubus was similarly direct in his response to him. McMath told
me, "I talked with him before he acted. He made no bones about it. He
said he had to have an emotional issue. Up to that moment, I was for
the guy. The thing that is so evil about Faubus is, he's no demagogue in
the usual meaning. He knew he was making a choice between entrenching
his machine, or pushing the state ahead. He knew what he was doing when
he made the choice."

But he had been helped in making the decision. It was help he had
looked for, and welcomed, as props for his rationalization. He got advice
from the local White Citizens Council brain trust, but most importantly
he got it from two old political flame throwers, Georgia Governor Marvin
Griffin, and Talmadge's little counselor, Roy Harris. Faubus will not today
concede the influence they had on him; questions on the point seem almost
to embarrass him. Griffin and Harris, of course, are quick to take credit
for swinging him to their convictions, and although this would mean
nothing without verification from other sources, verification is fairly
abundant. To quote McMath once more, since he was as close an observer
of both sides as there was around, "Griffin had a tremendous influence.
Faubus was still wrestling with himself. Basically he is a decent guy.
Griffin was the man who put his finger on the nerve in this thing. Griffin
was the guy."

*In coming before you for your support I come with
clean hands. I'm going to shell down the corn and let
you see it.*

Marvin Griffin, Running in 1954

*. . . the "if-you-ain't-for-stealing-you-ain't-for-segrega-
tion" modus operandi of Griffin's administration.*

Columnist Charlie Pou, in retrospect, 1965

Anyone living outside the manger of southern affairs would have a hard
time appreciating Marvin Griffin, that dung-caked savior of segregation
whose star of destiny moved upon a rueful Atlanta in 1954. Even for
southern connoisseurs of pungent politics, his administration was smellier
than most could take. A grand jury investigating the wreckage he left
behind found "perfidious conduct of state officials heretofore inconceivable in the minds of citizens. The operation of our state government by
the principles of cronyism and personal profit has dissipated a tremendous
amount of our tax money." Estimates of state losses through corruption
during his term ranged from $10 million to $30 million. Not one contract
of his $100-million rural road program was let on bids; all were disposed
via favoritism. Many of the roads have since had to be rebuilt. In other
matters, about two dozen state officials, including Griffin's brother Cheney,
were processed through the courts on a variety of charges; charges of
influence peddling against Cheney were eventually dropped. In the words
of Ernest Vandiver, who followed Griffin as governor, "The state of
Georgia was buying rowboats that would not float. Some were wisely
sent to parks without lakes." Equipment was paid for that was never
delivered. Buying was done on a political-family basis: Griffin's Board of
Education chairman wrote $11 million in insurance for the Georgia Port
Authority, and then split his commission with a Savannah meat dealer
who happened also to be the brother-in-law of the Port Authority chairman and a pal of Griffin's. Bread cast upon the water always seemed to
wash home. Griffin spent as much money one year on the roads in his
home county and the state highway chairman's home county as he did in

90

thirty-eight other counties combined. Herman Talmadge's uncle was on the state highway department's payroll but hadn't reported for work in two years. Sales tax collections were so loose that delinquencies were believed to have run into the millions of dollars—most of it impossible to trace. Double-bidding to rig purchase contracts was fairly common. As Griffin's term came to an end, Judge Douglas Thomas, impaneling a grand jury to investigate one of the scandals, observed, "There has been more uncovering of just plain thievery in the state of Georgia in the past six to eight months than in the entire history of the state."

That was probably an exaggeration, and Griffin was justified in responding in his own eloquent way, "Nuts. Just plain nuts. I ain't about to apologize for nothin'."

Comparing the Griffin era's ethics to previous administrations is useless because, after all, the newspapers of Atlanta had not been quite so steadfast in their pursuit of mischief during the administration of Herman Talmadge as they were during the administration of Griffin, so any solid comparison is impossible. This is a point which some Georgia politicians have mulled over until they came out the other end, arriving at the unique conclusion that Herman's administration, if the truth were only known, was probably even *crookeder*. One very responsible state official told me, "I think Herman's administration carried off the carloads where Griffin's carried off only the baskets. You know how they say in the Bible, 'Saul has slain his thousands, but David his ten thousands.' That's how I would compare Griffin to Talmadge." Such colorful appraisals are not, however, accompanied with supporting data.

Another reason Griffin might properly feel singled out unfairly for special abuse is that he inherited so many of Herman's cronies, such as those from the Talmadges' old home county of Telfair whom the newspapers accused of selling large quantities of pipe to the state but neglecting to deliver or install it.

Probably the main reason the Atlanta slickers found it so easy to dislike Griffin was that he, like Gene Talmadge, delighted in rubbing his rural power in the city's face. Those were the twilight years of the county unit system, that unique system by which a man was elected not by popular vote but by a tally of county electors whom the rural-dominated legislature had distributed in such a way that the courthouse gangs could beat Atlanta every time. Backed by the rural counties, a man could be elected governor with about 30 percent of the popular vote. Griffin was.

Rural kings were traditionally men who came right out in the open with ideas and quirks that made the sophisticates stand aghast; the more aghast, the more the rural following liked it. Such was the intent and success of Gene Talmadge's pasturing a cow on the lawn of the governor's mansion. Griffin's most memorable effort along that line was to spend half a million dollars of state money building a 400-foot pier into the river at his hometown, Bainbridge, for the purpose of eventually turning the drowsy rural shopping center into a bustling seaport. The town is 100 miles from deep water. He and some of his friends bought a surplus army landing craft and entered international commerce. They never got the boat to Bainbridge, but they did run it between Tampa and Havana several times, hauling chickens south and rum north, until the newspapers got wind of that rum traffic and gave him so much bad publicity he went out of business.

And another probable reason the city folks disliked and distrusted Griffin was that they undoubtedly knew, or at least sensed, that he was pulling their leg. A graduate of the Citadel and a smart rascal, Griffin was not the hick he enjoyed pretending to be. He was assisted by his looks: a big country grin, a bulbous nose that always appears a little sunburned, a fieldhand build. And to this he added a beautifully cultivated gaucheness of speech and an open and freely-expressed judgment of his own limitations and of the cussedness of a public that won't let a politician make a few mistakes. "Well, a governor can't be a Solomon," he told me plaintively. "He's just a ordinary man. Anybody shortenin' an account, the law covers it. It's just like one, two, three. Every time the auditor told me someone was shortenin' an account or embezzlin' I wrote the department head sayin' to discharge this person eee-*med*iately, and advised the attorney general to collect the missin' amount from the bondin' company. What else can a governor do besides run him off? But brother, they held me personally, individually liable for everything that went wrong.

"They use to talk about my plans to use the river for my boat. I told 'em, the Lord put the water in the river. There's a nigra boat paddler named Sebourne Primly that charges the doctors $3 a day to row 'em trout fishin. Don't I have as much right to use the water in that river as he does?

"They had a hearin' about somethin' else and the secretary of the Georgia Port Authority was in there about this other matter and then the matter of the little ol' boat came up.

"They say, 'What's that little ol' boat haul?'

"She say, 'Well, I don' know but I think manifest show refrigerators and something else to Havana.'

"They say, 'What they haul from Havana back to Tampa?'

"She say, 'Preserves and fruit and tobacco and rum and . . .'

"They yell, 'RUM! *Griffin's in the rum business!*' Headlines all over the paper that afternoon about it and they wrote about it for a week. Would they criticize the president of a railroad line because his trains haul liquor?

"My brother was an aide in my office. If I had it to do over again, I wouldn't put anyone in there kin to me. Somebody's got to be a scoundrel, a thief, a rascal and a blackguard, but it ain't got to be a member of your own family."

Griffin was feeling just as defensive about the press's judgment of his advocacy of segregation, and hurt by what this had done to him politically.

"The Atlanta papers—and I'm not complainin'—would lie about me. They'd say, Griffin ain't gonna get any of the nigra vote because he said he don't want any of the nigra vote, and why, hell, I never made any such statement. Now who'd make a damn fool statement like that? Niggers all over the state'd tell my hometown niggers, 'Yah, he say he don' want any our votes. We gonna 'commodate him.' I get along fine with my home niggers. I run 'em a segregated nigger page in my paper. They call each other Mister and Mizz and Missy in the stories, and that's theirs.

"*Time* magazine quoted me once sayin', 'The way to handle a integrationist is to cut off a limb of a blackjack saplin' and brain 'im.' That's a damn lie. I didn't say that. You know what a *brushy top* saplin' is? A brushy top saplin' is a small saplin' and it's got a hundred damn little ol' limbs and things. An' if they used to want to scare a race horse to get him out of the damn stall—they didn't have startin' gates here in Georgia —one fellow would get astride of him and another fellow out yar would git him a brushy top saplin'. They don't do one damn thing but make one hell of a noise—a swishin', you know. He'd hit down behind that horse, and by god they's off!

"I said, hit down behind these integrationists' with a brushy top saplin'! Well, *Time* says I say take a blackjack and club 'em to death. Well, that kind of talk wouldn't go over. That's just crap. I will say I was loose in pickin' a term they didn't know a damn thing about."

Expediency, which any politician must have a certain amount of, is an addiction with Griffin. The only trouble is, to do the expedient thing successfully a politician must be able to double back, and Griffin has cut himself off from ever doubling back on racial matters, and it's got him very upset. With the county unit system dead, as of 1962, and the Atlanta Negroes showing their vote strength, Griffin would mightily like to cut into that bloc now. He even attended a Negro nightclub a few months ago—apparently with no effort at secrecy, since the papers picked it up and he admitted it—but it's too late to erase the past. "The Atlanta papers have written so much about my being anti-Negro," he complained. "I don't think I could buy their vote for $200,000. If I had a million dollars I could get some, but how many? Niggers ain't fools." The handicap is pretty awesome. In 1962 when he ran against Sanders, Sanders got 2,300 votes in one Negro precinct and Griffin got three, a ratio that stirred Griffin to the morose joke, "Somebody voted under a misapprehension." If the times had allowed it, and if it would have been profitable, doubtless he would have out-Kinged Martin Luther. His racism was openly schemed. One time he described how he went about programming his campaigns. He said, "In north Georgia they're interested in the chicken business. They've got no nigras to amount to anything in north Georgia. Some counties don't have none. But they're really worse on the race question than the folks down here in south Georgia. Thata's what they are mainly interested in, niggers, chickens, and roads—to get out of that knee-deep muck in the mountains. So when I talk up there, I give 'em a couple of chapters on race. Occasionally I give the federal government hell. You can't ridicule the Negro race. Used to be, before the niggers got the vote, you could say what you wanted to about the race. But that doesn't go over now. Individuals in the race, yes, I pour the mustard to 'em. You can really tear after Martin Luther King successfully."

Griffin shows the same pinch of sincerity in discussing his previous assaults on the federal government. When he was halfway through his term as governor he met in Richmond with Governors Stanley of Virginia, Coleman of Mississippi, and Timmerman of South Carolina, to write a joint proclamation of opposition to the U.S. Supreme Court. Griffin, the most militant of the four, wanted to use stronger language, insisting that interposition means a state's right to *nullify* federal laws. It was mostly bluster. I asked him later if he really meant it. "Well," he answered, grinning his way through a masterful job of telescoping time, "a way back yonder South Carolina tried to nullify the laws, and I didn't feel that we could really at the final stage nullify federal laws. But if we got enough states to impose their states' sovereignty between their people and a federal act, if we could get enough of 'em, sort of *go in a wad,* it would have a tendency to slow this thing down. . . . It's a *sentiment* thing."

It is uncertain, in retrospect, if Griffin ever seriously intended anything by any of his statements or actions, including the easy shedding of friendships, except just to get ahead in a kind of pore-boy scramble.

When Griffin came back from overseas in 1946, Ellis Arnall made him state adjutant general. Griffin was politically ambitious. Prior to that he had run for Congress. As soon as he got back he started trying to run for governor. The first year, he threw a barbeque in Bainbridge and practically announced his candidacy. But the Atlanta papers didn't like Marvin Griffin, and justifiably. Griffin's previous stay in the capitol, as executive secretary to Governor Ed Rivers, had had its incorrect moments, most notably when Griffin participated in the curious pardoning of several hundred prisoners at the state penitentiary. There was another memorable moment in his career as executive secretary when he threw the former highway director out of office and down the stairs of the state highway building, for which Griffin was sentenced to twenty days in jail and a $200 fine but avoided the penalty by giving himself a pardon over the governor's signature.

Anyway, Arnall tried to promote Griffin, and he called the men who ran the Atlanta papers. He talked to their business associates and asked what they thought about taking Griffin as a candidate, and they said *no,* under no circumstances. If Arnall couldn't swing Atlanta to his side, then it was time, Griffin decided, to leave the Arnall-Rivers-Thompson crowd that he had followed successfully so far and switch to the Talmadge group. And that's where Griffin stood in 1948, running for lieutenant governor. When he took his turn at the victory barbecue at the Talmadge place in Telfair County, you could hardly have guessed he had ever even spoken to men like Arnall and Rivers and Thompson. Recounting how as a boy he would take stray cats to "a strange country where the timber is high, dumping them out and yelling scat!" he completed the analogy: "That's what the Talmadge administration will do with those other stray cats, Rivers, Arnall, M. E. 'too.' You know where we're going to dump them?"

"No!" came the choric response.

"Harlem!" shouted Griffin, and the crowd roared.

Griffin was Talmadge's lieutenant governor the next six years, and then he was chosen to be Herman's successor. The results of that race, which was a complete victory for Talmadge because it once and for all crushed the anti-Talmadge forces in the state and brought the Atlanta press to heel, were misread by Griffin. He thought it was his victory. Later he would try to be independent of Talmadge, even to challenge him for control of the machine, and Talmadge—at last smoothly in league with Atlanta powers—would destroy him.

Talmadge was aware that 1954 would be his last chance to set up his machine in such a way that it would go on functioning trouble-free when he left for Washington and the Senate. In selecting his successor, he was quite willing to forego old alliances and old debts. Fred Hand, who had been speaker of the House during the Talmadge era and had not only helped shape some of the administration's better programs but had in the early drunken days of Talmadge's term loyally covered up for his leader, now wanted to be governor. There was nobody else around of the old gang with equal ambitions and also with equal talents. Hand was no political genius, but he was smart enough, and scandal-free. Talmadge promised Hand he would stay neutral; when Hand heard the rumors that Talmadge was working against him, he said publicly, "I do not believe it. Herman wouldn't stab me in the back." Hand told me later he was aware that his back was already thoroughly riddled and that he had said that "just to make Herman feel bad." Unfortunately for Hand, his ties were not solely with Talmadge. He was related to the Callaways, the textile barons, and through them, and in his own conservative right as a legislator, had the blessing of a considerable portion of Atlanta big business. To Herman, this looked like a setup which might later free Hand of the Talmadge straitjacket to work out his own independent financing and appeal, so Herman decided to chance it with Griffin, who, though he had been with Rivers and turned on him and been with Arnall and turned on him, might be safe merely because if he turned on Talmadge he would have nowhere else to go. (Talmadge could not guess that the Bainbridge bumpkin would actually come to the point of seeing himself as being above the need for sponsors.)

When it was all over, Ralph McGill sized up Hand's and the *Constitution-Journal's* defeat as proof that Talmadge "has a state organization and influence much greater than any ever attained by his late father, Eugene Talmadge," and he judged that "when Herman Talmadge determined, with a certain ruthlessness, to by-pass a closer and more loyal

friend (Hand) and support Mr. Griffin, he did so with great astuteness."*
It was an astuteness the *Constitution* was never again willing to buck. The
Atlanta press and Talmadge have since then worked in almost total
harmony.

Temporary ill feelings that had come between Roy Harris and Griffin,
because of their opposite efforts in this campaign, soon passed away. The
morning after the election, Harris warned Georgia in an issue of his
Augusta *Courier* to watch out for "the little handful of people surrounding
Marvin," a prophetic warning. But it was not long before he and Griffin,
allies who never allowed disputes over ethics to interfere with their more
important task of fighting integration, were fighting it once more, shoulder
to shoulder.

Prior to their descent upon Little Rock, the best illustration of this
teamwork was the case of Dr. Guy Wells.

Wells was one of Georgia's more distinguished educators. He was
education advisor to General Lucius Clay and was a consultant under
Point Four in Libya, where he recognized the harm that this nation's attitude toward the Negro was doing to its relationship with other countries.
On his return he joined the Georgia Committee on Interracial Cooperation
and, just as the U.S. Supreme Court handed down its school desegregation
decision in 1954, he was setting out on his campaign to keep the white
attitude loose and friendly toward the Negro in Georgia. Rotary Clubs and
churches welcomed him as a speaker, for a while. He was, after all, the
much beloved president of the Georgia State College for Women at
Milledgeville, and was advocating nothing more radical than the theory
that the ability to cross national and racial boundaries is the mark of an
educated man.

After developing this theory at Paine College in Augusta (Roy Harris'
home town), Wells was identified in the next issue of the *Courier* as "a
traitor to the white people of Georgia." The next move was Governor
Griffin's. Wells was drawing a $518 monthly pension as a former teacher
and, because of his emeritus status, still holding a life and hospital insur-

---

* Herman's intimate friend Georgia Comptroller Bentley says, "Talmadge has
an affection and intense loyalty to his friends, but it's practical—he doesn't allow
it to jeopardize his future. He taught me one rule: If you have a friend and an
enemy, choose the friend—but don't weight the scale for that friend if he's vulnerable because it would make you vulnerable."

ance policy through the state. "To be drawing $518 a month pension," said Griffin with a grim nod at the *Courier's* reference, "Dr. Wells has been acting a little ugly." He fixed that; his state Board of Education ordered the State Teachers Retirement Board to cut off Wells' pension "if possible," and the state Board of Regents took away his life and hospitalization insurance by taking away his emeritus title. Wells was not permitted to appear before either group.

Rotary, for which Wells had once been a district governor, and the Baptist Church, which had once hailed him as "one of Georgia's first citizens," did not come to his defense. The *Constitution* and *Journal,* hastening to preface everything with the assurance that neither paper stood for "the philosophy which Dr. Wells now espouses," only wondered abstractly "if it is really safe to speak and think independently in America today."

To his credit, Faubus wanted to work his segregation mischief in his own style, without being linked overtly to the likes of Griffin and Harris. Having determined already to block Negro entry into Central High, he did not want his methods mucked up by the Georgia hellions. When he heard that Griffin and Harris were coming to Little Rock to speak to a Capital Citizens Council fund-raising dinner, Faubus telephoned Griffin to say that he understood "one of your party may make inflammatory statements. Our town is tense. If that's true, I'd rather you wouldn't come."

To which Griffin is reported to have responded, "Naw, I'm gonna give 'em hell on the constitution and Roy is gonna give 'em hell on the civil rights thing. But nobody will advocate violence."

And the dialogue is supposed to have ended with Faubus saying, "In that case, you're welcome. You and your party come stay at the mansion. I'm speaking out of town that night, but you have breakfast with me."

So Griffin proceeded to break his word by telling the Little Rock Citizens Council that blood would flow in the sewers of Atlanta before *he* would let one nigger enter a public white school, and little Roy chimed in with a yell of astonishment that any southern governor with troops at his command would not use them to bar the door to niggers.

While Faubus will not concede that Griffin had any persuasion with him, he does say—as is natural, since this would be further excuse for acting as he did—that Griffin's appearance ruined any chance of quieting down Little Rock so that the school could be integrated without the use of arms. Faubus says that "sentiment" around Little Rock hardened in the last two weeks before school opened and "one thing that triggered the change was Governor Griffin's speech. He told them there was no integration in Georgia, and people were coming to me saying, why does Arkansas have to have it?"

No doubt they were. But there were others who were coming to him and saying that Arkansas could have integration peacefully. With Faubus it was simply a matter of selective listening, with the third-term race in mind.

It's the best thing that could have happened to us, this
Little Rock situation. It's caused two things—people
are talking out loud now, and they're more deter-
mined than ever to fight integration. It's a fight for
freedom now. And it could go two ways nationally—
public opinion could swing to our side and take the
pressure off us, or it could swing agin' us.

                                              Roy Harris, 1957

Little Rock had been preparing for two years to make the opening of
school in 1957 a smooth and peaceful affair. The plan for integration,
although unsatisfactory to the NAACP because of its tentativeness, had
been approved (after a previous order) by the federal courts, approved
wholeheartedly by the Little Rock school board and by the mayor and
most important city officials, as well as by (so far as could be determined)
a majority of Little Rock's citizens.

Arkansas would have paid little attention to the group of disgruntled
white parents—The Little Rock Central High Mothers—who turned up
in state court five days before school opened to petition for a postponement
of the integration order, except that appearing with them, with no prior
hint of his feelings, was none other than little Orval, come to warn of dire
things, of bloodshed and mob violence, if integration were allowed. Not at
all! scoffed School Superintendent Virgil Blossom; it could be done peacefully. Ridiculous! agreed the school board, and appealed to the federal
courts to enforce its integration ruling.

But Faubus would not be talked out of the play he had pre-determined
with his staff two weeks earlier. On the evening before school was to
open, out marched his 270 National Guardsmen, and chaos was come. His
explanation for calling out the Guard was hardly more convincing than
Chicken Little's. He had received unimpeachable evidence that "caravans"
of unruly whites were on the way to Little Rock to do violence against the
nine Negro children who wanted to enter Central High. Guns, he had been
told, were being sold at an unusual rate. He had acted "prayerfully" in
the "conviction" that it would be impossible "to restore or maintain order"

100

if "forcible integration" were carried out. This statement was immediately suspected as being a rationalization of his actions, because ever since he entered politics he had said of integration that he was against only the "forced" type and that otherwise he thought it should be strictly a matter of local choice. Since all important local officials had chosen to integrate Central High, he could only dodge the appearance of going back on his word by labeling it nevertheless as a mysteriously "forced" situation. And there were other mysteries; when he heard that the FBI might take him into custody by force, for violating a court order, he wired President Eisenhower that he had "*certain evidence* upon which I acted to preserve the public peace."

The certain evidence has not unto this day been produced. As for the mysterious caravans that were moving through the night to descend with Caucasian wrath upon integrated Central High, where were they? The question was put to Faubus in a television interview and he responded, with a knowing side glance, that Arkansans didn't tell all they knew. The sheriff of Pulaski County said he had heard nothing about such caravans; nor had he, said the chief of police of Little Rock. In fact, an investigation by Federal District Judge Ronald N. Davies revealed that up to the moment that Faubus set the stage for violence, police had not had a single case of interracial violence reported to them.

Now, too, the governor began to refer to the January 1956 poll which supposedly had shown that 85 percent of the state's residents were in favor of continuing segregation; within two weeks after calling out the troops he added to this another poll which, he said, showed that 82 percent of the people of Little Rock agreed that violence would have occurred if the Guard had not been called. Both polls, as interpreted by Faubus, were quickly absorbed into what the *Gazette* hooted at as Arkansas mythology and attempted to set straight by reminding its readers that, contrary to Faubus's continual claim that 85 percent of the people had voted for segregation in the previous election, actually "56 percent of the people supported the most extreme of the proposals, the 'nullification' amendment, 61 percent supported Faubus' interposition resolution, 72 percent supported the most innocuous of the proposals, the initiated school assignment act, patterned after a Virginia plan since declared unconstitutional by the federal courts."

If Faubus' recollection of one-year-old history was cockeyed, so, too, was his reading of the present poll. Not even the poll-taker, Eugene

Newsom of Paragould, President of Mid-South Surveys, Orval's ouija board, could understand how the governor came up with 82 percent support for the troop call. "I can't say such and such a percentage of people say such and such a thing," Newsom protested to reporters. "I prefer to say that an overwhelming number favor what the Governor did." Well, no, he admitted, he hadn't exactlly *asked* them if they favored Faubus' action but he said he thought the question was *implied*. Under further questioning, Newsom said he had interviewed 300 people in Pulaski County (Little Rock), a county in which at that time there lived approximately a quarter-million people.

The truth and the governor were, it appeared, becoming more estranged in all areas of discussion. In the midst of the confusion and the conflicting statements that poured out of the capitol and out of the governor's mansion, one thing only was certain: that on September 3, 1957, as Harry Ashmore described it, "Little Rock arose to gaze upon the incredible spectacle of an empty high school surrounded by National Guard troops called out by Governor Faubus to protect life and property against a mob that never materialized."

Burlesque though it was, it was also the first time since the Civil War that a governor had even temporarily succeeded in interjecting himself and a military force under his control between the will of the federal government and the object of that will. Little Rock was now a national crisis.

"The lesson of Little Rock, Ole Miss, Freedom Ride and Birmingham," wrote *Look* senior editor George B. Leonard, "can be summed up in one sentence: He who deals with segregationists using reason and reason alone does so at his own risk. Rather, then, think of them as afflicted children who must be forced to walk: Be sympathetic and kind, but be firm." This would be especially good advice for dealing with segregationists such as Faubus, who are not segregationists by philosophy but, according to their calculations, by political necessity. In attempting to deal with Faubus as a reasonable person acting out of reason, Eisenhower and his helpers merely extended the cruel burlesque.

After throwing up guards around the mansion and secluding himself for a week, Faubus came out briefly to talk with Eisenhower in Newport, where the governor was surprised because the people in that town didn't seem to like him. Then he returned and secluded himself again, sleeping soundly, eating well and regularly, chatting by telephone with his son in college, and relaxing by reading books about his favorite character, Abraham Lincoln. Faubus has always seen himself as something of a Lincoln and once said he guessed he was the only governor in the country who split rails like the great emancipator.

"Like Lincoln," he is fond of saying in historic tones, "I am, like Lincoln, against political connivances." Sail on, oh ship of cornpone. "Like Lincoln, I stand with the people's right to decide for themselves, God directing." And, like Lincoln, willing to give God a little assistance.

He called off the National Guard; the redneck crowd got out of control; Ike sent in the federal troops under General Edwin Walker, saying that mob rule in Little Rock menaced the very safety of the United States and the free world. Within a week Faubus allowed his reading of Lincoln to be interrupted again. Back to the effete East he went under new coaxing, enjoying it greatly, to sit with four supposedly smooth "southern" governors (none of the real toughies, of course) and be persuaded, they thought, to declare his willingness to uphold law and order. But hadn't he already done that at Newport under the tutelage of Ike? He had come out, with Ike smiling and trailing along behind, to say: "I have never expressed any personal opinion regarding the Supreme Court decision of 1954 which ordered integration. That is not relevant. That decision is the law of the land and must be obeyed." There! Of course, he hadn't obeyed it, but he had *said* it. Now they wanted him to say something else, to be exact: "I now declare that I will assume full responsibility for the maintenance of law and order and that the orders of the federal court will not be obstructed."

Very well. The four mediators agreed on the wording. Eisenhower agreed to it. So did Faubus. Oh the happiness of these naïve mediators, treating him as a sincere rebel! Victory was theirs—until Faubus walked out of the conference room, said his piece and then added two poisonous words: ". . . *by me.*"

And so, with the peacemakers and Ike shrieking in the background that he had betrayed them, had destroyed the spirit of the agreement, that all their labor was in vain, Faubus sailed happily into the western sunset, back to his racial wallow, and held one of the press conferences he relished so much.

Q. Governor, they say you added the words "by me" at the end and that changed the meaning. Did you add those words and what interpretation, if you did, do you put on it?

A. Now then, just a minute. By adding the words "by me" you mean they wrote their statement and then wrote mine? I write my statements from this end of the line. They can write theirs from that end.

Q. Well, Governor, LeRoy Collins of Florida is quoted as saying "We went over every word of the statement carefully with Governor Faubus and it was my understanding that he specifically agreed to everything verbatim just as the President did." What would you comment on that?

A. That that is true. The negotiations were on the basis of those two points and I agreed to those two points.

He was playing with them, of course, the wiry-souled ex-fruit tramp, survivor of hunger and snickers and highway cheating; survivor of the broad tie in a narrow-tie town; he had slipped and smiled his way through a life that Governor Collins, the first-family patrician of Tallahassee, could not imagine and therefore, at the council table, could not cope with the product of. Sure, he was lying, just as he had many times before, and just as he would even more frequently in the future; it was the mark of the new gentility, the new loyalty to the southern guard. Faulkner knew: the conniving Snopeses would rule at last.

Faubus did not want to be unreasonable; he just didn't believe in "overnight" integration—this, his interpretation of an integration that was planned to stretch over seven years! No, he would not allow his lawyers to even stay in the courtroom and hear, or give, testimony before Judge Ronald Davies as to whether an injunction should or should not be issued to keep the governor out of the way of the nine Negro children. He would not permit it because Judge Davies had obviously "carefully screened" the witnesses so as to hear only one side. It's true, the judge was not to have the privilege of listening to Amis Guthridge, spokesman for the White Citizens Council, or James T. Karam, the Little Rock clothier and friend of Faubus' who was later accused of circulating in the mob with sly advice, or those legislators who traveled to Virginia as Faubus' emissaries to learn the ways of interposition. In their place the judge heard only such biased persons as the mayor of Little Rock, the chairman of the school board, the principal of Central High School, and the chief of police. It was obviously a frame-up. Faubus' attorneys stalked out.

Segregationists who manufacture their own crises to keep a fiery nimbus behind their personality, subject themselves to the same risk that a bullfighter risks, namely, a public that grows tired of old stunts, callous to blood, impatient with peril. The politician, like the bullfighter, can hold his fans only by moving in closer; eventually he will be tossed.

With Faubus, that moment came when he attacked *The Arkansas Gazette.* In some ways this was a popular thing to do, as it is always popular among country folk to attack "those lyin' papers" in the big city. Faubus did not lose votes by it; he lost face, beginning with the time in late October 1957, when the public had grown accustomed to and a bit bored by the tourists and troublemakers hanging around the high school, and Faubus moved in to stir up the lull a bit by accusing Harry Ashmore, executive editor of the *Gazette,* of planting a psychiatrist at one of the press conferences with the intent to publish the psychiatrist's diagnosis.

It is always a mistake for a politician to make a great to-do over the fact that somebody else thinks he is crazy, as Earl Long and George Wallace were later to learn, and the *Gazette* was not slow to spot the opening, Ashmore writing: "Although a few of our readers have suggested in letters to the editor that Mr. Faubus may be suffering from some abberations, this newspaper has never been that charitable in its own view.

"We believe Mr. Faubus knows exactly what he is doing—and we suspect we have earned his wrath because through accurately reporting his devious course step by step, we have shown precisely where he is taking the people of his state in the furtherance of his political ambitions, and the terrible price all of us are going to have to pay as a result."

For two years thereafter, the governor's highway patrolmen took turns removing the *Gazette* from racks and throwing them down storm drains. *Gazette* reporters who covered Faubus' speeches in the boondocks were singled out by the governor—"I don't want you to hurt that young man there, please, for my sake. It isn't his fault he works for a lyin' newspaper"—and while the farmers glared, worked up subtly by Faubus, the governor would act the protector's role. This hatred of the *Gazette,* too, was only pretense. He told more than one *Gazette* reporter privately that he thought it was the best newspaper in the state.

Face was lost too—except among those who, a year earlier, would have been willing to believe there was some foundation for the pornographic leaflets handed out by Jim Johnson's followers showing a cartoon of Faubus in bed with a well-known civil rights leader—or at least credulity was dented when Faubus charged that the troopers serving under General Walker were following Central High School girls into their rest-rooms. "Vulgar accusations," said Eisenhower, and most Arkansans were inclined to agree. "We'll prove it when the time comes," said Faubus, but of course a convenient time never came.

Southern politicians in moments of stress are usually forgiven their little aberrations, and Orval was, too. More than forgiven: prayed for as God's right arm, with 600 gathering on one occasion in the Central Baptist Church to ask God to strengthen Orval and smite the heathen Yankee soldier with pestilence. Although this was a time when Faubus was being hung in effigy in Canada, hissed in Providence, and, in Adelaide, Australia, described as "public enemy #1, one of the world's wicked men," at home he was moving into the first stages of a popularity that ended in an unbeatable political dictatorship. Elsewhere in the Deep South he was a legend emerging from the shadows of nonentity. His old friends in Georgia had not forgotten him. Griffin was especially busy; ever since the Little Rock trouble hit the headlines, city officials and attorneys and others had received hundreds of pamphlets, tracts, circulars, reprints and other white supremacy documents through the mail—much of it bearing the stamp of the Georgia state Department of Education. Swaddling Faubus against the blast of the world's contempt also were men such as Thomas G. Wilson, President of the Arkansas Bankers Association who, having his own curious conduits of information, announced, "Outside the press, the East likes Faubus." All efforts to bind up the wounds were refused by Faubus. When, in early 1958, Senator Olin Johnston of South Carolina said, "I think everyone would agree Little Rock is dead" (as an issue), Faubus commented icily: "He speaks for himself. I don't think an assault on the Constitution is ever a dead issue." He would do everything to see that it survived through the elections. Now the governor was on the road constantly, off to speak to a Billy James Hargis rally, off to address a segregationist rally in Houston. No longer merely a politician, he was now a performer, molding his pronouncements to every new stage, altering his voice and gestures even to each new audience. To the state AFL-CIO convention in Little Rock he declared that he was a loyal Democrat and would remain so; the same evening, only forty miles away in Pine Bluff, he said he would consider serving another party. He had become, he told one of his admiring throngs in New Orleans, "a child of destiny." But savor the full statement: Asked if he would consider being the Presidential candidate of a third party, the little man raised a hand slowly to his forehead and then to his hair, pressing a stray lock into place. He was thinking. "Yes," he said finally, "I would not rule out that possibility, but it would not be a party based on the segregation-integration issue. It would be based on states' rights." Did he think he would have a chance? The little man smiled modestly. "I have received support from *all* states." His eyes became faraway and glazed as he listened to the yoo-hoo of fate, counterpointing his own confidence. "I never asked to become what I am now. *But sometimes you become a child of fortune or circumstance.*"

There was the George Wallace of yesterday.

Is it necessary to record that Faubus' gamble paid off in the 1958 election? Offended by the presence of the army of occupation, his people backed Faubus (264,346) against Chancery Judge Lee Ward, the "law and order" candidate (59,385), and the Little Rock meat packer, Chris Finkbeiner, who charged crookedness in the Faubus political machine (69,173). The campaign served truth in one respect, in that now Faubus stopped pretending about some of his important past actions. For instance, when he first called out the National Guard, he said that he did it to preserve law and order. Later he shifted to the explanation that he was upholding states' rights. But now the fire of the campaign burned away sham and he openly boasted of calling the troops for the sole purpose of keeping out Negroes. There was in some of his speeches the sheen of madness, as when he warned of an imminent "invasion" of Negroes into the all-white hill counties, and when, on July 4, he likened himself to the fathers of the American Revolution and likened the federal government to oppressive King George. It did not matter that Faubus had raised the sales tax and expanded the income tax—necessary increases, perhaps, but in a normal year enough to banish any hope for a third term; it did not matter that he had been caught in many lies, or that he quite plainly had set out to ruin the reputations of several politicians and editors who had been of great service to the state. To most Arkansans, the sending of troops had been a declaration of war, and Faubus was their responsive shot. Choosing between the influence of two outsiders—Griffin and Ike—264,346 went along with the picaresque Georgian. The fear of seeming other than "loyal" to the state and its leader had such a grip on even many of its more sophisticated residents that an NBC show "Outlook," documenting the election campaign antics of Orval, was voluntarily censored off the Little Rock and Memphis stations. It was an election that was to shape the course of countless future campaigns throughout the Deep South. A guaranteed vote-getting technique of resistance had been established. *The Arkansas Gazette* correctly predicted: "The moderate position formerly espoused by many southern political leaders, and by this newspaper as a matter of principle, has been rejected by the mass of voters in this Upper Southern state and is now clearly untenable for any man in public life anywhere in the region."

If more proof of that were needed, it was supplied with the defeat of Representative Brooks Hays, manipulated by Faubus behind the scenes as an act of revenge against the man who had talked him into sitting down with Ike. Faubus now hated Hays (whom he has never forgiven, and still refers to as a "weak reed"), not because by agreeing to go to Eisenhower he had shown weakness; if anything, Faubus had shown himself to be more cunning than the President. No, not for that, but because Hays was a living reminder to the people of Arkansas that a politician could be an active segregationist and still haggle in a friendly philosophical way. Hays was so opposed to the integration ruling that he had signed the Southern Manifesto, although its wording was a little too tough to suit him. In the Stevenson conventions he had been the platform committeeman most responsible for working out civil rights planks that sounded acceptable to the North without sounding abominable to the South. Governor James Coleman, no softy on segregation, endorsed Hays by saying publicly, "The South needs you in her great struggle." The fact that he easily defeated Amis Guthridge, the Citizens Council blabbermouth, in the primary, indicated that it had not occurred to the people of his district to look upon Hays as an integrationist. But Faubus soon planted the idea, keyed to a special session of the legislature in which the governor was given a number of sweeping segregationist powers, including the power to close the schools at whim and set up a private school system (which he did for the 1958-59 session). Faubus also put to work his crony Claude Carpenter— a sometime member of his official staff, sometime Public Service Commissioner, and sometime finance chairman of the state Democratic Party —to lay the groundwork for the defeat of Hays in the general election. Emotions were very high; the feeling within the state was one of actual insurgency; emergency measures were being enacted regularly. In such an atmosphere the oddity of a serious write-in campaign against a strong incumbent does not seem so odd.

Three weeks before the election, Dr. Dale Alford, an eye doctor and the only pro-Faubus member of the school board at this time, announced. He was the chosen one. Then Kay Matthews, later appointed by Faubus to a chancery judgeship, worked out the wording of an opinion handed down mechanically by the attorney general that people wanting to vote for Alford could, for convenience, apply to the ballot printed gummed labels bearing his name. It worked very well, and when it didn't, the election judges would (after supplying the label in the first place) assist the illiterate in applying it. Even with such hanky-panky Alford won by only 1,200 votes out of 60,000—and many of the 1,200 came in, as was habitual in any election touched by Faubus, suspiciously late. Nevertheless, the very fact that Hays was beaten at all, even by the most skilled skulduggery, after winning in the primary, was a gloomier lesson than Faubus' staying in for a third term.*

At this point the South's hate wave was cresting; building up through the Dixiecrat movement, the political assassination of liberal Claude Pepper in Florida, the churnings of Talmadge and Harris and Griffin, it would soon break into a long frothing descent as if swept, still powerful, still dangerous, but always diminishing, on toward the shore very, very dimly seen. That the wave did not build higher (through intelligent legalistic defiances), with a resulting schism of much greater proportion than presently exists between the South and other regions of the country, can be, ironically, credited to Faubus' bungling defiance at this time. The encouragement of the mob at Little Rock unquestionably furnished the pattern for the encouragement of the mob at Ole Miss. Faubus' oath that he was "ready to go to jail" would be repeated again and again, with the same vacuous bravery, by men such as Wallace and Barnett. But at Little Rock the federal government had been forced to make a stand, and it had stood for force if force were necessary. The courts, too, in refusing to sympathize with a good-

---

* Time has found the two surprise adversaries remaining faithful to their divergencies. Hays, after completing a term as president of the Baptist Convention, became an official of the "socialistic" TVA, and then served as second in command of the Community Relations Service of the Justice Department. Alford, after running up the most flagrant hooky record of any Arkansas congressman, later fell out with and ran against his creator, but now is reportedly thick with Faubus again. The paths of Hays and Alford converged again in 1966 when they were among those who ran and lost in the campaign to succeed Faubus; both men this time shared the common fate of sounding too moderate up against the undiluted hater, Jim Johnson, the same Jim Johnson who had helped spook Faubus into creating the Little Rock problem.

hearted school board that asked further delays in the face of what it took to be an impossible situation, destroyed any residue of hope that the strategy of "General Longstreet dalliance"—(hold out just a little longer, boys, and reinforcements will arrive)—could effect any permanent reversal in the slow, slow inevitability of school integration.

There were other destructive forces at work on The Cause, some from within. The exposure of the monstrous graft of the Griffin administration in Georgia was occurring at about the same time. What this meant was described by Harris in a private memorandum circulated among friends: "Marvin, as governor, was the leader of the segregation forces in the South. . . . When the Atlanta newspapers began to expose the graft and corruption, the leaders in the other southern states began to fall away. Our whole effort fell flat. Our organization, on a southwide basis, floundered. The blow-up of Marvin Griffin's administration was the most severe blow the cause has had during the last six years."

A serious blow, perhaps, but because it was happening at home Harris exaggerated its importance. Nothing within the scope of Griffin's ability to do or leave undone could possibly rank in importance, negatively to the segregationists, with the forcing of the federal hand by Faubus. The white-vs.-white abrasiveness encouraged by Faubus had by 1960 exposed the nerves of the South to such an extent that it made much more effective, if it did not indeed make possible, the black-vs.-white sit-in movement and what Leslie Dunbar called "government by the street," that started in Greensboro and did not end in Americus.

If the wages of sin is spiritual death, as the crudely-lettered signs nailed to pine trees through the South proclaim, they is also sometimes materialistically bountiful. In January 1959, as anticipated, Faubus appointed the controlling member of the highway department and promptly forced the resignation of Herbert Eldridge, who for six years had kept at a distance the Arkansas politicians who wanted relatives on the payroll, contracts for friends, and asphalt for their favorite stretch of wilderness. Independence was no longer the hallmark either of Arkansas bureaucracy or of the Arkansas legislature. School teachers were openly solicited for political contributions; when the Arkansas Education Association said that it was, at last, time to take an interest in how the state's money was being spent, it was immediately threatened with an investigation for subversive activities. Although there were no indications, other than the illogical passion aroused by the Central High School affair, that Arkansas wished to throw in its lot with the Deep South, Faubus was committing the state to that anyway, by obtaining from the legislature a "free electors" law giving him power-by-crony to cast Arkansas's electoral votes any way he chose—a whimsical venture coinciding with identical laws being passed in Georgia, Alabama, Louisiana, and Mississippi under the guidance of the Committee for the Forty-eight States (another of the faceless disguises used by the old Dixiecrat crowd). Behind it all, of course, was the desire to be the controlling minority within the Democratic party or, failing that, move huffily into a third party.

Perhaps the best indication of the impregnable position in which Faubus now happily found himself was the manner in which he fobbed off criticism, hardly bothering to acknowledge it, much less answer it. He was blamed for the bankruptcy of the Arkansas Business Development Corporation, which carried 1,700 stockholders down with it; he was accused of using the welfare department politically, of double taxation, of firing people at the state hospital for political reasons, of meddling with nursing homes, of chasing away college presidents, of permitting brutality at the penitentiary.

He was charged with connivance in the organization of sixty insurance companies during the first five years of his reign, most of them going under and taking many Arkansas dollars. He was charged with secretly giving special tax favors to some out-of-state corporations operating in Arkansas, by changing their tax formula. Faubus only laughed and said he was "not in the mood to argue." He was publicly asked to deny that he had become a millionaire through ownership of one-fourth of the stock of the Foreman Cement Company, a subsidiary of the Arkansas-Louisiana Gas Company, which served him and which he served in such close harmony—but he declined to answer. When he was caught mailing out political letters to persons on the state welfare roll, a list that is by Arkansas law supposed to be secret, and asked where he had obtained the list, he smiled and said, "That's my secret."

The more he treated their accusations with contempt, the more his opponents railed at him. He was, they said, "one of the political pimples of history" . . . "the man with the stereo mouth" . . . "a dictator of disgrace and defeat."

It did not much matter when the charges were supported by data. In the 1962 campaign, McMath, trying for a comeback, pointed out that the state was paying only $50,000 more in welfare that year than it had a decade earlier—but the cost of *administering* the program had swollen by *$1 million;* that Faubus had $40 million in state funds scattered among friendly banks, bearing no interest to the state; much of that money was in banks "owned by the chain banker who is the silent partner" of the governor. Specifically he mentioned the First State Bank of Texarkana, which is tied by an interlocking directorate to Ark-La Gas Company; it had more than $2 million in state funds at that time to play with, paying no interest, while a less friendly bank, but of almost identical structure, in El Dorado, had only $70,000 in state funds. Faubus' only response was to damn McMath as "a hard core integrationist" who was "tied to those main street moderates from back east."

Although no one in Arkansas would suggest that Faubus sold out cheap, he has always given the impression that if he did sell out, he would be a bargain. In 1958, he made a great to-do about not accepting a bribe of $125,000, in connection with a race track franchise. One must take his word for it that a bribe was offered, but even assuming that such a thing took place, why the grand self-congratulatory act? "I could have taken that bribe and retired, and nobody would have been the wiser," he said. Retired—on $46,460 after taxes? Did he really mean that, except for a deep lode of innate honesty, he actually might have sold out and retired for $46,460? Possibly so, because in 1958, when William F. Rector, a Little Rock real estate man announced that as agent for a New Jersey corporation he could say the corporation, in reaction to the racial mess, would not establish a $10 million shopping center there, Faubus blew up and said Rector had queered the deal because he had failed to get some insurance business with the state a couple of years earlier. The insurance business Rector did not get would have brought him exactly $92 a year—which was 8/10,000ths of his income. This, because the umbilical to his dirt-poor boyhood had never broken, was typically Faubus' measure of a man.

Co-existence is very difficult to arrange with Faubus. Senator William Fulbright tried it by touring Europe and keeping mum during the Little Rock crisis—a noncritical favor which Faubus returned later by ridiculing Fulbright as an "addlebrained visionary" because of his tolerant views of the Cuban people. Power has not been accompanied by magnanimity. When in 1964 he was opposed by Republican Winthrop Rockefeller, who had done more than any other one man to lead the Faubus government out of the economic dark ages and who had tried to be a true personal friend of the governor's, Faubus identified himself as the only candidate who could be counted on to oppose immorality and atheism, going on to elaborate that "marriage is ordained by God and marriage vows should be observed," an obvious reference to Rockefeller's celebrated divorce from Bobo eleven years earlier and also to the three divorces, long past, of Rockefeller's second wife. "As a counterpuncher," one long-time political observer noted, "Mr. Faubus specializes in the low blow." It is the kind of blow he has used also to keep opponents of his legislative program in line. When the legislature passed an omnibus appropriations bill, much of which was not earmarked for a particular purpose but left to the discretion of the governor to spend as he wished—a clear violation of the Arkansas constitution—and when the legislation was challenged in court, Faubus counterpunched by saying the challenge was imperiling money for the state school for handicapped children, a ridiculous statement on the face of it because the appropriations for this school were only $50,000, but it served as an excellent emotional blackjack.

Strong-arm is not an extravagant description of Faubus' government. In 1961, a $90 million bond issue passed the house of representatives in ten minutes and passed the senate with less than a day's debate. But those were slow times by comparison with what the legislature would later do for him. In January 1964, the senate passed a $150 million bond issue in the length of time it took to call the roll. There was no debate, and since there were no printed copies of the bill many of the senators could not have known what they were voting on. Legislation was whipped through either chamber with the cry "Governor's bill! Call the roll." That was enough to do it. Special interests in alliance with the Governor got the same treatment. It was nothing rare to hear a legislator present a measure with the demurrer, "Don't ask me anything about it. All I know is this is the bankers' bill." Magic words.

It goes without saying that the legislature never even considered overriding a veto. Faubus was flanked by men who, influential in their own right, became surrogates of great power through his benignity. Such a one was William J. Smith, sometimes known as The Other Governor. An attorney (now "Judge" because of a one-month interim appointment to the Supreme Court), he was legislative secretary to the governor each session and his words carried great weight. "The senate will now go into a committee of the whole and hear from Judge Smith." Since he became so useful to the governor, Smith's law firm grew from three members to nearly two dozen, being the largest in the state and known as the firm to which one goes if he wants the extra-tough job done. A few years ago, it is said, Southwestern Bell was using another firm but wasn't getting anywhere with the Public Service Commission until one day the governor did Bell the great favor of calling its representative in and telling him, "You'll get skinned if you don't change attorneys," which Bell promptly did and wasn't skinned at all.

And yet dimly, in this self-serving jungle, the people seem to be signalling for an independence they will not claim because they do not know what to ask for, having experienced it so seldom. They, like the followers of Father Divine, have come to terms with the most important prerequisite for worship, which is that they assume the sins of their master, and Faubus—who started out campaigning in a broken-down Chevvy but later used a Thunderbird or a Lincoln, knowing that many people relish by proxy the successes of a scoundrel—understands that "children of destiny," whether leading blacks in Harlem or whites in Arkansas, best fulfill their role by not taking such reverence too seriously. Thus, after Faubus' legislature had turned down the idea of voting machines, the people eighteen months later voted to permit themselves that luxury. Faubus had said voting machines are "nice" but he was against them if the state had to buy them. Even now voting machines are only permissive, and many sections of the state do not use them; in these areas, which have come through so loyally with late votes for Faubus, violations of the election code became the rule. After the legislature had laughed at the idea of a permanent registration, the people eight months later passed it for themselves. Every constitutional amendment proposed by the legislature for Faubus since 1957 was defeated by the people. In 1959 (after the attempted purging of forty teachers in Little Rock for integration activities) the people had a recall election and got rid of the three Faubus members. It is very strange—Orval can win his own elections by lopsided margins but he cannot transfer his popularity to issues. And yet the people seem unaware of what by such actions they are saying; they will not listen to themselves; as if by the silent compact struck in that wild moment of embarrassment at Central High School, the majority of the people of the state have agreed not to notice Faubus' many failures.

And so they were stuck with him. Like the crazed mariner, he has hung on at the wedding celebration until his tale is told, and it has been a long, long tale. From time to time during his governorship it almost seemed the state would at last be shed of him. In 1962, looking pale and wan and claiming to have an ulcer, he went on television with a melo-dramatic flourish to bid his people farewell. He would not run again. "We have done many good things and made much progress together." Adieu. But, of course, he ran after all. In 1965, looking a bit haggard and puffy around the jowls, he again began talking of retirement. No one believed him. With mischievous skepticism the great *Arkansas Gazette* editorial-ist noted that Faubus had "ridden into more sunsets than Tom Mix," only to come out in the next reel with guns blazing. But this time he did step down. No one in Arkansas accepted it as a permanent thing. They knew he would come back to cash in all those favors stored up over the past dozen years by Faubus-controlled boards, regulating in a friendly way utility rates, highway contracts, banks, insurance rates, investment com-panies, trucking tariffs, liquor store licensing, and the university system.

People who have wanted to run against Faubus could not get money for the campaign. These boards and commissions—about 125 of them—are empowered to hire about 20,000 people and spend nearly a quarter billion dollars a year. In Arkansas, which still rivals Mississippi as the poorest state in the nation, the vote-seducing potential in such a disburse-ment of funds is evident, and Faubus has never made any effort to hide the fact that he used money to this end.

Very faithfully each campaign he wrote a letter to the state's 80,000 welfare recipients who regularly, in the spring of campaign years, got a $5 monthly increase (from federal money). He usually started a cam-paign with a "nut" of 150,000 votes. Add to that most of the 80,000 welfare people and many of the 20,000 state employes and their families, and also a high percentage of the 15,000 teachers, whom he kept happy with periodic pay raises, and Faubus was off and down the track before the starting gun. As a last touch, he sent the legislature ninety-three appointments just before packing his bags in 1967.

If he has been as unbeatable as any man in southern politics—aside from the reasons given already, which, actually, are subordinate to this—it is because he is a wizard at adapting, at doubling back on the trail to kill the pursuer. The last time John Kennedy visited Arkansas, Faubus publicly insulted his administration, with Kennedy present. Yet after Kennedy's death, Faubus sent out 1,000 Kennedy memorial stamps on envelopes cancelled in Boston to that many Catholic families in Arkansas, with a note enclosed saying how happy he was that on Kennedy's visit "there was no unpleasantness." In recent years, too, Faubus has often used the word "socialistic" to describe the federal government, but in addressing a farm organization recently he claimed that many of the Great Society ideas had originated in Arkansas and he promised to get as much federal money as possible to carry them on. True to his promise, Faubus used $3 million in federal highway funds, this on the sly, to raise salaries of the top state highway officials. Caught, he ordered the employes to return the money. "I was pushing a lot of these programs," he boasted, "while Johnson was still a conservative back in Texas."

Of all the acute ironies of Faubus' career, however, none exceeded his use, during the later part of his reign, of L. C. Bates as his advisor on the hiring of Negroes for state government—yes, L. C. Bates, husband of Daisy Bates, the leader of the Central High School integration movement, whose name Faubus once invoked to arouse his savage rubes. Furthermore, Faubus compacted with Bates never to hire a Negro who is not pro-civil rights. How did he explain this other face? Why, by claiming it's the same old face. "I've always been on a friendly basis with L. C." Nobody corners Orval Faubus.

And likely they never shall, for here is a man who, having set the South on fire, now nonchalantly alluding to a little trouble spot here or there in the country, offers himself as an arbitrator, as "someone who can stabilize the situation as much as possible." Why, it's Faubus the racial peacemaker! Strange that he was at first unrecognized. And now he has retreated to the hills to prepare other guises for other realms. Not far from the grave of his father, Sam, that fearlessly honest old fellow who was arrested during World War I for making "disloyal remarks," not far from the site of the shanty where he himself was born, Orval now pads over the carpets in a home whose foundation is as long as a football field (a quarter million dollar home bought, he says, from savings from his $10,000-a-year governor's salary) and ponders the best phrases for describing his *new* warlike character. At peace again with the Negroes, he is willing to be at war with the alien world. He is, he says, writing books— the "true" story of Little Rock, and his experiences as a soldier in World War II, and in them both is the subtle message: that America should be comforted, and the wrongdoers of the world should beware, because Orval Faubus is girding himself for new battles.

Just as he once heard phantom caravans tooling through the night, bringing arms to Little Rock, now he claims to hear phantom enemies stealthily approaching the ramparts of America. In such a situation, if such is true, wouldn't Arkansas and America feel much better with a man like Orval Faubus in the U.S. Senate? It is a question the boy from Greasy Creek is not too modest eventually to ask.

An Interlude:
Money

The South has more than a fair share of merchants of hate. They are financed, in general, outside its borders. A glance at the admitted list of campaign contributors to almost any of the more easily identified dema-gogue-reactionary southern politicians will show that the money comes from non-residents or from lobbying representatives of non-residents. . . . The most ingenuous of frauds, the American Democratic National Committee, founded admittedly for the purpose of defeating the expressed will of the people in a national election, operated almost entirely in the South. But the men who backed its operations financially were not southern. The native fascist groups of the South always disclose, sooner or later, that their dissemination of hate is in the interest of outside exploiters, interested in retaining the South in a colonial status and willing to utilize racial tensions for that purpose.

Ex-Governor Ellis Arnall of Georgia, 1947

For many years the comfortable theory that northern money nourished the roots of all southern political troubles was perpetuated by both moderate and ultra-conservative spokesmen for the region, understandably eager to clear away enough guilt to give the South a breathing space for its conscience. The greatest advance toward honest self-appraisal in the last twenty years, or roughly since the Dixiecrat Convention, has been the evolutionary exposure (and, in random ways, the South's confession) that its political ills have been increasingly financed at home.

Perhaps the imprint of northern silver at the time of the above Arnall complaint was still strong enough to excuse his laying the blame at the foot of Wall Street. There *was* northern money in southern politics, and political money deserves criticism proportionate to the distance it travels. Northern money is not especially insidious in itself but, after all, a big bankroller will not be as sensibly cautious about the calibre of campaigning his money supports if he does not have to live within the defective atmosphere it develops. What would otherwise be legitimate political strategy takes on a questionable virtue when its financial backers cannot control their forces, as recent events in the South show they often cannot.

In a vain and silly fashion, Governor Orval Faubus used to liken himself to a "burn man," which in logging camp parlance is the man who burns the tops and limbs of felled trees. "He must have a natural feelin' for fire," Faubus explained. "If he's a fraidy cat or too cautious he don't get the burnin' done. And if he ain't real smart, he's sure to start a forest fire." Considering the conflagration that spread out of Arkansas, Faubus has no grounds for bragging. But the analogy he supplies is useful to illustrate that when the match is tossed from half a continent away, there is not likely to be much control over the fire that results.

To this extent, *whatever* money came in from the North to back racist campaigns, distribute shrill broadsides against the federal government and especially the Supreme Court, and viciously to counter all government regulation and union efforts, was especially irresponsible money.

Of the twenty-two leading financial supporters of the influential Southern States Industrial Council (which wants to sell the Tennessee Valley Authority and believes "the great—the overriding—issue of our time is [*poverty? ignorance? enforced inequalities? no, no*] government control and regulations"), there are fourteen from above the Mason-Dixon line, with E.I. duPont de Nemours of Delaware giving four times as much as its nearest competitor in free-enterprise thinking, the Chesapeake and Ohio Railroad Company. Other big givers with northern headquarters include Firestone Tire and Rubber Company of Akron, General Motors, General Electric, and Household Finance Company. The primary purpose, almost the sole purpose of this organization, as with so many other industrial organizations in the South, is to propagandize. SSIC's program centers around a group of right-wing publications distributed to more than one million persons yearly, and a column written by the organization's vice president, Thurman Sensing, which is sent to more than 1,000 daily and weekly newspapers. The SSIC was set up in the mid-thirties to combat the NRA and it is perpetuated to fight unions. Sensing was a regular columnist in Herman Talmadge's ultra-racist newspaper, and his column continues to appear in a number of extremely right-wing oddity publications in the South.

The irresponsibility of the special interests—both northern and newly-southern—in this regard is recognized, not just rumored. Judge Roy Mayhall, former head of the Alabama state Democratic committee, said, "The racial smokescreen has been used by industry for as long as I can remember to elect their politicians." The smokescreen has not been thick enough in recent years to hide the resulting disaster from the world. Milton Cummings, one of the larger independent industrialists in Alabama, supported Mayhall's accusation: "It is common knowledge that big business like U.S. Steel and Goodrich have been subsidizing the White Citizens Council and the Ku Kluxers and the John Birch Society for years."

But all of the above-named mentors of southern politicians have for many years had southern branches, and as these branches were set up, the northern firms did not have to send in so much money to keep the South persuaded of what it is supposed to believe. As the South developed its own financial pockets, its own industry, and as transplanted northern business and industry put down roots and began to blossom with all the indigenous heavy-scented bigotry and cant, the New South could indeed boast that it is buying its own politicians.

Granted that Arnall's viewpoint was accurate shortly after World War II; it is much more sensible now to inspect the financing of southern politics for the close cooperation of *both* northern and southern money, since it is often impossible to tell their motives or their impact apart. After all, the money that has come South from such notable northerners as General Robert Wood of Sears Roebuck, and Pierre S. duPont, a vice president of E.I. duPont de Nemours (and, like Wood, one of the most generous supporters of right-wing, anti-union, pro-states' rights organizations), blends smoothly into the golden currents already flowing through southern political activities from the likes of such textile barons as A. G. Heinsohn, a heavy contributor to right-wing functions, and Roger Milliken, the chief financier of Republicanism in South Carolina. Money that came from the "southern" duPont family in Florida was spent on the same brand of southern politics as were the donations of the duPonts of Delaware, who, though "northerners," had as early as 1950 put half their investments in the South. Likewise, it would be academic to attempt to separate the support given to the Dixiecrat conventions by oilman J. Howard Pew of Philadelphia and oilman H. L. Hunt of Dallas and his lesser colleagues of Houston. The big money at the Dixiecrat conventions was oil money, but its donors were not troubled about which side of the Mason-Dixon they came from.

North and South, theirs was a common joy to hear the alphabetic litany of fear, chanted by such southern leaders as Herman Talmadge at the 1952 Democratic convention and Governor Allan Shivers the same year in his race with the liberal Ralph Yarborough in Texas—". . . the NAACP, ADA, CIO, COPE and other elements in this country who would destroy every vestige of states' rights and . . ."

And what do these monied interests mean by "states' rights"? The best answer is by example, and one of the best examples is in the operation of the Deering-Milliken textile-mill chain. Roger Milliken is the man in charge. He is a man of firm opinion. He "owns" the Republican Party of South Carolina, writes its platforms, bankrolls much of its activities ($500,000 worth in 1964, so the rumor goes). He is reported to have told intimates that it cost him $250,000 to lure Strom Thurmond into the Republican Party, but if that's true, he paid for something he could have got for free, because Thurmond didn't really have anywhere else to go. Milliken, an endorser of the John Birch Society, is a tough, no-nonsense employer. What he can't buy, he breaks. He is a great advocate of what he calls voluntary unionism, which sounds fair enough, but to Milliken, and in South Carolina, it has a special meaning: Shortly before Christmas 1956 he closed the Darlington Manufacturing Company, throwing 500 workers on the street, because they had voted to unionize. Desperate to get back on a payroll, on any terms, 83 percent of the workers signed a petition swearing never to even mention unionism again if he would keep the plant open and keep their jobs going. It wasn't enough to please Milliken. He wouldn't be satisfied, he said, if only 17 percent "hard core" union people were left on the payroll; he didn't want *any*. He auctioned off his machinery and moved out of town. People don't talk unionism and liberalism in Darlington and nearby towns like they used to before the strike. The

National Labor Relations Board has been trying ever since to make Milliken take a less granite attitude toward his workers, and *that* is what Milliken considers a threat to states' rights. Most southern industrialists agree with him. And, for that matter, most northern.

There is a way of life to be defended—jointly, North and South—and a way of life to be opposed. By 1944 there were clear signs that, if industry and big business were to maintain their political leadership in the postwar South, they would have to use the racial issue again to keep the middle and lower classes chopped up, suspicious of each other, and ineffective in attempting major social reforms. There were ominous signs of unrest. It was in 1944, for example, that the Southern Tenant Farmers Union, meeting in forty-one locals throughout the South, voted to push a program calling for the end of the poll tax in eight southern states, an end to racial injustice, an extension of social security and of National Labor Relations Board protection to all farmers and farm workers, a breaking up of big land holdings because "no individual should hold title to land which he and his family are unable to cultivate with their own labor power," the levying of a graduated land tax on all corporations holding more than the maximum needed for individual ownership, and the distribution to the poor of "forty acres and a steel mule"—a demand based on the unfulfilled promise of forty acres and a mule for each freedman in the Reconstruction. These radical demands were heard openly in the South only twenty-four years ago, and they very clearly constituted a dream that most men of means felt they must oppose. On the other hand, there was already in the South a way of life to be defended, perfectly illustrated in Mississippi where, even today, state law forbids factory, mill, or cannery owners from employing children *under fourteen years* of age; where children under sixteen years of age can't work more than ten hours a day *except in an emergency,* and where *sixty hours* constitutes the maximum work week for these youngsters. Industry intended to defend that kind of paternalism.

This was the focus, this and the fact that in Dixie only 20 percent of the eligible workers are today union members compared with the national average of about 36 percent; the disparity was much greater twenty years ago, right after the collapse of the AFL-CIO's much vaunted "Operation Dixie" that was supposed to sweep across the Deep South, bringing the blessings of unionism to all workers, but didn't.* The cauldron in which these economic matters were cooking was of primary concern to the Deep

South politicians and their paymasters right after World War II; the thought of miscegenation did not trouble them nearly so much. Nor did the Brown decision of 1954 switch the focus of their alarm overnight. In 1955, the year after the landmark school desegregation ruling, the leaders of the racist South—Eastland, Talmadge, Thurmond, Perez, Tom Brady, Rivers, etc.—met in Memphis at a convention of the Federation for Constitutional Government, the antecedent of the Citizens Councils, to plan for the coordination of all conservative groups across the South into what keynote speaker Senator Eastland called "a people's organization to fight the Supreme Court of the United States, to fight the CIO, to fight the NAACP and to fight all the conscienceless pressure groups who are attempting our destruction. *It will fight those organizations who attempt with much success to socialize industry and the great medical profession of this country."*

It was not the NAACP's later racial emphasis but the CIO and the specter of socialized production and medical care that then inspired the blackest fears. It was significant that the Federation for Constitutional Government elected as its executive chairman John U. Barr, a New Orleans industrialist and banker; he was an organizer of the Southern States Industrial Council, had been an organizer of the Dixiecrat convention, and was a veteran officer of the United States Chamber of Commerce and of the National Association of Manufacturers—a man who counted his racism in the countinghouse.

The mania for making a fast buck, or even a slow buck, is so widespread in the Deep South today that it remains in fact much more troublesome than racism; the mind of the South is much more preoccupied with it. President Kennedy thought it very strange (as did Arthur Schlesinger, Jr., who recorded the exchange) that Governor Ross Barnett, in one of his highly emotional telephone-plot conversations with the White House prior to the riots at Ole Miss, should—while the nation shrank from the blood cries in the background—thank Kennedy for helping Mississippi with its poultry program.

There was nothing unusual about it; Barnett was only clumsy enough to reveal to the world that with him, as is true with almost every important Dixie politician, the chicken market is more important than the public

* There were other, later impressive failures. Between 1960 and 1963, the Textile Workers Union spent $1.5 million in the Deep South and was able to recruit only *seven* workers!

peace. The dignity and spirit of this curious South has been so plundered by its own leaders that one will often hear the most remarkably revealing complaints, as when the Defense Department closed a number of worthless military bases in the South and thus provoked Representative Mendel Rivers of South Carolina (whose district contains a naval base, a Polaris submarine maintenance center, a Marine Corps air station, a Marine Corps training center, a Coast Guard station, a mine warfare center, an Army transportation depot, and an Air Force base, all generating a total payroll of $209 million a year) to rage: "It appears to me that the closing of these bases is being done purely for the sake of saving money." Everywhere there are those frenzied governors whom Leslie Dunbar, when he was Executive Director of the Southern Regional Council, properly called *"de facto* executives of the state Chambers of Commerce, who spend their time competing with each other as supplicants for new plants." It has been almost a generation since exploitation from the North was considered an evil fate. Unbelievable as it may now sound, with every Dixie Chamber of Commerce trying to lure northern industry with promises of semi-slave labor and free land and buildings, Senator James O. Eastland of Mississippi in 1948 complained bitterly that "our natural resources have been exploited by eastern capital as an outlet for investments to make huge profits from cheap southern labor." Exploitable resources and cheap labor are the very inducements which Mississippi and every other southern state use now to attract capital. So lovely has the prospect of being raped become that today many southerners feel the big problem is working out from under a deadening form of government that, behind the razzle-dazzle of legislative racism and the perfunctory drama of states' rights, seems hardly definable in anything but bordello terms. "We have talked," said Dunbar, "of state socialism and state capitalism, but what do we call governments whose chief affair is to entice and propitiate business?"

I started writing this in the sub-basement of the Florida capitol: a good place to begin measuring the Deep South. It is a building whose superstructure is appropriately half a foot out of alignment with its foundation. There is a sense of abandonment, a wistful archeological air about the capitol as of ruins nobody cares to dig. Pieces of the capitol roof go whizzing off in every high wind. The dome, supported only by legends and rotten timbers, is condemned. Ceilings sag. But the exterior is painted a fine, pure white, and from a distance—say, standing on the farthest hill across Smokey Hollow—the lines of the buildings are beautifully aristocratic.

As a symbol of southern politics this building is perfect. It is not ugly, but it is not sound. Underneath the white paint it is very rickety indeed. Government in the Deep South is in a condition of great disrepair as the result of the business–industry power faction's having ruled successfully so long on the simple principle that property rights are preeminent. In Tallahassee, as in most of the Deep South, the kaleidoscope of time and instincts works in weird patterns. On opening day of the legislative session, great bouquets are heaped high on every desk, slipping over onto the floor where the iris and roses and carnations are stacked around and in the tall brass spittoons, just as in other lost civilizations the brazen images were decked with flowers on festival days. Ralph Waldo Emerson visited Tallahassee and left calling it a "grotesque place." To some extent, politically, it still is, for here, as in all Deep South states, pine trees, potato fields, moonshine, paper pulp—not people—have run the government for generations; and there are only a few signs that the situation will radically change soon.

One hears considerable talk these days about how the cities hope for meaningful legislative reapportionment to acquire control from the backwoods. But it is significant how seldom these calls for reform come from industrialists and big businessmen, even though their headquarters are in the cities. These latter have no cause to complain. They have done very well under the rural legislators, many of whom are themselves bankers, insurance executives, timber squires, and who, for ends which he did not have in mind, would agree with that fallen angel of Populism, Tom Watson, that "gratitude may fail; so may sympathy, and friendship, and generosity, and patriotism, *but in the long run, self-interest always controls.*"

The dollar sympathies of the Florida legislature (a typical southern legislature) have been well known since the day in 1901 that it changed the law to permit Henry Flagler, vice president of Standard Oil Company and builder of the Florida East Coast Railway, to divorce his insane wife, and then changed the law back again—a gesture in Bible-quoting Florida that may have been even more significant than the 2 million acres of prime land the legislature gave him for his railroad.

The state's continuing concern for the well-being of commerce was illustrated fifty years later when it set aside two major rivers as "commercial streams"—which industry could, and did, pollute as it liked. Now the state is busily draining portions of the Everglades, a singular natural monument, so that private real estate speculators can have more land; and the Oklawaha River, generally considered to be one of the finest wild rivers in the nation, is being ruined so that a canal can be built across the state for the benefit of the barge industry (although Congress, for more than 100 years, said the canal was a senseless idea) and more real estate speculators.

In every one of the fifty legislatures the interests of the members are the same as those of big business and big industry, but this is especially true in the southern cloud-land of Xanadu, and therefore one must expect southern legislatures to be filled with men whose law partners are lobbyists and who themselves represent commercial clients before state commissions even while drawing their legislative salaries. The ethics and compassion of southern legislatures was well captured by Frank Trippett, a Mississippian now on *Newsweek's* national editorial staff, in his book, *The States: United They Fell.*

> Texas legislators who were about to appropriate several hundred thousand dollars to the state's animal wildlife board also heard officials testify that the state did not employ a single juvenile parole officer; thus children, on being released, were often returned to detention for want of supervision and guidance. It was at this point that a senator advanced a suggestion: why not put the delinquents under the animal wildlife board? His colleagues roared with laughter. Comparable hilarity bubbled up in a Florida hearing on prison conditions. The knee-slapper: one legislator suggested that, as an answer to the need for more cell space, psychopathic killers be placed in cells together. Could a couple of sick jokes reveal a fundamental legislative orientation?

Not long ago I heard a Florida senator helping to kill a conflict-of-interest bill by arguing that it wouldn't do any good to prohibit public utility commissioners from owning stock in utility companies because "they would just shift the ownership to their wives and children."

For a hundred years this region has been told that that which is inevitable is right and just, and our politicians have slyly learned to adapt this ethic for their friends. Since they *will* steal, it can't really be stealing. One playful southern official laughed when he identified himself to a congressional committee as "just a cheap politician, the only kind my region can afford"; it was a good joke, but it was not true, because actually very few of our Dixie politicians come cheap.

They can justifiably ask a high price. They do their chores well. Most southern states have no corporate income tax, no state property tax, no severance tax on natural resources; they make few demands on the paper mills, insurance companies, banks, mines, and timber companies to carry a proportionate share of the cost of government services.

South Carolina is a typical Dixie outpost in this regard. The basic tax from which the South Carolina state government operates is the sales tax, yet any manufacturing industry is exempt from it. If an individual buys fifty pounds of coal, he pays sales tax on it. The mill owner can buy 50,000 pounds tax free. The legislature did not forget the poor man, however; he was given two exemptions from the tax: Bibles and newspapers.

The managers of the South do not call this exploitation but rather "creating a friendly business climate." If encouraged, they will become almost metaphysical about it. For many years the economic affairs of South Carolina were run in the legislature by what was sometimes known as the "Barnwell Ring," a group of personally wealthy and business-oriented legislators who (like all wise old political bosses) like to pretend they do not exist, or that they are invisible, or at least that their power is greatly exaggerated and that actually they vote against each other—which, in South Carolina, is sometimes the case, when, for example, they cannot decide who should get the boodle: public-power attorneys or private-power attorneys. In general, however, their aims coincide remarkably. The two most influential members of the ring, and in fact the two who gave the ring its name, are state senator Edgar Brown, who as chairman of the Senate Finance Committee has been virtual dictator of state finances, and Sol Blatt, speaker of the house. Both hail from Barnwell (population 4,500) in Barnwell County (population 18,000), a rustic no-place about twenty miles east of Augusta, Georgia. The reason these rural statesmen are important to our argument is that they so blatantly have run the state for the special interests. Brown steered finances, by his own description, in such a way that "the big fellows like duPont, Stevens, Deering-Milliken, Fiberglass, Textron, Chemstrand, Lowenstein, Burlington, Bowaters and others . . . have confidence in our stability." Which means, of course, that "sales tax [but not on manufacturers] will continue to be the major provider." As for Blatt, he devotes his highly-paid legal skills to watching after the interests of the South Carolina Textile Manufacturers Association, the South Carolina Electric and Gas Company and most other private power companies.

They never describe their control of politics as originating in financial motives; their objective, they will tell you, has always been purely to preserve the South as the last outpost of fundamental founding-father Americanism. This is, in a way, true. There are many characteristics of the region that reflect exactly, as no other region in the country can do, the spirit of 1776. "The only revolution in which compassion played no role in the motivation of the actors," Hannah Arendt tells us, "was the American Revolution," which wrote into the new Constitution not one phrase in recognition of the misery of the 400,000 Negroes then in America. In terms of our beginnings, misery is an un-American reason for making revolutionary changes* and the U.S. Supreme Court's sweeping efforts to relieve misery among the Negroes can be justifiably seen by the South as of unfamiliar and even un-American origins.

"We have witnessed a revolution in our country," said Herman Talmadge, as though he had discovered something that wasn't being done openly, "a revolution which has taken place from the bench of the Supreme Court of the United States." And, since revolutions are supposed to be accompanied by spies and espionage, his elder colleague Richard Russell went on to explain how the revolutionists on the bench had all been hand-picked saboteurs, beginning with the selection of Earl Warren after a "secretive flight to Sacramento" by then-U.S. Attorney General Brownell, and continued thereafter by the Justice Department through a devious "process of screening" to make "sure that no man will be nominated who does not wholeheartedly embrace the 1954 decision of the Court on school segregation, which was admittedly based on psychology and Myrdal rather than law. . . ."

Hopped up by their relish for hocus-pocus and drama, southern politicians describe the situation in such breathless terms that one is inclined to laugh. But if they are psychotic about the details, they are very sane and correct about the change. There *has* been an "un-American" revolution, and concern for the inner man (call it psychology and Myrdal, or compassion) had a lot to do with it. To keep from paying for the results

* The Confederate Constitution, a highly "American" document in many respects, did not provide tax levies for the general welfare.

of this revolution has been the overriding motive behind the southern man of great property, just as it has been since Reconstruction days.

Although it has become not only unfashionable but almost incredible in an America that saw the U.S. Chamber of Commerce and the AFL-CIO *both* endorse Lyndon Johnson, to speak in terms of class conflict and to deal even obliquely with such symbols as The Capitalist and The Downtrodden, symbols that fitted more naturally into the world of Joe Hill, it is nevertheless true that the tension—or ever-present *potential* of tension—between these two economic extremes has more than any other one thing made postwar Deep South politics what it was and is, in a recurrence of what took place seventy years earlier when the South's rich planter class, tired of being taxed to pay for the social reforms of the Reconstruction Republicans and fearing that the reforms might take deep root, decided to cancel out economic conflicts between classes by establishing white racial unity from top to bottom. As Harry Williams describes the effort in his little study *Romance and Realism in Southern Politics:* "It was an admirable arrangement to head off any economic stirrings on the part of the masses. Indeed, it was understood that there was supposed to be no relation between politics and economics. . . . They elevated the race issue to subordinate economic or other issues that endangered their position." Williams sees the characteristics of this wealthy class—the Bourbons, the Redeemers—as these: "They believed in economical government, the type that furnished few services and collected few taxes. They thought that government should not interfere in social matters or regulate affairs. They preached the industrialization of the South through the importation of Yankee capital and the advantages of close cooperation with the industrial East. They were often of the planter class and they acted and talked like traditional southerners, but they were hardly in the old agrarian tradition."

Scarcely any change in details is needed to describe the "New" South's industrial mutants, who had no trouble rationalizing the revival of the old Bourbon gimmicks for emotionalizing the masses. Roosevelt, like the black Republicans, had had his spree of social reformations and new taxes, and the rich southerner of 1945 felt no better about that than did his grandfather of 1875. Niggers inching toward the ballot box must be stopped; the few southern liberals who had cropped up in the Great Depression must go; and all white folks must be unified against the union recruiter, the anti-Christ of the social gospel, and Yankee Washingon with its silly child-labor laws and minimum wages.

Their efforts have largely succeeded. At the organizational meeting of the Dixiecrat Party in Birmingham, 1948, the keynote speaker was Frank Dixon, former governor of Alabama but at that time counsel for the Associated Industries of Alabama, a wing of the National Association of Manufacturers. The AIA has hundreds of members, including the great northern corporations with plants in Alabama. At that same states' rights conference Olin Horton, associated with the Alabama Mining Institute, the coal operators' organization, was in charge of local arrangements. The philosophy of the Dixiecrat movement appealed much more profoundly to industry than it did to the upper-bracket politicians of the South, who, except for the scatterbrains and those who had been panicked by the hooting from the thickets, did not want to give allegiance to that strange party. Only the governors of South Carolina, Mississippi, and Arkansas, the two United States Senators from Mississippi, and about half the Mississippi delegation in Congress were there.

Aside from the industrial representatives, the most noticeable attendants at the Dixiecrat bonfire were men whom the Chicago *Daily News'* redoubtable Ed Lahey described compositely as "middleaged, in a seersucker suit, tieless, rednecked, and leatherfaced, the easily inflamed type whose idea of civic mindedness would be to volunteer for night duty to chase a union organizer out of town."

It has, in the last quarter century, been a wonderfully successful team, this, the industrialist and the redneck. Together they have trained the southern politician to treat the race question as being all-important and invisible. Their genius at this was nowhere better illustrated than when Donald Leslie, Sr., chairman of the board of Hammermill Paper Company of Erie, Pennsylvania, sitting beside Governor George Wallace, was cheered and applauded when he said that he had decided to build a $25 million plant at Selma, Alabama, because "my company had investigated the character of the community and received nothing but fine reports." (This was said within hours after 2,600 Negroes had been jailed or arrested in their efforts to bring about integration.)

The fruits of such cooperation may appear ridiculous to many people in the outside world, but the results are just what the redneck-industrialist-politician team set out to achieve. Teachers can be fired in South Carolina for union membership. Union organizers in Florida are fingerprinted. In several southern states, industry pays no taxes for the first ten years of residence. The executive director of one southern public utilities commission told me they did not try to control Bell Telephone because "one little outfit like a state finds it pretty difficult to deal with a utility that large." In Alabama industry sets its own ad valorem rates. No region has lent its rivers and streams so wholeheartedly to pollution by industry. Eastern coastal waters near the Georgia line once supported the greatest oyster and shrimp beds of the entire Atlantic coast—this was before industry won the right to pollute the rivers that feed the area. And best of all, unions in most of the Deep South really haven't a chance to thrive, with all the anti-picketing and open-shop laws. Despite job gains, per-capita personal income slips further behind the national average, and though time lost through strikes has doubled in the last five years, there have been few net gains in union organizing. Low as their economic life is, the rednecks mean to defend it against Negroes who want jobs and organizers who may want to give them jobs. A movie of the Selma marchers was taken around the country and shown to select audiences to prove that communists and villainous agitators were behind the disturbance; when it was shown to newsmen in Washington, the narrator identified various people as they appeared on the screen as being "a well known fellow traveler now working for SNCC" or "a former communist sympathizer now with CORE," etc. Ticking off the traitors one by one, he came to a white man of whom he said, "I don't know his name, but he is with the AFL-CIO." The newsmen laughed; but that was northern laughter.

Productivity is up; some industrialists say 15 percent above what can be got out of workers in the north. W. Cooper Green, former executive vice president of the Alabama Power Company, Birmingham, thinks he knows why: "A job is a luxury for these old farmers coming down from the hills. They've been living hard—on cornbread and fatback—and now they can go out and buy a TV set." People who have been living hard and who think that living easy is owning a television set are easily persuaded that any change would only result in something worse, and this fear has been, over the past generation, solidified into a political force.

Aside from this, the special interests have made doubly sure of their control of southern politics by raising the campaign ante to an almost unmanageable level. The stakes are no longer within reach of the general public. The interests who fear such things as unionization and who desire massive tax relief are best able to buy time by buying politicians. All politicians are for sale, of course, in a pleasant democratic sort of way, but for a long while the average people of the Deep South have simply been unable to stay in the bidding for their own leaders.

John Sparkman, for example, was elected Senator from Alabama in 1946 after spending only $75,000. To win re-election in 1966, Sparkman is believed to have spent nearly ten times that amount. Sparkman's career proves that the man with the big money does not always win; but it also proves that *even when the well-heeled candidate loses,* he shapes the future. In 1954 Sparkman, who was considered something of a progressive, was opposed by Congressman Laurie Battle, a mean campaigner. Doctored photographs of Sparkman and his Negro friends were circulated, as were the mysterious leaflets from the "Communist Party of Alabama" telling how it would be better for "the cause" if Sparkman were elected instead of Battle. But more importantly, Battle was so loaded with big business and big utilities campaign money he was nicknamed "reddy kilowatt." As usual, Sparkman was running as a poor boy. He won, and the margin was comfortable, but the money spent against him in that race caused something within him to freeze.

Whether or not Sparkman might have developed into something resembling a true progressive, we will never know; what we do know is that the golden armor worn by his losing opponent in 1954 left him shaken and permanently frightened and he has remained very, very respectful of the Big Mules of Birmingham and monied people everywhere to this day. Gladly he accepted the alliance and support in 1966 of the Chase Manhattan Bank of New York and other large banks, though he must have known they would expect favors in return when he stepped up to Chairman of the Senate Banking Committee in 1967.

Million-dollar campaigns are no longer unusual in that grits-and-gravy poor region where the average annual income is $2,000 or less. Carl Sanders won his race in Georgia with an expenditure of $1.5 million (one banker publicly subscribed to one-third of it). Marvin Griffin, ex-governor of Georgia, complained to me, "It takes at least half a million to run in Georgia now, and that doesn't leave anything for buying votes."

There are, of course, happy exceptions to the intimidating powers of the big bankroll. Several times in the 1950's, in races both for the governorship and for the Senate, Ralph Yarborough of Texas was drowned in a sea of opposition money from the big oil men. Out of sheer orneriness he finally prevailed with a seat in the Senate, but instead of becoming more conservative and more cautious in hopes that this would keep away the rich hobgoblins, Yarborough—who moves among his colleagues to a drum beaten by the ghost of his old idol Estes Kefauver—developed the most progressive voting record in the Deep South, a voting record, indeed, that would be judged progressive in any region. He is exceptional.

There are also some not-so-happy exceptions to the rule, although these exceptions can generally be accounted for as a kind of cancerous offshoot of the big-money cell. Sumter Lowry nearly made the run-off in Florida against LeRoy Collins in 1956 with an expenditure of only $100,000, but Lowry was using the same hate machine that had put George Smathers into the Senate in 1950, a machine which for several years remained well oiled with duPont money. Lester Maddox was elected governor of Georgia in 1966 not only without heavy financial support but despite heavy financial opposition. After Ernest Vandiver dropped out of the race with a weak heart, the Atlanta fatcats spent most of their money on the candidacies of ex-Governor Ellis Arnall and Bo Callaway, the Republican millionaire mill owner. As it turned out, the rich men of Atlanta didn't get their wishes in either direction, because Lester Maddox, with almost no money, rode into office on the crest of all the anti-federalism, anti-everything-ism that the insurance–Coca-Cola–banking fraternity had helped pay for in other years to get their own candidates elected. Maddox got a free ride on a very expensive emotional apparatus out of the past.

But the rule is still the rule: big money usually wins. One of the more entertaining sessions of the Kefauver Crime Committee hearings revealed that three men met in a hotel room in Jacksonville, Florida, and decided to buy Fuller Warren, then a candidate for governor in Florida, just as they might buy a race horse. Each man put up $150,000. Aside from this $450,000 kitty, Warren received only $15,000 from the public. The partner of one of these men wrote the bill subsequently passed by the Florida legislature which freed the billion-dollar citrus industry from all state taxes—a condition of bliss in which it remains to this day. One of the more important owners of groves and processing plants is Coca-Cola Company, which has so much to say in Georgia politics also.

A number of Warren's friends became wealthy men during his administration, but it should be added that he left office broke. It should also be added that although he at one time belonged to the Ku Klux Klan, his was one of the most moderate of administrations, and on one occasion, when several well-known northern Negro leaders came to town and he was afraid they might try to be served in a local restaurant and run into trouble, he invited them out to the mansion for lunch. The obligated politician is not always a bad politician.

There was nothing very unusual about what came out in the Warren campaign investigation, really, except that it *came out.*

It usually doesn't, though everyone knows southern politics has become big-money politics for big profits. Twelve years ago Cecil Farris Bryant, short of funds, dropped out of the Florida gubernatorial race with a whimper, going on television to charge, "The big man wants $2 back for every $1 he puts in—the little man doesn't understand. . . . I have always wondered if I could succeed as a politician without compromise—now I know." But four years later, campaigning in the costliest style Florida had seen to that time, Bryant apparently had adjusted, for a few months after taking office he was issuing written instructions as to which banks should benefit from the state business: "I think it would be unwise," he wrote confidentially, "not to include the First National Bank of Miami Beach and Frank Smathers [George Smathers' brother] in the picture. The Florida National Bank at Orlando, both in the person of its President and of Mr. Ed Ball, were active supporters. Unless there is some strong practical reason to the contrary, I would like very much to see that institution put in a key position in the financing." If those who paid for Bryant's campaign wanted a racial reactionary of the coldest sort, they got their money's worth.

Sometimes it's hard to tell whether money ruined the politician, or whether he got money because he was already appealingly ruined. Kissin' Jim Folsom of Alabama, whose Suds Bucket just wasn't deep enough, had to borrow from the Big Mules to pay off his first campaign debts, and the resulting obligations smothered his liberal plans (the obligations were, admittedly, assisted by booze, as I explain in a later chapter). Arkansas Power & Light used to own the governors of Arkansas, but Orval Faubus was the property of Ark-La Gas Company. The big man in Coca-Cola, Robert Woodruff, once introduced Herman Talmadge as "the best governor Georgia ever had and son of the second best governor." Just as business had loved Gene Talmadge for not passing any taxes, and for putting striking workers into a barbed wire compound, business loved Herman all the more for passing such consumer taxes as were needed to preclude spreading much of the burden to business and industry, and for tacitly encouraging Klan terrorism aimed at the union.

The bartering of Georgia politicians reached such an intensity among Atlanta's men of wealth that strangely candid peeves have been heard, as when R. E. Gormley, vice president of the Georgia Savings Bank & Trust Company, in debate with Citizens & Southern president Mills B. Lane, Jr., noted that Lane's bank controls 20 percent or more of the bank resources of the state and added pointedly, "The person or organization who controls the credit facilities of a state or nation will be able to not only control the economic life but also the political and social welfare. My contention has always been that money or credit is the most powerful dictator and the hand that controls its power may or may not use it wisely."

It has not always been used wisely in Georgia; the record of money dictators in the Deep South as a whole is very unwise. Of course it happens in every region, but the impact of big campaign money is much more disastrous in the South because, where the cost of chicanery is cheaper, you can get much more politician for your million, and where there is usually only one kind of thinking—reactionary—the money can be spent effectively only by pushing whatever happens to be trumps in that campaign. Is it hate the niggers, or hate the peaceniks, or hate the federal government? A million dollars can out-hate $500,000. Stumps were free but television isn't and—except for a rare Maddox—the days are gone when an underdog candidate could take a hillbilly band and a collection plate and go to the people, haranguing and begging them, and hope to compete with the deep velvet purses of the nouveaux Bourbons.

The result has been a Deep South in which the populace has once again had to be content with leaders who led them deeper and deeper into beguiling passions, intellectual snipe hunts in search of nonexistent interposition laws . . . exciting grass-fire rages that swept the Gulf crescent, only to be snuffed out in a new, massive defeat in the courts or in Congress: the frittering away of another generation—but all highly successful in making the people at once indifferent to and pliable to the things that were being done in the southern legislatures, and in southern governors' mansions, to establish the new Bourbonry in unshakeable power.

6

George Smathers, The South's Golden Hatchetman

The basic reason for mystery about money in a campaign is so the candidate may possess a conscience that is legally clear.

Fuller Warren, Governor of Florida, 1949-1953

Senator Joseph S. Clark of Pennsylvania in his book *Congress: The Sapless Branch* reminded the nation of what it should already have known, that astride the work of the Senate stands a small clique—"the Senate establishment"—which in secret agreement assigns members to committees with regard to seniority only as it strengthens the establishment, has absolute say over what legislation passes and what does not, controls the political careers of less powerful senators, and even dictates to some extent the choice of presidential nominees.

This establishment—also known as the "inner club"—is conservative but not partisan: "Democrat" and "Republican" are terms to which it attaches little importance. Southern conservatives are dominant, and among these, ranked just behind Senator Richard Russell of Georgia on the power ladder, has been (at least during the Kennedy and Johnson era) Florida's George Smathers, still a handsome, wavy-haired fashion plate, although in an unobservable and unspecified way, he claims, decaying inwardly.

Smathers is a unique politician in that he left his line on history, and

136

a significant line it was, not so much by what he has done in office as by the manner in which he was elected. Although as an individual exploiter of power and a dispenser of favoritism he has ranked high in Washington, it is in quite another role that he became such a notorious symbol in the South. More than any other politician, Smathers stands for the business–industrialist axe, weighted with bigotry and with fanatically misleading patriotism, that was used to hack the Deep South away from the rest of the nation after World War II in order that unionism and potential business-taxing reforms could be kept out of the region. He is the perfect case study of the southern politician who, having treated his constituents to the public orgy of a witch-burning, is thereafter left alone to the private orgies of serving special interests and himself.

He has been in a position to do this. While he was secretary to the Senate Democratic Conference (a post he resigned at the end of 1966), Smathers was officially in the Number Three position in the party hierarchy, right after the majority leader and the whip. Actually, through the establishment's clubbiness, Smathers had more influence than either Mansfield or Long. And for a time, after the passage of the 1964 Civil Rights Act, some political handicappers felt that Smathers was no longer trailing Richard Russell among Dixie's prestigious conservators in the Senate; the mighty Georgian has never regained the reverence he had before that fight got away from him.

But Smathers was not able to follow through on his momentary push to the top. His health and his spirits caved in; especially his spirits. Two days before the grand jury brought in an indictment of Bobby Baker, who had pulled some questionable deals while serving as secretary to the Senate Democratic majority, Smathers announced that he didn't know if he would be physically strong enough to run for his Senate seat again, in 1968. Later, however, when it was announced that the pre-trial hearings of the Baker case would be delayed several months, he recovered to the point that he was, he said, feeling "healthier than I have felt for two years." And when the Justice Department, by admitting that it had bugged and wiretapped Baker, thus guaranteeing that many of Baker's dealings and relationships would not be admitted into evidence, Smathers began to look well on the road to recovery. Florida's other senator, Spessard Holland, observed with little sympathy, "George says he's got a bad stomach, but I think he's just got a thin skin."

But whether he decides to run for re-election, or to return to Florida

to seek the governorship, or to retire from politics—this may be of concern to the special interests whom he has always served so well, but as
an historical matter it is of little consequence—Smathers has already left
his dent in history as the Deep South's Golden Hatchet Man.

1950 was the pivotal year, not only in his life but to a very serious
extent in modern southern politics, and as a result of his great Faustian
service to the bourbonocracy of Dixie in that year the mood of the region
went more determinedly to the right and to the rear.

Despite the Dixiecrat charade of 1948, there was still a base within
the Deep South for progressive politicking, if it could be shown that
progressive politicking was not fatal. And this was, indeed, being shown
in the career of Florida's Senator Claude Pepper, a "spread eagle orator,"
a tender-hearted, red-nosed Alabamian who came to the Senate in the
mid-1930's no great liberal, who in fact learned his ways about the Senate
as a protégé of Mississippi's Pat Harrison, but who fell in love with
Roosevelt and then carried forward what he thought was Roosevelt's
dream into reaches that the Deep South could only regard as dangerous
fantasy.

Pepper's handicap was that he had once been proved overwhelmingly
correct in taking a position that was very unpopular at the time. He had
stood almost alone—and certainly he stood alone in the dedication with
which he pushed the point—in demanding that this country get into World
War II many months before we did enter it, arguing that the longer we
delayed, the tougher and longer the fight would be. He was called a bloody
warmonger for that, and hanged in effigy and all the rest. Vindicated by the
historical turn of events, Pepper then seemed to crave betting on the long
shot, the unpopular cause, or at least the no-longer popular one.

After the war, he began asking for a more tolerant view of Russia,
for a quiet time in which the new giant could shed its gaucheness and
learn to live with the other giants. Domestically he pushed ahead with the
notion that those who have big money should be made to pay for raising
up the racial minorities and the white poor.

So long as Claude Pepper could get by with this kind of talk, there
was always the possibility that others would try it and would shake the
Deep South into new alignments. Pepper, it was obvious, must be hushed.
And there were other, more practical reasons for some to think so.

Perhaps the first signs of the Deep South's latest spasm of madness
could have been detected shortly after Friday, February 25, 1944. Like

William Jennings Bryan's fixing of the hour of creation, this may be excessively precise, but something did happen on that day which, spreading out from the reaction of a small but influential group, had a formative influence on that area's political frame of mind.

The U.S. Senate had just reconvened after a recess, and the first order of business was the reading of a message from President Roosevelt vetoing a revenue bill. With the war effort stretching the budget to the breaking point, FDR had asked for legislation to raise $10.5 billion above existing income, and had been given in return a bill that would have raised less than one billion. But worse, the bill had been used merely as the vehicle for special interests to truck through Congress several major exemptions and much tax relief. As FDR pointed out, the relief was marked "not for the needy but the greedy."

> It has been suggested by some—[Roosevelt's words came unexpressively from the clerk's mouth]—that I should give my approval to this bill on the ground that having asked the Congress for a loaf of bread to take care of the war for the sake of this and succeeding generations I should be content with a small piece of crust. I might have done so if I had not noted that the small piece of crust contained so many extraneous and inedible materials.

After twelve years of it, Roosevelt's wit was beginning to have something less than a magical effect on Congress, and immediately upon the clerk's laying down the message, many senators yelled for a vote, but Pepper, whose voice was the first heard after the message, insisted on having his say. It was at this point that the face of the South as it would appear to the world for the next twenty years began, like Dorian Gray's picture acquiring its first hidden wrinkle, to change for the worse.

Pepper, who regularly kept pace to a quixotic drum, was about to offend the wealthy once again, and this time they would launch a campaign that would destroy him once and for all as a potential spokesman for that long anticipated and most illusive of all bodies politic, "the New South." Certainly Pepper had never been the spokesman for the Old South, except in those depression years, perhaps, when his support even of the Townsend Plan was not looked upon as terribly radical and when FDR's social program was supported by most southern congressmen.

He knew that now, as on numerous other occasions, he was in the minority. He knew also that what he was doing was not likely to attract many votes, the public's grasp of revenue matters being what it is, and would most certainly anger the men on whom any politician must rely for the major portion of his campaign money. He could not, however, have guessed to what extent this would be true. The only immediate reward for him was an opportunity once more to indulge in the rolling phrase, and as he was one of the last of the Dixie politicians for whom this could be an irresistible temptation, he yielded to it; the ugly machine cranked out the golden words again, but this time to his ruination.

> I do not believe, Mr. President, there is one of us who will doubt that when most of us molder in the sleep of forgetfulness there will be a star that will shine in the history books and in the hearts of mankind, that will be as luminous and as fixed as the North Star. It will be the name of the leader of our party, Franklin Delano Roosevelt. He has held up the light of liberalism and of sacrifice. He has been the champion of many causes, of many downcast and oppressed people. I believe that when we vote today we will not be voting on the tax bill—if that were the only issue I would vote to override the veto—but we will be voting on what is to be the permanent course and character of our party.

Rhapsodic references to FDR no longer worked the same loyalties they had when he was still in his second term. Although most of the nation considered Bilbo rude to talk of making Eleanor the "First Lady of Liberia," there was a more general willingness to rebel at the dynasty.

Pepper, sometimes called "FDR's trial balloon," was punctured again. Seventy-two senators voted no. Only thirteen went with Pepper, and of these no others were from the South except Hill of Alabama. Old Carter Glass of Virginia, ailing and absent, sent word, however, that if he had been there he, too, would have voted with the President.

On the day following his speech—the only speech supporting Roosevelt's veto—top members of the Florida Association of Industries, a phalanx of the National Association of Manufacturers, met in Jacksonville, and personally chipped in $62,000 to begin the war chest to defeat Pepper. If they could not do it that year, they would never quit trying, and spending, until they had. The short-range results were easily counted, the long-range results inevitable. That year Pepper was re-elected by less than 10,000 votes although his opponent was a nobody, whereas in 1938 he had defeated five strong candidates by 68,000 votes. The next time he ran, he would be defeated, after the most elaborate crusade of political annihilation ever conducted in southern politics; and in getting Pepper, his opponents would wipe out the one eloquent voice for liberalism in the region.

The most important man at that Jacksonville meeting was Edward Ball, the baby-faced brother-in-law of Alfred I. duPont and the *de facto* boss of the southern arm, a billion-dollar arm, of the duPont enterprises which control the largest banking chain in the Southeast and are the largest landholder in Florida, owning at that time about half a million acres (both the number of their banks and the size of their landholdings have doubled since then). Ed Ball was the most important man who could be summoned to any political meeting in Florida. He probably still is, although today his influence, and interest, in politics is considerably diminished, largely because he has achieved just about everything he set out to achieve in the way of a satisfactory profiteering atmosphere in the state.

In Pepper's early political career, Ball had helped him win office, but now Pepper to him was "that Buzzard." Pepper had opposed him on too many issues. Ball would not stand for such opposition. He had supported Judge Ollie Edmonds against Pepper in 1944 and was disappointed that Edmonds had fought fair.* This time Ball intended to have a candidate who would fight dirty.

The Herald-Tribune called Florida at the time of the Civil War the "smallest tadpole in the dirty pool of secession," and this apparently was a pretty good appraisal of the status of the state at that time, since Tallahassee was the only rebel capital east of the Mississippi the federal troops didn't even bother to capture. But in recent years, especially in the post-World War II years, Florida's role as a shaper of what may or may not be the Deep South's last stand against creative federalism has been strangely underrated and usually ignored, one reason perhaps being that most of the country does not think of Florida as Deep South, forgetting that those Tallahassee legislators are operating about twenty miles from the Georgia border and about the same distance from Alabama. This is cracker country, moonshine country, stiff with the old social myths and political myopia.

But the main reason Florida is so important in the recent history of the Deep South is that it is the fief of Ed Ball. The Deep South that has since World War II given the rest of the country so much worry and that has tormented itself into a broken posture of resistance was to a great

---

* Ball was later quoted: "I told Ollie he couldn't follow the Marquis of Queensberry rules in a barroom brawl, but he wouldn't listen." (*Fortune*, November 1952)

extent shaped by the Ed Balls of the region, rich men with their own use for politics, which is of course to make money.

The foundation for Florida's political power structure was laid the day Ball's sister, Jessie, married Alfred I. duPont, a wanderer from the Delaware tribe. Little, roly-poly Ball—who loves to munch lime Life Savers and sip Jack Daniel's—played inlawmanship so expertly that today he and the Florida duPont estate are considered more or less as one. Ball is smart, aggressive, and, needless to say, very rich. It is a combination he used in establishing himself as the dominant political influence in the state, a position he enjoyed until the mid-1950's.

For most of the preceding twenty years Ball had owned, if not the legislature, at least several of the leaders of the legislature. He was not known to be a big spender for *supporting* a politician (one of Florida's ex-governors, who admits a close friendship with Ball, admits also with some bitterness that he was never able to squeeze more than $250 from Ball for his campaign), but he was reputed to spend with a frenzy to oppose any politician who crossed him. Pepper had bucked big business before. When federal investigators discovered southern fire insurance companies were taking in $52 million a year and paying out only $18 million, the Justice Department cracked down, and when it appeared certain the companies would lose in court they brought tremendous pressure on their congressman to vote to exempt insurance companies from the anti-trust laws. Pepper treated their request with contempt.

But this was the first time he had gone so formidably against the types of industry and business Ball himself was engaged in. The tax bill that Roosevelt was attempting to veto would have benefitted bondholders who had purchased their bonds in the speculative market for far less than their face value. As it happened, this was precisely the position of Ball and other duPont officials who had bought up Florida East Coast Railway stock at bargain prices; the railroad was still in bankruptcy although making excellent wartime profits. The bill would also have permitted the lumber industry to treat income from the cutting of timber as a capital gain rather than annual income—a great tax advantage. Ball is Florida's largest lumber dealer.

If ever there was a bill that seemed drawn to dream specifications for the southern duPonts, this one was it, and when Claude Pepper chose to oppose it, he did so with what now appears to be prophetic understanding of what would happen to his own career. "I do not ask," he told the

Senate, "that this country always keep a liberal party in power. I know how sentiment acts and reacts. . . . In politics the sentiments of action and reaction are artificial. Sentiments are created, and they in turn create politics."

The creation of sentiment is a specialty of Dan Crisp, Jacksonville public relations man. Working with an almost unlimited budget and from almost the moment that Pepper had quit telling the Senate about North Star FDR, Crisp managed in the six years following the veto to remake the thinking of Florida, and contributed in no small way to the revival of that peculiar type of shrill, alarmed, primordial chattering that has been the Deep South's voice in national politics for the past two decades. Crisp's was the only full-time, loaded organization in the South at that time dedicated to the one goal of arousing such nationalistic and racial fears that liberals could not possibly be elected. Crisp was Ed Ball's Machiavelli, and I say this in a complimentary way. In any age, Machiavellis are those skilled artisans who protect the politicians' conscience by doing the unconscionable things for them and bearing the guilt. The best of these artisans will often discuss their hatchetwork with open objectivity and pride. "The contrived build-up is a notable phenomenon in our time and much attention is being given to its techniques. . . . Moreover [as John Kenneth Galbraith has observed], those who set out to give the build-up . . . are rarely the kind of people who are reticent as to either their methods or their motives. They are likely to have an extrovert pride in both." Crisp does.

> Q. Was race a legitimate issue for you to bring up?
> A. The embers are always there. You can fan it into flame or leave it smolder. The same is true of religion. But the southerner votes on emotions less than the northerner. The southerner votes more on personalities. Issues would be a poor third.
> Q. What are your feelings about men like Russell and Holland and Smathers and Eastland? Do you think they are personally concerned or do you think they use civil rights the same way you use it?
> A. I think they use it the same way I use it.

"For the first few years we had no one in mind to elect," Crisp told me. "We just wanted to defeat Pepper. Those were my orders. Our effort was broader, but it all narrowed down finally to getting people in the frame of mind to vote against Claude. He was that much of a national symbol of liberalism. Out-of-state people also wanted to dump him and were willing to contribute big money. Ball gave some of the money, but his genius is in collecting. He collected money from lots and lots of big businessmen, big industrialists, oil men like H. L. Hunt, in all parts of the country. Republican politicians would go North to tap their usual sources and be told sorry, all the money was coming down for our work. We had it all right. We spent a couple of million right out of this office. The drawers in this desk were stuffed full of it. Radio men still come around to reminisce about those days. I'd pull open a drawer and shoosh! the money would come flying out. The federal people descended on me, but of course we were handling only cash so they had to take our word. Anyway, money isn't the only way to give. A company can give $1,000 worth of paper—these rightists operate on paper.

"But don't give too much credit to our bankroll. Power in politics is not whether you can accomplish something—I mean like getting contracts or gaining favors and so forth, because this can be done not with power but with money. You might say, well, money is power, but real power in politics comes to my way of thinking from whether or not you can elect a man or defeat a man. To do this, you've got to have organization. Conservatives may be in a better position in regard to money or accomplishments money can buy, maybe they are, but so far as electing or defeating candidates they aren't."

The U.S. Chamber of Commerce sent money, and so did the National Association of Manufacturers; the American Medical Association assessed members up to $25; and General Wood of Sears stood shoulder to shoulder with Montgomery Ward as a contributor, forgetting business rivalries in the bigger patriotism.

By the time Pepper ran for election in 1950, Crisp had gathered together the strands of all sorts of splinter groups—the Jeffersonian Association, States' Rights Association, Federation for Constitutional Government, Byrd for President, Thurmond for President, the Florida Tax Revision League—and had woven them into a noose for Pepper. Too, he had added his own deft creations: The Florida Democratic Club, the Anti-Pepper Campaign Committee of Volutia County, and the Democratic Club of Duval County.

"It is not necessary ever to have a real working group," Crisp explained. "Give me the names of three people and an issue and I can make it look like a very active, strong working organization. But this [the

Florida Democratic Club] happened to be a working group. It was headed
by Charles Sheppard [a state Representative], who was sincere and had
a lot of contacts, but he was primarily a figurehead. What happened was I
would call him on the phone and say this is a release you are about to
make. We had a lot of cooperation from the newspapers. We would
ghost write editorials and many papers would use them. By 1948 we were
bustin' the ass off Pepper in news releases from the Florida Democratic
Club. Aside from sending them out to every newspaper and radio station
in the state, we sent them to every P.O. boxholder and every rural delivery
box in the state—and those were the days when the P.O. and rural boxes
could swing an election.

"As for the Anti-Pepper Campaign Committee of Volutia County, we
were real proud of it because with a name like that Pepper wasn't likely
to get alarmed. One county wouldn't matter much, and besides he was
always strong in Volutia. Actually it was a statewide organization. The
same was true of the Democratic Club of Duval County."

Crisp was working as far as possible through official organizations by
getting friendly members to plant resolutions, such as the one passed by
the State Association of County Commissioners in 1948 which decried
Truman's civil rights program as "obnoxious, repugnant, odious, detest-
able, loathsome, repulsive, revolting and humiliating to all true Democrats"
—and since Pepper had said that Truman gave mere lip service to civil
rights, where did the resolution put Pepper?

Meanwhile Pepper was not oblivious to what was going on or to the
identity of his enemies, although Crisp insists, "I tried to tell him (later),
but I don't think he ever did understand the magnitude of what his side
had been up against or how well organized we were. I still don't think he
does." Pepper was not that naïve. When, in 1946, leaflets were distributed
at a rally which accused him of loving Russia more than he loved the
United States, of approving of labor racketeering and gangsterism, of
fomenting social equality between the races, and of wanting to control "the
air you breathe," Pepper knew things were rolling out of control and in
the wrong direction. He says today he knew he was up against the "most
formidable powers ever arrayed against a state politician," and he told a
friend of that day, "There aren't many Russians in the state, and labor
is in the minority. I have ears to hear and eyes with which to read, and I
know I'm going to have to stand up against terrific waves of public animosity if this continues."

Even as he accurately foretold the future, four years away, he took one more step to secure his defeat. The Florida East Coast Railway was in bankruptcy and Ball's St. Joe Paper Company, which had bought a slight majority of the outstanding mortgage bonds, was trying to get possession of the road. The Atlantic Coast Line Railroad was also trying to get control, and the issue was before the Interstate Commerce Commission for final decision. Pepper presented a memorandum to the Commission recommending that the line be turned over to ACL because Ball was a ruthless buccaneer. The railroad, wrote Pepper, would be considered by Ball as just one more cog "in one great machine which he operates and manipulates. . . . Every string which controls this vast empire runs right to the fingers of Mr. Edward Ball." And in a prediction which 1,200 former employees—locked out by the Florida East Coast line in the longest strike in railroad history—would now agree with only too heartily, Pepper said, "I feel that if the operation of the railroad is given to the duPont interests, my friends among the workers will regret it to the end of their lives. It is impossible for me to visualize Mr. Ball in the role of a benefactor of labor."

It was a double injury that George Smathers was the man Ball eventually picked to run against Pepper, for Pepper had been Smathers' first and best political friend, his sponsor and advisor. Smathers believed that destiny took precedence over friendship. But it wasn't destiny that called, it was Ed Ball, and it was an impersonal call at that. Smathers was not even Ball's first choice. Millard Caldwell, a former governor and today one of Florida's right-wing supreme court justices, was first choice, but he refused. Smathers was, in fact, fifth on the list. "We just used him as a vehicle to do what we had been doing for years," Crisp told me. "I don't know whether George would appreciate my saying it or not, but he was just a means to an end."

Verification of this comes from the *Orlando Sentinel*, the newspaper formerly owned by Martin Anderson, who has always been close to the Ed Ball clique. An editorial shortly after Smathers' victory reviewed the purpose of the campaign: "We were in that battle and we knew many of the key men on Smathers' team. They were for Smathers because they thought Smathers was a vehicle to take Pepper off their backs. . . . They gave their money, not willingly, but with considerable persuasion, to

Smathers for one purpose and one purpose only: To pry Claude Pepper out of his U.S. Senate seat. Nobody got any patronage from Smathers' victory. Nobody got any road contracts. Nobody built any bridges or ships and made a million dollars. Even if these key Smathers men had been looking for such loot, Smathers, a freshman senator, could not have delivered it. No, the key men in the Smathers campaign were for him because they hated Claude Pepper's political theories first, last and always."

A very willing tool, an enthusiastic recruit to the *bund* of McCarthyism, was Smathers—he and his "Order of Smathers Sergeants," an anti-communist force of what he called "red-blooded young Americans" recruited to "keep order on Election Day." In saying this, however, I give the late senator from Wisconsin undeserved prominence. Actually, Smathers showed *him* a thing or two about using the technique now known as McCarthyism.

Smathers was not always as he is now, at least not outwardly. He was, before Ed Ball picked him out of the crowd, known as a liberal, a progressive, a "Pepper man." He changed when it profited him to change and with great gusto, burying his old friend under an avalanche of slander and creating an atmosphere of ideological tension from which Florida, and some other parts of the Southeast, have since never really escaped.

Senator Pepper first heard of George Smathers in 1938. Endorsed by Roosevelt and certain to win re-election, Pepper was approached by Smathers, who asked that he be named head of the University of Florida campaign committee. Smathers was a handsome dog, 6'3", captain of the basketball team, champion debater, nicknamed "Smooch" for his conduct with the coeds. The campus campaign job was an insignificant one and Pepper was glad to give the likeable Georgie a leg up.

Smathers was no sooner out of college than he was back in Pepper's office asking that he be helped to an assistant U.S. District Attorney's post. Pepper got that for him, too.

Smathers did well in the attorney's job, and he did well in the Marine Corps during most of the war. Then, up he popped in Pepper's office again, asking for another job. It was June 1945, right after capitulation in Europe. Pepper recalls the incident: "He wanted to get out of the Marine Corps, which he called a Sahara. He wanted to run against Pat Cannon from the Fourth District. Somehow poor old Pat, who should have been a liberal from his background, got to be terribly antagonistic toward FDR and me. Every day he said something against us. So I told Smathers I would try to help.

"I went to [Attorney General] Tom Clark and told him this young Marine is a liberal and capable and I wanted to get him some job to get out of the service. So Clark gave him an assistant attorney general's job handling condemnation suits in land cases right in Miami, where he could start laying his political groundwork."

When Smathers filed against Cannon, his first campaign picture was taken arm in arm with Pepper. He was known as a Pepper candidate, a labor candidate. Pepper helped him write his speeches. At Pepper's request, the CIO supported Smathers, but, with understanding, behind the scene. He won easily.

The political Smathers of the mid-1940's talked about "our good friend Henry Wallace," and about being "grateful for the part Russia played in the war. . . . We have got to work with Russia. . . ." In the mid-'40's he saw his role in Congress being to help "stop the militarists. Americans are extremists. Last time it was disarmament, this time it will be 'the biggest and the best.' " The Smathers of that day introduced Franklin D. Roosevelt, Jr., to the Young Democrats national convention. Smathers called it an "honor" to be with that group and to be identified with FDR, Jr.'s speech, which was "realistic, affirmative and bold. It was in keeping with the liberal traditions of the Democratic Party as had previously been so well enunciated by the speaker's father, the late and great Franklin D. Roosevelt." Smathers thought so much of young Roosevelt's speech he had it put into the *Congressional Record,* and today one wonders how Smathers could ever have supported its statements—assertions that "human rights come before property rights"; pro-labor assertions that damn the "economic overlords of Wall Street"; praise for the Democratic Party as "the political party which for the last fifteen years has been identified with a policy of cooperation with the Soviet Union."

Only three years later, sniffing the winds of extreme reaction that were beginning to whip across the country, Smathers challenged Claude Pepper for his Senate seat with the accusation:

"The leader of the radicals and extremists is now on trial in Florida. Arrayed against him will be loyal Americans. . . . Standing against us will be certain northern labor bosses, all the socialists, all the radicals and all the fellow travelers. . . . Florida will not allow herself to become entangled in the spiraling spider web of the Red network. The people of our state will no longer tolerate advocates of treason. The outcome can truly determine whether our homes will be destroyed, whether our children will be torn from their mothers, trained as conspirators and turned against their parents, their home and their church. I stand for election on the principle of the free state against the jail state."

What had Pepper done to deserve this? He had proposed the Democratic nomination of Henry Wallace for President in 1948 (but so had he proposed Eisenhower) and had in turn been proposed for that office that year by Americans for Democratic Action. He had refused to help other Southern Senators in their filibusters. From 1945 on, he signed every petition for cloture. He supported the Fair Employment Practice Code, which Smathers called "that Yankee monstrosity." He backed World Federalists. He criticized Churchill's "iron curtain" speech as making accommodation with Russia more difficult. He was listed by *Pravda* as a good friend of the U.S.S.R. He attempted to cut our military aid program. He frequently attacked the National Association of Manufacturers. He supported all bills that called for an increase of minimum wages. He supported the Townsend Plan. As early as 1945, he recommended a national health insurance—both doctor and hospital for all people—tied to social security.

But Pepper had always been that kind of man, that kind of politician. Smathers claims he split with his mentor when the senator returned from Russia saying peaceful things about the communists. Smathers recalls that he was "shocked." He says he was also "shocked" when he walked by Madison Square Garden in New York and saw that Pepper was speaking on a program with Henry Wallace and Paul Robeson. If that was true, the shock reaction was curiously delayed. Pepper made his trip to Russia in 1945, even before Smathers came to him for help in getting out of the service. As for the Madison Square Garden incident, in 1946, it did not prevent Smathers from seeking Pepper's help in his first campaign.

The truth is that Smathers, always ambitious (he has admitted a yearning for a presidential nomination, and he has been talked of seriously as a vice presidential candidate), fell into Ball's pot of senatorial campaign money and refused to struggle. It was part of the national big push by big money, with contributions thrown around so flagrantly that the Senate set up an investigating committee, headed by Senator Guy Gillette, to see if there had been any skulduggery. Gillette did indeed study elections in Pennsylvania and North and South Carolina. But for some reason he never got around to Florida and Illinois (Dirksen won for the first time) elections.

The best-remembered speech of the campaign was Smathers' insinuatingly smooth: "Are you aware that Claude Pepper is known all over Washington as a shameless extrovert? Not only that, but this man is reliably reported to practice nepotism with his sister-in-law, and he has a sister, who was once a thespian in wicked New York. Worst of all, it is an established fact that Mr. Pepper, before his marriage, practiced celibacy."

It was a brilliant tour de force—"making Claude Pepper a pervert by assonance," as William Buckley summed it up in *McCarthy and his Enemies*—but more funny than effective. Not even north Floridians are that dumb.

Much more telling were the newspaper ads in which Smathers came right out and called "wily . . . oily tongued" Pepper all but a traitor. Still more damaging was the little book *The Red Record of Senator Claude Pepper*, which blanketed Florida a week before the balloting; nine tons of the book were shipped into Miami alone. The picture of Pepper standing by Paul Robeson circulated throughout north Florida. And the clipping, dated 1946, in which Pepper asked Americans to pray for Stalin. Smathers read it at every crossroads, then asked, "Did you pray for Stalin this morning?" And the often repeated remark that he was glad he wore the orange and blue of the University of Florida: "Thank God," Smathers cried from his sound truck, "thank God, I don't have to wear the crimson of Pepper's and Felix Frankfurter's Harvard Law School.* Alger Hiss is no classmate of mine."

The CIO drive to register Negro voters in Florida was publicly interpreted by Smathers as "the most dangerous invasion of carpetbaggers" since the Civil War, aimed at returning labor's "Charlie McCarthy" to the Senate. It was the sly work of "Red" Quill of the CIO Transport Workers.

And, for the moderates and liberals of Florida, there was the long piece in *The Saturday Evening Post* just two weeks before the election. Who was the author? None other than Ralph McGill, publisher of the

---

* If a person were inclined to take this sort of attack seriously, he would have to ask why it was that Smathers was always so close to Philip Graham, his fraternity brother at the University of Florida, who finished at the top of his Harvard law class and then became Frankfurter's clerk.

Atlanta *Constitution,* who still liked to play footsie with the Talmadge crowd and hadn't really made up his mind what he was, but was suspected in some quarters of being a fish-eating liberal. There was no question but that he thought Pepper was just what Smathers had been saying all along —a pinko. With obvious relish McGill quoted Smathers' denunciation of "those in government who are apologists for Stalin, associates of fellow travelers and sponsors of Communist-front organizations." Gratuitously McGill threw in his own description of Pepper's backers—"ultra-leftwing friends." Coming from McGill, this was the hardest blow of the campaign. Today, to his credit, McGill says he was tricked into writing the piece by Smathers' father and that he has had only great sorrow from the writing of it.

Against the big smear, Pepper tried everything, including humor. He would try to amuse his audience by tiptoeing across the stage, collar turned up, glancing furtively over his shoulder; then whisper into the microphone: "Joe? This is Claude. Got some secrets for ya." But Smathers had spooked Florida past the laughing point.

Frightened liberals switched to Smathers. Conservative Democrats, in which the state abounds, went to him *en masse.* Many Republicans registered Democratic to support the golden boy, the president of the Florida Young Republicans Club sent a letter to all members urging them to forget party ambitions just this once to support Smathers. He won easily, pulling most of his strength from the rural counties and riding over Pepper by 60,000 votes. *Life* magazine hailed the end of Pepper's "distorted liberalism" as "a blow to the Fair Deal nationally and a warning of the strength of the Communist issue which Republicans are sure to raise this fall."

Led by McCarthy, who had produced his little list of State Department suspects only three months earlier, and encouraged by Smathers' giant-killing election in Florida, the Republicans did indeed raise the issue— again and again and again.

So did some Democrats. Crisp took his campaign treasury and literature into North Carolina to help Willis Smith, former president of the American Bar Association, successfully unseat Senator Frank Graham on the issues of communism and the FEPC. Graham, a former president of the University of North Carolina, had led Smith by 53,383 votes in the primary. But then the "Florida Program" went into high gear. "If you want your wife or daughter eating at the same table with Negroes," warned a newspaper ad, "vote for Graham." Smith won by 20,000 votes; the eastern section of the state, where the Negro population centers, switched to him almost solidly.

"After the 1950 victories," says Crisp, "the rightist groups became inspired. We went Southwide and nationwide in the complete belief that we were going to set up a third party—a states' rights party."

Was the victory of 1950 worth it? Or did the campaign mar the victor as well as the defeated? Perhaps both. In a letter to a friend in May 1949, Pepper had with uncommon accuracy described what was about to happen to Smathers:

". . . interests who hate me and what I stand for have made it so alluring to him financially to oppose me that he couldn't resist. . . . It will be a spirited campaign, with his youth and handsome charm, energy and money, not to speak of all those selfish and shortsighted forces who will array themselves with him. . . . He may win, although I don't think so, but I have regretted to see what has happened to him, already, spiritually. He cannot prevent manifesting toward me extreme dislike, and he has been running away from the liberal side quite rapidly for some time. *He had bright promise and showed earlier, real conviction. By the time he has wallowed through a campaign with such as will be around him in major places, I am afraid he will be a very much transformed person. . . .*"

Toward liberals, the once-liberal Smathers now almost invariably shows a defensive sarcasm. He relies on the brittle "so-called" knife. The students who went to Cuba, disobeying the State Department, are "so-called American students." Liberals are "so-called, self-styled liberals." Typical was the sharp exchange between Smathers and Paul Douglas, in which the latter complained that the liberals of the Senate had, with their vote, bailed out the leadership again, although "We have indeed been exposed to continuous revilement and denunciation." With a sneer, Smathers replied: "I have no knowledge, and I doubt anyone else has, that the Democratic leadership wants to do anything but try to cooperate with the so-called, self-styled liberal group. It is my belief that the leadership wishes to cooperate and wishes to help these self-named liberals. . . ."

Incident upon incident has developed in Smathers' mind a hard callus toward liberals. He has never forgotten them for what they did to him at Tampa in 1952, trivial as it was. He was on the platform with Stevenson, although he had refused to support Stevenson's program. Claude Pepper was also on the platform. The crowd went wild over

Stevenson. When Pepper was introduced, he was also applauded. Smathers was booed.

The wrenching of his point of view from what at one time appeared to be its natural course seems also to have left him with an inability to think of the laboring class in kind or humane terms.

In 1961, a bill before the Senate would have given workers in commercial laundries (not the "Mom and Dad" type) a rising scale of wage protection, starting with a required minimum of $1 an hour and increasing in four years to $1.25 an hour. Smathers was against it. The laundries could not afford to pay $1 an hour, he said.

Senator Humphrey appealed to him: "This is not very good, clean work. It is hot, sticky and frequently stinky. The people who dig a ditch in front of the laundry are paid more than that. Yet we ask people who work inside the laundry—and many of them are women, frequently older women, who can't get other work because they are too old—we would ask them to work for less."

Smathers' response, significant of the deep transformation that had started with the campaign of 1950, oozed with contempt—Humphrey's argument, he said, "makes me bleed with him."

He steered President Johnson into a deal whereby, if the President kept the foreign farm labor minimum wage of 70¢, Smathers would vote the Administration tax cut. Next he pruned an amendment that would have given tax credit to parents sending their children to college. Then, having voted, he announced that he would have been happy all along to support the bill because much of the proposed cut benefited business. Johnson would not have had to sell out the migrants after all.

For years he had a major role in keeping the seafood industry employees, migrant farm workers, and workers in the hotel industry—all of whom are among the lowest-paid employees in Florida—from being placed under the National Labor Relations Board. He once proposed a five-member "court" to have absolute say in the settling of strikes. The suggestion terrified even Alf Landon, who said, "The totalitarian state is creeping up on us. . . . Smathers has proposed horrible and un-American legislation."

From 1950 to the present, Smathers has also shown a bitterness toward Negroes that had never been evident in his earlier career (it would have been unlikely, for he grew up in tolerant Miami). In his first Senate election year, he declared that he would gladly defend, free of charge, any policeman indicted for violation of civil rights. Fourteen years of police dogs and cattle prods later, he took the same harsh approach. After Martin Luther King's arrest in St. Augustine, Smathers offered to pay his fine if he would "get out and stay out of Florida."

When ten hard-pressed liberals filibustered the television satellite bill in 1962, Smathers raged against them: "In a democracy an opportunity is supposed to be provided for voting, and if a majority believes a proposal is right, I think they ought to have the opportunity to say so. . . ."* But after two months of filibustering the civil rights bill, he felt it was indecent even to talk of shutting off debate. His part in the filibuster was a prepared eighty-page speech and that amount again of extemporaneous questions, heavily laced with insults for Negroes and liberals, and sometimes for other minorities. At one point he praised Jews because they observe what he called voluntary segregation of their race—an observation that must have lacked appeal in Miami Beach. Another time, he said that ninety-two mixed marriages in the District of Columbia prove that integrated schooling produces interracial marriages. He insisted that outlawing segregation in schools had "set the South back fifty years."

Finally, driven to desperate spite, he asked J. Edgar Hoover to investigate the integrationist movement for communist domination or communist infiltration—just as, fighting Hawaii's statehood (too much racial mixture out there), he had asked Senator Joe McCarthy to investigate reports of strong communism on the islands.

If he has been a success since arriving in the U.S. Senate, it is a success covered with smudges, and therefore it is a success that has not permitted him to seek the limelight that he has always so feverishly desired. His face is familiar, but the name would mean little to most Americans. They have seen Smathers countless times in the television newsreels, standing behind Mansfield and Long and the President on the White House steps as they greeted newsmen after one of their Tuesday strategy breakfasts. But the junior senator from Florida seldom pushes to the front.

It isn't that he is modest. He simply would prefer to lie low until it is generally forgotten that he is the only senator on record as Baker's business partner. And that is just one of a long string of events that have made

---

* Many liberals were surprised when the liberal *Washington Post* joined Smathers in denouncing the small band of Senators who held out against the Telstar franchise. But at the time of his suicide, classmate and publisher of the *Post* Philip Graham was chairman of Telstar Corporation.

Smathers leery of publicity. Earlier, there were various land promotions that glowed in the dark of suspicion . . . and his close friendship with the late dictator Trujillo . . . and the Panama housing deal that died when exposed to sunlight . . . and the FCC scandals of 1958 . . . and the "dozen calls" from Smathers' office that helped swing a $1.9 million FHA loan for an old college chum to build an apartment house which promptly failed.

Although he may lack fame with the population at large, George (people who are inclined to distrust him sometimes call him "Gorgeous George") Smathers is a wheeler–dealer of the pre-Billie Sol Estes stripe, and his friendship is valued by industrialists and land promoters.

Businessmen interested in federal appropriations or in contracts with Latin American *jefes* know that Smathers can help; he is the second ranking Democrat on the Senate Finance Committee, and he served on the Foreign Relations Committee for enough years to have belted a few with the current strongmen of South America. He swapped off his foreign relations seat, however, for a spot on the Senate Judiciary Committee, to help the southern powerhouse that runs that influential committee—Eastland of Mississippi, McClellan of Arkansas, and Ervin of North Carolina. Together they have kept down any baseless hopes about a reform in the federal judiciary that runs the southern courts. Smathers has other uses, being a member of the Joint Committee on International Revenue Taxation and the Select Committee on Small Business. (To round it out with something for the home folks, he is also chairman of the Special Committee on Aging, a singularly unproductive group.)

For eighteen years—ever since he turned on and defeated Claude Pepper—Smathers has moved upward along an arc of growing influence. Without apology, he has scrambled into his position with much the same immoderate drive that marked the career of Budd Schulberg's Sammy Glick—sacrificing some friends, breaking some important promises, loyal when loyalty paid off.

What makes Smathers run? William S. White, likening him to Lyndon Johnson, calls him "tough, pragmatic." Another Washington newsman, whose narrower field has given him time to pay more particular attention to the Florida senator, describes Smathers as "vain, cunning, insecure and touchy."

He is reputed to have been among the late President Kennedy's closest buddies. The editors of *Look* counted him as one of only eight in the intimate "gang." Smathers and Kennedy went to the House in the same year, occupied adjacent offices in the Senate, frequently double-dated and partied together. Smathers was an usher at Kennedy's wedding and later a weekly breakfast companion at the White House.

It was a useful friendship—for Smathers. When he staged a fund-raising dinner for his campaign in 1962, Kennedy came down to Miami and spoke at it—and the kitty hit $10,000.* When Kennedy turned up in Palm Beach for a week-end, Smathers usually managed to get away from Washington for the trip, too—to let some of the Kennedy glamour rub off on his image in south Florida. But when Kennedy needed Smathers' help in the Senate, Gorgeous George more often than not was either absent or voting on the other side.

The Administration lost a badly needed $90 million from its space program on a 40-to-39 vote, because Kennedy's buddy was in the capitol steam bath. (That was the first excuse Smathers put out. Later he changed it to "out walking for my health.")

During Kennedy's first year in office, when momentum was critically needed for the Administration's new program, Smathers supported Kennedy only 47 percent of the time on 124 roll-call votes. He voted with the conservative coalition 76 percent of the time (more often than GOP leader Dirksen) in 1961 and 1962, and he helped scuttle Medicare and other key Kennedy bills. He voted in only 66 percent of the 229 roll calls during Kennedy's last year, thus becoming the second "most absent" man

* On that occasion, as on many other occasions, President Kennedy's dry humor indicated he was well aware that the profit in their friendship flowed always away:

"I actually came down here tonight to pay a debt of obligation to an old friend and faithful adviser. He and I came to the Eightieth Congress together and have been associated for many years, and I regard him as one of my most valuable counselors in moments of great personal and public difficulty.

"In 1952, when I was thinking about running for the United States Senate, I went to the then Senator Smathers and said, 'George, what do you think?'

"He said, 'Don't do it. Can't win. Bad year.'

"In 1956, I was at the Democratic convention, and I said—I didn't know whether I would run for Vice President or not, so I said, 'George, what do you think?'

" 'This is it. They need a young man. It's your chance.' So I ran—and lost.

"And in 1960, I was wondering whether I ought to run in the West Virginia primary. 'Don't do it. That state you can't possibly carry.'

"And actually, the only time I really got nervous about the whole matter at the Democratic Convention of 1960 was just before the balloting and George came up and he said, 'I think it looks pretty good for you.'

"It will encourage you to know that every Tuesday morning . . . we have breakfast together and he advises with me—Cuba, anything else, Laos, Berlin, anything—George comes right out there and gives his views and I listen very carefully."

in the Senate. Other Kennedy intimates were bitter. One called Smathers "the least enthusiastic friend a man could have." Smathers replied coolly, "The President understands."

This kind of political dubiety is nothing unusual for Smathers, but it seemed to be especially intense during the years his "friend" was in the White House. Omen of things to come was his statement in 1960 that Kennedy was personally attractive, but that the things he stood for were "obnoxious."

In April 1963, Smathers accepted a place on the Young Americans for Freedom advisory board, an organization which shortly thereafter brought into Florida several speakers who accused Kennedy of semi-treason. "Its initial purposes," Smathers said of YAF, "sound good to me." In May 1963, the senator joined with a number of outspoken Birchites to sponsor a testimonial dinner in New York City for Charles Edison, a bitter enemy of Kennedy, an editorial advisor to *American Opinion* (the Birch Society magazine), a national advisor for YAF, an endorser of the Manion Forum, and treasurer of Americans for Constitutional Action.

Smathers is now reputed to be a Johnson man. Certainly he owes much of his present standing to Johnson. In the mid-1950's, when Alben Barkley died, Smathers got Johnson to put him in charge of the Senate Democratic Elections Committee, the agency that disburses campaign money. For two years he ingratiated himself into the conservative establishment by almost ignoring liberal senators while handing out campaign funds generously to conservatives who did not need it, such as the late oil man Robert Kerr of Oklahoma.

Smathers made connections that way. And when Johnson appointed him "acting" Majority Leader in his absence, he made more. *The New York Times* found that he derived much of his power from the fact that he was "among those included in the inner sanctum . . . that a Senate Democrat can enter only when he hears that accolade, 'Lyndon thinks a lot of him.'"

Occasionally he has—with bad grace or bad planning, but ineffectually in either case—shown some loyalty to Johnson. At the 1960 convention Smathers held back the Florida vote as a favorite son on the first ballot, planning to give it to Johnson on the second ballot, which never came off. At the 1964 convention—first at Johnson's request, then at Johnson's angry goading—he made a nervous seconding speech for Hubert Humphrey. Then, to cancel whatever help he might thus have given Humphrey in the South, he spent an hour with newsmen explaining that he had been blackjacked into the speech.

Johnson has learned to be wary of the golden boy from Florida who takes campaign contributions from wealthy Goldwater delegate William Pawley with one hand and pulls Democratic strings with the other. On two occasions—if we can take the word of Bobby Baker—Johnson warned Smathers: "You double-crossed Claude Pepper, but you aren't going to double-cross me." Unless it improved his position, the senator wouldn't think of it.

After two terms in the House and nearly four terms in the Senate, Smathers has yet to put his name on a single important piece of legislation that was not designed to help a special interest. More specifically, several of the bills in which he has interested himself seem to have a bearing on the clients who patronize the Miami law firm that bears his name.

When reporters ask about such matters, Smathers assures them that he has not practiced law since he came to Congress and that his law firm "scrupulously avoids" taking any cases that may involve the federal government.

Smathers was in the vanguard of the legislative drive to get the oil-rich tidelands away from the federal government and into the hands of the states, whence they could pass less noticeably to the major oil companies. His voice was one of the loudest and most insistent in advocating unlimited importation of residual oil. The present import program has harmed the domestic oil industry generally, but it has greatly benefited Standard Oil Company and Gulf Oil Corporation. Both companies are clients of Smathers' law firm. They were not his clients until he went to Congress.

Smathers steered through the Senate a bill which he said was for the purpose of helping "the small investor" who had lost his investment to Castro. Lee Winfrey, then the *Miami Herald's* Washington correspondent, looked over the bill and commented: "More to the point, as far as the eventual aim of the legislation is concerned, are such corporate giants as Texaco, Standard Oil of New Jersey, and International Telephone and Telegraph Corporation, who lost property in Cuba valued at more than $50 million each."

He has been equally resourceful in protecting the interests of the insurance companies. A tax bill pushed by Smathers was judged by Senator

Albert Gore to be a great improvement over previous tax controls but, said he, "It will still leave the life insurance industry in one of the more favored tax positions within the Internal Revenue Law." Smathers had headed off sterner restrictions by initiating mild ones.

Among the clients of Smathers' law firm are these insurance companies: Lloyds of London, The Home Insurance Company, Union Marine and General Insurance Company, General Accident Fire and Life Assurance Company, Atlantic Mutual Insurance Company, and Insurance Company of North America.

Smathers has also championed legislation to require foreign air lines entering the United States to charge the same rates that American-owned airlines, operating overseas, are required to charge. Pan American World Airways, which operates only to other countries, is a client of his firm. (It is worth noting that when Bobby Baker, in June of 1963, arranged a meeting between Edward Levinson of Las Vegas and officials of Pan American World Airways to discuss bidding on gambling concessions in Pan American-operated hotels in Curaçao and the Dominican Republic, he was serving the interest of a Smathers client and of the Caribbean country with which Smathers had had the most intimate dealings; Smathers' firm represents a Dominican steamship line. More might be known about this happy coincidence if the Senate committee investigating Baker's affairs had not stopped short of questioning senators.)

Railroads are the special interest for which Smathers has worked most conscientiously. He spent 1966 vigorously opposing the Post Office Department's effort to liberalize the size and weight of parcel post packages. This would cut into the business of Railway Express Agency; the Seaboard Air Line Railroad, a Smathers client, owns 35,292 shares of REA stock. In 1958, by betraying an agreement congressional leaders had with the Administration, he got rid of the 3 percent cargo tax; it was the only tax cut voted that session and was characterized by *The Washington Post* as a striking job of "outmaneuvering." That same year, as chairman of the Surface Transportation Subcommittee of the Senate Commerce Committee, he held hearings that laid the groundwork for the Transportation Act. This act makes it much easier to drop unprofitable passenger service, whatever the public interest.

The Seaboard Air Line Railroad Company was no doubt gratified, but primarily this legislation was born of obligations to the Atlantic Coast Line Railroad, a Florida line which has been good to Smathers (as will be shown later), and more particularly the Florida East Coast Railway, the owners of which were largely responsible for putting Smathers in the Senate.

The Florida East Coast owners had additional reason to view Smathers with such affection, since he was the most eloquent spokesman for a 1962 amendment to the Internal Revenue Code that resulted in a savings of many millions of dollars for members of the duPont family.

After the longest antitrust court fight in history (thirteen years), it looked as if the duPont Corporation would have to turn loose the $3.5-billion stock it owned in General Motors. Much of this divested stock would wind up in the hands of individual members of the duPont family who, under the tax law in force at that time, would have to pay devastating income tax on it, just as though it were a dividend. The duPonts' golden cry of pain was heard in Congress.

Smathers, always a gentleman to the well-heeled gentry, especially duPont gentry, jumped in with men like Harry Byrd to help win passage of a bill that would give the duPonts a chance to pay the much softer capital-gains tax. In fact, this extraordinary piece of legislation—written especially for the duPonts—was so worded that, under certain conditions, they would have to pay no tax at all.

The Senate was obviously impressed with Smathers' argument about doing "grave injustice to millions of innocent stockholders" (there were about sixty-five of the Wilmington branch of the duPont family involved in this) and reminding the Senate that the duPonts' only sin was that they had "invested their savings in the American way, in the American tradition, to provide jobs." Smathers marshaled the entire debate in such a way as to make his colleagues think he was anxious for the well-being only of the Delaware duPonts. Not one—not even Senator Douglas, who was prone to say unkind things about Smathers—mentioned that there was another duPont, by marriage, in Florida: Mrs. Jessie duPont, who, with her brother Ed Ball, owned 764,000 shares of stock in the parent company, E. I. duPont de Nemours & Company, and 445,000 shares of General Motors, worth together roughly $250 million.

In early 1967, on the Q. and A. page of the Sunday supplement *Parade Magazine,* somebody asked: "What is meant by the statement 'Senator George Smathers is an operator'?"

To which *Parade* answered: "Smathers has many fingers in many pies, has been involved with Bobby Baker, the Teamsters, Eugene McGrath of Panama, many other affairs which have recently come to light."

That was incorrect only in the observation that they had "recently" come to light. They have been coming to light for years, but people are forgetful. Baker was just the latest.

Smathers thought a lot of Bobby Baker, and Bobby—who once boasted, "I have ten senators in the palm of my hand"—thought a lot of the senator, even going so far as to admit trying to rival Smathers' noted talents as a coxcomb. When Johnson was Majority Leader, Smathers (secretary to the Democratic conference) and Baker (secretary to the Democratic majority) had been the Texan's right and left hands. They were both Johnson protégés. Around town, Georgie and Bobby were cocktail playmates.

Scott Peek, Smathers' administrative assistant until 1964, was also Baker's pal, and joined him in business ventures involving Spiegel Stores, Seaboard Air Line Railroad, WERTCO (a real estate enterprise in Jacksonville backed by the Teamsters), and Mortgage Guaranty Insurance Company.

When the committee investigating the Baker scandal came upon the Peek connections, they studied them in such haste that Smathers did not come into the discussion. And his name might never have emerged in this context if, at the committee inquiry, Senator Carl T. Curtis had not confronted Milton L. Hauft, Baker's tax accountant, with the question: "Did Mr. Baker have any income from any joint venture with senatorial employes?"

Hauft answered: "With Mr. Smathers and Mr. Peek. The only ones I know of."

It sounded for a moment as though Senator Curtis had hit the jackpot question, but then committee chairman Everett Jordan shut off the flow.

Smathers will never forgive his colleague for that question. Days later, he was talking to a newsman in the corridor of the capitol when Curtis passed by. Pointing with the finger of a betrayed Caesar, Smathers said, "There is the man who got me in all this trouble." He feels even more bitter about it today.

But Smathers' worst enemy was himself. When newsmen came at him with questions, he panicked and sprayed them with suspicious, conflicting and often sour-funny answers. First he would not say anything at all. Then he came out with a formal statement that early in 1957, "some long-time friends" approached him with a land deal near the fast-developing Cape Canaveral (now Kennedy) space center, and "knowing of the difficult financial circumstances which my then administrative assistant, Scott I. Peek, was in, trying to raise a large young family on a limited salary, I asked him if he would like to buy a one-eighth interest in my share of the investment. Also, being apprised of the similar circumstances of Robert G. Baker who, too, had a young and growing family, I offered him a one-eighth interest in my share of the investment. Both of them took advantage of this offer and each of them gave me his check in the amount of $1,500."

(In the same year when Smathers was trying to help Baker in his "difficult financial circumstances," Baker filed a credit application in which he claimed a net worth of more than $800,000. Peek was earning from Smathers the maximum allowed by law for his position, $13,500, and was already involved in several profitable deals on the side.)

Dusting his hands of the whole affair, Smathers started to walk away. But escape wasn't quite that simple. J. Hilbert Sapp enters the case at this point. Sapp is a contractor and builder of Orlando, Florida, a city in which Smathers has conducted several profitable ventures.

Sapp, who contributed to Smathers' 1950 campaign, does very well as a defense contractor; he received more than $3 million for work at Cape Kennedy. Smathers said he did not know Sapp, had "never met him"; certainly he had never intervened to help him get defense contracts. Sapp agreed, "I really don't know him myself." But Sapp did remember selling $423,000 worth of land to a trust which included Smathers' cousin, Benjamin Smathers.

Now begins some interesting mathematics. Smathers had said he owned $12,000 worth (before selling $3,000 to Baker and Peek) or one-fifth of the trust. One-fifth of $423,000 is certainly more than $12,000—the amount Smathers claimed he paid for his share. Most people would say one-fifth was more nearly $80,000. Confronted, Smathers said, "I made an error. The Clayton brothers owned 60 percent and I bought 13-1/3 of the remaining 40 percent." But even that didn't figure out right.

Nor did Smathers' estimate of how much money he got back. He said it was $42,000. County deed records showed it was nearly twice that much.

Confronted, Smathers threw up his hands and said, "I simply don't know how much I've received. That may sound strange to you, but it's true." Smathers' office couldn't help. Workers there said a copy of his income tax for a crucial year was missing.

Tired of trying to make the figures add up right and tired of newsmen's nosiness, Smathers growled, "There's nothing wrong with this at all. I just seem to always catch hell." He added, pious with anger, "If this is wrong, this with Baker and Peek, they're going to have to rewrite the Bible, that part where it says we're supposed to help poor people."

Why was he angry? He had avoided any real inquisition, through the courtesy of his colleagues. Senator Jordan, who had started out saying, "We've got all on our hands we can deal with right now" but "we wouldn't hesitate to question senators if we feel their testimony pertinent," and even went so far as to promise, "we'll pursue this investigation wherever the facts lead," later decided that if the facts led to Smathers, maybe they were going too far. At that point he told reporters shortly, "We're not investigating senators."

Jordan's restraint may or may not have helped Smathers. For sure, it did nothing to clear the air, and it left under a cloud some names that possibly did not belong there. Among these was the name of Grant Stockdale, who had gone to Washington as Smathers' assistant when Smathers was starting out in Congress and who had later, partly through Smathers' influence but mostly through his own friendship with Kennedy, been appointed ambassador to Ireland. Stockdale had once had close business connection with the vending machine concerns that got the keenest scrutiny in the Baker inquiry. Just before Stockdale left for Ireland, he was served with papers in a $131,000 damage suit in which a rival firm charged him with using "undue influence" to gain contracts for vending services at an aircraft maintenance company in Miami. Subsequently, Stockdale's company, Automatic Vending Services, Inc., also got contracts totaling $500,000 a year at Patrick Air Force Base and the missile test center at Cape Kennedy.

President of Automatic was Eugene A. Hancock, who previously had been President of Serv-U Corporation, the vending company in which Baker owned stock and which figured so prominently in the inquiry. When Baker resigned his Senate post, Stockdale knew what was in store for him, if only by innuendo. "I hope I don't get cut up too bad," he said. "I haven't done anything wrong." December 1, 1963, Stockdale leaped from a thirteenth-floor window in Miami, hit a fifth-floor ledge, and was killed instantly.

Before and since the Bobby Baker flare-up, Smathers has been rigidly and loudly against any law that would require senators to disclose their financial dealings. When several senators voluntarily opened their files and let the public look, Smathers stood firm: "Senators are not like the officials in the executive branch [who are required to disclose their private interests]. We are elected and if we have an opponent worthy of the name, anything improper should be brought out."

That sounds like a bold challenge, but he doesn't really mean it. Nobody is more hurt and astonished than Senator Smathers when opposing candidates or newspapers suggest that there may be improprieties in his private affairs. And in a way it is understandable; the man is beset by many rumors. There is, for example, the rumor that he and his banking brother, Frank, went to the officials of the Pan American Bank in downtown Miami and said they wanted to buy in, adding, "If you don't let us in, we'll put up a bank right across the street and drive you to the wall." To which the Pan American group is alleged to have said, "Go ahead and try it. There hasn't been a national bank charter issued for downtown Miami in years and there won't be."

That is the extent of the rumor, but very much a fact is the charter which Frank Smathers, Jr., and six other businessmen have held since January 1964, for "The United National Bank of Miami," situated right across the street from Pan American. Perhaps Miami needs another bank downtown? Well, perhaps. But the new bank is *also* right across the street from the First National of Miami, the largest bank in the state.

The decision to charter a new bank, said big brother Frank, who is also president of the Miami Beach First National Bank, "is a vote of confidence in the future of downtown Miami." Former U.S. Comptroller of the Currency James J. Saxon, who granted the charter, was a very good friend of Smathers'.

Senator Smathers has always been keen for land promotion in Florida. When, at a recent subcommittee hearing, an investigator told of wading around in a Florida bog for two days, looking in vain for a lot that had been advertised, Smathers took the stand to testify that, even if such promotion were going on, he thought the Federal Government should not butt in. He considered most land frauds to be only a "human problem of overselling."

Smathers has been in a few land promotions himself. He was present at the ground breaking for the Central Florida Industrial Park (CFIP) in April of 1962. Dr. Paul Douglass, a Rollins College professor and an advisory board colleague of Smathers' in Young Americans for Freedom, reported later that on that occasion, "Senator Smathers praised the park and said he would do whatever he could to help it along."

Which is not surprising. Smathers owned part of it.

Central Florida Industrial Park is situated eight miles south of Orlando, near the Martin missile plant. If Martin prospered, so, supposedly, would the park. Late in 1962, Martin, Douglas and North American were selected from forty defense contractors to lay out competitive proposals for the design of a missile to be known as the Sprint and planned for cooperative use with the Nike-Zeus missile. Together the two missiles became the "Nike-X," which was announced the next year by Secretary of Defense McNamara.

In the spring of 1963, an evaluation board composed of experts from the Army and from Bell Telephone Labs—for which Smathers was to work so diligently to obtain the satellite franchise that year—announced that Martin had won over Douglas and North American. Bell is in charge of the Nike-X operation, on which the Defense Department has said it would in all likelihood spend $17.6 *billion*. Of this, probably half a billion will be spent at Martin-Orlando, and Martin officials claim that 60¢ of every dollar will go to subcontractors, those near at hand to get the work. As the slop-over occurs, subcontractors and suppliers at the Central Florida Industrial Park will be in a fine spot, just two miles south of Martin, to catch their share.

Less than a month after the Martin contract was announced, the Senate held its first closed session in twenty years. After four hours and nineteen minutes of secret debate, the Senators emerged to announce that they had, by a vote of 58 to 16, decided to support Senator Russell's amendment to go beyond the older Nike-Zeus anti-missile system and put their money on the Nike-X. It was a great day for Martin-Orlando.

Despite the appeal of its location, the industrial park got off to a slow start, and the owners had heavy mortgage payments to meet. At this point, Smathers' loyal friends, the Atlantic Coast Line Railroad, purchased 400 undeveloped acres along the park's spur track for $600,000. W. Thomas Rice, ACL president, said that Grant Stockdale, at that time chairman of the board of Central Florida Industrial Development Corporation, first came to him with the idea of buying it.

The park was also amazingly lucky to get the new Sunshine State

Parkway to come right by its door. The turnpike was originally planned to go sixteen miles south of Orlando. That was in 1955. Then plans for the park got under way and the proposed route for the turnpike started bending northward, until it came straight past the CFIP—despite the fact that a right-of-way so close to the city would be immensely more costly.

Several members of the Turnpike Authority were strong supporters of Smathers, whose part-ownership of the industrial park was not generally known. He says he has since sold out. Just how much he owned is uncertain. At first he wouldn't talk about it at all, saying, "When the Senate requires that all senators divulge their business interests, then I'll disclose mine." Later he said he had bought approximately 3 percent of the park, but strictly as a favor to Stockdale. "He said it would help him," Smathers explained.

On November 26, 1963, another man who had played a vivid role in Smathers' life was found dead in a run-down Miami rooming house; he had been dead for four or five days. He was Richard A. Mack, fifty-four, during his last months a chronic drunk, in and out of psychiatric clinics. There had been a time when Mack was considered a good bet to become governor of Florida or even U.S. senator. He had been a railroad and utilities commissioner in Florida for eight years, and then, sponsored by his friend Smathers, was appointed by Eisenhower to the Federal Communications Commission. Smathers had previously tried to get Truman to appoint Mack.

In February 1957, Mack and three other members of the seven-member FCC ignored the advice of a commission investigator and awarded a license for Channel 10 in Miami to Public Service Television, Inc., a wholly-owned subsidiary of National Airlines. A House subcommittee investigating misconduct in the FCC discovered that Mack had taken six checks totaling $2,650 as "loans" from Thurman A. Whiteside, a Florida attorney who had been hired by National Airlines to push its application. Mack and Whiteside had known each other a long while, and said their financial dealings stemmed from that long acquaintance.

Paul R. Scott, also a lawyer and a National Airlines director, defended Whiteside's role by saying he had learned that Smathers and Senator Spessard Holland were among those "contacting" Mack in behalf of another applicant, Colonel A. Frank Katzentine, owner of WKAT in Miami Beach. Whiteside's influence was supposed to just "neutralize" that of the Florida senators. Senators Estes Kefauver and Mike Monroney were also accused of intervening in Katzentine's behalf, and they admitted it.

But not Smathers. George T. Baker, president of National Airlines, declared: "If the Congress because of its self-made rules or because of the club spirit convicts Commissioner Mack for his wrongdoings and drives him out of office and lets these senators go scot-free, it will shock the American people." The House committee did not call Smathers to testify, and to this day he has given no further explanation or defense. At the time of the investigation, Smathers was one of Majority Leader Lyndon Johnson's closest aides. House Speaker Sam Rayburn, Johnson's mentor, flatly refused to let the committee call Smathers or the other senators to testify. "We're not going to invite them to come over," said Rayburn. "And if I were the senators I wouldn't come voluntarily." They took his advice.

Meanwhile, Presidential aide Sherman Adams had telephoned Mack and told him to resign. While Mack was protesting his innocence and imploring him to "wait until all the evidence was in," Adams had hung up.

At no time did Smathers come to the defense of Mack, who had been his political ally for years and who now sank quickly. After a fourteen-week trial which ended in a hung jury, Mack became so destitute and far gone as an alcoholic that the charges were dropped. Whiteside was tried alone and acquitted; he killed himself a little more than a year later.

None of this appeared to bother Smathers. He rode out the storm. Today, not one Floridian in a hundred even faintly recalls that on the day Mack and Whiteside were indicted by a federal grand jury for "conspiring to influence" the FCC, Representative Oren Harris of the House investigating committee angrily "corrected" the report of a staff investigator who had said Smathers also intervened—through Mack—in a Pittsburgh television case involving another of Smathers' seemingly countless "old friends." Smathers had put in a good word for Hearst's WCAE to get the channel. Pittsburgh Mayor David L. Lawrence lobbied to get the channel for Television City, Inc. Both won: Television City, Inc., got the channel after it merged with WCAE. They paid three other applicants $50,000 each, "for expenses." Representative Harris said they had done nothing improper.

As for the disputed channel in Miami, it was eventually taken away from National Airlines and given to L. R. Wilson, Inc. It comes as no surprise, then, to learn that Senator Smathers and his brother Frank had been executors of the L. R. Wilson estate. Smathers came out winner all around. As Meade Alcorn, then Republican National Chairman, complained, Smathers' innocence was made a matter of faith, "without a hearing, without testimony, without supporting documentation that [he] had done nothing wrong."

The amiable and lackadaisical Senate Majority Leader, Mike Mansfield, who can find merit in the most unlikely places, once called Smathers "without question, the foremost expert on Latin American affairs in this body." One who is not a member of that body, however, and who does not have the advantage of observing Smathers close at hand, may think the evidence of his expertness somewhat elusive.

His suggestions for correcting the Cuban situation vary from urging an immediate invasion of the island to recommending that the United States designate a special day of prayer for Cuba.

Of Smathers' several curious associations with Latin American leaders, none is more inexplicable than his close and lasting tie to the late dictator of the Dominican Republic, Rafael Trujillo. In this, of course, Smathers was not without company. A number of newspaper reporters took money from Trujillo. A well-known Miami columnist accepted $20,000 from the dictator to write a biography that has never appeared. Minor and major politicians throughout the South and up and down the east coast took money from Trujillo. Florida's former Governor Haydon Burns was once investigated on the suspicion of being an unregistered lobbyist for Trujillo. So if Smathers was, as Trujillo once called him, "a very good friend of our country," he was not the exception.

The senator made a number of speeches in behalf of Trujillo, in practically all of which he mentioned, one way or another, that "I do not think there is any doubt that the average farmer or workman in the Dominican Republic is very strongly in favor of the generalissimo." Smathers seldom missed a chance to count the Dominican Republic's "100 fine hospitals, more classrooms and more paved roads than any other country in Central America has."

When the Bay of Pigs had the country in an uproar and Senator Wayne Morse denounced those "seeking to wave the American flag into tatters in an attempt to whip up hysteria in this country for direct military action," Smathers responded scornfully that the solution to the problem was *not* "patience and more debate." He had expressed just as much impatience earlier when Castro said it might be three or four years after the revolution before Cuba could hold elections. But he had always displayed patience and understanding for Trujillo. When in 1960 it became evident that, unless he reformed, Trujillo would be deposed shortly by forces either within or without his country, Smathers visited him and got him to promise "free elections" within two years. The end of the thirty-year dictatorship could not be achieved any sooner, Smathers said, explaining with a tolerance strangely absent from his approach to Castro: "We are always a little naïve in thinking that because we have democracy in our country, and because of our love for humanity, people in other lands should have exactly the same type of government we have. But that is impossible—at least for the immediate future."

Those were oppressive days for Trujillo. The Organization of American States was saying that his regime was marked by "flagrant violation of human rights," and our State Department was demanding quick changes. In his time of need, Trujillo had at least three allies here: Senator Strom Thurmond of South Carolina hailed him as "a true and loyal friend." Senator Allen Ellender of Louisiana, returning from a trip to the Dominican Republic, had many kind remarks to make about the dictator, remarks in which Smathers concurred, which he indeed praised as showing his colleague's "courage."

When the aging dictator was deposed, Smathers called for a U.S. task force to go in and restore the good old days. Editorially aghast, *The New York Times* said it could "not imagine worse advice than that given President Kennedy by his close friend Smathers."

Precisely what role Smathers played in Trujillo's politics, or what role Trujillo played in Smathers' politics, may never be known. Some of Trujillo's most important palace records have disappeared, and a number of reporters have speculated as to their disposition. Robert Jones of the Indianapolis *Star* wrote that the files "are supposed to have been spirited out of the Dominican Republic and are believed to be in Washington. . . . The evidence is believed to be in the hands of certain officials of the U.S. government—but which officials not even the investigators seem to know."

Sometimes you must be patient if you want to discover just what is behind Smathers' concern for the welfare of Latin Americans. Early in 1961, he took the floor of the Senate to tell, in a funereal drawl, of the "slums which fester like great sores in Lima, Santiago, Buenos Aires, Rio, and Caracas, disfiguring the souls of the people who inhabit them." The situation was so bad, he said, that it would take 19 million homes to correct it.

But was the situation hopeless? No, not at all, said Smathers, as he introduced an amendment to the Foreign Assistance Act which would set aside $15 million specifically for building self-liquidating pilot housing projects in Latin America.

Nearly two years passed before the Senate discovered another side to his concern for homeless Latins. One of Smathers' dear friends, Eugene McGrath, was, among other things, operating an insurance company in Panama City. McGrath applied to the Agency for International Development (AID) to underwrite a $10-million loan (to be made by two large labor unions) for building 1,200 houses in Panama City. When Smathers made his heartfelt appeal to the Senate for building funds, he had talked of houses costing $2,000. McMath's houses, however, were to be priced at $8,333, a sum which William Gray, head of the economic section in the U.S. Embassy in Panama, said included an unduly generous profit margin (comparable houses built by the Panama Government cost $3,000 less).

But such quibbles came later. For the first year, the arrangement of the deal was made in complete secrecy. Joseph S. Farland, at that time ambassador to Panama, said he knew nothing about it until Smathers' administrative assistant, Scott Peek, summoned him to the senator's office where Smathers told him to give the project, then and there, his stamp of approval. Farland refused, saying he would need at least thirty days to study it. Smathers telephoned Farland's superior, Edwin Martin, Assistant Secretary of State for Inter-American Affairs, and warned that if Farland did not approve the project, he would take the whole matter to the Senate and try to get him removed as ambassador.

Considering the secrecy that prevails even between agencies within the State Department, and considering Smathers' demand for action-or-else from Farland for a project the ambassador had never heard of, Oliver L. Sause, Jr., head of AID's Central American section, was hardly being excessive when he said the matter had been handled "in an unusual manner."

Unusual or not, AID Administrator David E. Bell authorized the $10-million loan guarantee. Five days later, Ambassador Farland, saying it was all "most peculiar," resigned. He said Smathers' pressure had been too much: "When a senator—especially the only senator to attend the last birthday party of our late President—attacks an ambassador, especially a Republican ambassador, that Republican had damn well better look to his hole card."

Smathers, without directly denying Farland's charges of pressure, characteristically complained that he was being picked on. "I'm tired of taking the rap on this," he said, adding that he wasn't the only senator to lean on the State Department, "but I seem to be the fall guy."

After the project was exposed to the light by Washington newsmen, AID officials conceded that it didn't look as good to them as it once had.

So much for some of the rubble in the corners of his Senate career— quite enough to put many senators in deep trouble. But for some reason Smathers has generally escaped widespread criticism either at home or in Washington. "That's just George's way," say his friends. So say also his enemies. Not since 1950 has anyone expected him to act differently.

Something snapped when Ed Ball pulled him into a new shape. Most politicians can keep their true personalities separate from the tactics they sometimes use—eye-gouging during an especially bitter campaign, but then reverting to their normal stance. Smathers could not do it.

As his power increased, so did his isolation. His clique has fallen away: one by assassination, a few by suicide, several others by political defeat. One or two improved their income—from vending-machine companies, among other sources—and pulled away from his circle. But mostly the going has been via bad luck, as when Miami attorney Charles Ashmann, once Smathers' aide, received a three-year sentence for writing bad checks, peddling influence and embezzling $60,000 from clients. Many of the old loyalties, born of the old buccaneerings, can no longer be counted on, and this has left him shaken and reaching frantically for new alliances.

Pathetically, he keeps trying to reburnish his career with Wholesomeness. He introduces resolutions designating "All-American Family Week" and ordering a gold medal to honor J. Edgar Hoover. These gestures cannot keep out the gloom, which keeps washing back on him until he looks out on an America where the average person is "an angry, frustrated, worried man who sees his nation flaunted and degraded with the free world slipping away." His patriotism is as squally as it ever was and his foghorn warnings as doleful.

In his personal life he feels set upon. Innocent questions are received as threats. What did he think about the Walter Jenkins case? Who? Walter

Jenkins? Smathers—who for long periods had almost daily dealings with President Johnson's staff—was not sure he could remember Jenkins, once the most important member of that staff. "To my knowledge, I've never seen the man, nor have I ever heard of him or his duties."

Newsmen and their editors, he is convinced, are deliberately persecuting him. When an adverse review of his career appeared in *The Nation,* Smathers interrupted a vacation in Europe to fly back and counterattack. Painfully, painstakingly, he counts his clippings, including seventy critical comments from Drew Pearson since the year he won his Senate seat. He points to three critical references to him on a single editorial page of *The New York Times.* While Graham lived, *The Washington Post* tempered its criticisms; now it does not. When Clark Mollenhoff of the Cowles newspapers pursued him with questions, Smathers turned and seized the reporter's lapels in a frenzy of anger. Persecution everywhere.

Each session of Congress is more frantic than the last. Attempting to work both sides, he is caught in grotesque postures. Catering to the American Medical Association (always good for campaign money) *and* to the old folks back home, Smathers wound up voting both ways on the social security-medical care bill. He voted against the amendment, and then he voted for the bill that included the amendment.

After what was undoubtedly the most traumatic experience of his career—the 1964 election and 300,000 Florida Negroes going to the polls to give that state back to the Democrats for the first time since Smathers went to the Senate—he engaged in embarrassing lurches at survival, including, of all things, a vote for the Voter Registration Act in 1965. He got safely through 1966 and 1967 by delicately avoiding all subjects that might conceivably be controversial, while taking a firm stand against crime in the streets.

With the awakening of the black bloc, and with an accumulation of unlucky deals and public disclosures, he began complaining of being ill. His office is full of pill bottles. Every three or four months he disappears into another clinic—Mayo or Boston or Bethesda—and comes out with oblique remarks about being beset by an ailment that is "serious but not incurable." His staff says he has an ulcer and a spastic colon. He *looks* in great health. But the hidden thermometer keeps cracking and spilling its red vein of fear.

Washington observers began to talk. For a time his influence at the White House seemed not so great as before. Such whispers could hurt him, for he is a man who lives by a reputation of being able to extract favors. Not for him the dogged dissent of a Fulbright or the moral intoxication of a Goldwater. His genius is of a different sort—the political squeeze, the cloakroom swap; the nattily dressed deliveryman for the private interests.* But just when the whispers were becoming dangerously widespread, he stifled them all by persuading President Johnson to budget seven million dollars for the Miami boondoggle, Interama, an international carnival to be built in the middle of a swamp. (Just to prove that profiteering makes strange politics, there was poor Claude Pepper, now back in Congress, holding a shovel and working diligently at Smathers' side for the same pork barrel.) And just to prove that was no one-shot return of his old talents, Smathers turned out to be Johnson's ultimate advisor on the question of whether to suspend the 7-percent investment credit. According to a report in *Forbes* magazine, November 15, 1966, it was none other than Gorgeous George alone who sat up with Johnson until three o'clock one morning to make the decision. From such episodes it must be concluded that Smathers still has enough maneuverability that if he leaves the Senate, he will doubtless do so as he arrived, amidst a shower of golden coins and crackling greenbacks, the Deep South's real professional.

In the closing debate on the civil rights bill, after attempting in vain to get Smathers to soften and allow a vote, Senator Douglas remarked: "I always hope for redemption. I believe in the old hymn, which I used to sing in church as a boy:

> While the lamp remains to burn,
> The vilest sinner may return."

He said it half in jest, but only half, and anyone who remembers the Smathers of pre-1950 will want to sing along, but not with a great deal of hope.

* The latest high-cost maneuvering to come to light was the cleaning up of George A. Wackenhut's private detective firm by the Smathers law firm. Wackenhut, who was once briefly an FBI agent, used to squeak along on an income of $9,000. He wanted federal contracts. But federal agencies aren't supposed to employ private detectives. Smathers' firm, as Fred Cook points out in the May 15, 1967, *Nation*, "neatly solved this difficulty by splitting the Wackenhut Corporation like the amoeba—one part for investigation; a second, housed in a subsidiary corporation, for guard and security duties. Once this Smathers legerdemain had been performed, federal agencies seemed to become fascinated by the previously little-known Wackenhut Corporation. NASA, the Atomic Energy Commission and other federal enclaves poured millions of dollars into Wackenhut's lap to protect them from subversion and intrusion. . . . Wackenhut [did] $17,755,514 worth of business in 1965."

7

Jim Eastland,
Child of Scorn

Laws against adultery, fornication, sodomy, incest, and bestiality were known in the laws of Moses. They are basic in the Ten Commandments. They are found in the Roman Law. They were in the Common Law of England. They were in the law of the colonies when the Constitution was adopted. They have been brought forth in the laws of the forty-nine states. They inherit their efficacy from ethics and religion, and have been fed on spiritual meat. These laws are known wherever the spirit of decency flowers and men look up through the mist at God. In only one place are they held in low repute; that is in the U.S. Supreme Court, where we find nine men appointed for life dissenting against the judgment of mankind.

Senator James Eastland, 1959

The Negro is different because God made him different to punish him. His forehead slants back. His nose is different. His lips are different, and his color is sure different. . . . We will not drink from the cup of genocide.

Ross Barnett, 1959

Equally spaced around the periphery of the rotunda of the capitol in

174

Jackson, Mississippi, are four columns, in each of which is a niche, but there are no busts of heroes there although that is what they were intended to hold. Instead, in two of the niches are, temporarily at least, portraits of Mississippi's two Miss Americas, a tribute in chivalrous counterpoint to the rhapsody of Mississippi Supreme Court Justice Tom Brady, "The loveliest and purest of God's creatures, the nearest thing to an angelic being that treads this terrestrial hall is a well-bred cultured southern white woman, or her blue-eyed, gold-haired little girl." A third niche, when I was last through Jackson, was filled with a cardboard football schedule for the University of Mississippi.

Bronze and marble political *lares* had never occupied their proper places, I was told, because the legislature could never agree on the four greatest politicians Mississippi had turned out. That *would* be a puzzler. Of course by Mississippi's standards Theodore Bilbo would be toward the top of any list, but even though there is a rampant. Bilbolatry in Mississippi whose devotees would like to see the little man reproduced on every floor of the capitol, the fact that his life-size statute dominates the floor below might make it difficult to get his head into one of the four niches. Still, he would be a strong candidate.

So would Hugh White, who probably saved Mississippi from being auctioned off when he set up the then-revolutionary scheme of luring industry into the state with long tax moratoriums. Although the favoritism of his Balance Agriculture With Industry program was unfair to the lower income group—whose sales tax, even on groceries, bears most of the weight of state government—and although many fly-by-night industries abused the deal (some of them move in, sop up the taxless benefits, the cheap labor, and then go into bankruptcy or leave the state after dark), nevertheless, for all its drawbacks, BAWI kept Mississippi from ruin. A niche for Hugh White.

Who for the other two? Fielding Wright, the Dixiecrats' smudged vice-presidential valentine, who went sniveling back to Stevenson in '52? Hardly.

The only possible choices would be between James Plemon Coleman, Ross Barnett, and James Eastland—Coleman because he is the slickest politician Mississippi has turned out since Bilbo, Barnett because he is probably the dumbest politician ever produced by the state; oddly enough, either quality may get a man to the top in Mississippi.

Coleman was the last of the aristocratic governors; not truly aristocratic, of course, but such as is so designated in Mississippi, where the landed gentry claims a bloodline that disappears kindly into the ground-mists four or five generations ago, an aristocracy of certitude that nothing will ever change. Coleman was the last response to that certitude, come just as it was unraveling and tearing along the edges into strange new fears and uncertainties. He was the last governor to be elected on the premise that there was nothing to get very excited about. This was not an especially courageous position to take. Although when he pulled it off in 1955 the Deep South was already a year into the first shock of the school integration ruling, strongholds of genosecurity such as South Carolina and Mississippi did not think the law would ever have to apply to them; their only confusion lay in how best and most absolutely to duck it. Coleman's approach—legal trickery—made him, to outsiders, seem a moderate; but this was at best the white man's moderation. The Negroes hated him then; they still do. They hated him because he was effective.

They hated also the injustice of being subjected by a man who was praised widely in northern newspapers and magazines as a progressive fellow. Of course, in a way he was: he wrung through the legislature a law permitting the recall of those corruption-inclined satraps, the county sheriffs; he temporarily cleaned up the Gulf Coast gambling joints where tourists were being fleeced of $300 million each year; he at least cut down on some of the cruelty at the state penitentiary; and, by streamlining the executive department, he built up a sizable budget surplus without increasing taxes. Moreover, for the sake of encouraging the industry that Mississippi had been pimping for since Hugh White's revolutionary program started in 1936—industry which might stop the 40,000-a-year exit of Mississippians—he talked soothingly. God knows, considering what happened when the next governor talked otherwise, this was no small thing. "What we need," said Coleman, "is peace and quiet. What happened in Clinton, Tennessee, will be like a boil on the side of Mt. Everest compared to what could happen in Mississippi." He knew his people. He was never keen on the Citizens Council; this claptrap jingoism was contemptible to him because he did not believe in wasting time with the obvious. "Integration is no more possible here than it is for the Mississippi to run uphill." Any efforts from outsiders would be efficiently deflected by a legal thrust. Big (6'5", 245 pounds) Cousin Plemon had gone off to Ole Miss with a wagonload of sweet potatoes to barter for an education; the potatoes had rotted, but he had stayed on to become one of the law school's sharpest graduates, an authority on Civil War military strategy (with a library of 400 Civil War books), an educated farmer with a farmer's arrogant assurance that nobody is smarter than himself. There was, when he limited the comparison to other Mississippians, some grounds for that assurance. He was not supposed to win the election in 1955; nobody had won the governorship on his first try in thirty-two years. Coleman did it by being the most *accurate* segregationist among five very strenuous segregationists; that is, he itemized his record, a record that included very little ranting and considerable frustrating of blackmen. Mississippi Negroes remember him best for his handling of the Willie McGee case when he was attorney general: "Elect me as your attorney general and I'll handle Willie in a way you'll like," Coleman had promised, and sure enough, Willie, whose only crime was that he had lived with a white woman apparently with her consent, went off to be electrocuted, convicted three times of raping her. Nobody in the South was better than Coleman was at finding flaws in the NAACP's legal petitions for school integration, or enjoyed more the hunt for them. He would stay up all night on such a case, savoring the search, tickled at the prospect of burying the petitioning Negroes under a load of legalisms.

Whip 'em legal-like, that was his way. When Fielding Wright swore a mighty oath in the '55 campaign that he would allow his body to be pierced by one of them federal bayonets before he would bow to integration, Coleman said that was silly "theatrical talk. The bayonet stage will never come to pass with Coleman as your governor. There are ways to keep schools open without using bayonets. Police power is a weak straw that has been broken by more than 500 decisions of the U.S. Supreme Court since 1883." Coleman believed that the way to beat the federal government would be to pass a new state law every time it was needed and then fight all the way to the U.S. Supreme Court. "Any legislature can pass an act faster than the Supreme Court can erase it," he said. Before he went to his inaugural ball he mused, "I believe in preserving segregation, but I don't believe in making war. In the first place, I am a loyal American, and in the second place you can't win." His inaugural address included the assurance, "Mississippi will be a state of law and not of violence . . . despite all the propaganda which has been fired at us, the country can be assured that the white people of Mississippi are not a race of Negro killers." Repeatedly he warned in private conversation, "Mississippi has been completely ruined once on the race question. God forbid that it should be allowed to happen again. We owe it to both races to see that it doesn't. A weak or frenzied leadership could make this state a battleground." When Ross Barnett went off to defend John Kasper in Tennessee, Coleman remarked, "If a man like John Kasper ever enters the state he'll have a butterfly net around him before he gets his mouth open." Negroes were still getting only the janitorial jobs in the new industrial plants he was bringing into the state, but at least they were not being badgered *en masse*; in a way Mississippi for the four Coleman years was the calmest state (outside of South Carolina and Florida) in the Deep South. There was no serious talk in Coleman's circle of "banning" the NAACP.

Coleman also maintained the last vestiges of a loyalist Democratic organization. Mississippi had followed after its Fielding Agonistes, down the precipitous Dixiecrat path of '48, and it was to leave the party again in 1960 and 1964. But in 1952, Coleman, reputedly almost singlehandedly, kept Mississippi at the Democratic convention and in the Democratic column, and he repeated this performance more easily as governor, in 1956. In many respects, Coleman's regime was the last of the relatively subdued Mississippi Old South, before it was replaced by hysterical rearguard guerrilla warfare. His attitude, loyally southern but calculatingly loyal, was not to be heard in Mississippi again until the blight of Barnettism was partly burned away by new federal laws and the economic fears of Mississippi industry.

Looking back on Coleman's regime from this distance in time, one can only be awed by the intricate duplicity of his political genius; any doubt about that genius, or its intricate duplicity, was certainly dispelled on the occasion of his acceptance by the Senate Judiciary Committee as appointee to the Fifth Circuit Court of Appeals. At these hearings on July 12 and 13, 1965, he was presented as (1) a sly defender of the Negro and (2) a monstrous defender of the intractable and often violent Mississippi white man. It would have been impossible for a Mississippi governor in the 1950's to be both. Which side was correct?

U.S. Attorney General Nicholas Katzenbach had his job to do. Lyndon Johnson was paying off old convention debts to Mississippi, and Katzenbach was carrying the satchel. Of course, said Katzenbach—opening with anything but disarming candor—Coleman was a segregationist governor, but "when the full picture is considered, we see not the caricature of an unyielding white supremacist but a man who was frequently willing to take great political risks to support moderation and respect for law and order when the opposite course would have been the politically expedient one."

Then Katzenbach ticked off Coleman's "heroisms"—the State Sovereignty Commission "dwindled to virtually nothing" during his term; he favored donating state land, despite editorial outcries from the state's leading newspapers, for the use of an integrated veterans' hospital; he refused to purge the state textbooks of pro-integration statements; he criticized Governor Faubus' course of action during the Little Rock school crisis; in 1959 Coleman invited the FBI to come in to investigate the Mack Charles Parker lynching case; he opposed a legislative investigation of the 1962 riots at Ole Miss, contrary to the wishes of Governor Barnett.

"Some say," Katzenbach remarked dead-pan, with what must be the most pathetic defense of extremism on record, "some say that Mr. Coleman is a racial extremist. *In the context of Mississippi politics,* he could not be so classified in any sense of the term. . . . In the context of Mississippi political life, these were acts of genuine political courage."

The other side saw Coleman's record a little differently. Clarence Mitchell, the NAACP's Washington director, said it seemed mighty odd to him that the information compiled by the FBI in the Mack Charles Parker lynching, after being put into the hands of Governor Coleman and other Mississippi officials, just sort of evaporated. Mitchell had tried to warn the FBI. He had tried to warn then-Attorney General William Rogers "that it would be unwise to give information which had been assembled by the Federal Bureau of Investigation to the government of Mississippi because inevitably this information might find its way into the hands of those who were accused of the crime." But Rogers wouldn't listen and, recalled Mitchell sadly, "The information got there and subsequently nobody was ever convicted for that crime. It is a fact which I believe the FBI would support, that this was one of the most comprehensive and effective investigations that they ever conducted. It would seem to me, therefore, that certainly the question ought to be raised in these hearings of what happened to that information after it reached the state of Mississippi and also whether it did in fact get into the hands of those who were counsel for the persons who were accused of the crime." (Later Senator Sam Ervin of North Carolina, who was chairing the special subcommittee handling this hearing, did ask Coleman about it, in an offhanded fashion, and Coleman said it was a ridiculous notion, and that satisfied Ervin completely.)

John Lewis, chairman of the Student Nonviolent Coordinating Committee (SNCC), who had been released only ten days previously from a Jackson, Mississippi, jail, had a few observations to make about Katzenbach's claim that Coleman was more moderate than Faubus. Devastatingly, Lewis simply quoted from one of Coleman's 1959 campaign speeches:

> Let us examine the record. Nobody can argue with the record. When the schools were integrated at Hoxie, at Van Buren, at Fort Smith, and other places in Arkansas, Governor Faubus made no effort to stop that integration. When trouble flared up in Arkansas, Governor Faubus made no effort to stop that integration. When race mixing finally got to the state capitol at Little Rock, he did not try to stop it. Do you believe it would be right for me to refuse to fight until it got within the shadow of the state capitol at Jackson? Do you believe it would be right for me to let the NAACP integrate Lexington, or Greenwood, or Macon without raising my hand to stop it? In my view of things, if I were to follow this policy, I would not be the governor of Mississippi, I would simply be the governor of Jackson. I have adopted the rule of stopping integration anywhere it raises its head, regardless of the town, and I have enforced that rule.
>
> Governor Faubus had done nothing about race mixing at the University of Arkansas. I could not follow him on this. When they attempted to mix the races at the University of Mississippi, I stopped it cold. Many of you have heard Governor Faubus say on nationwide television that his son attended an integrated college. I cannot follow the governor in sending his son to an integrated college. I have sent my son to the University of Mississippi, where the races are apart. People ordinarily do not send their children to schools that they do not approve of, and I feel that if I were to send my son to a mixed school I would be publicly approving of race mixing, and I would be setting an example for the entire populace to follow. . . .
>
> In a speech which he delivered on June 13 at Biloxi, at the Mississippi Bar Association, Governor Faubus said that the people ought to be allowed to mix the races in the public schools if they wanted to, or that they should be allowed to keep the races separate if they wanted to. That might please both sides, but that is not the policy of the state of Mississippi. We believe that it is to the best interest of both races that they have their own schools throughout the state and that everybody operate under the same rule.

Jim Eastland 181

> *Therefore, I could not follow Governor Faubus in supporting local*
> *option on segregation.*

And if the Senate committee wanted actions, not oratory, Lewis could cite those also: Coleman's signing into law the repeal of the state's compulsory education laws in 1956, which was the normal southern preparation for closing the schools to block segregation; the same year, signing laws requiring railroads and bus companies to maintain separate waiting rooms and toilets for intrastate traffic; signing, the same year, an act giving businesses the right to choose their customers. In 1958—this is perhaps the most notorious episode of Coleman's time in office—Clennon King, a Negro professor, applied for admission to the University of Mississippi; he was whisked away from the registrar's office by state patrolmen, held secretly for two weeks, committed to an insane asylum for thirty days, and then forced to leave the state.

Coleman was always pretty proud of the way he handled the Clennon King case. Just two years before the Senate confirmed him for the judgeship, when he was running for the governorship again in 1963, he boasted, "The point of this story [about King] is not the fact that one man was kept out of Ole Miss. Rather, it shows that we know how to protect your rights in such a way that the federal government could find no excuse for putting hands on the state of Mississippi."

The really strange feature of these committee hearings was that as late as the year 1965 the same old southern double-back would get by unchallenged. For instance, this exchange, when Senator Jacob Javits attempted to get nearer to some of that strange southern linguistics.

Senator Javits: "Governor Coleman, first I would like to ask you to define what you consider to be a segregationist as you use the word?"

Mr. Coleman: ". . . It is not a term that I like or ever did like. *I don't think it is a very accurate term. I don't think we have segregation in the true sense of the word in Mississippi or ever had.* But we have had some rules for the separation of the races in certain activities such as in the schoolroom and other things that partook of a social situation, shall we say. But again, that is all gone. Whatever segregation was, why, it has been destroyed in this country by decisions of the Supreme Court and acts of Congress as I see it, Senator."

He said he didn't think "we ever had segregation in retail establishments," but then admitted that he had signed a law making that very thing an institution. He admitted that he might have said, as the newspapers quoted him on March 17, 1963, that there would be no racial mixing in the schools if he were re-elected, but, what he *meant* by that, Senators, was, well, "I want to point out that nowhere in that statement did I say that that would be accomplished by defiance of the Supreme Court of the United States or by open rebellion against the country. I had in mind actually trying to operate . . . as I did the first four years on the basis of personal peace and good will among the people of Mississippi which worked very beautifully during those four years."

And finally Coleman was asked directly by Senator Javits if he had boasted of sending Clennon King to a mental institution and then chasing him out of the state.

Mr. Coleman: "Senator Javits, of course I did not run him out of the state. . . . Now, right after this thing happened, and after he was submitted to this mental examination in good faith, why I was amazed to find a lot of people thinking it was just a gimmick. . . . *However, in the give and take and fisticuffs of a stump campaign in Mississippi, I made the statement that you say I made. . . ."*

Some people believed him. Among these was Ralph McGill of the Atlanta *Constitution,* who wrote the committee on behalf of Coleman:

> . . . Because of the fact that the Negro was very largely de-prived of the ballot and of education, he was therefore not able to function fully as a citizen. Statistics show that the white southerner, because he, too, was captive of a restrictive system and also suf-fered educational and economic lacks, participated as a voter far less than did white citizens of other states.
>
> This produced a situation in which the southern politician of good will and purpose and integrity often had to make public state-ments which never jibed with his deeds on his character. This was a matter of political survival. For generations in the South even our best men had to seek office in this manner. A look at the speeches by Governor Coleman and a similar look at his deeds and obvious character will illustrate this point very well.

McGill only said a look; he didn't say a close look.

Bouncing against Coleman's administration in a rhythmic animosity were the careers of Paul Johnson and Ross Barnett, both of them Cole-man's political enemies then and today.

Among the many reasons Johnson feels ill toward Coleman is that Cousin Plemon, by manipulating himself into the governor's mansion in 1955, held Johnson away from that prize for eight long years. Having been defeated twice previously for the governorship, Johnson actually campaigned in 1955 on a whine, "It's Paul's turn." Not even Mississippi could go along with this approach to the governorship as nothing more momentous than a time at bat.

The trouble with Paul Johnson's career is that he was never able to free those instincts that would have permitted him to deal easily with either the good people of Mississippi or with the peckerwoods, a distinction in class that was once roughly defined as the difference between involuntary manslaughter and murder. Peckerwoods ride by and shoot into Negro shanties at night; good people refuse to distribute federal surplus food to hungry Negroes in the winter, thus insuring their eager return to the fields at $3 a day come spring (it is not unheard of for Delta Negroes to die from cold and malnutrition in the winter). It is the difference between those who, merrily sucking a jawful of Red Man tobacco, are willing to work and sweat to dig a grave in the night to hide their murder, and that smaller group whom Hodding Carter called "the uptown Ku Klux Klan"—men of substance who would not think of night riding, either to kill or to catch a killer; they are the Rotary Club of Indianola who did their civic duty by buying more riot guns for the local police when the SNCC youngsters came to town, not the farmers who later burned down the Freedom Labor Union's headquarters. Nine low-class white men were convicted of bombing Negro homes in McComb, an offense that could have brought death penalties, but it was a middle-class judge who put them on probation with the excuse that they had been "unduly provoked" by civil rights workers who were "of low morality and unhygienic."

Being a timid man, an indecisive man, Johnson was unable either to soothe enough of either side, as Coleman could, or arouse enough, in the fashion of Barnett. Son of another Governor Paul Johnson—whose "average man" program provided for free school textbooks, old-age pensions, care of indigent children, and support of charity hospitals; the program was fought and crippled by some of the Delta legislators in 1950—Johnson *fils,* it is generally believed, wanted to carry on the ideas of his father, but after three defeats the drive to reform became merely a drive to be elected, at any price, and so he decided to hitch onto the whipping coattails of Ross Barnett.

Of Ross Barnett, who in 1959, on his third try, won the highest elective office in the poorest state in the nation (at that time, average income: $1,173), the kindest and most accurate thing that can be said is that he is bone dumb. Canny, yes. He started life one of ten children in a poor farm family. After working his way through college and law school as a barber and janitor, he became the most successful damage-suit lawyer in Mississippi, earning $100,000 a year. There was a standard joke around Jackson about the poor yokel who asked another, "If you was knocked down by a car, which doctor would you call?" Answer: "Dr. Ross." Nevertheless, dumb. Well remembered by reporters is that moment when Barnett took over as the registrar at the University of Mississippi to bar James Meredith. Get the scene: Barnett in the doorway. Here comes Meredith, the only Negro within 200 yards, surrounded by a sea of white marshals. Barnett: "Which of you is James Meredith?"

Doug Starr, who covered the capitol for the Associated Press the first two years Barnett was in office, says the governor held only five press conferences during that time, all of which were worthless because to any serious question put to him by a reporter Barnett would invariably reply, "Well, what do you think I should do?" And he meant it; he was asking for advice. Perhaps some of it was only absentmindedness; he was perpetually abstracted. He never looked a person in the eye, never looked where he was going. Backing into the propeller of a plane, he was laid open from shoulder to hip; but it did not change his ways. He meandered through life. He went into the next county to dedicate a new highway, and when he started his speech, opening with a comment on how happy he was to be there, he couldn't remember where he was. At one of the Southern Governors' Conferences, he planned to make a speech in which he would accuse the national Democratic Party of borrowing from a program laid down by the Soviet Communist Party in 1928. Ruminating over the remarks he was about to make, he kept asking an aide, "Now tell me again, what was it that happened in 1928?"

He reveled in politics, the wild promises, the wilder accusations. To be elected he promised so many jobs that the lineup of expectant applicants sometimes stretched back forty yards from his doorway; desperately he seized control of state agencies that were supposedly autonomous and squeezed jobs out of them. It is said, perhaps only in fun, but it does not exaggerate the situation he found himself in, that at the time he was going through his ordeal of making good on campaign promises the U.S. was having difficulties with Red China and a reporter asked Governor Barnett "What do you think of Matsu and Quemoy?" His reply: "They're good men, and I'm sure I can find a place for them in Fish and Game."

Having blustered and profaned his way into the governor's office, Barnett found that he had no program for the state, no ideas to fulfill, and so he settled down to chat with cronies who soon filled the hallways and the offices of the executive suite, laughing and hooting and telling tales. Barnett loved it and encouraged it. It was open house every day, with great clots of people standing around gossiping. Many an important letter or legislative bill was signed by Barnett on a hallway wall, after one of his harried secretaries had hunted him down and dared interrupt some visiting farmer's earthy story.

Governing without purpose, he turned to vacuous and often silly pastimes, renovating the mansion with garish luxury (gold-plated bathtub faucets) and presiding over the DAR-inspired purging of the school textbooks (out went Sandburg and MacLeish). The million-dollar surplus Coleman had left in the state treasury was promptly sopped up in frivolities and boondoggle. For the first time, state funds were channeled through the Citizens Council. Those sketchy reform plans that the legislature had made—for instance, to improve conditions at the state penitentiary—were discarded as being unnecessary.

Mississippi is not made up entirely of fools. In 1961 students booed Barnett at a football game—many of them undoubtedly the same students who, two years later, feeling their insularity threatened, looked to the North with inflamed eyes and cheered the old buffoon as he raised his fist and in a tremulous voice cried, "I love Mississippi! I love her people! I love her ways!" He had been the butt of jokes, an elevated ambulance chaser fit to be ridiculed; and then, strictly by the accident of national stresses, he was being cheered by his people again. But the most unbelievable note of irony was struck when he was taken seriously by such sophisticates as U.S. Attorney General Robert Kennedy, gulled into an impossible position by Barnett's *ad hoc* telephone script.

> Kennedy: Can I rely on you that there won't be any violence?
> Barnett: Yes, sir.
> Kennedy: I am taking a helluva chance. I am relying on you.
> Barnett: There won't be violence. . . . No one will be armed.
> I will be in the front line and when Meredith presents himself, I'll do like I did before. I will read a proclamation denying him entrance. I will tell the people of Mississippi now that I want peace and we must have no violence. . . . When you draw the guns . . .
> I will step aside and you can walk in.

Kennedy: I think it is silly going through this whole facade
. . . of your standing there; our people drawing guns; your stepping aside. To me it is dangerous, and I think it has gone beyond
the stage of politics.

Not for Barnett it hadn't; for him "it" was right in the middle of the
stage; and him *with* it, and the nation, and the eyes of the world, and
however unwillingly and feeling silly, the Kennedy brothers. It was a coup
that Coleman could not have pulled off. He would have tried something
rational, he would have pulled a legalism, and the episode at Ole Miss
would have ended with Meredith ensconced amidst grumps and curses but
no violence. Dull Barnett, with his mind half on the poultry market,
successfully led everybody into the slough and thereby became what
Hodding Carter accurately called "the dominant political figure in Mississippi as long as he lives."

James O. Eastland has, during his twenty-five years in the United
States Senate, been called many things. In the Delta country, which arches
along the Mississippi River from Memphis to Vicksburg, he is referred to
with real affection by the white folks as "Our Jim." Elsewhere in Mississippi affection diminishes to merely the typical appreciation of the South
for standard fare: political hominy grits, tasteless but substantial. Robert
Hearin, the affable president of the First National Bank of Jackson, one
of the two largest banks in Mississippi, is downright proud to be a friend
of Jim Eastland, whom he calls "solid, you know what I mean, really
solid."

Washington has reacted to him across a wide spectrum. FDR saw him
as just another Dixie pitchman, open to trade. ("That's all right, son,"
Roosevelt told him after Eastland's first race for the Senate. "I got quite
a kick out of those anti-New Deal cracks. But now you're elected and
we've got to play together. You can come see me whenever you want to.")
Eisenhower feared him and allowed him to handle Republican patronage
in Mississippi. Lyndon Johnson's love of power includes that vested in
Eastland, with the result that they seem chummier than they really are.
("They're like brothers," says Wilburn Buckley, Eastland's home secretary, with considerable exaggeration.)

But generally, the descriptions applied to Eastland outside the South
reflect a deep bitterness and fear. Even Westbrook Pegler, who stands
second to no man as a wacky conservative, attempts to hoot him down as

an "illiterate in good standing." Clarence Mitchell of the NAACP has publicly expressed various designations of loathing for Eastland, ranging from "stinking albatross" to "accessory to murder and treason" to "mad dog loose in the streets of justice."

Getting his Senate colleagues to appraise his character publicly is not easy, but the late Herbert H. Lehman, once senator from New York, damned Eastland as "a symbol of racism"—an estimate with which most southerners would agree, but with a different intonation. *Time,* after one of its mysterious polls, marked him as the "nation's most dangerous demagogue." I. F. Stone offers a briefer sketch: "Mississippi McCarthy."

Intimates of the senator are quick to press upon inquirers the portrait of him as a devoted homebody who avoids the party circuit in Washington to be able to spend more time with his family and with his real-life detective stories, which he reads at the rate of two a day; as a good planter, a kind planter, who "never whips his niggers and would fire any white worker who did"; as a pillar of the Democratic Party who has helped keep Mississippi from going officially Republican (as if, in the light of the 1964 election, this mattered much). The private image of Eastland as a kindly paternal planter somehow keeps getting gobbled up by his carnivorous public image, however, and despite the best efforts of his friends and family it remains true that none of America's anti-southern cults has more devotees than the one that directs its hatred at Senator James Eastland. He, more than any other extant politician, seems to symbolize what intellectuals, seekers, mystics and mavericks are trying to remove from the world.

Exactly why this should be true is more complex than is the man who inspires such feelings: a rather simple man, really, as simple as Sunflower County, his home and birthplace, where 70 percent of the population lives and dies in uncomplicated peonage, where violence (e.g., Emmett Till) flows out as naturally as the passage of seasons, and where one can easily stand in the middle of the Delta's steaming sameness and honestly believe that the world goes straight out forever, flat all the way and overripe, and made by a God who in His infinite wisdom gave Adam a cotton allotment.

It's hardly enough to say that Eastland is hated because he is an old-school segregationist. Strom Thurmond is shriller and Leander Perez more savage, and yet they are judged to be merely disagreeable curiosities. Is it because he is so effective in his hyper-conservatism? But he isn't very effective: he has never had a fraction of the success or following in Washington that Harry Byrd could command even in the ailing days at the end of his career. Although he has few rivals as an accomplished vilifier of the Supreme Court, this separates him from most other Deep South politicians only in the matter of decibels.

Eastland does not draw dislike from any specialty: he is adept at irritating in many ways. If he is dangerous, it is only as the embodiment of the southern middle class at bay. He is, though very wealthy, middle class in every way. Like Miniver Cheevy, James Eastland, child of scorn, loves the days of old but does not know what to do about it. "We are living in an age," he wails, "where everything old is evil. Old values are being swept away and pseudosophistries substituted." His emphasis on chivalry is rather odd at times. He seemed less concerned that three persons were slain and more than 300 wounded at the Ole Miss riots than that some of the coeds were reportedly forced to flee their dormitory in their nightgowns. And when dozens of Negroes entered the registration office of Mrs. Martha Turner Lamb in Greenwood, Mississippi, demanding that their full citizenship be recognized, Eastland was not so much perturbed that a revolution was at hand (although that did annoy him) as he was that a group would "push themselves into the office of any public official, much less the office of a *lady* public official."

However, there is a leak in the quaintness that deflates it to mere dullness. In frequent public statements Eastland has shown his concept of the law and of the Constitution to be that of a recipe book, wherein every problem is indexed and where one need only turn to the right page to find the proper formula. The Constitution speaks but is not to be interpreted—except by some psychic communication with the founding fathers. "I say," says Eastland, "that the fundamental of all fundamentals in our system of government is the premise that the Constitution of our country shall be interpreted strictly in accordance with the understanding of the members of the Constitutional Convention who submitted it and the states which adopted it."

Persons who expect imagination or eloquence from Eastland are always disappointed. Pat Watters, Southern Regional Council writer, heard Eastland at a fund-raising dinner for the Georgia States' Rights Council, and described him as "a disappointment, a sing-song speaker who often lost the tune, a stringer-outer of sentence structure, a constructer of swimming syllogisms, a citer of confused communist-front charges, and in this performance anyhow, a bore." Watters expected too much: Eastland, with his raspy repetitions, is usually a bore. He mistakes excess for eloquence—

as when he charged that the NAACP is backed by organizations "of all shades of red . . . the blood red of the Communist Party . . . the almost equally red of the National Council of the Churches of Christ in the U.S. of A."—and has neither the guttersnipe charm of Theodore Bilbo nor the raging excitement of Richard Russell at his best. Eastland is simply excessively trite. At an outdoor Citizens Council rally in Montgomery, the crowd became so bored with him and began to drift away in such large hunks, Eastland threw away the last seven pages of a thirty-page speech.

Carefully lettered on the wall of the Freedom Democratic Party's shanty headquarters in the Negro slum of Indianola, county seat of Sunflower County, is this dogma:

> There are rich people
> And poor people.
> Middle class people
> Are the same as
> Rich people.
> They have more things
> Than they need.

That is another clue to Eastland as an object of hate. He stands preeminently for the preservation of a world in which the middle class so outdistances the poor class that even to mention a "middle" begs the question. In any real sense there are only two classes: those who have what they need and those who do not.

Although he is not the largest landholder in Sunflower County, Eastland's 5,800-acre plantation, acquired by his grandfather at $1 an acre and now worth between $500 and $700 an acre, makes him a multimillionaire. In addition he has leased a 1,300-acre plantation near Vicksburg for raising specialty cattle, and holds stock in the First National Bank and the Deposit Guarantee of Jackson, the state's two largest and politically most influential banks.

Telephone operators in Sunflower County earn $200 a month, stenographers $200 a month, sales clerks $20 a week and salesmen $50 a week, mechanics $1 an hour, electricians $1.25 an hour, medical technologists $200 a month, bookkeepers $175 a month. (Figures taken from a salary list issued by the Indianola Chamber of Commerce to entice new industry and business.) However, contrary to what a northerner or westerner might suppose, these workers—all white, of course; jobs of that type are not open to Negroes—are not the deprived class. They are, like

Eastland, members of the *wealthy* middle class of Sunflower County. They have something; they have, by comparison with the Negroes who work on Eastland's plantation, more than they need. So when the National White Citizens Council movement was born in Indianola in 1954, a movement that originally was said to be made up of "respectable middle-class" white people, it's no wonder that Eastland was one of the organizers and the chief speaker. In the unreal world of Mississippi, the clerk, the burgher and the planter stand shoulder to shoulder not democratically but in the aristocracy of the full gut.

Of the 46,000 residents of Sunflower County, 68 percent are Negroes.* Most of these Negroes are in *families* earning less than $1,000 a year, with children nine and ten years old working a full day in the fields to bring the family total to even that much. Full-time Negro maids in town are paid $8 a week. Two-thirds of the residents must expect to subsist on federal food handouts at some time during the year.

If life for the Delta Negro is uniformly low, so are his spirits. Many feel that even on the bare-survival terms of service that the white planter has laid down, they are being cheated. One woman who sharecropped with her husband for sixteen years said they quit and went into day laboring because their white landlord stole so much from them. The last year they worked their twenty-five-acre sharecropping spread, they had good results: thirty-two bales. Cotton was selling at about $200 a bale that year, and they were supposed to get half of it—or $3,200 for their share. Instead they received $500.

"There's too many ITS in 'croppin'," she told me with still sturdy good humor. "You plants it, and you prays over it, and you works it, and you chops it, and you picks it—and then, at the end of the season, they *takes* it."

Delta Negroes are bound to the plantations in such a way that many find it hard to get away. When a chopper is in debt two-thirds of the year and paying off the debt the other four months, it is difficult for him to accumulate enough money to gather up his family and leave. Yet total despair from being at cross purposes with the white planters has filled the slums of Indianola with self-exiled laborers. Eastland has called these unhappy people communists. Squatting in the dirt with a group of them

---

* These and other figures that follow are either from Indianola Chamber of Commerce records or from U.S. Census Bureau records, supplied by the Indianola C. of C.

one day, beating away the flies and smelling the grayish green water in a nearby ditch that Negro children played in, I asked them to tell me about Marx. They didn't know anybody by that name; but they knew ol' Eastland. They knew some of the Negroes on parole from the state penitentiary he was working for nothing. They knew an awful lot about being hungry. One boy, fourteen, who had been working in the fields for three years before he and his folks walked off in disgust a month earlier, said that a typical meal at his home was butterbeans and bread.

What else?

"That's all, butterbeans and bread." And sometimes, he said, just one and not the other.

If they had not left their farms in protest, many of them would have been kicked off anyway. The rapid increase in the use of cotton-picking machines and weed-killing chemicals has brought heavy unemployment to Sunflower County, as it has to much of the Delta. Between 1950 and 1960, Negro farm jobs fell off 48 percent. The unneeded Negroes are looked upon as a nuisance. "Negroes," said one planter, "went out with the mule." If they are not yet gone, they are going. In the last decade, hunger and despair have driven 22 percent of them out of Sunflower.

Many of those who remain and who are uppity enough to protest tell of slave conditions. The whites resent such expressions. One woman who works in the government allotment office in Indianola told me sharply, "Why, the niggers that live out there just love it. That's been their home all their lives." Slavery was the expression used by Andrew Hawkins when he testified before two congressional committees. Hawkins, a Negro cotton picker who is an official with the hardly-existing Freedom Labor Union, said that Negro cotton choppers who live on Eastland's plantation earn less than 30 cents an hour *when* they work, which often is less than two days a week. He said that many Negroes on Eastland's plantation were forced to make and sell bootleg whiskey just to stay alive.

"Just bunk, all bunk," said the senator.

Eastland's office invited me to visit the plantation and see for myself: "Talk to anybody who works there. We've got nothing to hide." But Clyde Rutledge, general manager of the plantation, refused. "I don't want you talking to the niggers. Next thing, every reporter in the country would want to be interviewing them." So I went in by the back route that night, escorted by a nervy Negro man who lives in nearby Ruleville. There is plenty of moonshining going on, all right. My guide introduced me to three part-time moonshiners living within half a mile of each other on the Eastland place. He assured me there were numerous others, known to him because he patronized them (and the heavy stench of sour mash told me he was not lying). "Drinks pretty good, too," he said. "Leastways it gets you drunk." Price: $5 a gallon, nearly as much as a tractor driver earns from Senator Eastland for a full day's work.

The Negroes who work for Eastland appear to live no worse than others on the Delta. Their shanties are the usual weathered bare boards, no plumbing, no toilets at some shacks and outdoor ones at others, no insulation (and it gets *cold* on the Delta), broken furniture, screens off, windows out, leaky roofs. Four persons to a bed is nothing uncommon. At one place we stopped my guide just hauled off and urinated in the front yard (dirt) while the conversation went on. And why not? Dusk had not settled into night and there were four shanties within view, but the spectators would understand because there wasn't a toilet within three miles.

There are teen-age children on Eastland's place who have never been to school because they have never had the clothes to wear; there are children nine years old who work from sunup to sundown. Some of Eastland's workers have never tasted beef. One woman said she had eaten turkey only twice in her life: once when she got a turkey from comedian Dick Gregory,* and the other time, back in the mid-1950's, when she bought a turkey on the installment plan. At a tractor driver's shanty the family meal that night had been biscuits, molasses and salt meat. Tractor drivers are among the elite force; for a twelve-hour day they earn $6 and work nearly the year around. Cotton choppers earn only $3 a day and have only a four-month work year.

Meanwhile, at Sunflower County's six Rotary Clubs, four Lions clubs, four VFW posts and seven garden clubs the life of service and fun goes on about as usual, conscience clear. For in Washington, speaking their true beliefs and desires, assuring them that what they do is right—that *they* are not to blame for the Negro's condition but the fact that "our natural resources have been exploited by eastern capital as an outlet for investments to make huge profits from cheap southern labor"—is the potent voice of Our Jim (who will gross an estimated quarter of a million dollars this year).

---

* The Ruleville Citizens Council responded to the influx of Gregory's turkeys by sending two 'possums and a sack of sweet potatoes to Chicago.

Our Jim says: "We have no voting qualifications based on race, none at all, and anybody who's qualified can vote." (As late as 1966, his home county had registered fewer than 3 percent of its Negro population.)

Our Jim says: "I am against any organization which indulges, which promotes, racial and religious prejudice, hatred and bigotry." (He has supported the John Birch Society, the Citizens Council and every major white-supremacy organization that has popped up in the South in the last twenty years.)

Our Jim says: "I have never engaged in a filibuster. Southern senators have never filibustered but we have conducted campaigns of education." (He has done service in every anti-civil rights filibuster that has taken place in the Senate in the last twenty-four years.)

Our Jim says—or until a few years ago he was still saying it—"there's not a Ku Klux Klan chapter in the state of Mississippi."

These are not lies; they are the true expressions of how one region sees itself, and itself in relation to the rest of the world. Such views, the result partly of individual myopia and partly of regional madness, forestall any outside persuasion, and the nation, seeking dialogue, is thus frustrated to the point of rage and turns easily on Eastland because he tells his southern myths with such bland sincerity.

On the wall of Eastland's office is a photograph of Mary Ann Mobley, Miss America of 1959, inscribed, "To a great statesman and loyal Mississippian." He *is* a loyal Mississippian, and this loyalty, combined with his hold on the chair of the Senate Judiciary Committee, has given Eastland both the motive and the position to shape, retard and pervert the civil rights movement more than any other man in America. The Judiciary Committee is one of the two or three most important committees in the Senate; some believe it to be *the* most important. It handles not only all civil rights bills but all judicial appointments, including appointments to the Supreme Court, and oversees all appointive jobs in the Department of Justice.

For many people, the theory of committee structure by seniority reached its most indefensible point in 1956, when Eastland became Chairman of the Judiciary Committee on the death of Senator Harley Kilgore, a liberal from West Virginia. The promotion was made on the recommendation of then Democratic Majority Leader Lyndon Johnson. Only two senators spoke out against the appointment: Wayne Morse of Oregon and Herbert Lehman of New York, who received their reward from the

southern press by being called "two racist demagogues" (Richmond
Times-Dispatch) and "leftwing pinkos" (Jackson, Mississippi, *Daily
News*). Other senators who might have been expected to gag at the
promotion took the position that they were made helpless by the seniority
system.

But the next year, when Majority Leader Johnson laid his committee
slates before the Senate, with Eastland again tabbed for the Judiciary
chairmanship, Paul Douglas of Illinois was finally moved to point out that
the Senate and Johnson were not helpless, as they pretended, because
they did not follow the seniority system when it pleased the inner establishment to ignore it. Although Senator Estes Kefauver of Tennessee
(usually on the outs with the establishment) had four years' seniority
over Senator John F. Kennedy of Massachusetts, Kennedy had been
named in his stead to a coveted seat on the Foreign Relations Committee.

Some observers were well pleased by the Eastland appointment. Fulton
Lewis, Jr., remarked that "Kilgore was a constant critic of big business
and sought unremittingly to prod the government into more antitrust bills.
Eastland is not likely to react the same way." (Eastland has indeed not
reacted the same way. Not once has he initiated an antitrust investigation;
and when four steel companies refused to surrender cost data subpoenaed
by Senator Kefauver, Eastland told them, "I don't blame you at all.")

For his part, Eastland appeared not to understand what all the quar-
reling was about. "Of course I'll be an impartial chairman of the Judiciary
Committee," he said publicly, "and carry out my duties to the best of my
abilities"; privately, he gave his word of honor to two delegates from the
NAACP that he would do nothing to block the progress of civil rights
bills to the floor.

The New York Times credits the Eastland influence in the Judiciary
Committee and its Civil Rights Subcommittee, of which he was chairman
before advancing to chairmanship of the full committee, with bottling up
122 civil rights bills. In his 1966 campaign, he boasted that the number
was actually 127—"not one ever emerged."

Eastland held up appointments within the Justice Department, attempting to evoke the promise that federal troops would not be used to enforce
civil rights laws in the South. He would brag in speeches around Mississippi of how "in time there was so much pressure built up from various
members of the committee who wanted to get their nominees approved,
I was able to get the Judiciary Committee to approve or reject bills and

to name judges I wanted." As a matter of course since he became chairman, Negro nominees to the bench have been kept waiting nine months to a year for confirmation, and Jewish nominees have frequently had to wait just as long.*

Eastland was correct when he boasted of his bargaining power. Thurgood Marshall, counsel for the NAACP, was nominated September 26, 1961, to the Second Circuit Court of Appeals. One year later, less two weeks, he received confirmation by Eastland's committee. There had been a purpose to the delay, as Attorney General Robert Kennedy is said to have discovered one day when, meeting Eastland in the corridor, he was accosted with this quasi-threat: "Tell your brother that if he will give me Harold Cox I will give him the nigger" (meaning Marshall, now a Justice of the Supreme Court).

Marshall thereupon ascended the Second Circuit bench and Cox, Eastland's old college roommate and protégé, became a federal judge in the circuit that handles most of the Deep South's civil rights cases. Cox's tenure there has been distinguished by such acts as calling some Negro civil rights defendants "chimpanzees," protesting by letter to the Justice Department about its "lousy" civil rights cases, threatening on one occasion to jail then-U.S. Attorney General Nicholas Katzenbach for contempt, and throwing out indictments against seventeen men charged with the murder of three young civil rights workers near Philadelphia, Mississippi—a triple murder which Eastland, by the way, persisted in calling a "hoax" until the bodies were actually dug out of the mud.

The cumulative effect of this kind of delay and barter within the Judiciary Committee is such that for some time Eastland was considered no joking matter. One can scarcely raise a smile now by recalling the days when Eastland's Internal Security Subcommittee voiced grave concern because the Young Pioneers were circulating leaflets advocating "Smash the Boy Scouts!" Gone, too, is the time when no Washington cocktail party was considered complete unless somebody came up with the quip

---

* Quite often Eastland's actions have given off an anti-Semitic odor. In 1965, when a group of lawyers headed by Morton Stavis of Elizabeth, N.J., represented the Freedom Democratic Party in its effort to unseat the five Mississippi Congressmen, Eastland said that Stavis had been an attorney for Communist Party members appearing before the House Un-American Activities Committee and that Stavis *had changed his name in 1939 from Moses Isaac Stavisky!* Well, said Stavis, so what? He had changed his name legally and openly; understandably he saw Eastland's mentioning the change to be "ill-concealed anti-Semitism."

that the two southernmost parts of the United States are Key West and James O. Eastland.

Grimness set in. It is understandable—since so many bombings, burnings and assaults have occurred contrapuntally to Eastland's propaganda litanies in the Senate—but it is also unfortunate, for some of the finest off-Broadway farces have been played in Eastland's committees.

If all the column inches Eastland has put into the *Congressional Record* in connection with that shapeless social nebula which he calls communism were placed end to end, "they might stretch," as one Washington wit calculated, "from here to sanity." In pursuit of what he conceives to be his duty, Eastland has filled the *Record* with a riot of accidental humor. Describing one civil rights meeting in Atlanta, Eastland concluded, with an air of intrigue uncovered, "It is perhaps significant that almost one-third of those present at this conference wore beards."

Deeply shaken by what he called the "invasion" of Mississippi by the National Lawyers Guild to help participate in the 1964 summer project of voter registration, Eastland set out to show the world just what sort of spies and subversives his state was having to deal with. He gave Henry W. McGee, Jr., of Chicago as an example. "When he was fourteen years old," Eastland told a no doubt puzzled Senate, "Henry W. McGee, Jr., was reportedly a member of the International Workers Order, Lodge No. 751 at Chicago." That membership was nineteen years previous, and apparently Eastland realized that it did not strike his colleagues as something to get terribly upset about, so he threw in a few things that Henry McGee, *Sr.,* had done that displeased him.

John Tillotson, another invader, was guilty in Eastland's eyes because at the University of Minnesota he had led a student protest against atmospheric nuclear testing. On several occasions he had stated his opinion that "nuclear war won't solve anything" and had even written rather sharply about the campus ROTC. These revelations failing to arouse the Senate to much alarm, Eastland again ended lamely with, "there is more which could be said about young Tillotson if security reasons did not prevent it. He is an outstanding example of a second-generation communist-in-prospect. In fact, he might even be called third generation. His father was a communist; his mother was a communist; his grandmother was a communist. . . ."

Eastland followed up with other examples of his politico-Mendelian discovery.

Persons who have been called unwillingly to appear before Eastland's Internal Security Subcommittee will quickly point out, however, that such entertaining boobishness *is* accidental and incidental to the injury of reputations which takes place there. Although witnesses regularly complain of his bullying tactics, the senator insists that he conducts his committee business in a fair and untroubled manner. A friend of Eastland's who has sat in on numerous executive sessions of the Internal Security Subcommittee said, "I never saw Jim really mad except once, and that was when a nigger referred to him as 'ol' Eastland.' I've heard others call him just Eastland, and he didn't seem to mind that, but this was the first time he'd ever been called 'ol' Eastland,' and he got so mad he got red in the face and his gray eyes got cold, and I thought he was going to knock that nigger out of his chair. Jim was so mad he was grinding his teeth. Nobody but a communist nigger would have called Jim 'ol' Eastland.' "

Eastland believes that any witness should be allowed to have an attorney, but he also feels that attorneys willing to defend communism, former communists or suspected communists—even if Eastland's suspicions are the only ones aroused—must be prepared to share the obloquy of their clients. The records of his committee's hearings are full of instances when he has called an attorney a communist for no reason than that he represented an unpopular cause or a "suspect."

Nor it is possible to clear oneself with Eastland if he is convinced that his suspicions are correct. The best example of this is the case of James Dombrowski, who has probably been subjected to more brutal unfairness over a longer period of time than any other integrationist on the senator's list. Dombrowski has been a marked man among congressional investigators from as far back as the early 1940's when he was executive director of the Southern Conference for Human Welfare. The SCHW was suspect: it stood for integrating the races. It gave awards to dubious people like Governor Ellis Arnall of Georgia, now a wealthy corporation attorney; on its advisory board were people like the late folklorist, J. Frank Dobie, who was noted for being about as subversive as a cactus. Later Dombrowski became Executive Director of the Southern Conference Education Fund (SCEF), an organization whose openly announced and overriding aim was to put an end to segregation in the South.

Dombrowski has sworn under oath before the Internal Security Subcommittee that he is not now and has never been a communist. He did so in 1953 and Eastland made no attempt to prosecute him for perjury, so by normal rules this should have meant that thereafter Eastland would treat him as though he believed him. But it wasn't enough.

For two decades congressional investigators had been itching to get their hands on the SCEF's files. Four years ago, Eastland figured out a way to do it, with the cooperation of the New Orleans police and of the hoked-up Louisiana Joint Legislative Un-American Activities Committee.*

Early in October 1963, the New Orleans cops, with several legislators trudging at their heels, marched into the SCEF's headquarters and started tearing the place apart, literally. They also invaded the homes of former Orleans Parish Assistant District Attorney Benjamin E. Smith, the SCEF treasurer, and Bruce Waltzer, Smith's law partner. The legislative committee's counsel explained that they did not give the FBI advance notice of the raids because they were afraid the FBI might have had to tell Attorney General Kennedy who, in turn, would have tipped off the Reverend Martin Luther King, who would have warned Dombrowski.

When the raids were over, the two attorneys and Dombrowski had been charged with criminal conspiracy (a charge later thrown out by a state judge), and while they were running around trying to get out of that accusation, the twenty-year collection of extremely important data was being carted off from the SCEF. The state legislative committee released the records to Eastland within twenty-four hours of their removal.

Months later, Eastland returned the records, but only after every piece had been photographed. Since then he has been reading into the *Congressional Record* portions of private letters to and from Dombrowski.

Protected as he is by the ponderous fortifications of the Washington establishment, Eastland is not an easy man to beat; but from time to time the inner vein of excess that has mucked up his whole career breaks out again and he defeats himself. That happened in his now-famous effort of 1956 to bully *The New York Times*, which had, he felt, been unkind to him.

Under the guise of seeking out communist influences everywhere in the American press, Eastland set out specifically to get the *Times*. He has always denied that the paper was a special target, but figures make the denial silly: twenty-nine of the thirty-five witnesses called to executive sessions of the committee, and fourteen of the eighteen witnesses called

---

* This fascinating organization recently investigated, and cleared, the Ku Klux Klan, finding it to be only a "political action group" with "a certain Halloween spirit."

to public sessions, were past or present members of the *Times* staff; in the latter group, a fifteenth witness was the brother of a present employee of the *Times*.

Among those summoned by J. G. Sourwine, counsel for the Internal Security Subcommittee, was one Robert Shelton. Correction: *He* was not summoned. Another Shelton's name was on the subpoena, but Robert Shelton was the newsman the committee's subpoena server insisted on hauling in. It was a clumsy, needless mistake, as Eastland was to learn, but at the moment he didn't seem to care: one Shelton was as good as another for his purpose, which was to blacken the name of the *Times*, and since Robert Shelton was an employee of the *Times*, he would do.

But Robert Shelton refused to cooperate. When the grilling began, he read into the record this statement:

> I am involved in these hearings as a victim of accident. The subpoena first served to me was originally made out in the name of a person who does not work on my paper. A committee aide, when told that there was no such person on the *Times*, insisted on knowing if there was anyone with a similar name employed there. There were a few, but the only one that interested your man was the sole similar name in the news department, mine. At the executive hearings the committee counsel tried without success to link me with a certain New York newspaper. He was unable to establish any connection because I never worked for the paper under discussion. Yet I have been called back here today. It appears to be just another step in a campaign to discredit the paper for which I work.

Too bad, said Eastland, but he would nevertheless have to answer the questions.

"I won't answer, because I am a victim of accident," Shelton insisted.

Thereupon he was charged with contempt of Congress. Although by the time the thing got to court Eastland and Sourwine knew they were in the wrong, they attempted to bluff it out. Sourwine claimed that Robert Shelton was exactly the man they wanted and that they had subpoenaed him on the basis of information supplied in an informer's letter. Shelton's attorney, Joseph L. Rauh, Jr., took the position that Sourwine was not telling the truth, and by the time the case came up on appeal the informer's letter could not be found. Eastland fared even worse. Seventy-seven times he answered Rauh with either, "I don't know," or "I don't recall" or "I don't remember."

The New York Times investigation was unquestionably among the most notorious held by Eastland, but he testified in the Shelton appeal that he could not remember any details of the hearings.

> Rauh questioned: You can't remember one detail, can you, Senator?
> Eastland: No, sir, I certainly can't.

Were the hearings even legal? Eastland insisted that he had had the authorization of the subcommittee for holding them, but he could not remember when the subcommittee was called together to give the authorization, or where it met, or who was there or what was said. He could not remember Shelton, or who issued the subpoenas for him and the other witnesses, or whether a record was kept of the meeting or how many witnesses were called. He could not remember any of the testimony, he could not remember any legislation that was pending at the end of the hearings. He did not know Sourwine was supposed to have a letter regarding Shelton, nor did he know what disposition Sourwine had made of it.

But none of his lapses of memory strains credibility more severely than Eastland's forgetfulness of the John T. Watkins case. Four years before the Shelton appeal, Eastland had taken the floor of the Senate to introduce five bills, recommended by the American Bar Association, to "correct certain decisions of the Supreme Court which have weakened our internal security." Ticking off the five, he said that of all the subversive decisions, none was so bad as that of the Watkins case, in which the court held that the House Un-American Activities Committee had to show relevance of questions about a person's associations. The decision infuriated Eastland: "In the Watkins case the Supreme Court abrogated the right to judge a man by the company he keeps. The Supreme Court has in effect created a new 'First Amendment right,' which it has designated the 'right of freedom of association,' and has held in effect that a man's association with communists are his own personal business, and that he cannot even be asked about such associations without invading his right of privacy."

He had reason to be furious, for just the previous year the Watkins precedent had been used by the Supreme Court to slap him down. Back in 1955, when the Eastland committee was pumping Matusow for all those commie pipedreams he later recanted, Harry Sacher, a New York attorney, was called to testify. The committee (only two members were present) started off slyly, asking Sacher about Matusow, but then switched—the Supreme Court later referred to it sarcastically as a "brief excursion"—to asking him questions about what he thought of proposed legislation barring communist attorneys from practicing, and then sneaked in three questions about the possibility of his being a member of the Communist Party, past or present.

But Eastland was trying to weasel around with the wrong man. In his way, Sacher was tough. As an attorney for the eleven communists tried before Judge Harold R. Medina in 1949, Sacher had so bedeviled the judge that he spent six months in jail for contempt. That had removed none of his scrappiness, and when Eastland started prying into his political affiliations, Sacher told him to go to hell.

Eastland cited him for contempt. Sacher went to the Supreme Court, and the case bounced back to the court of appeals with the advice that this conviction be reviewed in the light of the recent decision in the Watkins case. The appeals court ignored the advice, reaffirming the conviction. But by a 6-to-2 decision, the Supreme Court overturned the lower court in 1958 and freed Sacher, with Eastland screaming in the background about "an unconscionable restriction on the legislative power."

Such was the unhappy effect that the Watkins case had had on Eastland's career prior to his taking the stand to be questioned by Rauh:

> Q. Do you recall ever having listed the Watkins case, among others, as being pro-communist?
>
> Eastland: I *think* so. I think I listed a number of cases as being pro-communist, but when it was and what was in what I said at the time, the *Congressional Record* speaks for itself. *I don't recall.*
>
> Q. But now to ask it more generally, Senator, you do agree with me that you have called the Watkins case decision pro-communist?
>
> Eastland: I say I could have, yes. I *think* so.
>
> Q. All right. Now the Watkins case was decided in June 1957. My question is very simple. Were you following the principles of that case back on January 6, 1956?
>
> Eastland: I don't remember at this time what the Watkins case held.
>
> But Rauh became nettled and pushed on harshly:
>
> Q. Senator, in your entire—you just referred to the fact that you tried to be fair to all the witnesses that come before your committee?

Eastland: Yes, sir, we have tried very hard to be fair with all the witnesses.

Q. Can you name a single witness who has ever said he didn't remember as often as you have said it this afternoon?

Eastland: Well, I don't know, but there are very few men in this country, except a judge, that hears as many witnesses as I hear.

Q. I asked you a simple question.

Eastland: Well, I know. I caught the implication in your question.

Q. I was asking you if you could name one witness before your committee that ever said. I don't remember, I don't recall, I don't know, as often as you said it.

Eastland: I can't answer that question. I don't know. . . . I just tell you I don't remember anything about it. This was eight years ago.

Q. Senator, do you have any idea how many years back your subcommittee goes in asking witnesses about things?

Eastland: Well, we try to get what they remember, of course, what the facts are.

Q. How far back do you go?

Eastland: Well, that depends on the case. . . .

Q. Have you ever, at your hearings, ever counted up the number of times a witness has said, I don't remember, and used it as a question of his credibility, Senator?

Eastland: No, sir.

Just as his old friend and mentor Joe McCarthy was never again so cocky after his encounter with Welch, the public character of Eastland has noticeably limped ever since its encounter with Rauh. Too many people in Washington could answer the questions Eastland suddenly could not answer; too many could remember the brutal overhauling witnesses had received in his committee when they could not dredge up transient events from the depths of twenty or thirty years. Spread across the nation in a million reprints is Eastland's messy little innuendo regarding Chief Justice Earl Warren's failure to remember random reports issued six years earlier by a California legislative committee, when Warren was California's governor. "Certainly," Eastland told other senators with a knowing look, "certainly Judge Warren cannot claim unfamiliarity with his own state official reports on such an important subject."

After the Rauh cross-examination, Washington was no longer quite so willing to accept Eastland's basic premise that forgetfulness is a symptom of treachery.

Considering their impact upon our times, it is ironic that Mississippi's two most notorious living sons are political successes by accident. Of the two, Ross Barnett is more of an accident than Eastland, but Eastland is an accident, too. If the insurrection at Ole Miss had not occurred during his first term of office, Barnett would be just another gray face in the fog of Mississippi's political past.

Nothing so dramatic established Eastland. He started out as a second-choice interim appointee. Governor Paul B. Johnson, Sr., had hoped to name Eastland's father to fill the vacancy brought about by the death of Senator Pat Harrison. But Woods Eastland, a power in Mississippi politics, didn't want it, so the largesse was passed on to his son. Up to that moment, Jim Eastland's earlier political star seemed to have burned out. Ten years before, he had won state-wide attention as a member of the Mississippi legislature. He and two other legislators, Courtney Pace (now Eastland's administrative assistant) and the late Kelly J. Hammond, became known as the fighting Little Three; they tried to push through the rather progressive program of Governor Theodore Bilbo, but were frustrated by the reactionary Big Four, including Walter Sillers, who has been in the Mississippi legislature since 1916 and who for the past twenty years has been speaker of the Mississippi house.

Eastland strictly followed Bilbo's lead; Bilbo made him. Still, he gets full marks for backing what he did: money for highways (there was scarcely a paved road in Mississippi at the time), free textbooks, money for TB hospitals, etc. But all that was a decade past, and Eastland, retiring from the legislature when Bilbo left the mansion, had settled into dabbling in law, luxuriating in the family wealth, living the typical life of a spoiled planter's son, and doing little about politics. Taciturn, unimaginative, ineloquent and humorless, Eastland—United States senator by appointment—arrived in Washington amid few predictions that he would stay long, or make an impression while he was there.

But Washington did something that Eastland could attack, and from the attack he drew strength. This was 1941, edge of wartime, and the Office of Price Administration put a price ceiling on cottonseed oil just as Eastland arrived in the Capitol. There were few topics that Eastland was competent to speak on, as even his friends admit retrospectively, but one of them was agriculture, especially cotton. The OPA regulation would have cut the cotton farmers' profit in half; it would have reduced his own family's income by many thousands of dollars. It was enough to make

Eastland—who customarily cannot rise above a low C in rhetoric—sound drivingly persuasive. The regulation was killed. And immediately Eastland was a hero with many of the home folks. He had slain a regulatory giant, or at least cut off a finger.

Eastland had been appointed for eighty-eight days, until a special election could be held, on the promise that he would not be a candidate. He kept his promise on that occasion, but the 3,500 letters that had come to his office praising his work in the cottonseed-oil fight pointed to a following that he did not want to waste, and the next year he came out as a candidate against Senator Wall Doxey. It was a tough fight, with Bilbo taking the stump to denounce his one-time protégé, but Cottonseed Jim, whose principal tactic consisted of attacking President Roosevelt, won by 16,000 votes.

If Eastland had grown up in the county of his birth, it is doubtful that he could have made the political grade. But his father moved from Sunflower County to Scott County and there Jim was raised, not returning to the Delta to live until his mid-twenties. The significance of this is that the Delta is traditionally the home of the Mississippi aristocrats, the wealthy planters. But the voting power lies to the south and the east, where the rednecks live. The only resident of the Delta who has ever been elected governor of Mississippi, for example, was Fielding Wright, and he made it only because he was first automatically boosted to the position from lieutenant governor on the death of Governor Thomas Bailey. The impoverished rednecks do not normally trust Delta moneyed men. Eastland has the best of both worlds: born among the rich and reared among the rednecks, he carries both blocs.

For the first ten years after he defeated Senator Doxey, Eastland was nobody in Washington. He was only one more southern vote, which went predictably for low tariff, against labor, for the administration's foreign policy, and against social reform. Inarticulate, inconspicuous, with few noticeable interests outside agriculture, Eastland represented his mostly impoverished constituents in such a style that one of his Senate colleagues of that day now recalls: "To make Jim believable, I had to keep reminding myself that his grandfather actually rode with General Bedford Forrest. Jim didn't seem to be much. In fact, if you looked at him very long, he would begin to disappear, like the Cheshire cat."

The Eastland that the world was later to know and that civil rights workers were to hate began to emerge in the early 1950's, clutching with quiet desperation at the coattails of Senator Joseph McCarthy. As chairman of the Internal Security Subcommittee, Eastland's goal was the same as McCarthy's, and it was from McCarthy that he learned the headline profit to be had from attacking the Supreme Court. Subcommittee records of those days reveal cooperative exchanges such as this between the two men:

> Eastland: The court seems to be issuing one pro-communist decision after another.
> McCarthy: You're so right.
> Eastland: What explanation is there except that some communist influence is working within the court?
> McCarthy: Either incompetence or the influence you mention.

Not content merely to call the Court communistic, Eastland worked up some statistics to "prove" it. Between 1943 and 1953, he said, the Court had still leaned toward patriotism, ruling in favor of the communist position only fifteen times and against the communist position nineteen times. *But then came Warren.* In the next five years the Court sat in judgment on thirty-nine cases in which the struggle between the decent people of America and the communists was evident, *and in thirty decisions the communists were sustained.* Guess who was the least loyal member of the bench in both the number and percentage of evil votes. That's right: Black. He voted to sustain the commies every time, said Eastland. Douglas was not much better. (Many spectators of the Eastland Game began to wonder if they understood the rules, however, when he disclosed that *Frankfurter* was also a heavy offender.) Tom Clark was counted the best of the anti-communist wing of the court, but even he had voted with the reds eighteen times by Eastland's reckoning.

Being communistic was bad enough, but to top it off, the Court was also—and perhaps still is (Eastland has not brought his Court index up to date)—lewd.

One would not suspect it to look at Eastland, but he is very sensitive to sex matters. They affect him very strongly. When he thinks someone is getting out of line sexually, he never just suspects him of being a *little* out of line. For one instance—a careful search of his public utterances will disclose many others—on February 3, 1965, in a colloquy with the junior senator from Mississippi Mr. Stennis, about some civil rights "agitators":

Stennis: The white boys and white girls would live in Negro homes. They would sit in the courthouse square on park benches, and they would love and hug and go down the streets holding hands. I am speaking of the white girls and white boys in the groups that came in.

Eastland: I know of several instances in which members of the group were syphilitic and the Public Health Service had to take charge.

Stennis: Yes, I heard of that, too. The mores, customs and traditions that the people there were taught in their youth were flouted daily in the faces of both races. . . .

Eastland: I know of an instance in my hometown in which a Negro woman cut her husband up because of his attention to one of those white girls.

This is vintage Eastland. Where Stennis saw only loving and hugging and holding hands, Eastland perceived running flesh sores; where Stennis measured the result as merely flouting customs, Eastland envisioned bi-racial rolling in the hay. When it comes to sex, Eastland goes for the ultimate accusation.

And so in 1959 when the Supreme Court approved the distribution of *Lady Chatterley's Lover* as being something less than pornographic, East-land was immediately spewing the bench with accusations of its being willing also to approve coaching in "bigamy, or sodomy, or miscegenation, or even rape." Likewise when the Supreme Court released the movie "The Miracle," which had been banned as sacrilegious in New York, Eastland said the Court had essentially "put the cloak of immunity and its stamp of approval on adultery." It was only a matter of time, he suggested, before the Court was approving "sexual perversion" and "bestiality," two items which up to that point had been mentioned by no one on or off the Court but Eastland.

On the death of McCarthy in 1957, Eastland became the nation's number-one patriot, his only rival being William Jenner, who was to retire the next year. Having learned so much from his fallen comrade, he could be expected to eulogize McCarthy as needing no "vindication and no justification before the bar of ultimate justice and the throne of his God. His heart was pure: his purpose was noble."

Equally pure of heart, Eastland was the Senate watchdog to protect individual licenses. His was the loudest voice raised in the Senate against the federal marshals' treatment of townspeople in Clinton, Tennessee.

When local thugs attempted to block integration despite a court injunction prohibiting force, marshals threw them in irons. Eastland saw this as unnecessarily harsh treatment for contempt, but when other senators entreated him to read into the record an explanation from the marshals for using irons, he refused to do so, saying he would stand on the description of the incident supplied by the attorney for the arrested fifteen men—"a very able, very responsible, very respectable, and one of the ablest trial lawyers in the United States." The attorney so applauded was Ross Barnett, representing the Clinton defendants at his own expense.

That wasn't Eastland's only statement on Clinton. When the county attorney went to the Clinton High School and explained to the students that the court's injunction applied to them too; that it meant the court would no longer tolerate "throwing of ink on books, books belonging to the state of Tennessee, the messing up of lockers, the threatening notes to teachers, the filthy language to fellow students, the pushing and shoving of other students [Negroes]," and that they could no longer gather in gangs and beat Negroes going to and from school, Eastland wailed: "These children have been told by responsible authority that they had no freedom of speech, they had no freedom of assembly . . . and that their minor peccadilloes and misconduct" would be punished. "Neither Hitler nor Stalin was ever guilty of more ruthless thought control."

In the field of civil rights, Eastland has preached resistance to law—sometimes in the form of individual defiance, sometimes as legislative interposition or nullification—but not hypocritically, for he has preached it as much in Washington as in Sunflower County.

His counsel was especially inflammatory in the periods leading up to two of the worst outbreaks of racial violence—at Little Rock and later at the University of Mississippi. Much has been written, quite justifiably, about the influence of Georgia king-maker Roy Harris and Georgia Governor Marvin Griffin on Arkansas Governor Orval Faubus in inciting him. Strangely, however, little credit has been given to Eastland for his effect on Faubus. Inasmuch as Eastland's advice came from next door, not three states away, it was probably even more effective than that of Harris or Griffin.

To hear Eastland talk—as he did talk to organizations all over the South—about "weak-kneed politicians in the border states," the segregation battle in the South depended solely on Faubus' standing firm. "If the southern states are picked off one by one under the damnable doctrine of gradualism," he told the American Legion at Tupelo, shaking his head like a distress lantern, "I don't know if we can hold out or not." Oh, it sure made him depressed to even think of Faubus who, he predicted, "will not take action and, as a result, racial integration has already started." Apprised of Eastland's comments, Faubus of course said he was not a weak-kneed politician and he would, too, take action.

When Eastland first "took up" international affairs, he followed a path already beaten by other senators from the Deep South—straight to Generalissimo Rafael Trujillo. Eastland became one of the Senate's most outspoken defenders of the Dominican Republic. On a goodwill tour of that country, Eastland and Jenner were invited to speak to the legislature. They competed to see who could praise more richly. Jenner said that because the Generalissimo had refused to "drift with the tide," he had turned the Dominican Republic into an "island paradise." But Eastland easily won the contest of praise. "Your Generalissimo," he told a legislature that for thirty years had been too terrified to act as anything but Trujillo's rubber stamp, "is one of the great men of the free world. With him leading your government, this leader of all Latin America—you lead for freedom; you lead for honor; you lead for religion; and thank God you lead for common sense."

Later on, when he began to feel that he really knew something about foreign affairs, Eastland would warn the Senate against admitting Hawaii to the Union because "the economy of Hawaii is communist-controlled." Furthermore, he said, the commies had taken over the Hawaiian legislature. When other senators pointed out that the FBI had made a detailed study of possible communist infiltration into Hawaii and had found that there was a maximum of between forty and sixty communists out of a population of 635,000, Eastland retorted: "What is there in numbers? We have seen, all over the world, a small minority of communists taking over one country after another." (Just as, one might have added, a small minority of the electorate sends him to the Senate each six years.)

By this time, such was the reputation throughout the country of Mississippi's senator, that when Meade Alcorn, Republican national chairman, and Paul M. Butler, Democratic chairman, agreed in 1958 to wage a fair campaign and avoid using vilifications and scurrilous attacks, they could not come to terms on whether mention of Eastland and Faubus as Democrats fell within that definition. Alcorn said he thought it wasn't exactly vilification to remind the public that Eastland wore the Democratic label, but Butler protested that it was hitting below the belt.

It is likely that Eastland would have turned out to be much the same person he is today, McCarthy or no McCarthy. Acting independently, he proved his own mettle in the election of 1954, the only real challenge— and it was not great—he has had since he beat Doxey.

It came from the late Lieutenant Governor Carroll Gartin, a kind of moderate. Tired of his largely nondescript life in the Senate, Eastland had said he wasn't going to run in 1953. By the time he changed his mind, a lot of people had got behind Gartin. The Lieutenant Governor would not have been there to get behind if he hadn't been snookered into running by James Coleman, who wanted him out of the way of his own ambitions. Coleman got Governor Hugh White to run a survey on Gartin's strength, and it showed—thanks to some interpretation by Coleman—that Gartin would carry three-fourths of Mississippi's eighty-two counties.

"Nobody," said one of Eastland's aides, laughing at the memory, "nobody but a goose would have believed the survey. I could have named thirty counties that would have voted for Eastland if his name was just on the ballot, no matter what kind of campaign he ran."

Eastland won all but twelve counties, and he lost three of those by fewer than 100 votes. It was a good test of Eastland's popularity. In Ruleville, which he sometimes calls home, he lost only two votes out of 500, and as one Eastland aficionado pointed out with justification, "It's pretty hard not to make at least a dozen enemies in a town like this."

Popularity is perhaps not exactly the right word for it. Eastland may sometimes arouse a tenuous identification with the masses, but he is no "popular" campaigner in the manner of Eugene Talmadge or James Folsom or, going back to his own state, Theodore Bilbo. He has no flair, but only the sureness of a native son in voicing the meanness the rednecks feel.

In the 1954 campaign Eastland took his place just below Vardaman and Barnett as a true-blue demagogue, but, then, the times were made for him. His campaign opened only a few days after the Supreme Court handed down its school-desegregating decision in the Brown case—"Black Monday" in Mississippi.

At once he was inciting defiance. "I know that southern people, by and large, will neither recognize, abide by nor comply with this decision," he said. "We are expected to remain docile while the pure blood of the South is mongrelized by the barter of our heritage by northern politicians in order to secure political favors from red mongrels in the slums of the East and Middle West."

Again and again he repeated the boast first made at his old home town of Forest, his face filling with blood as he leaned across the rostrum and rasped out an account of his negative powers:

"After 1950 they [that is, the civil rights measures] were blocked in the Civil Rights Committee. Do you know why? Because of seniority I was maneuvered into chairmanship of the Civil Rights Subcommittee. Yes . . . Eastland of Mississippi [tapping his chest] . . . became boss of the committee that had all of the civil rights bills! And they said I broke the law and so I did! You know the laws says the committee has got to meet once a week. Why, for the three years I was chairman, that committee didn't hold a meeting. I didn't permit them to meet. I had to protect the interest of the people of Mississippi. I had special pockets put in my pants and for three years I carried those bills around in my pockets everywhere I went and every one of them was defeated!"

Today his aide Buckley, who was formerly Senator Pat Harrison's aide, feels that history of that sort should be edited and revised.

"That talk of a pocket for the civil rights bills was just campaign talk," says Buckley. "He used to say, 'I'm going to get my wife to make a larger pocket. I'm going to have her sew 'em up in there.' That was just campaign talk. Confidentially, we *did* play on race in '54.

" 'Course, Eastland was nothing like Vardaman, who used to talk about God's making niggers from an ape's skull, and a frog for the nose, and a skunk for the armpit, and the ashes of hell for color. But anyway, what a man says in a campaign is one thing, what he does up there in Washington is another."

Buckley's argument would be more convincing if Eastland had not filled the Washington air during the closing years of the war—when he was not running for office and therefore not being called on for any special theatrics—with statements about the Negro's physical, moral and mental inferiority.

Speaking of the Negro soldier, he had said: "He has disgraced the flag of his country. He will not fight. He will not work. Yet we give him preference. We discriminate against the white soldier in order to get some Negro votes."

This was not just talk to please the home folks. Buckley says that Eastland advised General Dwight Eisenhower privately to put Negro soldiers in work battalions, not on the front lines, because they couldn't be trusted, "and Eisenhower did, though he denies it now."

His contempt for the Negro cannot be blamed on war-torn nerves. Two years after the war he was still saying, "The mental level of those people renders them incapable of suffrage." And in the same period he said that Mississippi didn't need a poll tax because, "If southern states wished to do so, all they would have to do to confine their electors to one race would be to provide that no man who had been convicted of bigamy or unlawful cohabitation, or who was guilty of adultery, should vote. That would give us an iron-clad control over our elections."

Nor was Eastland's advice to flout the Supreme Court's decision "just campaign talk," as Buckley insists. In 1955, a year after he had been re-elected, Eastland was still advising the Mississippi White Citizens Councils, and the South Carolina Association of Citizens Councils, and the Patriots of North Carolina, and many nameless groups across the South: "Southern people will not be violating the Constitution or the law when they defy this monstrous decision. They will be defying those who would destroy our system of government. You are not required to obey any court which passes out such a ruling.

"In fact, you are obligated to defy it. The law is what the people make it, and a ruling is no more than public sentiment makes it."

And in his most famous speech before the Senate—a speech that has been reprinted and, according to Eastland, put into more than a million hands—he said:

"The question is asked, will the South obey this decision of the Supreme Court [the Brown Decision]? Who is obligated morally or legally to obey a decision whose authorities rest not upon the law but upon the writings and teachings of pro-communist agitators and people who have a long record of affiliations with anti-American causes and with agitators who are part and parcel of the communist conspiracy to destroy our country?"

The favorite son of Sunflower County won again in '66 because he was running against a dull Republican nobody, Congressman Prentiss Walker, a chicken farmer whose political career flowered in Goldwaterism. The Eastland-Walker race had its lighter side, as each man tried to get Mississippians to set sanity aside long enough to look upon the other as an integrationist. Walker appointed a Negro to the Air Force Academy —by mistake—but Walker, who is the friend of no one in Washington even approaching the seat of power, had the advantage in one respect, in being able to allude to Eastland's sometime friendship with that old renegade President Johnson; he also mailed out thousands of picture postcards showing Eastland with his arm around Bobby Kennedy (surely dating from the era when Bobby was an aide to Eastland's late pal, Senator Joe McCarthy).

Just to play it safe, Eastland opened the campaign season by introducing legislation to replace the almost demolished Internal Security Act of 1950 with a stiff anti-subversive law. But for some reason, the old Eastland fervor seemed to be missing from this electioneering gimmickry. Once again he took the floor to name a long list of "subversives," but the flabbiness of this pitch became quickly apparent when the best he could denounce were those who had participated in a "sing-in for peace" at Carnegie Hall.

He is a political worrier. After one of his campaign spiels to the home-folks, he turned to a bystander, within earshot of *The Washington Post's* Andrew Glass, and asked plaintively, "Wouldn't you say that was a thoroughly reactionary speech? I don't see how the Republicans can get to the right of that."

There are politicians in Mississippi who *could* have given him trouble. Eastland has a wide following but does not command deep political loyalties; nor has he given much loyalty, either to party or to individual politicians, except for the last governor of Mississippi, through whom he discharged the debt he owed Paul Johnson's father for appointing him to the Senate. Eastland even spoke for Governor Johnson in his last campaign: an unusually energetic show of commitment. The ties between Eastland and Mississippi's junior senator, John Stennis, reportedly came close to fraying when, a few years ago, Ross Barnett talked of running against Stennis, and Eastland did nothing to silence him.

In reality a partyless politician, he has not since 1948 cleanly broken with the National Democratic Party. That year, spouting the Calhoun nonsense about how to force the Democratic Party to come begging simply by refusing to vote the ticket, Eastland went Dixiecrat.

He never again made that mistake, though he did nothing in 1964 to try to change the course of a white electorate that gave 87 percent of its support (in some areas of the state 95 percent)—highest in the nation— to Barry Goldwater. He simply kept quiet, at least publicly, as did Stennis. But even silence from the South is sometimes appreciated in Washington;

today they are the only Mississippians in the capital with any power, although of course the power they share is quite enough for a state of only slightly more than 2 million people. Stennis is the chief pork barreler for the state, being second only to Richard Russell on the Armed Services Committee and ranking high enough on the Appropriations and the Aeronautical and Space Science Committees to keep NASA money flowing into Mississippi. Eastland's share of the power depends almost entirely on his ability to exert a negative influence and in that regard he seems to be dropping off sharply.

In recent years he has apparently given up trying to fill a role he once fancied for himself, that of the Great Arouser. Describing himself as "with a fever, weak, and can hardly stand up now," Eastland staggered to the Senate floor in 1948 and sounded the call: "The South is a sleeping giant. We hold the balance of power in this country. We can save the country. There must be a grass-roots organization in every hamlet of the South. The people must be informed of the dangers involved and of the results if the South is crushed. This all-southern organization must be pushed. There must be mass meetings. The people are ready! The South can be saved!"

Despite his fevered heroism, the nation wasn't saved that round, and neither was the South, but six years later Eastland was ready to try again, this time linking his talents with those of other southern leaders such as Strom Thurmond, John Bell Williams, L. Mendel Rivers, William M. Tuck, Fielding Wright, Herman Talmadge, Sam Jones and Coke Stevenson. This was the Memphis meeting where, to nobody's surprise, the chairman of the executive committee turned out to be none other than that old faithful alarmist John U. Barr, the New Orleans industrialist who was a prime mover in everything from the Dixiecrat movement to the campaign (conducted in league with Clarence Manion) to offer the nation T. Coleman Andrews for President.

That organization didn't catch on at all, but meanwhile Eastland was busy on the establishment of the White Citizens Councils of America—same goals, same leaders (for a while), same format—in Indianola, Jackson and other points in the South. Of all his organizational efforts, this one alone can claim to be in even moribund condition. The Citizens Council feels no gratitude to Eastland for its survival, though he did try to keep an alliance with it through favors, and in the past couple of years he has been subjected to the irony of being criticized by the Council and the Klan for not doing all he could do to stave off integration. Shaken by the virulence of this grass-roots criticism, Eastland imported Wallace from Alabama and Leander Perez from Louisiana to support him during his 1966 election and certify him as a true-blue reactionary.

In this groping about for something to lean on there is a very true symptom of Eastland's declining role in American life. The Citizens Council and the Klan have grounds to complain, not because of what he has failed to do, but because Eastland has done all that he can do. The nation may have to go on living with Judge Harold Cox for some time, but the nation is not likely to be forced to take another like him. James P. Coleman was not Eastland's choice for the Fifth Circuit Court of Appeals. No man who as governor of Mississippi had said "We cannot defeat the whole nation" would be Eastland's choice, but after talking it over with Senator Stennis, Eastland knew that Coleman was the best— or worst—judge Congress would accept from Mississippi, so he went along with the nomination. Even that much compromise indicates a withering away of Eastlandism.

He has had his period of negative strength, although even that has been exaggerated: mutilated and late, some civil rights bills nevertheless eventually, and regularly, reached the Senate floor despite Eastland's efforts to stop them in committee. Now there is scarcely anything left to stop. In 1966 he went around the countryside boasting that his committee was the "graveyard of civil rights bills," but he failed to mention that the voting rights legislation of 1965 was sent to his committee marked with a specific return date, rendering him powerless, and when Congress wants to do more for civil rights, it can be done in the same way. His Committee is no longer a hurdle for such civil rights legislation as a majority of the Senate wants passed; it is an ashcan for bills that a majority of the Senate finds troublesome, such as open-housing bills. He is no longer a weapon for the Klan but a tool of timid, middle-class suburbanites everywhere, which, however rude they can sometimes be, usually stop short of lynching.

In the Internal Security Subcommittee, he had his fling as the grand inquisitor, but of late the appellate courts have indicated they will hold him down to being merely a pest. When he talks of forcing all Americans to wear an exit permit when they cross their national border, and to forbid all world travel to "certain classes" of Americans, not many take him seriously; not many know how to take him at all when he charges that the FBI is sometimes used "in furthering the leftist revolution."

Old friends, old allies are falling away. An increasing number of Eastland's colleagues on the Judiciary Committee—including even that rational segregationist Sam Ervin of North Carolina—are racing to see who can most speedily dissociate himself from the Eastland-Sourwine position. When an Internal Security Subcommittee publication identified the American Friends Service Committee as "a well-known transmission belt for the communist apparatus," the sharpest denunciations came from within the committee itself.

It will take time—time first of all to forget some of the heartache that his leadership has brought—but by and by the nation will again be able to see Eastland as the pathetic absurdity he really is but does not mean to be. What has Mississippi left in him? One vote, and the native talent to stand straightfaced and without embarrassment before the Senate and predict: "Some day, Mr. President, the people of this nation will come to realize what they owe to the people of Mississippi. . . ."

An Interlude: God and Bob Jones University

> This war we're in [over desegregation] is basically a
> fight between the believers in a Supreme Being and
> the atheists.
>
> *Senator J. Strom Thurmond*

When Henry James said that one is as unlikely to find Christianity in American life as to find a centerpiece on a billiard table, he could not have been speaking of the Deep South or of Fundamentalism, the Deep South's favorite brand of Christianity. It is everywhere and seeps into everything, but especially into politics, and it goes much, much deeper than protests of a dramatic but superficial type, as when Cotton Ed Smith walked out of the 1944 convention to protest a Negro minister's giving the invocation.

In the back country they may quarrel over foot washing and using the single cup, and in the cities they may split over immersion and Arminianism, but when it gets down to the spiritual nutcutting, an impressive majority stands four-square together against the anti-Christ of liberalism that seeks man's perfectibility through his own efforts; stands four-square for the God who created the world in six days without the aid of evolution or urban renewal.

These are not snake handlers, operating along the keening edge of religious hysteria. They are the intellectually and emotionally flat-footed middle class, from millhands to merchants, and they are not looked upon as queer or rare, because in their neck of the woods they are not.

216

These people will not, in our lifetime, give up. And the reason why they do not give up, the reason why the problems that confront the Deep South today are not much different from what they were sixty years ago, is that these southerners are not just waging a political and economic war against change—although they are waging that, too—but a religious war.

Nowhere is this more impressively demonstrated than at Bob Jones University in Greenville, South Carolina, whose directors include Senator Strom Thurmond and Congressman William Jennings Bryan Dorn (S.C.). Bob Jones University's ministerial graduates preach to an estimated one million Americans every Sunday (5,000 preachers with an average congregation of at least 200), not to mention the many millions these ministers reach via radio programs each week, and the 800 missionaries in ninety foreign countries who supply the world with one image of America.

"If you would take the preachers that this school has put into the pulpits of America out of the pulpits," an executive of the school told me, "and remove from the mission field the graduates of the school who are serving the Lord there, there would be a tremendous void created in the realm of Biblical Christianity." There would indeed.

Bob Jones University bills itself as "the world's most unusual university," and when one measures it against what normally passes as higher education in this country, the title hardly seems excessive.

It is not so much a college as a bastion. In the minds of those who run Bob Jones University—which, for all practical purposes, means Bob Jones, Jr., Bob Jones, III, and Bob (Lefty) Johnson, lifetime business manager—this school is the last strong campus outpost of Fundamental Christianity. Wheaton College also makes that claim, but in recent years Christians who keep track of such things have begun to suspect that Wheaton harbors a professor or two who believe in evolution. If that is true, Bob Jones University may properly claim today to be foremost among the nation's Fundamentalist colleges. Its mission: to turn out men and women graduates who will oppose liberalism in all forms.

There are other colleges which share its beliefs and follow them faithfully, but none of these can rival BJU in size—3,500 students; or in wealth, which is sufficient to give the Joneses will power to refuse a $2-million grant offered them by a tobacco-family foundation. Nor can these others match it in renown. This is the school that dismissed Billy Graham as a student for breaking rules, later gave him an honorary Ph.D., then reversed itself again and damned him as a heretic in an argument that still rattles the Fundamentalist world. This is the school that counts Governor George Wallace among its illustrious honorary alumni, and among its more illustrious directors George Grant (who, until the Republican fluke threw him out of office, was Alabama's most conservative congressman), and U.S. Senator Frank Carlson of Kansas, the dedicated Baptist who sometimes presides at those Washington prayer breakfasts for President Johnson.

The late Bob Jones, the founder (who frequently referred to himself in just that way: The Founder), was the greatest evangelist of his day, and his day was that of Billy Sunday. The Reverend Sunday was, despite a lot of ex post facto character building, more acrobat than minister. Jones was the real thing: by the time he was forty, he had converted a million people. And when he hit a town, things happened. People didn't just march down to the mourners' bench for an evening's catharsis and then forget it. The fear of God hung over the community long after the Reverend Jones had departed. When he preached in Dothan, Alabama, the people decided to close the brewery, although it was their chief industry. Fifty years later it is still closed.

But in the late 1920's, evangelism had passed its heyday; it was, in fact, beginning to get a shopworn reputation. That's when the Reverend Jones "got the call" to become an educator. He opened a college in Panama City, Florida, but the 1929 crash wiped it out. He opened again in Cleveland, Tennessee, and had built up an establishment worth $2,250,000 before he sold out thirteen years later and moved to Greenville, South Carolina—enticed there in part by an offer from Greenville business leaders of 185 acres on the outskirts of town.

One of the most apparent defects of Fundamentalism is that, like John Wayne impersonating a Roman soldier at the Crucifixion, it runs to vulgarities: religious art that glows in the dark, rinky-tink hymns. In an incongruous way, BJU tries to move against this tendency: incongruous because, although the school rails against the world's depravity and the degeneracy of man, it promotes activities that would attract the worldly. It has a cinema department that ranks just behind USC's and UCLA's (though, of course, no BJU graduate would seek a Hollywood career); a music department equipped with 100 pianos and twelve organs; and an art gallery that offers a sprinkling of Botticelli, Tintoretto and Titian.

The arty touch is brought to fruition in Dr. Bob Jones, Jr., the fifty-

eight-year-old balding president of BJU, who considers himself quite a
Shakespearean actor and assigns himself a top role in almost every play
the school puts on. As a dying Lear, he can mutter a creditable "Pray
you, undo this button," but when he mounts the political pulpit critics
sometimes seem to detect a note of meanness and arrogance, in statements
such as: "I am not so disturbed about the enemy bombs that may be
dropped upon our American cities as I am about the termites of moral
decay in the foundation of our American society." But his oratorical style
sometimes flits off in other directions, and he can just as easily sound
downright precious, as in one sermon when he described a Biblical scene
in these terms:

> [John] saw the face of the ocean in its laughing mood when
> little wavelets, like frisky kittens, romped with strands of seaweed
> about the angles of the beach. On stormy nights, John, by light-
> ning's flashes, glimpsed the bosom of the sea heaving in anger
> beneath the insults of the wind and the lashing of the tempest. He
> watched the pouting tides pull their lacy gowns of foam about them,
> turn their backs, and sulk away from the beach. He watched the
> enamored billows fling themselves upon the rocky breast of those
> chaste shores and, being repulsed, die of love unrequited, to be
> trampled underfoot of their fellow waves as they in their turn
> rushed up to kiss the sands.

It is a style that would have made the old evangelical roarers gift their
teeth.

And then there is Bob, III, thirtyish vice president of the school and
expertly versed in the policy. He runs the school when his father is out of
town, which is three-fourths of the time.

It is not quite enough to say the Joneses run the place; they permeate
it. When students or faculty quit the school, they will as often as not assign
as one of their main reasons a disgust at what they felt was a deification
of the Jones family. "Standing up for Dr. Jones" is common calisthenics
at BJU. On the other hand, many of the alumni are quite content to pay
almost worshipful respect to the Joneses. One alumnus told me, "If I were
on the other side of the globe and Dr. Bob told me to come, I would put
down whatever I had at hand, and leave immediately."

For such dominating educators, the Joneses do not have the best
credentials, as the world goes. Mostly they are laden with honorary degrees from such places as John Brown University, Siloam Springs, Arkan-

sas, and Muskingum College, New Concord, Ohio. But they can afford to take whatever sneers are directed at them on that score. How many other college executives own the establishment, lock, stock and Bible—a $28-million going concern—which they can sell whenever they want to move on?

In that $28-million bundle are two radio stations, including one of the most powerful FM stations in the Southeast, sending out classical music, gospel music (but no crass foot-stomping singing, like the Stamps-Baxter outfit), Bible messages and, almost as important in a religious way, messages from such eminent right wingers as Carl McIntire, Billy James Hargis (who has an honorary Ph.D. from Bob Jones), Dan Smoot, Major Edgar Bundy and Howard Kershner. Not to mention frequent religio-political tidings from the Joneses themselves.

BJU is an object of amusement even to some hard-shell Methodists and Baptists, largely because of its strictness and because of the inbred quality of its faculty. Of about 150 regular faculty, only ten hold doctorates, and of these, four got their Ph.D.'s at Bob Jones University. BJU officials long ago learned that the best way to find teachers who believe as the BJU administration believes, and who are willing to submit to the regimen of the campus, is to train their own. Only twenty members of the faculty failed to take at least some of their studies at BJU, and most of the faculty got degrees from there.

Appropriately, since the Jones family controls the school with a firm hand, there is a dominating "family" atmosphere about the place. As part of their pay, the faculty is given room and board. When a husband is hired to teach, his wife is under contract, too—to work however she can. Teachers are paid according to their needs; an instructor with four children will earn more than a professor without a family.

No one goes to Bob Jones to teach without knowing what awaits him, but even among the initiates the air sometimes gets too thick, and some of those who leave are highly critical of what they left behind. Dr. Bob, Jr., has a word to say about that kind of apostate: "We fired a fellow from Bob Jones University once. He went out and said we were all crooked here. Looks to me like if he were an honest man he would have quit long ago rather than work with crooks. Brother, if we were crooked and he knew it, and still stayed on all those years, he was guilty as we are."

This professor had been fired for voicing criticisms. The first and most important rule at BJU, for both faculty and students, is: *No griping*. Dr.

Bob, Sr., was fond of telling the BJU students in chapel, "If you don't like it here you can pack your dirty duds and hit the four-lane highway." Faculty members who get out of line can be fired on ten days' notice. Dr. Bob, Jr., says: "We do not believe that a man in this school which has taken the Biblical position in every particular, right down to the tales of creation, we do not believe it is a just usage of the term academic freedom for a man to be able to say in the name of academic freedom, 'I'm going to teach evolution or free love in this school.' Academic freedom here boils down to the ability to say anything you want to say so long as it doesn't offend the Bible. We wouldn't tolerate any teaching in this school that was opposed to the Biblical position."

The regimentation of the faculty, however, is lightweight compared to the rules that run the student body.

A student who is merely caught inside—not necessarily buying anything, just inside—any of a dozen anathematized stores near the campus is automatically dismissed from BJU. These are stores—drugstores and grocery stores, as well as eateries—that obtained liquor licenses over the protests of the college. Also the students are *not* allowed to:

> Listen to jazz on the radio, or sing or play it themselves.
> Go into the gym in mixed groups.
> Date off-campus without written permission.
> Sit or lie down on blankets anywhere on the 185-acre campus.
> Leave the campus after 10:30 p.m.
> Borrow anything from townspeople.
> Release any information to newspapers without getting it approved by the administration.

In addition, there are some general regulations for everyone. Students are warned that anybody who "occupies his time excessively with games such as checkers, chess, puzzles" will be considered "irresponsible" and kicked out of school. Cards are absolutely taboo—even "Wheaton poker" (rook). Freshmen women may have two dates a week, sophomores, three a week, juniors, four, and seniors can date as often as they please. But "date"—except by special permission and with chaperon—means on-campus, and it also means for no more than two hours. Couples aren't allowed to stroll around the campus holding hands, either. (And remember: *No blankets.*) If they aren't attending a concert or other campus activity, they may sit down and talk in the student lounge—always keeping a six-inch space between their bodies on the couch.

Male freshmen may leave the campus three times a week in the daytime (checking out first), and liberties are moderately increased over the next three years. Freshmen must go in pairs, to chaperon one another.

The parade-ground crackle is awesome. Students rise with a bell, and go to sleep with a bell; they must attend all chapels; they must go to all meals; they must study at certain times and not study at certain other times; they must wear certain clothing (stockings for the girls at all times; for the boys, ties to class, coats at evening meal); girls must not loiter in the halls; and all classes must open with a prayer, and all discussion groups close with a prayer.

The school administration admits that only students with the most Christian grace will last beyond their freshman year, but those who do, says The Founder, are well rewarded: "If you ever feed on heavenly manna, garlic and onions can never taste good any more. If you go back from Bob Jones University after all that you get here and feed on the husks that the swine eat, you'll be like the prodigal son. It won't satisfy your hunger."

These regulations of time and place are as nothing compared to the regulations of thought, which are considered quite normal by an administration that at the same time describes the National Council of Churches as "a totalitarian group, just as dictatorial as Rome itself." In the light of that condemnation, the regulations could appear hypocritical; actually they are entirely consistent with the regional impulses to balk at every order that comes from a foreign source (Washington, say) while demanding strict adherence within the region to every communal tradition.

Dr. Bob, III, says proudly: "We're unusual in our objectives to teach the student *what he believes*. Most schools would be appalled at this statement, but committed as we are, we don't throw out a bunch of theories to them about the religions of the world and philosophy and this sort of thing."

Put in another way, the college teaches its graduates to act from pre-thought, not to think. As Dr Bob, Sr., was fond of saying: "This is not the age of the *thinker;* it's the age of the *doer*. If you try to think crossing a highway or street, some fool will run over you." And the best way to insure that their graduates act in a prescribed way is to spend four years, as the president says, "teaching them what they think." Leave no doubt about it, for, as Dr. Bob, Jr., counseled one chapel group, "What's doubtful is dirty."

Large corporations reportedly are wild about the Joneses' well-drilled graduates, who stay at their desks until the factory whistle blows, do not gripe about management policies, do not loiter around the water fountain, and obey all office rules. "I've had Bendix recruiters tell me they would much rather come here than go to Harvard or Yale," said Dr. Bob, III.

But the mold of institutional conformity does not extend to the institution itself. Because of rampant inbreeding, lack of Ph.D.'s on the faculty, shortage of curriculum, and methods of paying its teachers, the school could never win accreditation by a regional college association. But even if it could, the Joneses would refuse to belong, because, says Dr. Bob, Jr., "They dictate your administrative policies to you pretty much. One of our objectives has been *individuality* in education."

It goes without saying that a BJU graduate does not go out into the world marked by what Arnold called "the sweet reasonableness of Jesus," for that was not the purpose of his four-years' training. Right is right and wrong is wrong, so why be reasonable about it? Dr. Bob, III, does not dodge the point. He acknowledges that BJU students, faculty and graduates deserve to be called zealots and, in fact, views the term with favor:

> A man ought to be zealous for what he believes, when his belief is founded in the word of God, which is unfailing. Yes, like Goldwater, yes, that's right, that's right. There's nothing wrong with being an extremist. Look at the communists. You'd certainly have to say they're extreme. They lay down their life for the cause of godless communism. Anything for the state. Why shouldn't a man who has been given the gift of eternal life by Jesus Christ be ten times more zealous in the spread of the gospel? There's nothing wrong with being extreme in the cause of right.

This certitude sets the BJU student aside as a man to be reckoned with. One boy, hitchhiking back to BJU for the fall term, was picked up by an Episcopal minister, who had his car radio tuned to a jazz program. Without asking permission, the BJU student switched off the radio and launched out in a talk meant to liberate the Episcopal priest from his sinful ways. And this boy was not even a ministerial student. The ministerial students are something else again. In a typical year they distribute a quarter-million Bible tracts, hold 30,000 services in churches around Greenville (sometimes irritating the resident pastor by criticizing him), stop an estimated 80,000 citizens on the street—or roust them out of their homes—to talk to them about their need of Christ. They are relentless.

Founder Jones, who enjoys creating "sayings," frequently said, and his disciples repeat after him, "You can go as far as you like with a man of good will down the same road without compromising. Compromising begins when you go a step down the wrong road." And that, the Joneses will tell you, is why today they are the harshest opponents of the Reverend Billy Graham. He went down the wrong road; he compromised by getting on the platform with unbelievers, even with Catholics. For a while they were all for him; that was back in the days when Billy had the blessings of such men as the Reverend Bell Riley, the anti-Semitic, anti-Catholic war horse of Fundamentalism. Billy sounded all right then, and even up through the early 1950's when he was helping McCarthyism along with observations such as, "Over 1,100 social-sounding organizations are communist or communist-operated in this country. They control the minds of a great segment of our people. . . ." He sounded all right to the Fundamentalists when, to the joy of the industrialists who were moving into the South in a big way, he described the Garden of Eden as a place where there were "no union dues, no labor leaders, no snakes, no disease."

But anyone who lives by passing the plate among variegated cultures knows when to change, and that's Billy. These days he not only speaks to integrated crowds, he insists that they be integrated. These days he says pleasant things about the National Council of Churches, and cottons up to Cardinal Cushing.

If these actions disappointed most Fundamentalists, they downright infuriated the Joneses. The Founder, who tempered his crustiness with a balanced sentence, said he once told Graham, "To be an evangelist, the Lord wants a man to have brains in his head, grace in his heart, and guts in his belly—and you don't have any of them." The Joneses take turns ridiculing Graham for all sorts of things, some illusionary, some real enough: he spends more money on advertising than Barnum & Bailey; his original revival in Los Angeles, the one that first won him national fame, would have failed but for the prompted "testimony" of gambling, horseracing movie star Stuart Hamblen; the head count of the "saved" at Graham's revivals is phony because he plants workers throughout the audience who go down, at a ratio of two to one, with the people who surrender to Christ.

When the Joneses started to oppose Graham, around 1955, "our own friends thought we had gone absolutely berserk," says Dr. Bob, III, but now many Fundamentalists agree with the Jones position. Ask them for a formal stamp of shame, and they will call Graham "leader of the new evangelical movement." That may not sound especially damaging outside the Bible Belt because those who take religion in a relaxed way may find it hard to understand just how violently critical of the "new" evangelicals the Joneses and their followers can be. With them it is a matter of e-ter-nal damnation and no fooling. After pointing out that communism, in its effort to conquer the world, is using the Russian army, the fifth column and collaborators, Dr. Bob, Jr., draws this analogy: "Satan in his war against God and His word uses three similar forces . . . Modernism, Neo-orthodoxy and the New Evangelicalism. Of these three, the last group is the most dangerous." That's what they think of Billy. And if these Goldwater supporters had any doubts about whether they might have been doing Billy Graham an injustice, all misgivings were dispelled when they saw him praying over Johnson's inauguration. That old devil compromise had won again.

The last time I talked to Dr. Bob, III, he seemed troubled by the direction of some of my questions. "Please let me make it clear," he said, "that Bob Jones University is not a political partisan institution. We have both Democrats and Republicans on our faculty and represented in the student body. We believe in the old-fashioned, Christian Americanism which made this country great—those principles of freedom of thought and expression, of personal integrity, strength of character, freedom for all, pride of nation, et cetera. Because we believe strongly in these things, we desire to see them maintained, *but we do not play politics here at Bob Jones University.*"

BJU, which he says does not play politics and certainly not partisan politics, holds Americanism conferences now and then. At a recent one, Arkansas ex-Representative Dale Alford spoke on "States' Rights"; Dr. Billy James Hargis spoke on "The President—Ignorant or Untruthful? The Facts on the Danger from Communist Infiltration"; Harry T. Everingham (president of We, the People) spoke on "The United Nations, Socialist Trap for American Freedom," and Dan Smoot spoke on "Liberalism." Earlier Americanism conferences were similarly oriented.

When Governor George Wallace of Alabama was awarded his honorary doctorate from BJU, Dr. Bob, Jr., praised him as "a David warring against the giant, Tyranny. Men who have fought for truth and righteousness have always been slandered, maligned and misrepresented, but you, Mr. Governor, have demonstrated by your overwhelming victories that there is still in America love for freedom, hard common sense and at least some hope for the preservation of our constitutional liberties."

Early in 1963, Dr. Bob, Jr., wrote to every student at the college:

> If the Peace Corps were in the hands of honest, able, and intelligent men and if the Administration were trustworthy and would not take the attitude that lying is a legitimate tool of government, the idea of the Peace Corps might be basically a good thing. However, unfortunately the situation is entirely different. The President's brother-in-law is the head of the Peace Corps, which has been made, in effect, a sort of personal army for the promotion of the Administration's impractical, unrealistic, and unsound philosophy. . . . In Latin America it is being used to work with Roman Catholic schools and organizations and is, therefore, promoting the worst kind of religious totalitarianism while politically it represents the most liberal point of view.*

Despite this seeming evidence to the contrary, Dr. Bob, III, is trying to tell the truth when he says the college does not play politics. If it does not *sound* like the truth, that is only because he illustrates in a perfect manner what I said at the outset: In the Deep South—or wherever Fundamentalists operate, for that matter—politics and religion are so closely intertwined that sincere, honest fellows like the Joneses can play the devil out of politics and think they are just minding their Scriptural business.

"Our graduates are not crusaders against social depravity and political injustice," says Dr. Bob, III, with what may seem strange candor. "They are warriors against sin, and the Scripture refers to the Christian life many times as a spiritual warfare. So our efforts are not primarily for the purpose of making a better world, but rather to spread the good news of salvation. . . . When we deal in social and political matters, we deal only where they have some bearing upon the work we are doing and upon the lives and interests of individual, born-again Christians."

Who can unscramble that kind of thinking? Shake the kaleidoscope of politics ever so slightly and it begins to look like a baptismal.

---

* When this letter came to the attention of Bill Moyers, then deputy director of the Peace Corps and later one of LBJ's top aides, his diplomatic poise slipped a bit. He responded in a letter to Dr. Bob, Jr., calling him an "uninformed, prejudiced, arrogant, self-righteous and immature character" who resorted to "trash." Dr. Bob, Jr., replied that it was "time some of you arrogant, highhanded, and radical bullies got it through your thick heads. . . ." and circulated copies of the exchange very widely. Nothing nourishes the reputation of a Fundamentalist like a good fuss.

In a rather noted radio exhortation to the Negroes, The Founder once said:

> You might be over there in the jungles of Africa today, un-saved. But you are here in America where you have your own schools and your own churches and your own liberties and your own rights, with certain restrictions that God Almighty put about you—restrictions that are in line with the Word of God.

That is nonlanguage at its purest and most childlike: *"Your own liberties and your own rights with certain restrictions."* This is the logic of nonlogic, and it puts an entirely different complexion on what, coming from one less committed, would sound like racism: "If you are against segregation and against racial separation, then you are against God Almighty because He made racial separation. . . . It is no accident that most of the Chinese live in China. It is not an accident that most Japanese live in Japan. . . ."

Using nonlanguage, the Fundamentalists can sneak up on you pretty close before you know what they have in mind. Dr. Bob, III, started off on the subject of race:

> I don't want you to . . . don't misconstrue this as an attack upon the Negro—it's not. We love the Negro people. Some of the finest Christians I've ever known were Negroes. In fact, they put me to shame. And I have looked at several Negro Christians and wished to God I could be as Christ-like as they are. And among Christian Negroes there is no strife between them and us—we are brothers in the Lord. I'm for the Negro being able to have rights, to be able to ride on the bus with the white man, to eat at a restau-rant if he wants to, to have education in a state institution—he pays taxes like everybody else and he should have the privileges his tax money brings. I believe this and I'm all for it.

He seemed to be heading toward a modest pitch for integration, but I knew he wouldn't make it all the way. I remembered that panel in the Sistine Chapel showing God reaching across space to touch the finger of Adam, whose arm was outstretched as he slept, to wake him to life. The drama of the painting is in the participation of the spectator; the finger of God and the finger of Adam are only a little apart, but the imagination of the beholder must be the bridge; he wants it to happen, the movement of the painting is toward that touch, and so it *does* happen. This young man sitting across the desk from me, godlike in his certitude, was also stretching forth a finger to touch the Negro into a life of fellowship. But there was still the small gap, in this case requiring *his* imagination to effect the bridge, so I knew it would never happen. Fundamentalists have no imagination. Hearing them reciting the mysteries of Revelation, one is almost tempted to credit them with the imagination of a Blake, but this is foolishness. For people who insist on cramming 2,000 years of history and science into the ark of the covenant, the height of creativity is to quote chapter and verse. He went on:

> But now understand this. God's ways are not man's ways, see, and man in his condition can't see and will refuse to accept the judgment of God. Now, very frankly, and I don't think there is any way around it—and it's been the position of most conservative Bible scholars—that Ham and the Canaanites, the sons of his son Canaan, were cursed of God because of their indiscretion and sin and looking at their father naked when he was drunk after the flood and mocking him. God had blessed Ham, Seth and Japheth, the sons of Noah. He couldn't bless them and then turn around and curse them. His dealings with men are consistent and just, so he cursed *one* of the sons of Ham—Canaan—and he decreed that he would be a servant's servant.

I asked if that wording is in the Bible.

> Yes, sir. "Servant's servant" is in the Bible, 20th chapter of Genesis, I think. Until we have our redeemed, supernatural bodies in Heaven we're not going to be equal here, and there's no sense in trying to be. Here's what I say. The Negro—and I'm not, it's not my own feeling—but a Negro is best when he serves at the table, when he does that, he's doing what he knows how to do best. And the Negroes who have ascended to positions in government, in education, this sort of thing, I think you'll find, by and large, have a strong strain of white blood in them. *Now, I'm not a racist and this school is not a racist institution.* I can't stress that enough. But what I say is purely what I have been taught, and what I have been able to study in the teaching of the Scripture.

The fact that today there are more Negroes than there are tables to be waited on does not alter the scriptural necessity of his being a servant's servant.

I turned the talk to the United Nations. Partisan or nonpartisan, the UN is a political topic, and I felt that it would give us a breather from religion.

But to young Jones, the UN is very much a doctrinal topic:

Another thing, we believe the Bible teaches, and Bible scholars for years have taught this—it's nothing new—that in the end of time there's going to be a heading up into a one-world federation. Then the god of this world, Satan, will have free rein in the lives and affairs of the people here. He's called the man of sin, he's called the beast, the anti-Christ—he's going to rise to power and take all nations of the world together.

This one-worldism, this collectivism of religion, of politics, of everything, of all nations, this ecumenical movement in religion is another thing pointing in that direction. I mean, it's unheard of in the history of religion that the Catholics, and the Protestants, and the Jews, and all the cults are getting together into one big church. I saw the other day in the paper where a Catholic ordained a Lutheran, I believe it was, and on that ordination committee was a Southern Baptist, there was a Holiness man. I believe a Church of Christ man was on it, a Presbyterian and Methodist were on it— it is hard to believe—it's inconceivable but it's happening through all denominations. The Southern Baptists for years have been *the* conservative religious big denomination in the country. But now, there are overtones of uniting with the Northern Baptists which I believe will come to pass in five or ten years at the most. It's amazing how fast these things are heading up. And it may be that the United Nations . . . whether it's the agency through which this anti-Christ would work or whether it's merely preparing the people, getting them used to the one-world concept, so that his takeover would be easier, is another matter. It may be a new expression of "brotherhood of man"—which we don't believe in; there's not a word about the universal fatherhood of God and universal brotherhood of man in the Bible—but it is all a part of the plan to get the people of the world together for the takeover of the anti-Christ. The Bible is very clear on that.

The trouble with liberals, he said, is that they think man is inherently good and can perfect the world, whereas actually men are inherently degenerate.

How widely is this doctrine preached in the pulpits of America? It is safe to say that at least half the churchgoers of the Deep South are subjected to it regularly, although in this region only a fraction of it is preached by BJU graduates. Just as the John Birch Society finds the Deep South not especially hospitable, for the reason that groups see no reason to band together to push what the entire community has agreed on for years, so the BJU graduates by and large turn elsewhere to do their proselytizing.

The good BJU word is passed along in a second wave, as it were. Pillsbury Conservative Baptist Bible College in Owatonna, Minnesota, is the fifth largest of its kind in the nation. Its past president, Dr. Monroe Parker, has all three of his degrees from BJU and is a member of the BJU executive board of trustees. At least one-third of that faculty is from BJU. Dr. J. R. Faulkner, vice president of the Tennessee Temple Schools & Seminary, Chattanooga, is a graduate of BJU, as are a great number of the school's faculty. Dr. Tom Malone, founder and president of the Midwestern Baptist Seminary in Pontiac, Michigan, is a BJU product; he preaches to about 2,000 parishioners every Sunday. Dr. Linton Johnson, president of Freewill Baptist Bible College, Nashville, is a BJU alumnus; as is Dean Pierre Guillermin of Southern Methodist College in Orangeburg, South Carolina.

The Most Reverend James Parker Dees of Statesville, N.C., holds an honorary Doctor of Divinity from Bob Jones University. Reverend Dees is bishop of the only "Fundamentalist Episcopalian" church in the country, the Anglican Orthodox Church of North America. He organized the church and made himself bishop after quitting his priesthood in the Protestant Episcopal Church because the latter belongs to the National Council of Churches of Christ, which Reverend Dees believes to be a communist swamp. Reverend Dees has been a member of the editorial board of the Citizens Councils' publication of Jackson, Mississippi, and is a member of the policy board of Liberty Lobby. A brother in Christian arms is Henry Grube, founder and pastor of the Greystone Bible Church of Mobile, Alabama. Reverend Grube was a member of the first graduating class of Bob Jones University, the *original* school, in Panama City, Florida, and holds an honorary doctorate from his alma mater. He is an honorary "Colonel" on George Wallace's staff, works closely with ultra-conservatives such as Dr. Carl McIntire, the radio evangelist, and among his minor coups was the prevention of the use of fluorides in the water system of Mobile. Fluorides may stop tooth decay; but you never can tell, the commies might have some other use for them. Anyway, if God had wanted fluoride in the drinking water, He would have put it there.

Dr. Dallas Billington, pastor of the Akron Baptist Temple, where nearly 10,000 show up every Sunday, holds an honorary Ph.D. from Bob Jones and is on the board of trustees; Dr. G. B. Vick, pastor of the Detroit Baptist Temple (9,000 a Sunday), frequently speaks to BJU chapels and attends the annual Bible conferences at the school; Dr. Lee Roberson, pastor of the Highland Park Baptist Church in Chattanooga, largest Baptist Church in America with a reported 20,000 membership, is a popular speaker at BJU and is sending his daughter there. The school has many other friends, not tied to it by degrees or trusteeships, but strongly by philosophy. Among them are the Reverend Al Janney, pastor of the New Testament Baptist Church, Miami, Florida, and the Reverend Dr. W. A. Criswell, pastor of the largest Southern Baptist church in the nation (Dallas, Texas, 18,500 members) and a close friend and spiritual adviser to H. L. Hunt. The Joneses call Criswell the best of Southern Baptists. He is the chap who, in cahoots with billionaire Hunt, sent out 200,000 copies of a sermon before the 1960 Democratic convention warning, "The election of a Catholic as President would mean the end of religious liberty in America." The Hunt-Criswell leaflet, which *The New York Times* called "one of the most widely circulated pieces of campaign literature," prompted a Senate investigation and the threat of an indictment. However, personally Dr. Criswell and the Joneses don't get along too well. Their fuss is over the virtues of Billy Graham, who is a member of Dr. Criswell's congregation. Because of the ugly things the Joneses have said about Reverend Graham, Criswell called old man Bob Jones "a senile crackpot" and Bob Jones, Jr., "a juvenile crackpot" (which he must have meant only by comparison with the elder Jones, since Junior is nearing 60).

On and on and on goes the fellowship of—to use their own word—zealots, through the rich Farm Bureau strongholds and into the lonely country-come-to-town industrial excesses of Christian America, where they are earning more and enjoying it less, or think they are, and want to kick Mammon in the arse for old time's sake.

Bainbridge, Georgia, is a typical stronghold. This is the home town of Marvin Griffin, former governor.

One of Griffin's close friends is the Reverend Dr. Charles Bishop, pastor of a large Bainbridge Baptist church and a graduate of whom BJU boasts. He is a member of his alma mater's executive committee, having equal vote with the Joneses in the general policy making of the college. A very dapper Mississippi native, Reverend Bishop was Georgia Senate chaplain under both Griffin and young Talmadge. He graduated from Bob Jones University in 1945 and came to Bainbridge the next year. His church has grown from a membership of 100 that first year to its present 1,150 members. It owns a city block.

Since his church life is separate from the college itself, one may fairly use Reverend Bishop as a measure of what the more influential BJU graduates hope to do as propagandists in the world. He told me without any show of defensiveness: "I have no hesitation in giving my political views from the pulpit if they are backed up by the Bible.

"For instance, there is plenty of good Biblical support for segregation. In the 13th chapter of Nehemiah, starting at, I believe, the 23rd verse, it tells how the people of Israel were intermarried with the children of Ashdod, and how Nehemiah cursed them. We believe Nehemiah was a spokesman for God in this cursing. Intermarriage like that is bad, whether it is between the children of Israel and the children of Ashdod, or between blacks and whites."

A nucleus of conservative businessmen in Bainbridge sponsors speakers from outside; Reverend Bishop often handles the billing. They have had such speakers as the Reverend Kenneth Goff, a professional ex-communist anti-Semite (his topic: "The 1964 Election and Moscow's New Plans for the United States"). Reverend Bishop is their enthusiastic supporter:

> Yes, sir, I tell my congregation when these men are coming to town and ask them to attend. And I quote from their speeches in my sermons.
> These are bad days. I watched the Presidential inauguration on television. There was a 300-foot bar with fifty bartenders. I couldn't believe it. Just before that, I saw Billy Graham talking. One preacher and fifty bartenders, that's the ratio of this Administration.
> There's good reason to mix religion and politics. I think if you would go back and read history starting with Reconstruction, you would find every major political development in the South had a strong religious motive. We have found that Fundamentalist Christians and conservative politicians have a lot in common. Without the Fundamentalist Christian behind him, Goldwater would never have carried the Southern states he did carry. In my church, we gave out thousands of copies of *A Texan Looks at Lyndon*.

There are eight Bob Jones University ministers in southwest Georgia who have large churches. The Reverend Bishop continued:

> We didn't endorse any political candidate. We just gave out the truth. We felt if we could do that, our people would vote conservative. We didn't get into politics exactly. We talked more about government responsibility and that sort of thing. Like the wheat shipments to Russia. God never told people in the Old Testament

to go in and feed people who were against Him. The Russians are atheists. The communist astronaut said he did not see God up there.

We also try to teach our people—yes, from the pulpit if necessary—about the communist slave countries. We mention specific items that come in from those countries. We find out the brand names they go under. We got the City Council to pass a law saying you've got to put up a sign if you sell those items and get a special license. Most of the merchants agreed not to carry the goods.

Reverend Bishop has been telling the people of southwest Georgia how to save their political souls on daily radio broadcasts for nineteen years. Five other like-minded ministers, in as many different towns of southwest Georgia and north Florida, also take part in the radio assault. Together they blanket several hundred square miles.

Sometimes Reverend Bishop "takes over" the radio station. Warming up for the last Presidential election, he called the station manager and suggested that instead of buying spot space now and then through the day, why not let him buy the entire day and see if he couldn't get somebody to pay for it later? The manager agreed, and Reverend Bishop let fly: with tapes of Governor Wallace, tapes of Carl McIntire, of Dr. Bob Jones and Dr. Bob Jones, Jr., Dan Smoot and allies. All day. And Bainbridge citizens paid for it, just as he suspected they would. He pulled the same thing later at the radio station in Albany, Georgia.

For those who have the Bob Jones outlook on life, the satisfaction of the 1964 Presidential election—perhaps it can even be said, the victory of it—was in losing, as it was in those years when they went Dixiecrat. They knew that the route they were taking could lead nowhere but to certain defeat. For the southerner, joy is still to be found in lost-cause rebellion just for its own sake, but the quest for political defeat also springs from a desire for spiritual justification. He who would find his life must lose it, yes, that too, but there is also the old notion of the elect, set apart not by love but by suffering.

"There would be something wrong with our testimony and our outrage if all people thought well of us," said Dr. Bob Jones, III. "We don't ask the ungodly to think well of us. We don't ask the church people to think well of us who know nothing of a personal relationship with Christ. It doesn't bother us when they criticize us."

When the lying columnists, when the National Council of Churches sit in the seat of the scorners—the politically victorious scorners—it's all right; for as this fresh-faced young zealot says, almost kindly: "We can be certain that those religious systems that do carry political force and are accepted by the world in general are not of God but of the devil, and are being used by Satan to draw sincere and seeking men away from the truth of the Word of God."

Strom Thurmond;
1948 and All That

Climaxing his talk, Thurmond leveled a scathing blast at the world communist movement, declaring in one breath it was "a power-seeking, God-denying, man-and - material - worshipping, amoral force operating from base of territories it dominates, by conspiratorial tactics of subversion, infiltration, propaganda, assassination, genocide, espionage, political and economic blackmail, all under the cover of nuclear holocaust, through the apparatus composed of agents, tools, opportunists and dupes of all ethnic origins and nationalities, bent on the unswerving goal of world domination and subjection, and the recreation of man himself into the common mold of an obedient slave to the minority for which communism was designed to appeal—the minority which it has ever since captivated, and to the minority—may it ever grow smaller —which may in the future be so blind spiritually and so engrossed materially as to be stricken by the soul-destroying disease promulgated and spread by Marx and his successors."

Press Release (Longest Breath Ever Drawn in Senate) from Senator Strom Thurmond's Office, March 1962

235

Almost all the southern delegates to the 1948 Democratic convention supported Senator Richard Russell of Georgia for the Presidential nomination; then, having thrown their votes away once, a group of these recalcitrants hurriedly left Philadelphia to reconvene in Birmingham, Alabama, and determine how they could throw them away again. The method they decided upon was to form a third party, the States' Rights Democrats (better known as Dixiecrats), and to run Strom Thurmond, South Carolina's governor, as their Presidential candidate, with Mississippi's governor, Fielding Wright, as his ticket mate. Thereupon the strategists followed their oil-rich patrons to Houston, where a formal convention was held, the nominations made, and another lost cause launched.

Strom Thurmond was the perfect candidate to lead this enterprise.

A stranger will almost invariably approach Thurmond with scorn and leave him with wonder, for he is the Great White Nonesuch of southern politics. His term as governor was uninspired; at one time he was rated as low as any politician can be and still solicit a campaign fund; as a Democratic senator he was one of the least efficient and as a Republican senator he stands all alone in that respect. Senators don't like to be seen in league with him. For all the respectful attention he gets in the Senate, he might as well be, as one of his colleagues described him, "a leaky faucet in an empty house." And yet he holds South Carolina and a surprisingly large part of Dixie in thrall.

The first time I dropped by his office in Washington he was having a staff meeting. He has these meetings at least once a week; they are a combination pep talk, lecture on Politics 301, and sermon. He was telling the youngsters on his staff about how the Constitution does not allow the federal government to monkey with religion. He ended by saying, "There's *just so much power,* and you've got to decide where it will be put: in the states or up here." It was, I discovered, a perfect key to his view of the world—a Ptolemaic world of metaphysical absolutes, where love and hate and jealousy and power and truth are not limitless, but bounded; where qualities and impulses can be weighed by the pound. It is a world of pure blood. It is a world of one Eden, one Hell, one Heaven, one Right, one Wrong, one Strom.

Is there an editor anywhere in the country who has not been exhorted by one of Thurmond's letters to help bring God back to America? Has there ever been a congregation of the far-right within commuting distance

of South Carolina or Washington, that Thurmond has not addressed?—
Dean Manion's forum (at least eight times), the meeting of Union
Members Against Compulsory Union Membership (calling for "the faith-
ful application of Christian principles to all economic activities"), Politi-
cal Action Conference of Human Events (at least four times), the
Christian Admiral Bible Conference, Americanism seminars of the Jaycees,
The Congress of Freedom, Inc., etc. etc.

Hardly a week passes that the *Congressional Record* is not enriched
several times by his pious observations, or by others' thoughts that he has
looked upon and found good, even such homegrown lines as:

> The Supreme Court made a decision today
> To put God out of the schools in the U.S.A.
> And now the problem that we have to face,
> Is what will become of the human race.

Casting these shriveled kernels of corn in all directions, Thurmond rides
his pale nag toward a private Apocalypse, sincerely vexed by the bleak
future of the human race and determined that its mortal sin of moderation
will not be traced to his life. "In the final analysis," he told a little South
Dakota chamber of commerce in early 1967, "it is not only the fate of
our society which is at stake but a final judgment on each of our personal
lives. In considering this judgment, it is not amiss that we consider the
judgment of the church in Laodicea, which was in these words from the
Book of Revelation: 'I know thy works; thou art neither cold nor hot: I
would thou wert cold or hot. So then because thou are lukewarm, and
neither cold, nor hot, I will spew thee out of my mouth. . . .' Can we, or
will we, escape the same judgment?"*

With a scowling omnipotence keeping tab of every action, one can
never let down one's guard under pressure. There is the code, and one
must keep it. When President Johnson made his "shameful" We Shall
Overcome speech in April 1965, said Thurmond, "I did not clap one
time, even though Lady Bird was looking right at me." He finds nothing
amusing in his, on the one hand, holding fervently to a trusteeship in the
ultra-Fundamentalist Bob Jones University, where the Catholic Church is

---

* Not only does Thurmond love to quote directly from the Bible, he is also
expert at dropping Biblical phrases into the natural flow of his speech, without
attribution, as in one of his Dixiecrat Presidential campaign speeches, opening with
the consolation of Jesus: *"Let not your hearts be troubled* by false reports that the
States Rights ticket . . ." etc.

looked upon as the Whore of Babylon, and on the other hand filibustering by the hour against repeal of a portion of the Taft-Hartley Act by quoting at great length from the writings of Jacques Maritain and St. Thomas Aquinas. That which was heretofore considered evil, in his hands becomes good; it is the one unmistakable attitude of the fanatic, and that, of course, is what Thurmond is, proudly, loudly, avoiding the infamy of the church in Laodicea. God will not spew *him* out, for he is *hot*. Like every good fanatic, Thurmond is convinced that the only way to be sure that right-eousness prevails is to implant it and enforce it with an iron hand. This is why Thurmond, a retired major general in the Army Reserve, has indicated that there may come a time when the military will have to take over. In 1962 he asserted that the reason the military had not felt the need to challenge civilian authority was that the Pentagon had never been faced with what he called the "predicament" of having to choose between "the orders of the commander-in-chief and the Constitution which it is sworn to uphold and defend." He said further that if Congress should somehow slip up and allow the President to issue what Thurmond and other mili-tarists consider to be an unconstitutional order, the Pentagon would have no choice in such a "predicament" but to rebel. Lately he has been sound-ing restless, as though the time for the military takeover had arrived. During his 1966 campaign for re-election, Thurmond called President Johnson "a traitor to the nation as well as to the South." Obviously, his heroes in brass might have to move at any moment.

The lack of the light touch, of the spirit at ease with itself and others, of the assumption that life does not stop where there is a balancing of forces—the absence of these things from his orientation is noticed mainly by his frequent substitution of rich gaucheness. He does not like jokes on himself and he does not know how to joke with others. In closed sessions of committees, members often pull each other's leg. Thurmond sometimes tries to join in, but he does so with a heaviness that is almost belligerent. When, at the conclusion of his twenty-four-hour, nineteen-minute filibuster, he announced, *"If I had the time,* I'd tell you all the decisions handed down by this Supreme Court," he was rattled when other Senators and the gallery guffawed. Nor could he understand why they laughed at the last statement in his filibuster, that he intended to vote against the Civil Rights Bill.

After grilling Robert F. Kennedy for hours preparatory to his being confirmed as Attorney General, Thurmond leaned across the table and handed Kennedy a pamphlet—"A Scriptographic Presentation of What Everyone Should Know About the Constitution"—twenty-four pages of cartoons and drawings meant to carry the message to grade-school children. "Anyone can understand this," said Thurmond with an earnest frown, "I urge you to study it." He was neither joking nor mocking; he was gravely concerned about educating Robert Kennedy, who, looking down at the silly little booklet in his hands, as one senator present recalls, "obviously didn't know whether to laugh or to cry." It is a reaction Thurmond often leaves with his victims.

This devotee of prune juice and calisthenics once seriously accused Olin Johnston of immorality because he had entertained Sally Rand in the governor's mansion. A grim Calvinism runs through his career, *sometimes* with admirable results. As governor of South Carolina he enforced unpopular laws that other governors had found much easier to ignore; slot machines in American Legion clubs were not safe from his axe. As governor, he ordered the arrest and trial for murder of white men involved in a Negro lynching, the first time this had ever been done in South Carolina. As a judge he had pursued principle just as relentlessly, deploring his inability to give a Negro rapist more than forty years in prison (the jury had asked for mercy). Earlier, as an attorney in private practice, his air of righteous certitude won freedom for a woman accused of filling her husband with three shots in front and three shots in the back; Thurmond planted and cultivated the idea in the mind of the jury that if the husband had been a proper southern gentleman, a little ol' charge of buckshot in his back wouldn't have been fatal. For such a man, forcing a Senate investigation of the State Department and of the Defense Department for "muzzling" generals—something he did almost single-handedly and which many considered quite an achievement—was really nothing.

The states that gave their electoral votes to Thurmond as the Dixiecrat Presidential standard bearer in 1948—Alabama, Mississippi, Louisiana, and South Carolina—tell the story of both his success and his failure. They are the super-South, the nerve strand that has been peeled slick, stretched taut between the poles of Black and White, and twanged. They are the hippies of segregation. Georgia, Arkansas, Florida, Texas, North Carolina, Tennessee can't touch them. Thurmond once proclaimed that "Mississippi and South Carolina are the two most democratic states in the nation," and while this at first appears to be a prima facie absurdity, it gathers sense when one realizes what he means by democracy: namely, that the lowliest individual in the community has the same right as the highest to pursue his personal sonofabitchery to the point of rebellion, so long as it does not violate the customs of the state. This is a definition of democracy that many other South Carolinians happily subscribe to, and have been subscribing to since the days of Calhoun and earlier. Coming from Edgefield County, Thurmond would almost be disloyal if he did not. Edgefield was the home county of Travis and Bonham, two of the rebels who died in the Alamo; it was also the home of Chancellor Wardlaw, who wrote South Carolina's ordinance of secession; it was the home of Congressman Preston S. Brooks who, to avenge a slur on the name of U.S. Senator A. P. Butler (of Edgefield), caned to the Senate floor Senator Charles Sumner of Massachusetts and thereby helped establish the atmosphere in which reconciliation over the disputes leading to the Civil War was impossible; it was the home of Ben Tillman, who led the farmers in revolt against a state government controlled by Charleston and Columbia aristocrats with the Luciferian cry, "I had rather follow the majority to hell than these men to heaven." Edgefield County has turned out ten governors and nine lieutenant governors, most of them searing individualists. It is also the home of the state's oldest newspaper, the Edgefield *Advertiser,* whose present editor, W. W. Mims, has on at least one occasion backed up his political opinions in a sidewalk fist fight and who has advocated the establishment of a modern Confederacy.

In such an atmosphere one is rather inclined to go along with Hegel's notion that the essence of Spirit is activity, that the spirit of a people (nation, region, state, even county when it is as closely knit as Edgefield) erects itself through deeds into something objective, and that the individual appropriates this spirit, "enabling him to have a definite place in the world—to be *something."* The supposed "myths" relating to the South's differences, then, would not be myths at all, so long as they prompted the people of the region to *act* as if they were real and in the cumulative effect of such acts create the spirit which the people believed they had in the first place.

The most influential shapers of South Carolina politics since World War II were James Byrnes, Olin Johnston, and Strom Thurmond. Byrnes is now old, infirm, and important still in South Carolina politics mainly as a legend; Olin Johnston died in 1964, leaving the Democratic party numb and almost palayzed (or so it seemed in that bleak year) since he *was* the party.

Thurmond is, however, very much alive. And the reason for his political virility may be that he so excellently represents the kind of people with whom the South abounds: God-fearing, salt-of-the-earth folks who swim in the same rivers they dump their raw sewage into, set up auto junkyards next to college campuses, feel that poached eggs are only for sick people, and are convinced that all priests and nuns have intercourse and bury their babies under the nunnery. They are a proud race of men who don't want charity, partly because there isn't a legislature in the South that puts out a welfare check large enough to live on. They fear the nigger, who may or may not be standing at the gate of the factory but who the boss *says* is standing there carrying a through-passage card from FEPC and ready to take their jobs. Don't try to figure them out; they will vote both for an Olin Johnston *and* a Strom Thurmond. Way down deep, of course, the mill hands among them hate their bosses. Underpaid and insecure on their jobs, they loved Olin Johnston for giving them a forty-hour week when he was governor and voting against the Taft-Hartley Act (the only member of the South Carolina delegation to do so) when he was senator.

On the other hand, South Carolinians have eaten cold gravy so much that any job, even one on which they are gypped and threatened, is better than none at all. Remembering the old, lean days and not enjoying the memory, they are willing to let the boss get by with just about anything. Helping the boss to get by with anything is where Strom Thurmond comes in.

Ever since he entered politics Thurmond has been running for something—constantly, with painful earnestness, with or without encouragement. As soon as he was through running for President on the Dixiecrat ticket in 1948 he was off again, breathlessly, running for the U.S. Senate two years away, and when he lost that he was off again, running, getting his second wind, running for an opening not yet in sight.

It was this mad verve which was both the strength and the weakness of Thurmond's challenge of Olin Johnston's Senate seat in 1950—a campaign that in many ways was symbolic of South Carolina and Strom Thurmond in mid-passage. The reason he is in the United States Senate today is that he learned how to change his ideals 180 degrees, betray those who had previously supported him, manufacture new enemies, and be an

242   GOTHIC POLITICS IN THE DEEP SOUTH

instrument of revenge for South Carolina's most ardent opportunist, James Byrnes. He must also be credited with having learned how to overcome great obstacles and animosities. One need look back only to his 1950 campaign to see how far he has come, with so little to offer, in rallying the people of South Carolina behind him. In 1966 Thurmond polled 25 percent more votes than the next-most-popular winning candidate on the ballot; he could run as a Know-Nothing or a Bull Moose and carry the state without much difficulty. This is quite a change from his fortunes, and his prospects, in 1950.

Although South Carolina had romped off with him into the Dixiecrat briar patch in 1948, the state was not yet in the grip of an hysterical anti-federalism. Its froth could not match Thurmond's own; nor could it yet accept as normal the raving and head-standing and pell-mellness that is now accepted as just part of Strom Thurmond's political genius.

In his unreasoning anger, Thurmond was ahead of South Carolina, and this is one reason he lost in 1950. It should be understood, however, that this anger was not a virulent racism. Indeed, race was not a central issue at all, and if either of the two candidates was at a disadvantage in regard to a "softness" on race, it was probably Thurmond. Johnston twitted him for having invited a Negro governor of the Virgin Islands to spend the night at the mansion during Thurmond's governorship (it was done by mistake) and for having appointed a politically potent Negro doctor to a state board. It was Thurmond who, as governor, had sponsored the first state industrial school for Negro girls, the first state parks for Negroes, more Negro health services, and more trade schools for Negroes, in addition to helping abolish the poll tax. Thurmond was on the defensive about these things, and he in turn accused Johnston of being a big booster of the Fair Employment Practices Committee and other heinous Tru-manesque developments. But, still, it was not the kind of racism that had once flourished in South Carolina, back in the racy old days when Cotton Ed Smith called a Negro friend of Mrs. Roosevelt's a "greasy black wench," and when Cole Blease (who served the state as governor and U.S. Senator) vowed he would be happy to lead a lynch mob to protect the purity of white women. It was not even the kind of racism flourishing elsewhere in Dixie. In the midst of the 1950 campaign, the U.S. Supreme Court struck down segregation in railroad dining cars and ruled that the University of Texas law school must admit Negroes. Across the border in Georgia, Herman Talmadge immediately worked up a good lather: "As long as I am governor, Negroes will not be admitted to white schools! The line is drawn! The threats that have been held over the South for four years are now pointed like a dagger ready to be plunged into the very heart of southern tradition!" Such theatrics were notably absent in South Carolina. The Cole Blease–Ed Smith–Herman Talmadge approach had passed away into deeper subtleties, and in fact for the moment seemed hardly to figure at all in South Carolina politics as a talking issue.* The vilification of the present-in-time-and-space Negro, the physical Negro, was shifting to vilification of the "Negroization" of the Federal Government, a fearful, dusky phantom that seemed to seep out of all things "liberal." This was a new concept that the middle class and upper class could, without shame, fear and hate also, for he was not merely hungry and ignorant and wanting help in many ways, but he was pushing forward as the Grand Affront, knocking at the gates of precious institutions and leaving smudges on clean old traditions. One no longer talked about it so directly; more and more one merely denounced the liberals, or the CIO "outsiders." But everyone knew what these things stood for. In perfecting this sign language, South Carolina was several years ahead of the rest of the South; Mississippi is only today catching up.

But even though Thurmond did not sound any more racist than Johnston, and even though his political record in this regard was better than Johnston's (who, when *he* was governor, had wiped the Negro out of politics by establishing the white primary), still the Negroes of the state— operating behind the unfathomable but often accurate instinct that has meant the Negro's survival in Dixie—turned against Thurmond almost to a man. Their voting strength was still minuscule in 1950, but Thurmond lost only by 25,000 votes and many feel that the Negro vote spelled the difference. Why did the Negroes feel that way about him? Mrs. Modjeska Simpkins, who has since World War II been one of the more influential Negro leaders in the state, says that "Strom vilified Negroes in 1948, when he was running Dixiecrat, and we swore vengeance on him." This hardly

---

* And does so—on the *surface*—much less today. In 1966, House Speaker Sol Blatt, seventy, opposed a bill to require all children between the ages of seven and sixteen to attend school, using an argument that in another era would have been overpowering but in this instance was only embarrassingly divisive. Weeping actual tears, Speaker Blatt shrieked at his colleagues: "Do you want some sixteen-year-old nigger holding the hand of your granddaughter in the classroom?" The House heard him to the end in shocked silence—and then voted against him, 73 to 32.

holds up as an explanation; Thurmond had sounded like just about any other 1948-vintage states' righter. A more curious, but perhaps more solid, explanation came from her when she added much later, "Of course, part of Thurmond's trouble is he's on the defense. He knows that people know about the Negro girl he schooled at Orangeburg. She used to come to the mansion and get shopping money when he was governor. All the Negroes know about that." As I traveled around the state, I discovered for a fact that every politically-conscious Negro (as well as many whites) *did* bring that faceless Orangeburg co-ed into their conversation, sooner or later, when they talked about Thurmond. Though apparently without foundation, it was one of the most widespread political rumors I ever saw wrapped around a state: that Thurmond had a paternal interest in a Negro girl. I never talked with anyone who had ever seen the girl, but she certainly lived in their minds. And the odd part of it, to me, was that instead of crediting Thurmond with good faith for sending this legendary girl to college, many of the Negroes I talked with somehow seemed to hold it against him that he did not recognize her more authoritatively, although this would of course have been politically fatal.

There were others who viewed Thurmond's candidacy in 1950 with bitter abhorrence, but none more than some of the state leaders of labor who felt that he had betrayed them. In the 1930's and early 1940's, he had traveled under the banner of the New Deal. When Thurmond entered the governor's mansion in 1946, labor's heart was light. For the first time since Reconstruction, leaders of what were once known as the "submerged masses" were invited to a governor's inaugural. This, however, was about the last thing labor got from him. Union leaders, who were then trying mightily to get a real foothold in South Carolina and expected him to give them a leg up, never forgave him. Nor, by 1950, did he want forgiveness; by that time labor's vastly overrated drive to "take" Dixie had been crushed by the industrialists and their redneck allies, and Thurmond disclaimed his former alliance with the defeated troops. Four years made quite a difference. Whereas in 1946 he had eagerly sought CIO support and endorsement (and had received it), in 1950 Thurmond was willing to use the CIO as a spook, warning his countrymen that the CIO supported Olin Johnston (as it did) and that "the same forces" that tried unsuccessfully to re-elect Senator Claude Pepper in Florida "are trying to re-elect Johnston." It was clear that Thurmond was ready to cut himself off from all but the true believers, and in this respect his future was beginning to shape up.

Labor's enmity was of no critical importance; its ranks were certainly not enormous and, such as they were, they were far from united on any subject. Of more importance was the enmity of the "Barnwell Ring," a legislative group that represented some of the more powerful vested interests. Thurmond, needing an issue and a whipping boy for his 1946 campaign for governor, had run against the Barnwell Ring and had squabbled with its leaders ever since. These were potent enemies.

But neither the Negroes, labor, nor this group of fat cats hurt Thurmond nearly as much as he hurt himself. When the campaign began, Johnston paid for a private poll which showed he had only 30 percent of the electorate in his pocket. He told a close friend that if he could win re-election by 1,500 votes he would consider it a great victory. He need not have worried—Thurmond, in a sense, was on Johnston's side.

He made a fool of himself. He went around the hustings thumping on his chest and orating on the blessings of physical purity. He had stood on his head for a *Life* photographer to prove that he was fit to marry a woman much younger than himself—and the folks of South Carolina never let him forget it. "Hey, Strom, stand on your head for us!" And he sometimes did. He stood on his head too much ("That," Johnston would say slyly, "can make a man addled"), and came up talking. He jabbered, and flexed, and jabbered some more; he talked himself out of the running, and by the end of the race, a great swatch of South Carolina seemed thoroughly sick of him.

With his defeat by Johnston, Thurmond's future outwardly could not have been less promising. The ragtag unionists were through with him; many conservatives felt they could not trust him, for he was plainly not a team man. Also, following his career like scavenger fish, were those rumors that would not die—and still won't—of his involvement with the principal in the notorious Sue Logue murder case.

But the sophisticates who thought he was through obviously did not take into consideration the fact that in the minds of many South Carolinians, he still represented the grimly determined, humorless, righteous, guileless prohibitionist hick who, like Ben Tillman, without desiring real reform was ready to buck "the powers"; many South Carolinians, in short, could identify with him.

Four years later—four years filled by Strom with an everlasting shaking of hands and monotonous speechifying forays out of his law office in Aiken to keep himself always at ready—an organization, perhaps the slickest organization ever to be put together in South Carolina, would be placed at his disposal; he was to be the human cannonball, the weapon of vengeance which Jimmy Byrnes would fire at Washington as the opening shot in a war that would end with the Republicans and neo-Republicans wiping South Carolina off the national Democratic map. From 1944 to 1954 was only ten years, but they were ten long, bitter years for Byrnes, and he intended to use Strom well. Best of all, as it turned out, Byrnes—who, unlike Strom, has a kind of sense of humor—could accomplish it in the name of fair play.

One cannot help wonder what party politics would be like in this country if men like James Byrnes and Strom Thurmond were very numerous. Today Byrnes calls himself an independent Democrat. But back in the 1930's and early 1940's he was acting anything but independent; he was, except for Claude Pepper, perhaps the foremost spokesman for the New Deal in the South, war mobilizer under Roosevelt and a Roosevelt appointee to the U.S. Supreme Court. He snuggled so deeply into the Roosevelt bosom, in fact, that he felt Roosevelt owed it to him to make him his 1944 running mate. That didn't come off, and Byrnes has always felt that labor bosses put the squeeze on Roosevelt to keep him from getting the vice-presidential nomination. When he became governor, Byrnes retaliated by having a right-to-work law passed, kicking the labor representatives off the industrial commission, and passing a three-percent sales tax, a retrogressive tax which always offends labor.

Although Byrnes became Truman's first Secretary of State,* he could not be loyal to the man whom he considered a bad substitute for himself in the Presidency. Within a matter of weeks after leaving Truman's cabinet, Byrnes was seeing in the Democratic program something he had never noticed when he was privy to the highest Democratic councils—"creeping but ever advancing socialistic" aims. So in 1952 he went out in support of "my chief," Dwight D. Eisenhower. Eisenhower rewarded him by

* In this role he is likely to go down in history most infamously, according to Gar Alperovitz, for being the one most persuasive with Truman of the political—not military—necessity for dropping the atomic bombs on Japan. The one overriding question for future biographers to answer is whether ruthlessness or spitefulness was the chief motivating impulse in Byrnes' life.

appointing him as one of five delegates to the UN General Assembly in 1953. Again Byrnes felt betrayed, believing that "my chief" should have been more generous than a mere UN delegateship; and he was miffed by Ike's integrating acts, so he was ready to switch again in 1956, going this time for the hopeless ticket of Harry Byrd of Virginia and John Bell Williams of Mississippi. Williams' most noteworthy act up to that time had been to lead a Congressional investigation into the evils of forced school integration in Washington, D. C.

Despite his fickleness in national affairs, or partly because of it, Byrnes' political machine and popular following were awesome. For example, in the race for governor in 1950, Byrnes, seventy-one, purring around from speaking engagement to speaking engagement in a chauffeured limousine and dropping ponderous revelations of how "the more I see of the world the more I think of South Carolina," won without trying. The newspapers, like other parts of the state's power structure, were almost all for him. The other eleven candidates—a sufficient number to kill off each other—might raise real issues, but it did no good. One candidate complained quite accurately that the newspapers of the state were deifying Byrnes: "If he does go to town, there is an editorial. If he doesn't go to town, there is an editorial."

It was this kind of hauteur and popularity that Byrnes used so effectively to make Thurmond his instrument of revenge. The deed began when Burnet Maybank—who had gone to the U.S. Senate as Byrnes ascended to the U.S. Supreme Court under Roosevelt—died at his summer home in Flat Rock, North Carolina, on September 1, 1954. There was sorrow, no doubt, but there was a great deal more confusion, because this was only three days before the deadline for candidates to get their names certified to appear on the ballot. This was Wednesday. State law says candidates must be certified sixty days before the general election. The sixty days would begin at 6 p.m. Friday. Maybank had been running unopposed, so his name was the only name the state Democratic committee had under consideration.

Another state law permits the party's state executive committee to nominate a candidate when insufficient time remains after a candidate's death to hold a primary election. Thursday, the day after Maybank's death —demonstrating unseemly haste, some felt—Democratic party leaders caucused to consider how they would handle the situation.

Meanwhile, Byrnes had started calling for a primary to be held within thirty days, certification deadline or no certification deadline. He was also trying to get the executive committee to nominate him. At this point his idea was not to help Thurmond but to be a candidate himself. Byrnes had let the state committee know through a friend that although he had twice announced publicly he would never again be a candidate for a public office, he would submit to a draft.

This, however, was something not even the South Carolina Democratic Executive Committee could swallow. That organization is, and has been for a decade, just about as lukewarm to the national party as a "Democratic" organization can be, but when Byrnes expected them to back the man who two years earlier had been the main organizer of the Democrats for Eisenhower, he was asking them not only to frustrate the will of the national party—which wouldn't have bothered the committee too much —but also to lose face. For the same reason, the committee considered Thurmond out of the question, for he, too, had helped Ike in '52.

Others such as Congressman William Jennings Bryan Dorn and Donald S. Russell, then president of the University of South Carolina, were panting for the post. But State Senator Edgar Brown, wheel horse of the "Barnwell Ring," who had been on the executive committee since 1914 and was considered anchor man, had it sewed up.

After the funeral services for Maybank, and while most of those who had attended were on their way to the graveside rites, Brown and other members of the state committee were peeling away from the cortege and heading for a backroom conference to wrap up the nomination. Brown, who had been soliciting support almost from the moment of Maybank's last heartbeat, could see victory at last; he had been unsuccessful in two previous tries for the Senate. When the executive committee chose him, it meant his name was the only Democratic name that would be on the ballot in November. Nothing, surely, could stop him now. And once in office, he would be almost impossible to defeat. For years he had been the most powerful man in state government, with the alliances and commitments that should have made for an unbeatable machine. There was hardly a corporation in the state that did not owe him something for services rendered on the senate finance committee. Defeat by a Republican in the approaching election was out of the question, because the Republicans were still an ingrown clique of patronage hunters, and—the best reason of all—despite a five-minutes-to-midnight attempt, they had failed to get a candidate certified for the ballot.

Immediately after his nomination there was some talk of write-in opposition, but Brown did not take this talk seriously. Never in the history of the country had a write-in candidate been successful for a U.S. Senate seat.*

Even as Brown dreamed of the certainty of his victory, the furies were about to descend on him and ruin him. There was a time when Brown was Byrnes' dear friend. Byrnes had been best man at Brown's wedding. Brown had supported Byrnes politically for forty years. But Brown had refused to leave the Democratic party at Byrnes' behest in 1952—and Byrnes was still smarting over that. Now was a chance for revenge; the revenge was auxiliary to Byrnes' main purpose, but it would be sweet nonetheless.

Everything was in readiness. Byrnes, giving up his own ambitions for the Senate seat but still feigning neutrality as to who should get it, was on the telephone from the beginning and for weeks thereafter ("day and night" by his own description) marshalling the support for Thurmond that had always been Byrnes' or which in recent years was only waiting to be recruited by him. He had the 1952 Democrats-for-Eisenhower machinery still oiled; part of this overlapped the 1948 Dixiecrat group, and what didn't overlap was—as only Dixiecrats can be—ready to go. Fourteen of the sixteen dailies and seventy-three of eighty-six weeklies in South Carolina were ready to support the Byrnes–Thurmond putsch.

Meanwhile Brown was being killed with kindness from out-of-state party leaders. When the South Carolina press began clamoring for a write-in candidate, national chairman Stephen A. Mitchell said he doubted that the people of South Carolina knew how to write well enough to elect a write-in candidate, and Harry Truman, whom the people of the state despised for his civil rights program of 1948, and Major General Harry (Deep Freeze) Vaughan, Truman's former aide, were giving their support to Brown—support which Brown wildly attempted to repudiate, saying that Truman was "an ill man" and didn't know what he was doing.

Thurmond—that "now-I'm-a-Democrat, now-I'm-a-states-righter, now-I'm-a-Republican, now-I'm-an-independent, now-I'm-a-what-have-you," as Brown rather accurately described him—played his part well, for

* When Roy Harris, in nearby Augusta, heard Thurmond was contemplating the write-in route, he went over to counsel him against it. "I sat in his office all morning waiting to give him my advice," Harris recalls, "but he was so busy on the phone talking to people urging him to run I never did get to tell him why I was there. After a few hours of that, I saw how wrong I was and sneaked out."

once not talking too much, for once letting the smarter professionals and the newspapers talk for him, while he, fittingly, played the people's quiet martyr who had been deprived of the chance to do what he so loved to do—RUN—and Byrnes adroitly made it seem that in South Carolina's being denied a Democratic primary all civilization was going down the sewer: "Freedom of religion, freedom of speech and of the press can be secure only so long as the average man and woman enjoy freedom of the ballot." The state executive committee, by following the South Carolina constitutional allowances, just didn't know what they were endangering.

143,444 pencil-totin' Democrats-Dixiecrats-Republicans-States' Righters rescued freedom of religion, freedom of speech and of the press by writing in "Strom Thurmond" or "Srom Turmon" or something similar 143,444 times, sometimes so illiterately that Mitchell's estimation of the writing abilities of South Carolinians almost seemed to have merit, but the state attorney general had ruled that the writing didn't have to be very exact. Brown got 83,525 votes.

It was the first time in the nation's history a write-in candidate was elected to the U.S. Senate. It was a sensational campaign; nevertheless, a great many South Carolinians must not have cared much for either contender, for the total vote represented only slightly more than one-third of the qualified voters in the state that year. But it did not matter if two-thirds of the voters were too embarrassed, or too disgusted, or too apathetic to vote. The only thing of importance to Byrnes was that his hatred for the memory of FDR, hatred for fate, for history, and for his old party comrades on the Potomac was complete. He was sending Washington a strange bedfellow indeed.

The governor of North Carolina once responded, when Thurmond questioned him about his constancy, "Sure I like you, Strom, but I ain't no damn fool about you." Other political heartstrings vibrate in like manner. Few U.S. senators seem to give a damn about this strange colleague who feels that cooperation is a sign of weakness—of what he calls "partyitis." But far from being dismayed by his deepening isolation, Thurmond almost seems to encourage it. If other senators insist on pushing him into a lonely position, it has not been without continuing help from him.

Thus for Thurmond the 1957 Civil Rights Bill—which was to other southerners made barely palatable by the nonenforcement compromises managed through then-majority leader Lyndon Johnson—was rich food and drink, for it gave him an opportunity to lose all by himself, with a flourish. Other southerners had agreed not to filibuster the bill further, but to fall back to the next trench, in exchange for these compromises, and because—most importantly—to filibuster would only have called more attention to their defeat when it came, as it was bound to come.* The agreement would only be successful in this latter purpose, however, if it was respected by all southern senators. A maverick would do double damage, both calling attention to the defeat of the South *and* making the nonfilibusterers look like traitors to their region.

Apparently without weighing this subtle possibility, Thurmond, on August 28, at 8:54 p.m., moved onto the Senate floor with his malt tablets, a small box of munchables, and an armload of texts which he used to interlard dissertations on Constitutional law, the Bible, the sanctity of the home, and various lengthy mumbles, to hold the floor for the next twenty-four hours and nineteen minutes: a new and still unbroken filibuster record.

It mattered not to him that his monotonous, meaningless cascade of words was appreciated from the balcony during the night hours only by his pretty, young wife, the NAACP's Clarence Mitchell, and an unidentified man who sometimes fell asleep and snored quite loudly. Historic moments usually have a hard time shining through their intrinsic dullness, and this was no exception. Barry Goldwater twice came in with some remarks about the military pay bill, allowing Thurmond to duck into the men's room for relief and into the cloakroom to chomp some ground meat. He got other sketchy relief from questions by a few northern Democrats and some Republicans. But of southerners, only South Carolina's other senator, Johnston, who despised Thurmond, gave any help, and that reluctantly.

From Senator Herman Talmadge, who knows that in Washington demagogues cannot afford to escalate comparatives of demagoguery, came immediate denunciation of Thurmond as a double-crosser. After Talmadge

---

* Frank Smith, ex-congressman from Mississippi, recently explained, "When Lyndon Johnson promoted the strategy that changed the 1957 bill to a voting rights measure, the southern senators did not resist to the point of cloture because they realized that the right to vote was the one issue on which not enough northern and western senators would help them."

had frumped and fumed at the "grandstand of longwinded speeches" which "in the long run could wreak unspeakable havoc upon my people," other southern senators rushed across to shake Talmadge's hand. And they all but gave a standing ovation when Georgia's senior senator, Richard Russell, coldly denounced Thurmond as a traitor: "If I had undertaken a filibuster for personal political aggrandizement I would have forever reproached myself for being guilty of a form of treason against the people of the South."

This momentary fury on the part of the South's other hard-line senators was followed by a permanent wariness. They walked around Thurmond. He was dangerous. He was not a team man. He could not be trusted; he only wanted to fix his hold upon his Senate seat, at whatever cost to other southern senators and to the region itself. This is what they said then and what they have never stopped saying. He said he did such things out of principle. But his Washington critics were not so sure about that. There had been rumors that George Bell Timmerman, Jr., then governor of South Carolina, was eyeing Thurmond's seat in the next election. Thurmond's "valiant" filibuster would make effective opposition unlikely. And, looking at a wider horizon, it was believed by many of his detractors that Thurmond nightly put himself to sleep imagining he felt an underground surge toward a third party in the Deep South—a lullaby that was followed by dreams of himself as this movement's leader; maybe in 1960, maybe in 1964, maybe. . . . The record of that filibuster would come in handy then.

Perhaps for similar reasons in 1964 Thurmond again failed to see the delicate strategy of the southern bloc in permitting, without much protest, the appointment of Florida's ex-Governor LeRoy Collins to the directorship of the new Community Relations Service, a post created by the Civil Rights Act for settling racial squabbles. Collins was, and is, no integrationist by any means; he is a soft man, bonded in southern tradition, not likely to become a pushy reformer. If the southerners had to put up with a federal agent, they could not, from their position, find a better one. But Thurmond, like his mentor Byrnes, was wrapped in petty grudges. He had been gravely offended in 1963 when Collins, then director of the National Association of Broadcasters, addressed the Columbia, South Carolina, Chamber of Commerce with these strong words:

We have allowed the extremists to speak for the South . . . how long are the majority of southerners going to allow themselves to be caricatured before the nation by these Claghorns . . . Dixie battle cries . . . have been employed to incite sick souls to violence. . . . How many Sunday school children have to be dynamited to death? How many Negro leaders have to be shot in the back? How many governors have to be shot in the chest? How many Presidents have to be assassinated? . . . It is time the decent people of the South told the bloodyshirt-wavers to climb down off the buckboards of bigotry.

What Collins was saying was that segregation could not be maintained if the South got the rest of the nation completely down on it—excellent strategic advice, but Thurmond did not read it that way. He thought, for some reason, that Collins was talking about him. And it was in revenge that a year later he grilled Collins at the nomination hearing, expertly dragging out of Collins' past certain happenings to suggest that the Collins of the 1950's, back when the political going was toughest and when he was still governor and could have helped the Negroes but didn't (he left office in 1960), was not the Collins who now wanted to polish his national image in the community-relations job with an eye on those 400,000 Negro votes back home, where he still had political ambitions. Under Thurmond's prodding and gouging, unhappy Collins acknowledged some of his past actions and statements with the explanation: "A great deal I said in the old days—. . . it reflects a sincere feeling, but later events bring a modification of one's thinking. . . ."

It was, Thurmond left no doubt, a very weak-kneed attitude, indeed a hypocritical attitude. His complete incomprehension of the Deep South's new techniques for resisting change has made him the clown of the Senate.

On the last day of the Senate Commerce Committee hearings to consider the nomination of Collins, Senator Thurmond was sulking outside the door, hoping vainly that his absence might prevent the accumulation of a quorum, when Senator Ralph Yarborough of Texas came cheerily down the hallway, shook Thurmond by the hand and, still hanging on, playfully pulled him toward the hearing room.

"Come on in, Strom," he said.

Then Yarborough tried to turn loose, but couldn't. Thurmond was hanging on. "I'll make an agreement with you, Ralph," he said. "If I can keep you out, you won't go in, and if you can drag me in, I'll stay there."

Newsmen and Senate staffers gathered around, as what started out as a tease (on Yarborough's part; Thurmond was taking it seriously all the way) turned grim. Thurmond pressed for a showdown. The men took off their jackets, circled warily for a moment, and then thudded together— Thurmond a trim 175-pound physical culturist and Yarborough, with his classic senatorial paunch. After a couple of ughs and wheezes, Yarborough was on the floor; then Thurmond let him up, but in a moment he was back on the floor, his face red and his lips frozen in a gummy grin. Thurmond perched on Yarborough's chest–stomach, saying repeatedly, "Tell me to release you, Ralph, and I will."

Aides tried to break it up. Senator Frank Lausche, arriving late, scolded his colleagues for risking a heart attack. For ten minutes this amazing athletic stalemate continued, until word was passed to the committee chairman, Senator Warren Magnuson, who came out and sternly ordered them to arise. Considering the way things are, it was highly appropriate that Ralph Yarborough, the South's most liberal senator, should have been tripped and flattened; by the same measure, it was even more appropriate that Dixie's champion was Strom Thurmond.

10

George Wallace:
A Potpourri of Style

I thank God for George Wallace of Alabama. He is a
true son of the South. I wish I could call him President
Wallace.

Ross Barnett, Introducing Wallace
at a Citizens Council Meeting in 1965

I don't believe in the kind of discrimination that offends anyone.

Governor Wallace, 1964

At a meeting of an Alabama legislative committee where one of Governor
George Wallace's power-grabbing bills was under loud debate, a state
senator demanded that his colleagues tell him, "On what meat does this
little Caesar feed?"

It was not a difficult question. George Corley Wallace, who is a hungry
fighter, feeds on the meat of ambition, and with good reason, for he is the
strongest politician to come out of the South since the death of the
Kingfish, Huey Long, a generation ago. Wallace—the Little Judge, the
Barbour Bantam, the greatest disturber of the political peace in this generation, a neurotic, raving egotist, a skilled imitator of political gimmickry
that others had shown to be useful, but at the same time possessing more
imagination and drive and artistry of debate than all the other contemporary Deep South politicians put together—has ignited the same bonfires
of love and hate that were lit in Huey's day.

255

One should immediately make this distinction, however: Huey Long never depended on racism for his popularity, while Wallace has seldom depended on anything else, in one guise or another. Looking further at this distinction, one may become fearful for the cause of tolerance. Long, who based his appeal on economics ("Every man a king"), could have polled between 3 and 4 million votes in 1935, a secret survey conducted by the National Democratic Committee discovered, which was quite enough to frighten Roosevelt. But in 1964, ignoring economics and concentrating *solely* on the composite Federal–Negro–Commie threat, Wallace could have polled about 3.5 million in the nation as a whole and could have taken 18 percent of the southern vote, just 2 percent under Goldwater; this was according to the Gallup Poll. Other surveys were more generous. John Bucci, a poll taker with an admirable record in forecasting privately for Governor Scranton and for the Kennedy family, believed that Wallace could have won more electoral votes than Goldwater. He saw Wallace carrying Mississippi, Alabama, Louisiana, and possibly two other southern states—a possible total of 55 electoral votes. Apparently in agreement with Bucci and shaking at what the 1964 election would mean without the South (it would have meant his winning only Arizona), Goldwater then pleaded, "This is the first time in my life that a man has appeared on the horizon who might put enough votes together to form a third party. I would hope in his wisdom—and he is a very able man —I would hope that he would withdraw."

Nor did the wildfire enthusiasm among racist guerrillas end with the 1964 election; six months later a Louis Harris poll showed Wallace's popularity throughout the South at a high of 79 percent. And the election of his wife Lurleen in 1966 on a side-show platform—over a field of opposition candidates that included the state's attorney general, two former governors, the incumbent agriculture commissioner, one of the most powerful state senators, a former congressman of national reputation, and the best known Republican in the state—verified his continuing domination of Alabama politics. By early 1967 the Gallup Poll showed Wallace could get 13 percent of a presidential vote; late in 1967 the Field Poll, in an independent survey of California, reported that Wallace could capture 12 percent of that important electorate in a three-way race with President Johnson and any one of five leading GOP possibilities.

By early 1968 Wallace's potential was evident everywhere, and there was deep concern, first of all among the Republicans, secondly among those who feared that with Wallace on the prowl anything could happen. *The Washington Post,* not given to hysteria, editorialized that Wallace's candidacy might so split the vote that no one would get a majority and thus the final decision would be up to the House of Representatives—a direful eventuality to the liberal *Post,* which summarized its fears: "What is unmistakably clear is the fact that a flirtation by any large number of voters with a third party under present circumstances might subject our Constitutional system to the gravest strains that have been experienced in many decades."

For months there had been confusion about which party Wallace would hurt more. In 1967, columnist Joseph Alsop predicted, "If the Republicans did extra well north of the Mason-and-Dixon line, Wallace's subtraction from the Democratic vote in the South could defeat President Johnson outright." But a year later he saw the situation more accurately: "The Wallace candidacy will go far towards re-electing Lyndon B. Johnson." For a time the Democrats tried to pretend that Wallace would hurt them nationally. Senator Thomas J. McIntyre of New Hampshire, after meeting with President Johnson in January 1967, announced, "We've got to be aware of Mr. Wallace." But this was Democratic quackery. It was the GOP that stood to lose. The reasons were clear: If George Wallace weren't in the race, the Deep South would probably go Republican, as it had for Barry Goldwater in 1964. Outside the South, the extent to which Wallace would subtract from normally Republican votes would depend, of course, on how conservative a candidate the GOP put up. A Louis Harris poll late in 1967 showed Wallace taking 13 percent in a race with Johnson and Romney, 11 percent in a race with Johnson and Nixon— but in any event quite enough to serve as the best safeguard that President Johnson could possibly have. And it was this aspect of his candidacy that made him without question the most important third-party politician since Theodore Roosevelt's fling as a Bull Moose.

Wallace's motives were not accepted by all men as being pure. Governor Claude Kirk of Florida, the South's leading Republican, accused Wallace of being in the pay of President Johnson. There were other rumors around Alabama. Ex-Governor Folsom assured me that Wallace and Johnson are "thick as thieves." He said that Johnson stirred up the school guidelines issue just before the gubernatorial primaries in 1966 to swing the white voters solidly behind Wallace. And Folsom wasn't the only one around Alabama saying that sort of thing. Wallace called this "ridiculous," and it probably was, but the rumors illustrated very well the kind of shocked fantasies that Wallace's candidacy aroused both in the South and in the nation as a whole.

Except for the incumbent President, no man in America could move into national campaigning with a larger following already organized; and not even the President can claim so much spirit among his followers. Wallace's popularity with the southern lower, lower-middle, and farmer class is such that he is sometimes referred to as the "governor of Dixie." And his surprisingly successful forays into the North as a buccaneering presidential nominee have disclosed the deep veins of intolerance that no man in contemporary politics can tap with such contrived innocence as George Wallace. The Catholics of Baltimore, the Wisconsin "Poles, Italians, Germans and *other* lesser breeds," to use Wallace's own undiplomatic phrase, and the cold middle class of Indiana—in startling numbers in 1964 showed a preference for this little man who told their discontent in crass parables. The backlash of '66 showed that they are still there, awaiting the return of their smooth messiah.

The national press is sometimes sentimentally forgetful of who makes up Wallace's national constituency, and why. Wallace's three-state campaign in 1964 was properly understood by most reporters as the most toxic kind of racism. Magnolia deodorant could not disguise the stink of that Oriental Junket.* But sometimes these days the national reporters, even the best ones, seem to be getting tolerant of scented bigotry and interpret it as something else. Tom Wicker, the adept chief of *The New York Times'* Washington Bureau, typified this dangerous shift in the April 1967 *Harper's* when he apologized for Wallace ("what he has really 'stood up' for is the age-old streak of 'practicality' and earthy common sense in mankind") and, for bad measure, threw in an empirical, unsound psychoanalysis of that element of society which has heretofore given its heart to him (". . . it is not so blatant a thing as racism, or even violence, but the old basic natural instincts of self-preservation, survival of the fittest, kill or be killed, that George Corley Wallace, Jr. appeals to in practical men. . . .").

* Called so by some reporters because of Wallace's way of avoiding the mention of Negroes. For example: "If some social engineer in Washington decides your union doesn't have enough Chinese Baptists and Japanese Lutherans, they'll put them in there and put you out of work."

Really? Did those Klansmen kill Mrs. Viola Liuzzo because they were afraid that if they didn't, she would kill them?

And just who are the "practical men" who eagerly anticipate Wallace's Presidential campaign? ,

Gerald L. K. Smith, famed anti-Semite, alerted his followers across the nation to begin petitioning to put Wallace on the ballot. Klan czar Robert Shelton has said, "We made him governor and we must make him President." The Imperial Wizard of the Interstate Klans (Maryland and Virginia) wired Wallace his "100 percent support." *The Fiery Cross*, official Klan newspaper, editorialized: "Governor Wallace may never be President, but the psychological impact upon our enemies to this possibility is our greatest word weapon, and we dare not let this great man fade from the national scene." J. B. Stoner, the moving spirit behind the uproariously anti-Semitic, anti-Negro National States Rights Party, said, "Our slogan is the same as in 1964. Governor George C. Wallace— Last Chance for the White Vote!" Impatient in Wisconsin are the Liberty Amendment Committee, which is dedicated to the repeal of the income tax, and the Christian Freedom Fighters, who desire to "put more Christ into politics." John Birchers such as Tom Anderson are rooting for him: "Unless the Republicans nominate a true conservative in 1968," says Anderson, "Pa Wallace is a cinch to run, a cinch to carry the South, and a long-shot bet to throw the election into the House of Representatives." The White Party of America (described by the late American Nazi leader George Lincoln Rockwell as a "bunch of disgruntled Nazi Party members who swiped my mailing list and defected") awaits the second coming of Wallace.

Wallace's success with the more orthodox politicians of the South is much more iffy. Even Governor Maddox of Georgia, strangely fickle, has announced that he doesn't like third parties. When Wallace heard about this, he told a group of Alabama political underlings that Maddox "doesn't have much character." When Maddox heard about that remark, he said Wallace was just sore "because he doesn't have me in his pocket"; when Wallace heard about that reply, he said something that can't be repeated here. It was a typical experience for Wallace at Presidential campaigning time. Politicians who court him in other seasons, flee him then. When Leander Perez' forces moved in late 1967, continuing the fight into 1968, to take the traditional Democratic ballot symbol away from President Johnson and give it to Wallace, Louisiana Governor McKeithen—although agreeing with the things Wallace stands for—set about to protect the President's prerogatives. The Democratic leaders of the South for the most part still find their threads of money and power and prestige interwoven too thickly with the national party to warrant risking it all on a mere matter of ideology, as Wallace asks them to do. It was rumored that Roger Milliken, the millionaire textile baron who owns the Republican Party in South Carolina, bought Wallace out of the 1964 race to help Goldwater; but one of Wallace's closest friends said the real reason Wallace got out in 1964 was that "he couldn't get a single important southern politician to support him." This time Wallace says he doesn't care how the politicians treat him or whether they want him. "I'm going over their heads," he said. "I'm going to the people."

He knows the people are capable of Roman displays of adoration. At a Labor Day program in 1963 when Wallace shared the speakers' platform with two congressmen, Senator John Sparkman, Surgeon General Luther Terry, and several big men in organized labor, Wallace was not supposed to speak first, but he finagled it around so that he could. On hand were about 4,000 people. When Wallace finished speaking to them and left, all but about 400 left with him, yelling encouragements to him in his fight with the "feds" and forming a spontaneous motorcade of honor for his trip out of town.

Since then his popularity has become more tumultuous, more open, adulatory. Letters to the editors of Alabama newspapers commonly refer to Wallace as "our beloved governor." Grover Hall, a former editor of the *Montgomery Advertiser* and a close friend of the governor's, does not exaggerate when he says that "the man on the street is a religious supporter of Governor Wallace's." Like the followers of Mohammed, those who "Stand up for Alabama" (Wallace's war cry) believe that anyone who falls in battle against "the social engineers of Washington" (Wallace's phrase) will go straight to a segregated paradise. Some powerful southern politicians compete for his friendship. Senator Jim Eastland, running for re-election in 1966, considered himself extremely fortunate to get Wallace to come over to Mississippi and say a few things about what a fine segregationist he is—as if, unbelievably, a word from Wallace were stronger proof than Eastland's own record. Pictures of the two together were a major campaign weapon.

Yet even a man of Wallace's staggering popularity must expect to lose some support when he gets a reputation—as, in some quarters, he now has the reputation—for debt and taxation, favoritism, hypocrisy, and ruth-lessness.

He is a man of private crudities (shortly after he was elected, he telephoned a Montgomery businessman and said plaintively, "I just called you up to kiss your ass some more") and hidden insecurities. Continued opposition can make him literally sick; after a steady barrage of insults and challenges on the floor of the Alabama senate from Bob Gilchrist (the most indefatigable opponent of Wallace's in the legislature for four years), Wallace called Gilchrist to his office and said earnestly and plaintively: "Bob, if you'll say something good about me, I'll say something good about you." At the same time, Wallace dotes on grudges and nothing seems to please him more than a chance for revenge.

Shortly after President Kennedy's assassination, Judge Roy Mayhall, of Jasper, then chairman of the State Democratic Committee, made an impassioned talk to a Young Democrats meeting at which he laid down the theme that "we are all to blame for his death." Wallace, who had been in Dallas the week before the assassination visiting with oil Croesus H. L. Hunt and damning the Administration in speeches before right-wing groups, was incensed by Mayhall's charge.

For days thereafter, every visitor to Wallace's office was brought up sharp with the question, "Do you think I helped kill Kennedy?" When the visitor assured Wallace he did not think so, Wallace would flare back, "Well, Judge Mayhall thinks I did." Brooding on this for a time, Wallace finally decided to unseat Mayhall, who had been a circuit judge of high repute for twenty-one years, and, bringing the full weight of his office and machine into that campaign, he did defeat the judge.

There are those in Alabama who, knowing Wallace's sensitivity to slight, think his present rage against Lyndon Johnson may stem from the time of the Kennedy funeral, which Wallace attended. On this occasion, Johnson held a reception, and Wallace went through the receiving line. Johnson pumped Wallace's hand industriously enough—but Johnson's eyes were on Governor Rockefeller, the next man in line. Johnson failed to look Wallace in the eye! The little Alabamian considered this a calculated insult and he returned home fuming against the president.

One of his most intense grudges whirls around Oregon Senator Wayne Morse, who, during Alabama's school-integration fuss, called Wallace a "punk." Wallace retorted that he would "rather be a punk than a pink," and suggested that Morse "should have his head examined."

Saying so, Wallace left himself wide open to a cruel revelation. The next day Morse took the Senate floor:

> I have been informed from several sources this morning that the governor of Alabama has raised some question concerning the psychiatric soundness of mind of the senior senator from Oregon. I am perfectly willing to let my record on that score speak for itself. But I would have the record at this time show the following information:
>
> Official records concerning the governor of Alabama will show that Governor Wallace entered active military service on October 20, 1942, and was honorably discharged on December 8, 1945, with the grade of sergeant in the Army Air Corps. His military specialty was that of flight engineer, with nine combat missions completed in B-29s—a brilliant military record of dedicated services to his country. . . .
>
> During service, he was hospitalized from April 9, 1943, to June 3, 1943, for acute cerebral spinal meningitis. *He was also hospitalized in September 1945 for severe anxiety state, chronic, manifested by tension states, anxiety attacks, anorexia,* and loss of weight. . . .
>
> He filed claim for compensation in June 1946 and in December 1946 was granted service-connected disability for *psychoneurosis,* for which an evaluation of 10 was assigned.
>
> He was last examined by the V.A. in November 1956, when he gave his age as thirty-seven, and stated he was married, had three children, and was occupied as a circuit judge. *He was tense, restless, and ill at ease, frequently drummed the desk with his fingers, changed position frequently, sighed occasionally, and showed a tendency to stammer, resulting in the diagnosis of anxiety reaction.* The 10 percent rating was continued.
>
> Since Governor Wallace has not been examined since November 1956, it would seem to be appropriate for him to volunteer to be examined at this time.

Wallace replied that Mrs. Luce must have been right about Morse's being kicked in the head by a horse.

When two nationally known politicians begin calling each other batty, the exchange soon becomes a bit harsh and undignified, and one might have expected both men, when their tempers went down, to make an effort to forget it. It hasn't been that way with Wallace. He never loses an opportunity to drag Morse into a discussion to needle him some more, beating the straw of Morse's distant reputation with a furious flailing—"Well, at least I have a paper that certifies I have 90 percent of my faculties, which is more than Wayne Morse can claim!"

There are some today who think that Morse has given the only possible clue to other actions taken by Wallace. Once he went on a foot-stomping tirade in a closed meeting of the Legislative Council, demanding that his irritating enemy, then-Attorney General Flowers, be impeached. Being virtually incoherent on this occasion, Wallace never did make clear why he wanted Flowers impeached; that is, on what specific grounds. One member of the council said later, "I have never seen the governor quite so worked up. It was embarrassing to most of us. Some of the hardier souls laughed."

Although the VA has not examined Wallace in a dozen years, reporters who have accompanied him on some of his out-of-state visits say that the nervousness is never far beneath the surface, and when he approaches what looks to be a hostile crowd he will begin to make low, fluting noises, and flick his fingers, and a tick will sometimes begin to nag at his cheek. In private conversations with legislators and minor state bureaucrats, he is prone to outbursts, though publicly he is markedly cool under even the most hostile questioning. When he feels crossed, he seeks his revenge quietly and seldom brags about it publicly.*

Wallace has been ruthlessly adept at removing from the field of contention any semi-liberal politicians of enough popularity that they might challenge not only his omnipotence within Alabama but also might challenge the atmosphere in which he operates best. Carl Elliott was that kind: A moderate by national standards, a liberal by Alabama standards, Elliott had been appointed (through President Kennedy's influence) to the House Rules Committee, only the second Alabamian ever to get on that most powerful committee. Thus Elliott became a small cloud on the

---

* He prefers to brag about those times when he didn't seek revenge. Proudly he told me: "Couple of years ago, Governor Dempsey of Connecticut wired me criticizing, and they were about to tear down New Haven around his ears right then. Pat Brown wired me that they knew how to live together out there—Nigger-Americans, Spanish-Americans, Polish-Americans, Italian-Americans, French-Americans and all sorts of hyphenated Americans—and while I was reading his wire, the niggers was burning down Watts. A lot of people told me I should wire him back, 'I told you so,' but I don't believe in making political capital out of that sort of thing. A reporter asked me if it didn't please me to see Brown's troubles, and I said it certainly did not please me to have that sort of thing happen. Governor Egan of Alaska wired me and said I should stop causing all the racial trouble and I drafted a wire saying he must have caused the Alaska earthquake with all his loud talk, but I didn't send it. I don't like to stoop to that level."

horizon, and Wallace set out to blow him away. The United Conservation Coalition of Alabama—drawing its members from the White Citizens Council, Ku Klux Klan, John Birch Society, and the right wing of the Republican Party—in 1964 distributed a half million sample ballots, headed with Wallace's warcry, "Stand Up for Alabama." Congressman Carl Elliott's name was left off the sheet. By the time Elliott discovered what was going on, and raised enough money to pay for a statewide television show (he had to go heavily in debt personally) it was too late. Elliott lost; and since then he has been steadily slipping in prestige. A potential challenge was gone. Wallace denied having anything to do with it, but it is common knowledge among principal Alabama politicians that, in fact, it was Wallace's scheme from the beginning.

Most politicians both lust after and despise the press, but with Wallace these reactions are more extreme. I once asked him why he kept complaining that the press had mistreated him. He answered petulantly, "*Time* magazine said I picked my teeth with a soiled toothpick. And a fellow on *Newsweek* called me up and said, 'I'm a good Mississippi boy and I understand you, Governor, so let me travel with you and give you a good story,' and I said, 'O.K., come along, podnuh; I know you won't write it right, but come along.' And I took him in to eat with me, and he wrote in his story that I ate with a sucking sound." He is a plain man, disdaining the banquet circuit and preferring to have a hamburger at Turk's Place, with plenty of ketchup. He is a peevish man, quarrelsome and full of grotesque animosities ("I don't want to be a poodle dog for pinkos. The national news media is lying, distorted, left-dominated, communistic-minded. . . ."). One advantage Wallace has over just about every other major politician on the scene is that he's accessible, amiable in argument, and loves to gab. I dropped in on him at the capitol at 5 p.m., without appointment, and he invited me in for three hours of rapid-fire talk and chain smoking (cigars). Because he routinely curses liberal newspapers and magazines, some local newsmen doubted that he would talk to me at all, which shows they don't know their governor *de facto* very well. In his strange jungle of journalistic evils, my employer, *The Nation* magazine, is seen as no more liberal than the *Birmingham News* and the *Alabama Journal,* although these latter are about as liberal as the *Chicago Tribune.* "Let's go across the hall and talk," he said. "Maybe I can persuade you differently about things." In this kind of private debate he is a sportsman. But in his public teasing of the press, he is more often a bully. I asked

him if he did not in fact abuse the press, but he denied it. "No, I protect
the press. Sometimes I used to talk about a particular reporter being in the
crowd and what his paper or magazine had said about Alabama. I would
say: 'And here's *Esquire*'—their reporter had more hair than you ever
seen—and I would point him out and say something about him, or about
the *Los Angeles Times* man. After a while, when a little woman with an
umbrella came up and threatened the reporters, and some steelworkers
said, 'Here's the sonsofbitches, let's get 'em,' the reporters came to me and
said, 'Governor, these people are going to harm us if you don't help us';
so thereafter I would tell the crowds: 'Now, let's treat these reporters
polite and show 'em and the rest of the world that we are just as cultivated
and refined as anybody anywhere.' " This trick of "protecting" reporters
after arousing the crowd against them is something Wallace picked up
from Faubus, who often used it in the hot days after Little Rock. He will,
at a campaign rally, single out a Yankee reporter to goad and harass
and then come around later and tell the reporters he meant nothing
personal about it. Sometimes he goes to the trouble of warning fresh
reporters of what he will say about them on the stump, with the same
admonition not to take him seriously. Is all this a hoax? No, it only means
that Wallace has reached that plateau of arrogance eventually reached by
all strongmen, from which they assume that the feelings of others are their
playthings.

But it also reveals that gross vein of meanness that runs through so
much of Wallace's career. Blood and violence and physical reprisals lace
his conversation, but always thrown in—for Wallace is a God-fearing
Methodist who would not sanction violence for any other purpose—to
show what a place of peace and rationality, relatively speaking, the Deep
South is. "If a white man poked, pinched and fiddled with a nigger woman
on the street here, he'd get the hell knocked out of him by a policeman.
Same if a nigger man did that to a white woman. We know how to live
together down here. You can walk through the nigger section without
fear. A nigger can walk through the white section. We've got good
law enforcement in Alabama." (He said this the day after the third
church burning in a week in Lowndes County, and about a month before
someone tried to dynamite Federal Judge Frank Johnson's home in Montgomery.) He told *New York Times* reporter Tom Wicker, "Of course, if
I did what I'd like to do I'd pick up something and smash one of these
federal judges in the head and then burn the courthouse down. But I'm

too genteel. What we need in this country is some governors that used to work up here at Birmingham in the steel mills with about a tenth-grade education. A governor like that wouldn't be so genteel. He'd put out his orders and he'd say, 'The first man who loots something what doesn't belong to him is a dead man. My orders are to shoot to kill.' That's the way to keep law and order. If you'd killed about three that way at Watts the other forty wouldn't be dead today. But most governors are like me. They got too much education. They're too genteel." The South is a place of law and order, but the North is not, and because he is genteel he is forced to suffer outrages when he travels North. "Northern politicians are always complaining because we don't give protection down here. Hell, Martin Luther King can come to Alabama without protection, but when I go to Boston they have to lead me through tunnels for protection."

Talking violence, he is a man whom violence follows. Some newsmen who have accompanied him on speaking trips have been beaten by the Klan types that flock to him, and he has not always tried to interfere. He excused himself by saying that "it might be a good idea" if some of his opponents were thrashed. At a rally in Atlanta, where he spoke from the same platform with Georgia's chief Klansman, Calvin Craig, and with the fastest gun in the restaurant business, Lester (Axe Handle) Maddox, two Negro men were so badly beaten with metal chairs that they were hospitalized; Wallace did not speak out to stop the violence. Wallace denies it, but Al Lingo, then head of the Alabama state police force, claims that Wallace gave the word that sent horse-mounted troopers riding over the Selma demonstrators and clubbing them to the ground. President Kennedy did all but call his name when he laid the blame for the bombings that resulted in the death of four Negro girls in church; Senator Morse did call his name and said his hands "are dripping with blood." To review Wallace's career is to see that this is really not a melodramatic description.

Perhaps only a politician could accept the explanation as an excuse for his actions, but it is nevertheless worth pointing out that Wallace's blood-letting and his association with blood-letters was a conscious, and by his standards a justified, part of his maneuvering for power. As with so much else that marks his career, this is easily traceable imitation.

Over the mantelpiece of the fireplace in Wallace's office in the capitol is a huge grinning portrait of Bibb Graves, who has been Wallace's hero since he was a young man. Graves was Governor of Alabama from 1927 to 1931, dropped out a term because he had no Lurleen to take his place, was re-elected to the 1935-1939 term, dropped out for the required four years again, and would have been re-elected in 1942 if he had not died. Some proposed electing him anyway. Until the coming of Wallace, there had never been another personality-based political machine in Alabama to compare with Graves'. Wallace's entire career has been patterned after Graves'. Like his predecessor and idol, who had no political creed, Wallace is not burdened with a philosophy. And, like Graves, Wallace has believed it necessary to build his political fortress partly on a foundation of scum. Graves tried to be elected governor in 1922; not only did he fail, he failed badly. Four years later, however, he was washed happily into office on a wave of his new friends, the Ku Klux Klan. And although the Klan as a formal, organized force diminished in the coming years, the friendships developing from that secret order remained a key to his popularity.

Wallace has followed a similar route to power. In his first campaign for governor, in 1958, Wallace barely made the run-off against John Patterson, the candidate of the Ku Klux Klan. Wallace greatly desired those 75,000 Negro votes in the run-off, and so, while he said nothing about improving race relations, at least he gently knocked the Ku Klux Klan. Very gently. But still, it was a knock. He refused to speak to any KKK rallies. Patterson crushed him.

Thereafter Wallace, like his old idol, became a man of the Klan, and success followed. "They out-niggered me that time, but they'll never do it again," he told friends, vowing that thereafter he would earnestly seek the support of the fringe (the fringe is very wide in Alabama).* Since then Wallace has surrounded himself—joyfully, arrogantly, abundantly—with the toughest oddballs in town. He has tailored his line to cotton-patch fascism: book censorship, suppression of free speech, tolerance of violence, absolutism in state government.

Robert M. Shelton, Jr., head of the United Klans of America, has

* So well did Wallace learn the subtle niggering admired so much in Alabama campaigns—wherein one mentions beatniks and federal snoopers and other understood code words for racism—that when John Patterson tried to make a comeback in 1966 against Lurleen, he found that the incumbent had preempted the act and now he, Patterson, was in the same role Wallace filled in 1958, left with nothing to talk about that appealed to the rabble. Sadly the old racist told a meeting of campaign workers, "You can talk about roads and schools and old-age pensions all day and the crowds will stand there and watch the traffic go by."

been on the most intimate of terms with Wallace since 1962, openly soliciting funds for the Wallace campaigns that year and again in 1966, and he is now out soliciting presidential funds. Bill Jones, Wallace's press aide and presidential campaign manager, complains privately to newspaper reporters, "These guys like Shelton just use Wallace's name to raise money to put in their own pockets," but if this is embarrassing to Wallace, he has never given any indication of it. He refuses to disavow Klan support, saying, "I'm glad to get support from anyone except gangsters and communists," and shutting off further questions with, "I made my statement about the Klan in 1958"—whatever that was. When then-Attorney General Richmond Flowers announced plans in 1966 to investigate the Klan, newsmen asked Wallace if he would give assistance. Wallace replied coldly, "Let's move on to something important." How deeply the Klan is officially imbedded in Wallace's government is a matter of wobbly speculation, but some clues have been found. The U.S. Bureau of Public Roads in 1964 accused the Wallace administration of forcing an engineering firm to hire Klan chieftain Shelton as an "agent" for $4,000. A few months later it was disclosed that the head of the Klan Bureau of Investigation had been hired by Wallace to, of all things, investigate the Klan for the state. Wallace said it was an accident. One of Wallace's closest cronies and advisors is Asa (Ace) Carter, head of his own Klan in Birmingham in the 1950's, where he gained some passing notoriety for being accused of shooting a fellow Klansman who was so foolish as to inquire of Carter what he was doing with all the dues. Carter, too, was very active in soliciting money for the campaigns of Wallace in 1962 and Mrs. Wallace in 1966.

But Wallace's regard for the Klan goes farther than mere kickbacks and conversation. Legislation to restrict the sale of dynamite and thereby inhibit Klan bombers was killed by some of Wallace's men in the state senate. In 1963, when the Federal Bureau of Investigation was preparing a tight case against the bombers in Birmingham, Wallace stepped in and had them charged and convicted of a much lesser crime, and thus destroyed the FBI's chances for really putting them away. At a Klan rally, Wallace's chief muscle man, Al Lingo, sat on the platform with the Klan speakers and was introduced as "a good friend." When a civil rights worker was killed in Jayneville, Lingo brought a bondsman to assist the accused slayer.

Having grown to political lustihood in a state where there is a right-

wing nut—a very appropriate pun in this instance—of 100,000 or more
(judging from the faithful bloc of that size who give their support to the
perennial flaming-sword candidate, Admiral John Crommelin), which is
a handy margin to have in case of a tight race, Wallace can surely be forgiven for supposing that the same strategy that has been so successful
in Alabama will pay off as he moves again into the national arena. Barry
Goldwater disavowed the Klan, but Wallace considers himself much
cannier than Goldwater; *he* won't disavow *any*body. If Goldwater could
count on the little ladies in tennis shoes, Wallace feels he can get not only
their votes but those of their T-shirted sons who work in the mills around
Gary, Indiana, and in service stations and bars along the eastern shore of
Maryland, and in defense plants rising from the steppes of Los Angeles.
"Indiana was the birthplace of the Klan, you know," Wallace will tell
you, inaccurate, as usual, in his knowledge of history but instinctively
accurate about the depth of that dark corner of Indiana's soul.

Wallace's acceptance of support from the far right was, of course,
followed by appointment of supporters to good jobs. Two of the most
prominent right-wingers in the state were appointed by Wallace to the
Alabama Textbook Selection Committee. Textbooks are screened for
what he calls "writers with possible connections with communist-front
organizations." He asked the FBI to clear the authors. When a reporter
reminded Wallace that the Attorney General's list includes KKK affiliates,
Wallace said he wasn't interested in those, but only in authors "who front
for commies." High-school history books used in Alabama identify the
Klan only as an organization set up to combat the "oppressive" Reconstruction legislatures in which Negroes were given a voice; its latter-day
violence is not mentioned.* Like the right-wingers he is trying to appeal
to, Wallace seems sincerely to feel that much of the nation's troubles
come from the eggheads. "The intellectual morons," he calls them, and
he is fond of telling redneck political crowds, "Those intellectual morons

* Possibly one explanation for Wallace's using books as mere political tools is
that he doesn't have much to do with books in his own life. He told me he reads
"mostly magazines." I asked if he read any books at all, and after studying for a
long moment, he answered, "Well, I even read *Das Kapital* once, but I couldn't
understand it. I like to read books like *Lee's Lieutenants.* I like books about the
Civil War best, about people dying for a cause, brave men, North and South." He
was asked a similar question in Baltimore in 1964; his head snapped back as though
he were dodging a punch and he answered: "That question is 'bout to get me.
'Course I read Socrates, Plato and Aristotle and all those folks. And Machiavelli."

with all their theorizin' couldn't see Castro was a communist, but you people with just common sense could see that just by looking at his picture, just by instincts. The instincts of a common-sense Alabamian is better than the brains of a New York intellectual moron."

Wallace's experience in college left him with little nostalgia for the place. He was not the outcast po' boy he likes to pretend; in fact, he was offered membership in a fraternity and turned it down because, he said, he felt it might handicap him if he later went into politics. This suspicion of college students who "have it soft" continues. While 7,000 White Citizens Council members roared approval at a Jackson, Mississippi, conclave, Wallace threatened: "Personally, I'm tired of fighting communists 10,000 miles away from here and letting them run rampant in our country. If we catch any dudes trucking with the enemy in any university I have anything to say about, we will just expel them out of that college." (He was referring to students protesting the Vietnam war.) On another occasion he damned "people pooh-poohing around, sitting up in their ivory towers with a bunch of sissy britches." He told me that, if he were President, one thing he would do that Johnson hasn't done is, "I would have the Justice Department grab them by the long hair—these intellectual morons, these professors, these students tearing up their draft cards, raising money and blood for the Viet Cong—and have them charged with treason, have them tried and put away. . . . We're at war. It doesn't matter whether Johnson had the legal right to send the troops over there."*

In his last year as governor he attempted to get the legislature to pass a law forbidding any Alabama college to let a communist on its campus.

---

* I reminded him that when President Kennedy sent the National Guard to Tuscaloosa to throw him out of the schoolhouse door, he bitterly accused Kennedy of acting illegally. If he were for supporting Johnson, even if he sent the troops to Vietnam illegally, how could he have protested Kennedy's sending troops to Alabama's university, even if illegally? Wallace's response was a typical readjustment of the rules of the game, "That was different. I didn't have to be on the soldiers' side at Tuscaloosa. They were on my side. As [Deputy Attorney General Nicholas] Katzenbach walked by them, some of the soldiers called him a dirty bastard and a sonofabitch. They said: 'Why don't you get out of here, you dirty bastard,' and things like that. I think if Katzenbach and his crowd had laid a hand on me, the soldiers and the troopers there, well, they just wouldn't have allowed it. I know that General Graham, we didn't see eye to eye in all things, but I think he would have asked to be relieved before he would have ordered the troops to lay a hand on me. The Birmingham papers reported he said: 'It is my duty to take over.' Why, hell, everybody knows he said: 'It is my *sad* duty.' "

The reason for the law escaped both lawmakers and educators, none of whom could ever remember a communist trying to speak on an Alabama campus. Wallace was turned down.

The fluid, informal academic community found it easier to battle Wallace than did the commercial enterprises that could be subjected to economic reprisals. For example, newspapers that opposed Wallace on major issues were threatened with forfeiture of advertising from the state-ran liquor stores. School officials who opposed his anti-federalism were threatened with loss of state money. Legislators who opposed him were sometimes—depending on how powerful they were in their own right—threatened with the loss of road funds in their districts. He backed himself with two spy systems—one for politics, the other for social action. The network of political informers was made up of thirty officials, each assigned his special county or two counties, with the responsibility of reporting directly to Wallace any behind-the-scenes political activity that takes place there. The other secret police force, unmatched anywhere in the country, was made up of special investigators who compiled files on civil rights workers and newspaper reporters covering civil rights activities, and "subversives and anyone else who might cause us trouble."

He worked secretly with Liberty Lobby, a right-wing organization, in the preparation of a "biography" aimed at promoting him in '68; the biography presents Wallace in a pro-Negro light, telling how he has had fist fights to protect Negroes. That for the northern audience. At home he ordered the cutting off of salaries to teachers whose classes drop below 63 percent of normal enrollment—this to discourage school children from staying out for protest marches.

If he is hated by many outside the South (when he went to New York in 1963 to appear on television, there were more security precautions taken for his protection than had been taken for Soviet Deputy Premier Anastas Mikoyan; barricades lined 49th Street from the Avenue of the Americas to Fifth Avenue and closed Rockefeller Plaza; there were hundreds of policemen on hand), he is, obviously, revered by the right-wing everywhere. He recently broke his hand punching a punching bag; a right-wing organization asked for the discarded cast to preserve it for posterity.

Looking back on Wallace's early career, it is difficult to see the point at which he laid his grappling hooks in the South's heart. Before he became governor he was nothing much, an assistant attorney general, then a circuit judge. In the latter office he won a little publicity by fussing with FBI agents and threatening to throw them in jail if they butted into his business. He went through some contrived feuding with federal officials over the disclosure of voter registrations, but this kind of noisiness did not set him much apart from many other southern railers at that time, and it would do so even less today, for threats have become commonplace. In 1966 when Wallace threatened to throw two Negro agents from the Office of Education in jail if they ever came back to Alabama, it hardly made the newspapers.

His early political name, such as it was, shone mostly from the reflected glory, and notoriety, that came with his being a Big Jim Folsom man; Folsom's south Alabama campaign manager, in fact. To understand the evolution of George Wallace, one must go back through Big Jim's career and pick up a few of the pieces, for Wallace is there all the way, at first riding piggyback on Big Jim's strength and later leaping over Big Jim's weakness into the governor's seat.

The recent history of Alabama might have been a far different cycle, even a socially progressive cycle, if James Folsom had not had such a weakness for booze. This is accepted lore in Alabama; nobody tries to hide it, least of all Big Jim, who rarely gave a speech in his attempted comeback of 1966 in which he did not acknowledge his boozy past but vowed that that was all over with. And it probably was. The ruin was too great to think otherwise. Shuffling through the 1966 primaries once again —no longer a drinker "since I had that saving brain operation"—still talking about "peace in the valley" and offering to give his cast-off shoes to friendly old Negroes in the crowd; his last cakewalk of defeat, a nice guy finishing very close to last.

Ah, but it might have been otherwise on another important day. Many genies of speculation, and wispy guesses of what might have been, curl out of the bottle that plagued his career. Nobody who loves Alabama politics could watch the giant, slightly stooped hulk once again on the hustings without pondering the possibility that Alabama might never have had a George Wallace for governor if Big Jim—who, up to that crucial moment, had stayed sober the whole race—had not gone on television the last night of the 1962 first primary feeling very, very good.

There was that hideously embarrassing moment when he got to burping and chirping and hooting at the other candidates for imitating his campaign pitch. Just a bunch of me-too candidates, they were. . . . *"Mee too! . . . Me*too *. . . mee*too *mee*too *mee*too*mee*too! *. . ."* It went into the record book, sorrowfully for those who admire him, as Big Jim's Tweety Bird speech. (The *Montgomery Advertiser* called it "the night the cuckoo in the clock sang itself to death.") Naturally, the church folks, of whom Alabama has an ample number, didn't like it one bit, and Big Jim lost his chance to get into the run-off by 1,163 votes. Suppose that he had got to contest Wallace in the second primary. Could he have beaten him? Perhaps; it would have been a close race.

But in any event this was just the last of a series of defaults of leadership brought to Alabama by genial Jim, drunk or sober, liked by even his enemies, perhaps because he was always so ineffectual in opposing them. At first hated and feared by the Big Mules of Birmingham, later they paid for his campaigns as a sure guarantee that they would not be bothered. Big Jim never bothered anybody. Some of the folks around him looted the treasury, but he went out of office with little more than he came in with. True, he was a bit extravagant at times. In his first term he spent $140,000 of the state's money for a sea-going 95-foot yacht, which he named after his wife, and during the final year of his second term he spent $54,260 in state money for yacht parties. Then, too, there was the squadron of seven state planes which Big Jim sometimes augmented with the Alabama National Guard Air Force for buzzing college football games. ("I am ordering every jet, every C-47 and everything that can roll on wheels, much less fly, to fly over the Gator Bowl. . . .") There was some ugly talk that paroles could be purchased from the Folsom pardon and parole board, and Big Jim scorned this as "just smear and conspiracy," but he did acknowledge later, "If I can find some excuse to turn somebody loose, I'll always do it." During the last fifteen months of his first term apparently some good excuses were found because 1,600 paroles and 354 outright pardons were granted. Two prisoners found paroles waiting for them when they got to prison; one asked the deputy sheriff to hang around so he could ride back to town with him. When one of Folsom's closest chums, Dock Commissioner Ward McFarland of Mobile, was found guilty of evading his federal income tax, was sentenced and thus lost his civil rights, Folsom said he could go right on holding his state job anyway. Big Jim said it wasn't McFarland's fault, it was the fault of foreign aid, which demanded too much "dump money." Folsom had a battery company and forced the state to buy from it. When reporters inquired about the ethics of this, he replied, "I don't know why others should get the gravy. I'm governor."

But if there were chicanery and shysterism, these were well balanced by great amounts of low comedy. He publicly praised an invocation as "a damn good Baptist prayer"; when a snooty newsman from Ohio made derogatory remarks about Alabamians' racism, Folsom rebuked him, "Trouble with you-all up North is you'll sleep with a nigger, but you won't get up in the morning and eat breakfast with her." Sometimes, in his first successful campaign, he would be hung over and, excusing himself from speechmaking while the Strawberry Pickers struck up a few more tunes, he would lie down on the sidewalk and fall asleep. At a between-campaigns political rally to which Averill Harriman had been invited, once again Folsom stretched out on the stage and went to sleep. When it came his turn to take the microphone several aides tried to hoist the six-foot-eight-inch governor to his feet, without luck. Finally he became conscious enough to raise up on an elbow and say he felt too humble to follow such a great man, and fell back. A couple of years before his second successful campaign, he was arrested for drunk driving; the highway patrol was always following him, trying to catch him doing something wrong. Big Jim acted as his own attorney, told the jury what a great governor he had been and how he had been sick since, and broke, and got to crying and mopping his face and begging them not to convict. They didn't. Riding down in the elevator with reporters Folsom laughed and joked about how he had fooled the jury. At a southern governors' conference, at which he was supposed to lead a panel discussion on atomic energy, Folsom announced, "I'm supposed to report to you on atom bums but I don't know anything about atom bums so I'll just say hello and now I think I'll retire to the bar." At these governors' conferences it was commonplace for Folsom to be barefooted. In his second campaign, all sorts of cancelled checks from liquor companies and other assorted evidence of payoffs and kickbacks were brought into the campaign, but Folsom brushed it all aside by saying, "My ol' mammy told me when I got in mud fights, now don't you try to rub it off, Jim, just let it dry and it'll fall off." When he went to New York, he was met by a welcoming committee of forty fashion models, all of whom he proceeded to kiss carefully and elaborately while

2,000 spectators watched and applauded. Big Jim Folsom to Alabamians meant hoopla. He held press conferences while drinking champagne. His first inaugural parade, four miles long, was the biggest Alabama had ever seen; but his second inaugural parade—coming after numerous scandals, including a bastardy suit—found "The Little Man's Big Friend" heading a twelve-mile parade including 126 bands.

He could arouse this kind of affection because he was a kind-hearted fellow, truly desiring to bring peace and brotherly love to his state. Openly he spoke of the Negroes as "our colored brothers and sisters—our Christian brothers and sisters—back in the back there." That was after the Brown decision, after Alabamians were beginning to fire up over the race issue. "Negroes constitute 35 percent of our population. Are they getting 35 percent of the fair share of living?" He appealed to Alabamians to "do more than talk" about helping the Negro. He tried to get the poll tax abolished, tried to liberalize voter qualifications, tried to get more state parks for Negroes. He did win an anti-mask law, aimed at the KKK. "Let us join the people together again. Let us furnish leadership for our colored people. You were raised amongst 'em. Go down in the black belt and the white folks talk more like the Negroes than the Negroes do. Their two colleges aren't even accredited. They've got just eight trade schools and they want two more and they're entitled to them. Last year we turned our bad face to the world. They took pictures of mobs running around the streets of Birmingham. They was taking people out at night, floggin' 'em and mutilatin' and castratin'. Next thing they'll be wantin' to cut ol' Big Jim. Let us have peace in the valley."

He invited Representative Adam Clayton Powell to the mansion for cocktails (an act of hospitality which still haunts him), and when word got out that he and Powell drank scotch together, Big Jim didn't try to lie out of it. His standard reply was, "Shucks, you folks know old Big Jim don't drink nothing fancy like that. I drink hard likker just like you." When the segregationists—who once had tried to have him impeached as an integrationist—abused him about not caring if the schools were mixed, he twitted them by promising, "No Negro will be forced to go to school with white children as long as I'm governor." Over and over again during his last term, ending in 1959, he denounced the white councils, said "nothing based on hate can exist for any length of time in a Christian democracy. I favor white, red and black councils. I cannot lead this state if I base my thinking on hate." Remember, he was saying this to his people when, in the next state to the east, Herman Talmadge and Marvin Griffin were doing all in their power to stir up the people to new pitches of hatred. If it was only talk Folsom was giving, still that was a very valuable thing.

The only fault that can be found is, however, a tragic one: he could have given more than talk. Assuming the legislature was too hard-line to even consider the voting reform bills he offered, or the bi-racial commission he proposed, Folsom nevertheless had the wherewithal to fight the legislature more successfully than he did, or tried to do. He scoffed at the resolution of nullification passed by the legislature—but he did not veto it. The legislature passed a law disenfranchising 400 Tuskegee Negroes, and Big Jim cried out against such an undemocratic act—but he did not veto it. (It wouldn't have done any good, since the bill was passed unanimously, but if the law had been challenged by Folsom this at least might have kindled courage into debate.) He did not appprove of the pupil placement law—but he did not veto it. In each case, his only show of resistance was not to sign the bill, and allow it to become law through expiration of time. In economic matters, Folsom, although under tremendous pressure, refused to allow the militia to be used as a strikebreaker; but he signed a bill requiring merchants who sold Japanese textiles to put up signs confessing it and thus (the legislature hoped) identify themselves shamefully as un-American. He damned it as an "economic force" bill and said he would not sign it. That was Saturday. Monday, he "reluctantly" did so.

But of all the episodes in Folsom's career that mark his unique thirst, if not his weak nature, none illustrates it better than Autherine Lucy's effort to get into the University of Alabama. The rioters came, and out she went. And where was Big Jim? Today he says he would have sent the National Guard to keep order, as the Negroes expected and begged, but, "I was leaving it up to the police to let me know if they couldn't handle it." Many Negro leaders at the time suspected, however, that he was simply too deep in his cups to take charge. That would figure. Douglass Cater, touring Alabama not long thereafter, reported: "A British correspondent who interviewed the governor recently noted that he looked tired and exceptionally care-worn. Leaving the office, he remarked to an assistant that Folsom seemed under great tension because of the racial turmoil in Tuscaloosa (University of Alabama) and Montgomery. 'Tension, hell. He's just got a hangover this morning that's about to kill him.' "

The single touch of genius evidenced by Folsom in two terms (1943-1947 and 1955-1959) was that while he acknowledged the reality of the racial problem, he saw the southern political treatment, and the North's reaction to it, as a farce. "The Yankees and the southerners," he told me, loosening his top trouser button to get comfortable, "give each other hell up in Congress, and then they get in the backroom over cocktails and say, well, we put it over on the folks again. It's been going on for a hundred years. Bobby Kennedy was the Cecil B. DeMille at Tuscaloosa, just like he was at Oxford. But people are getting wise to that sort of thing." Tragically, the time came when Folsom was no longer the man who could lead his people toward such understanding.

No southern governor ever took office on such a cresting popularity: The legislature was against him; the big-city press was against him; the industrialists and big businessmen of the state were certainly against him. But he had faith that Henry Wallace, whom he greatly admired, was correct in predicting this to be the century of the common man, who was very much for Folsom. He drew the battle line in such a way that no one could mistake it. Against the powerful right-wing Farm Bureau Federation and the State Extension Service—and their allies, the Big Mules of steel, mining, and shipyard interests—he allied himself with the National Farmers Union and the followers of Aubrey Williams, close friend of Franklin D. Roosevelt's, whose radical views were the focus of a New Deal controversy in 1944 and who now headed up the 900,000-circulation *Southern Farmer*.

And so they went to war. And Folsom lost. The things he wanted to do for Alabama were, ironically, not to be done in any impressive fashion until the coming of George Wallace. The social reforms Folsom wanted, Wallace wanted. It must be conceded, despite some of his more obvious hypocrisies, that the lunch-pailer and the small farmer are the constituency closest to Wallace's heart, as they were to Folsom's, and when he shouts, "We did this for the working people of Alabama," he means it, and he sees no inconsistency in the fact that what he does for them is often done in a style that sets back the state fifty years.

But Folsom had fouled the banner they had fought under, and Wallace got nowhere until, as editor Grover Hall put it, "he shed himself of Jim's malfeasance, misfeasance and every other kind of feasance."* He got nowhere either, pity the times, until he turned his back on Folsom's racial kindness. Wallace could justifiably contend there is a causal connection between that turning and his success.

Wallace's first real notoriety came in 1958 and early 1959 in an episode rarely mentioned any more, although at the time it was widely gossiped; it is important historically as a perfect sign of the strategy on which Wallace was to build his highly successful career: the strategy of challenge, surrender, and bluster—always used in that order.* The date is also significant, being immediately after he had lost his first bid for the governorship to surly, rough-talking John Patterson; Wallace was convinced he had been too gentlemanly in that race, and now he was out to correct that defect.

Representatives of the U.S. Civil Rights Commission were in Alabama to look into charges of voter discrimination. They asked to see voter records of Barbour County and Bullock County, in Circuit Judge Wallace's district. With a great flourish of frustrating the commission, Wallace

---

* There are still campaign movies floating around the state, dating from the 1954 campaign, which show Wallace standing before a crowd yelling: "If it's Folsomism, I'm for Folsomism!" But because of the shadiness that brought general disrepute to the Folsom regime, Wallace today pretends he was not close to Big Jim. He told me: "No, I wasn't for Folsom. I was against him in 1946. But then I got five trade schools through the legislature, and I was thinking about running for Congress, although I would never have run against George Andrews—he is the greatest congressman, so far as I am concerned, and I stand for everything he does—but I was thinking about it, and I asked Folsom to put one of those schools in my Congressional District in case I ran, and he said he would. I guess I told him I would do anything he wanted, if he would do that. So six or seven years later he decided to run again, and he came to me and said: "You remember what you promised," and I said: "Yes, I said I would give you my support," and he said: "No, you said you would do anything I asked, and I am asking you to be my south Alabama manager." Well, I went to Governor Chauncy Sparks and asked him what I should do, because I didn't want to do it, and he said: "Did you promise?" and I said: "Yes, I guess I did," and he said: "Well, you'd better go ahead and do it then because you can't break your word in politics." So I said to myself: "Well, maybe I can have a good effect on Jim's administration"—that's how I salved my conscience.

"Well, so Jim was elected, but then I saw that those who was around him was drinking and stealing, and I got out because I figured they would all wind up in the penitentiary. 'Course, I don't like to go into that now, because Jim is sick in the head and all that."

* I must modify this, however, to say that in one important episode he challenged without surrendering and, in fact, forced the federal government to bluster a considerable amount itself. This was in his opposition to the school guidelines of the Civil Rights Act, which will be discussed more fully later on.

impounded the records and turned them instead over to county grand juries. At that point U.S. District Judge Frank M. Johnson, Jr., of Montgomery issued an order to Wallace to make the records available to commission agents.

"These characters from the evil Civil Rights Commission and Justice Department were backed to the wall—they were defied and backed down," Wallace proclaimed. "This 1959 attempt to have a second Sherman's march to the sea had been stopped in the Cradle of the Confederacy."

Actually what happened, as official court records show, is that when Judge Johnson told Wallace to surrender the records or go to jail for contempt, Wallace—although he claims he didn't—surrendered. While giving the appearance of defying them, Wallace made secret overtures to the civil rights agents. Contained in the court record is a sworn statement by civil rights agent A. H. Rosenfield describing a night-time call from Wallace in which he offered the records after turning them over to the Barbour County grand jury. Wallace angrily denounces anyone who says he gave up the records as "an integratin', scallywaggin', carpetbaggin' liar." But in reputable circles the story persists that Judge Johnson threatened Wallace with a five-year sentence in the federal penitentiary—long enough to prevent his running for governor in 1962—if he didn't back down, and that Wallace, to escape the contempt conviction, went contritely to Johnson's house at night, and made peace.

Johnson, a law-school classmate of Wallace's, was too gracious to go into details but he did say that Wallace had obeyed the court in a "devious" manner.

And did this total defeat in any way crack the veneer of Cock Robin rebellion that already was solidifying on Wallace's career? Not at all. Crowding the courtroom to hear Judge Johnson dismiss the contempt action were about seventy-five farmers and small-town merchants, some of them saying to anyone who would listen that *they* would pay George's fine if it came to that, some of them even wearing their old Win With Wallace buttons of the previous campaign, and all convinced from a mystic inversion of logic that what they were witnessing was a victory for The Little Judge.

Far from trying to get people to forget the episode because he did not win, Wallace made it the central theme of his victorious 1962 campaign.

"I called Judge Johnson publicly in 200 speeches on the stump and on TV a 'integrating, scallywagging, carpetbagging liar,' " he told me in happy recollection, "and I said, 'He ain't got guts enough to do anything about it.' A lot of people said I shouldn't say that. They said people don't like that kind of rough talk. They came to me in droves and said, 'Please don't say that again.' But I went on saying it, and I'm still saying it. By the time my campaign slogans become clichés, other people are using them."

This was the first step down his weird trail of victorious defeats. Also, it was from this embarrassing experience that Wallace developed his almost psychotic dislike for federal judges; insulting Johnson specifically and all federal judges in general has become a stock maneuver. The federal bench, he asserts, "doesn't have enough brains to try a chicken thief" (a threadbare quip he picked up from Georgia's ex-Governor Marvin Griffin). On one occasion, denying that he was mad for power, Wallace argued, "If I wanted power, I'd sell my state out and become a federal judge." And another time, he suggested that Judge Johnson was somehow a traitor to the South because he sent his own son to a private, segregated school, whereas Wallace's son attended a desegregated school. Interestingly enough, there was a quasi-populist smack to his argument, a smoldering class anger, as he sneered at Johnson for finding it easy to issue all those noble desegregation rulings because he could *pay* for segregation, whereas, "It just so happens that many working people can't afford private schools. My son has to bear the burden of school desegregation along with the rest of the people."

There have been modern southern politicians who were far greater, certifiable populists than Wallace; much more flamboyantly anti-communist; more colorfully anti-federalist; more devastatingly opposed to home-grown liberals; and some who were just as strikingly anti-integration. Wallace's fame as the standard-bearer of segregation rests on his supposed *success,* in the successful scope of his challenge; and in that supposition there is some irony. For the truth is that, although Wallace has stubbornly taken the message of segregation past the Canadian border, east to the Potomac, and west to the Cuckooland of California, no southern politician has in fact done more to advance integration not only in his home region but throughout the nation.

As his defeated opponent, the late Ryan de Graffenreid, remarked when Wallace moved into the governor's mansion in 1962, still breathing fire and brimstone: "It's been the same pattern in every state where you have a loudmouth, rabble-rousing governor. They have brought the walls of segregation tumbling down on their heads."

De Graffenreid was a prophet.

Wallace's effect on Washington lawmaking has been amazing. His bungling of the Birmingham upheaval led directly to the Civil Rights Act of 1964, his bungling of the Selma disturbance led directly to the Voter Registration Act of 1965 (sometimes nicknamed the George Wallace Citizenship Act) and his veto of a community action project in Birmingham had a similarly swift reaction. "Several of us were trying to get rid of the veto and getting nowhere," said Representative William Ford, a member of the House Labor Committee. "Then Wallace vetoed the community action program and the next day we got a unanimous Democratic vote to change the law. We couldn't have done it without George." Wallace's stubbornness was the direct catalyst for the Fifth Circuit Court's school desegregation order, issued in 1967, which blankets the Deep South.

In his inaugural address Wallace promised "segregation today, segregation tomorrow, segregation forever." But forever lasted only five months, at which time Alabama became, as a result of Wallace's resistance, the first and only state forced to operate under a specific statewide court order not to interfere with desegregation procedures. Almost from the beginning of his term all state universities have been integrated, as well as all big-city public-school systems and a number of rural systems.

Oxford, Mississippi, under Ross Barnett's direction, was a tragedy. Tuscaloosa, Alabama, under George Wallace's, was only a farce.*

Stumping the state in 1962 Wallace had promised, "I shall refuse to abide by any illegal federal court order, even to the point of standing at the schoolhouse door in person." For several years it had been standard stuff in the South for candidates to swear that they would go to jail, or bare their breast to federal bayonets, before surrendering to Washington. Wallace's vow was a little different; different enough, at least, that it caught the public's imagination, and Wallace knew that he had better go through with it, though he had no stomach for the melodrama. The stage was the University of Alabama. It was easy enough to stand in the schoolhouse

* Wallace sent State Police Chief Al Lingo and Hunter Phillips, later Wallace's security chief, to Oxford to report back on how that kind of crisis was developed, but either they weren't accurate in laying out the formula or Wallace didn't understand, because his crisis pooped out. The authority for their trip to Oxford is *The Wallace Story,* by Bill Jones, Wallace's former press aide; The American Southern Publishing Company, Northport, Alabama.

door, but what next? Wallace had been a champion Golden Gloves boxer as a boy. Should he draw on that training and sock Deputy Attorney General Katzenbach, or whoever sought to get past him?* Should he grab hold of the door jamb and hang on? Should he resist until federal troops or U.S. marshals carried him away, and should he then scream and kick? Standing in the doorway is not a simple thing to program, not if you are a high official who wants to come out of it with a little dignity. In the preliminary negotiations with the Department of Justice, Wallace offered to step aside if Katzenbach would come at him with fifty marshals. But the Attorney General, shuddering at the memory of what happened to the Oxford scenario worked out with Barnett, said no deal. Finally they had it all agreed on: Wallace was given a podium and a microphone to make his little speech; while television cameras purred, he would hold up his hand like a traffic cop as Katzenbach approached; then the National Guard general (temporarily federalized) would step in; Wallace would salute him, there would be a compassionate exchange between these two southerners, the general saying it was his "sad duty," Wallace consoling him, "I know this is a bitter pill . . ."; and then Wallace would step aside, surrendering not to the federal government but to a southern soldier acting under duress. Everyone went through his part just right and the timing was perfect, but for some reason the show was a flop.

Wallace had pulled out all the dramatic props—National Guard, state troopers, edicts—but nothing clicked, either on the college or the public-school level. As a matter of fact, his sending guardsmen around to peaceful school systems and his issuing and rescinding orders to open and close various schools were received even by some of his most loyal backers as the actions of a mad man. The *Montgomery Advertiser*, his most devoted supporter, called him a "wild man" and regretted his having made "a monkey out of himself." Some mothers suggested publicly that Wallace should be hanged. Huntsville Chief of Police Chris Spurlock said of the "shameful" closing of the schools, "If it isn't evident to all the world today that the executive head of our government is a sick man, then, by God, none of us are discerning enough to read the facts." Local school-board officials in Huntsville and Mobile, who wanted to integrate and go on with their business, charged Wallace with interfering in the same way he condemned the federal government for doing.

* I asked him why he didn't hit Katzenbach. Wallace said he had a temper, "but not that kind. I haven't hit anyone for years."

It was his most unsuccessful stunt, and he was only too happy when the guard was federalized and withdrawn, and the schools were all open again. Lamely he apologized for his defeat: "I can't fight bayonets with my bare hands." There *were* no bayonets. And when someone called this to his attention, he responded even more weakly, "I never have said I was going to win in this matter. I said we were going to awaken the people to the danger of an omnipotent federal government."

The *Alabama Journal,* a Confederate-conservative newspaper that has been one of the few to steadily see Wallace as an inept defender of the southern life, editorialized at the time:

> Our files are incomplete on the subject, but it appears that our governor holds the Southeastern Conference title for the most desegregation in the shortest time. How long will his fire-and-fall-back tactics fool the people? Most of them are still fooled by the mock warfare in which the administration has volunteered itself, and the state, as the losing side.
>
> Our melancholy conviction is that they will be fooled for a long time, because they want to be fooled. Just as the people in London were soothed by the sound of anti-aircraft guns firing at nothing in the early stages of the blitz—a calculated ruse to convince them that Britain was fighting back, thus to bolster their morale—so does Wallace continue to set off impressively noisy blanks. The people love it, sad to say.

The fact that they are blanks is known to most of Alabama's leaders, which accounts for the fact that they first received his tirades with shrugging unconcern. One Alabama college president, appraising Wallace's "successful failure" as a segregationist, said, "I would term the governor a pseudo demagogue, because he really doesn't believe what he says about the race question. He uses it only as a technique to get the vote of the nonsophisticated white man." The fact that they knew what was going on, however, lulled the business community into a position which they sorely regret today. For the first couple of years of his term, the rich men of Birmingham paid no attention to him. He rather amused them, in fact, voicing in his lowbrow way their own discontent. They would retire to the club room at the Mountain Brook Country Club to cuss the federal government, even as they made another million or two doing business with it; meanwhile, Wallace had taken the leadership of their Klan–union workers and thus had taken control of the state. By the time the rich men put down their glasses and stopped cussing the government, it was too late to hold back the Wallace wave. This is the situation today: Alabama big businessmen, who had grown so accustomed to running the state's politicians that they thought it could never be otherwise, fear Wallace and his rednecks. The innocent demagoguing they permitted because they understood it (after all, they had helped *pay* for it) has kicked back on them. This has been Wallace's only lasting victory, but in his political heart, which beats to Big Jim's anti-Big Mule tempo, it must be a sweet one.

One must, however, also acknowledge several spectacular temporary successes; Wallace can thank the timidity of the federal government, rather than his own strength, for them, and therefore for the artificial aggrandizement that has made him a national candidate. Not long before the '66 primary, one of Wallace's closest aides, speaking for the governor, said, "Let them register the Negroes. Let them bring down every Negro in Harlem and register them too. We'll still win."

It was a safe prediction. While the Negroes had a quarter million registered to vote in 1966—more than three times the number when Wallace first ran for governor—that was not yet enough of a bloc to swing a one-issue campaign. *However,* if the Justice Department had sent down federal registrars to all the counties where Negroes requested them, and if 70 percent of the Negroes had been registered (certainly not an impossible number), at least they could have put their choice, Attorney General Flowers, in a run-off with Lurleen, and *that* would have been the kind of psychological turning that could loosen Wallace's grip on Alabama.

In addition to a languid implementing of the Voter Registration Act of 1965, the U.S. Justice Department has virtually shown collusion with Wallace in its refusal to enforce other laws. Although Wallace was placed under a court order in 1964 to refrain from interfering with the desegregation of Alabama schools, he did nothing but interfere for the next two years, and yet the Justice Department did not try to have him cited for contempt. The best proof of Wallace's temporary success is the fact that only Mississippi can claim a smaller percentage of school integration. The blustering and bombast of Wallace has noticeably slowed down the U.S. Office of Education from enforcing all the congressional acts and all the court edicts that it has at its disposal. Alabama loves to watch Wallace bluff the USOE, and he kept up this form of entertainment even after he was out of the governor's office. One of the first things he dispatched Lurleen to do after she became *pro forma* governor in 1967 was rally the legislature into a special session and use one of his tested rebel scripts. The results were all he had hoped for.

There she stood, The White Goddess of the Black Belt, reciting incantations and spells, warning the U.S. Office of Education that (snap snap snap) she intended to hire more state troopers to fight anyone sent down to enforce the Constitution and that (boomlay boom) the federal judges who keep trying to expand school integration "better understand what the people of Alabama mean!" Then Queen Lurleen stamped her foot, and the aroused natives of the Alabama legislature yippeed and yahooed their appreciation, and the jungle drums beat ceaselessly through the night. In faraway Washington, sitting around the USOE campfires, Commissioner Harold Howe III and his safari mates heard the savage yells and shivered. God! It was those man-eating Dixiecrats again. Should they push on, or turn back? USOE explorers do not have the dauntless nature of a Lord Greystoke. Seldom have they acted with the calm awareness that southern politics never produce a new threat; decades and generations pass, but only the actors, never the lines, change in this creaking morality play.

"They have made their decree," she cried, "now let them enforce it!" Shouts and stomps. Whistles. They liked that; the South always had. It was an ancient, if not a venerable, line. Her husband had said much the same thing, with some of his privileged rococo embellishments, after the passage of the Civil Rights Act in 1964: "The liberal left-wingers have passed it. Now let them employ some pinknik social engineers in Washington to figure out what to do with it." The words Mrs. Wallace used were the precise ones employed in 1956 when Governor Allan Shivers of Texas refused to send state police to protect Negro students trying to integrate the high school in Mansfield. And, of course, the first southerner to emboss them in history was Andrew Jackson, more than a century ago, after the U.S. Supreme Court had invalidated a Georgia law stealing some Indian land: "[Chief Justice] John Marshall has made his decision, now let him enforce it."

What a pitiful sight it was, really, the earnest little woman standing there, sometimes almost in tears, come far since her days as a dime store clerk but not so far as to realize that every other statement she made was an historical cliché. She threatened to interpose the powers of the state police between the federal courts and the schools. Poor thing, George had even pawned off the doctrine of interposition on her. Pennsylvania had used it in 1809 and had been so embarrassingly squashed that only southerners would touch it thereafter, but for some reason they grew to love it. It has been enunciated dozens of times by southern governors and legislatures, without a speck of success. After the Brown decision in 1954, every legislature in the South pulled it. Alabama did itself, in 1956, although the governor of the day, Kissin' Jim Folsom, allowed as how the resolution of interposition was "a bunch of hogwash." And here was Lurleen dishing out some more hogwash, just as George had in 1963 when he declared everything but secession and called out the state troopers to keep the schools from integrating.

All federal officials who deal with Wallace should bone up on southern history, for the fear of Wallace cannot reasonably survive the knowledge that his career—notwithstanding the noise of parochial success that surrounds all he does—is closely and consciously patterned after the careers of politicians who were keyed either to a hopeless cause or to the lowest element of the electorate. It may be, at times, a winning combination in the Deep South, but certainly not nationally.

Over a loveseat in Wallace's mansion is a picture of William Lowndes Yancey, that oratorical fool whom Alabama once loved and still reveres, like Wallace, for leading it astray. Two years before the Civil War, Yancey went up and down his state asking, "Is the Constitution a fixed, unchangeable, immutable rule of conduct for Congress; or does it stretch, expand or contract, with each change of public opinion?" To him the answer was a shrill "fixed!" Southerners are Fundamentalists with the U.S. Constitution, just as they are so commonly Fundamentalists with the Bible. The meaning that was good enough for John Hancock is good enough for them. Since variances in education were anticipated by the Founding Fathers—"every citizen should receive an education proportioned to the condition and pursuits of his life"—the South is baffled when it asks only separate but equal, not separate and classified. "I say that the fundamental of all fundamentals in our system of government," Senator Eastland admonishes the Senate with the fervency of a circuit rider, "is the premise that the Constitution of our country shall be interpreted strictly in accordance with the understanding of the members of the Constitutional Convention who submitted it and of the states which adopted it." Its unalterable meaning is as sacred as The Word on the first Pentecost. And yet even the primitive concept that stirs this loyalty is a regularly replenished invention, a fiction. As with so many other night-blooming fictions in this region, this one too is passed as a rider to the Race Question. The lie is in the pretense that anyone could give an interpretation to the Constitution that would meet total agreement; the lie is especially and most dangerously in the pretense that the South would be reconciled to a consensus interpretation no matter how carefully the text is followed. This has been the special lie of the Deep South since before the Civil War. Of all the things that have not changed, this is foremost.

But being a good southerner, Wallace's Alabama predecessor, Yancey, did not mean by "fixed" that the Constitution should speak with one voice through one authority, as he made clear when it was suggested that the difference between the North and the South be submitted to the U.S. Supreme Court for settling. He called such arbitration a "monstrous doctrine," because only the sovereign states "should determine whether their reserved rights had been invaded." Each state would judge for itself. Nothing is so flexible and various as a "rigid" interpretation of the Bible or the Constitution. Here in the Bible Belt, the 1776-Belt, we southerners want no Popes, no Supreme Court with a final say. That should be left up to each preacher, each sect, each politician, each state. "I've got as much right to interpret the Constitution as anyone else in this country," Herman Talmadge said in 1956 when asked on his way to the Senate if taking an oath to uphold the Constitution meant that he would uphold civil rights laws too. "I'll be bound by what Herman Talmadge thinks it means." Whether you own slaves or utility plants, or merely represent those who do, it is a mighty useful attitude for turning aside regulations. And so we find Wallace declaring on several occasions that he intends to obey all the "*legal* laws" of the land. That sounds a bit shifty, and it is. Before a law can be considered a "legal law," one must do more than merely test it in the courts. One finds out if the people want to obey it; or at least one guesses at the people's sentiments in the matter.

Wallace is another Yancey, although Wallace's opposition ("lousy, no-account black and red court") is not quite so eloquent as Yancey's. One helped get Alabama into the Civil War, for which he was sainted. There's still no telling the depths of the defeat Wallace is preparing for Alabama; but knowing his people, Wallace knows that victory is the only thing he has to fear.

Next to a fire-breathing position against integration, Wallace planned his winning race for the governorship around promises to stop corruption in state government.

Shortly after he took office, he sent the liquor agents packing. Liquor stores in Alabama are state-owned, and liquor agents—there were usually about 100—had to do nothing but drift around from store to store talking up one brand or another. They were paid by the major distilleries, not by the state, and they were paid well—one of them drawing $52,000 the last year he was on the job. The governor got to appoint the liquor agents, so it was an arrangement that was just one giant piece of payola—recognized as such by about everyone in Alabama.

When Wallace wiped out the system, he was widely applauded for it, though his manner of doing it drove all the major distilleries out of the state (Old Houndstooth took the place of Jack Daniel's on the liquor-store shelves for four years). Even though prices went up, and even though sales declined so sharply for a time that the highway patrol was used to help business, still, Alabamians for the most part were happy to settle for inferior firewater because, hallelujah, the old liquor-agent racket was gone! Graft and corruption, gone! Alabama was on the way to clean government.

Or was it? It wasn't long before capitol watchbirds began to hear of one Wallace friend who was making a killing selling office supplies to the state, another Wallace friend who was getting wealthy selling black-topping to the state highway department. Wallace had rid the state of liquor agents, but soon in their place came the textbook agents (reportedly $800,000 disappearing via that route), and insurance agents (reportedly $600,000 going to Wallace pals) and highway agents (reportedly one agent alone drawing a 1 percent fee from the $100-million road bond issue).

The highway agentry stirred the biggest stink when Rex Whitton, administrator of the U.S. Bureau of Public Roads, wrote Wallace that he was jeopardizing the state's road program by requiring consulting engineers on federal highway projects to hire his friends as agents—a violation of federal regulations. Judging from several of the names on the list, it appeared to be a clear case of Wallace's returning favors for bloc votes.

Governor Patterson had deplored the free spending of the Folsom administration, but Patterson had been no slouch at it himself. In addition to a press secretary, he had had a radio-tv secretary and a personal photographer. He had sold five of Governor Big Jim Folsom's seven planes, but had later bought four others, and before he left office he had been using state funds to hire lawyers for his brother, Maurice, who had served as his state finance director and been accused of misusing $950,000 in state funds. Said Wallace: "Sinful."

Wallace promised that there would be no more wasting of state money. In his inaugural speech he said, "The big wheeling cocktail party boys have gotten word that their free whiskey and boat rides are over." And so they were. Whiskey isn't served in the Wallace mansion.* And one of the state's two yachts was sold.

But Alabama found out that there was more than one way to skin a state's kitty. Wallace, who had decried the seven-plane air fleet that had developed under previous governors, paid a quarter-million dollars for a Lockheed Lodestar for out-of-state trips. (Big Jim had a point: "At least you can fish from a boat.") With him on these trips would be half a dozen highway patrolmen as bodyguards, a sizeable public-relations staff, and many important appointed officials. These were no inexpensive ventures, especially when Wallace specialized in television appearances. No full accounting of his presidential campaign expenses in 1964 was ever made. Wallace doesn't know who takes in what. He says he raised nearly $400,000 himself in 1964, running for President in three states, but nobody knows where it all went or if it's all gone. Statements filed in Baltimore Circuit Court showed Wallace spent $90,000 in Maryland. The Indianapolis *Times* estimated the Wallace fund in Indiana at $50,000. If he spent as much in Wisconsin as in Maryland and Indiana together, that still would leave $100,000 unaccounted for.

And this may explain some of the excitement that accompanies a Wallace campaign. It is like joining the troupe of a traveling faith healer. Under the great flapping tent of a Wallace race—while The Master lays his hands on the bedridden faithful and bids them, "Stand up for Alabama! Stand up for America! Stand up for God!"—his friends are

---

* He started off in his 1962 campaign saying ". . . and I won't be drunk either" —an allusion, of course, to Big Jim. By the time the campaign was over he had stepped up his purity to the statement, "And I don't drink, either." He made good on his teetotaling, although former Attorney General Flowers says it is a change of pace: "I've drunk this room full with him." I asked Wallace about that. He said, "No, I don't drink. And I never did except socially. When I was about a sophomore in college I took a drink; in fact I took about three, and on the third one I strangled and I never have been able to stand the smell of whiskey since then. I was given an eggnog at a party once and didn't know it had whiskey and when I put it in my mouth I had to spit it right out. It was embarrassing. Sometimes with Flowers, when he was drinking, I would have a little glass socially. I'm not against drinking. I just don't drink, that's all."

profitably going through the crowd. Bucket-begging campaigners operate at road blocks,* other campaigners appeal for contributions on radio programs, others use mail solicitation. Some sell tags, some sell lapel buttons, some sell bumper strips. For example, *The Councilor,* the Citizens Councils of Louisiana's newspaper headquartered in Shreveport (circulation 250,000) and considered by many to be the most robustly anti-Semitic, anti-Negro publication in the South (specializing in Negro-white sex stories), was pushing three-color, Wallace-for-President license plates as early as 1966, and advising its readers, "It's little things like this that add up to win the biggest of battles." It really wasn't such a little thing, to *The Councilor.* The tags cost $1.25. By mid-1966 they had sold 60,000 and they were confident of a 100,000 sale by the end of the year. With a 60 percent mark-up, that's not bad.

There are other indications that the love for Wallace is partly tuned to the ringing of cash registers. He is widely blessed by the old right-wing workhorses and by the new ones who want to get into the business, because every time a new gut-plucking candidate like Wallace comes along it means new vigor for their membership and therefore their income. Some are quite candid about it. The Citizens Councils of America are sick and emaciated. The only reason they aren't dead is that Lurleen Wallace stirred things up again with her campaign and election, and then George Wallace gave further mouth-to-mouth resuscitation. William J. Simmons, the councils' executive director, says that when Lurleen won her big vote, "we turned the corner then" and the crisis was past. The councils would survive, however leanly—but only if George really ran for President and didn't just talk about it. For months Simmons went around the South complaining because Wallace hadn't formally announced; it was hurting business. As Wallace goes, so go the White Citizens.

Although the fringe that hangs on is doing better economically, Alabama is in some ways not. In fact, economically the state could be judged to be in something of a mess.

Of course, it all depends on whether or not a person favors deficit financing. If he likes it, he will like Wallace's way of operating. Alabama's budget droops beneath the weight of more than $450 million bonded

---

* These road blocks are, I think, a southern phenomenon. Solicitors simply stand out in the middle of the highway with their pails and make cars slow down, and then panhandle for the cause. Sometimes state and local police help tie up traffic to make things easier.

indebtedness (and even as this is written there is talk of adding on at least another $150 million)—twice the bond debt that existed when Wallace came into office and 700 percent higher than it was eleven years ago (during the same period the federal government's bond debt rose only 14 percent). It is anticipated that the state highway department will soon be paying one-third of its income (from gasoline tax, etc.) for debt. Without new bond issues, the highway department would be bankrupt. Under Wallace, Alabama has reached the point that it is paying $50,000 a day in interest alone, on bonds issued without a vote of the people.

How has he got by with it? Well, one reason is that the people recognize that Alabama was in such sad shape that something had to be done fast, even if it was done in the wrong way. But Wallace also got by with it because he was a sharpie. In a special legislative session he rammed through a $100-million bond issue for highways amortized in such a way that not one penny will be repaid until four years after he has left office— and, just as important now, not until Lurleen has stepped down. It's fancy, but costly: interest on those bonds will run to more than half the principal. He had *said* he needed only $60 million for highways, but he got $100 million—the extra $40 million, as one practical legislator admitted, was used "to buy us with county roads."

Typical of the economic glossolalia that guides the state's finances is the undirected and confused junior-college and trade-schools program. This was Wallace's baby, and he got the legislature in 1963 to give him $15 million to build five junior colleges and five trade schools. Or at least that's what the legislators thought they were voting on. As it turned out, the number of schools wasn't written into the bill, and by the time Wallace's floor lieutenants and friends were rewarded with placements, the state wound up with twenty-eight junior colleges and trade schools. Wallace had to go back and get another $15 million from the legislature in 1964. In 1965 he begged another $8.3 million. What started as a $15 million program ended at $38.3 million.

He borrowed, taxed, and spent more money in his four years than any other governor in Alabama's history; in fact, he almost doubled taxes, and with them he increased old age assistance, eased the requirements for getting on state pensions, increased state participation in the federal old-folks' medical-aid program, raised teachers' salaries, raised the budget for public schools and the budget for higher education by more than 25 percent, and increased workmen's compensation.

"I'm no ultra-conservative," he says honestly, "because those ultra-conservatives are conservative about just one thing—money."

These are smart political moves. One of the pillars in ex-Governor Folsom's old political machine was composed of the state's 110,000 pensioners. Wallace went out for that bloc support and got it. (On the other hand, since Alabama's prisoners can't vote, the prison system customarily gets about half what it needs to operate even at minimum standards. Only Mississippi and Arkansas put less into their prison systems.)

Wallace likes to pretend that the state is booming under his touch. But from time to time the truth slips out. He asked President Johnson to protect the Selma marchers because Alabama was too poor "to bear the burden," as indeed it probably was; the cost of this protection ran to more than a quarter million dollars, which is not the kind of sum Alabama can throw around. He has built many school buildings, but not so many as he claims; some of the schools he boasts of building were completed in the administration of his predecessor. Nor is he exactly generous about giving credit to the federal government; he takes credit for building the new field house at Auburn University, although it was done with federal funds, and all over the state the roadsides are dotted with large signs: "THE WALLACE HIGHWAY PROGRAM, Largest in Progressive Alabama's History . . ." with these proud words flanked by reproductions of a Confederate flag and an Alabama flag. Missing is the U.S. flag, and missing also is mention of the fact that the federal government is paying 90 percent of the construction. Wallace boasts a great deal about the prosperity he has brought by luring industry to Alabama, but Red Blount, one of Alabama's top industrialists, said: "Business doesn't come to Alabama because of Wallace. These businesses build for forty to fifty years. One governor is in for only four years (or, with his wife, eight). It's ridiculous to say they came because of Wallace or through his efforts. They came because of Alabama's natural resources and what the state has to offer." Wallace's "prosperity" has many holes in it. While in the last five years per-capita income has increased in Alabama a little faster than in the rest of the United States, it is still only 68 percent of the national average, third from the bottom among the fifty states, with only Mississippi and Arkansas beneath.

In this impoverished context, Wallace's vaunted economic "populism" takes on a different shade. In the last analysis, one must judge the degree of populism behind a welfare or a public-works program according to who pays for it. In Alabama, it is the consumer who pays. Alabama is one of the top three or four greediest consumer-tax states in the nation. The state sales tax is now 4 percent. Most Alabama cities add on another 2 percent. And that's across the board—groceries and medicine and newspapers included. (The Farm Bureau—which, along with the banking and insurance lobbies, is one of the three most politically potent groups in the state—loves the sales tax as a source of income because the material its members buy—farm machinery, seed, fertilizer, etc.—is exempt.)

When Wallace came to office, he had a reputation as being a fighter against the sales tax. When he was in the state house, he filibustered a sales-tax increase to death by introducing dozens of amendments and then speaking on each for ten minutes (the only way he could filibuster in that body). But to get the money he wanted for his program as governor, Wallace allowed a pyramiding of sales taxes—although for weeks he had been swearing to organized labor that he would not sign the bill to increase the tax.

Wallace had *proposed* a tax on utilities, a tax on insurance premiums, and an escheat bill. But these were just put up to make the poor man feel better; as Wallace must have known, they didn't have a chance of passing. Only the escheat bill got as far as a floor vote. It is generally felt that Wallace used them only as scare tactics to make banks, insurance companies and power companies get behind the increase in the sales tax.

Paradoxically, he kept taxes off big business and industry, yet the money leaders fear and distrust him; he piled new taxes and debt on the people, and they love him.

Wallace has not escaped the domination of big money, but he has come closer to escaping it than most southern politicians. Along this line of thought, it is interesting to speculate as to why Wallace did not run against Senator John Sparkman as either a Democrat or a Republican; for not only did he first say he might run as a Democrat, he also—according to the House Republican Congressional Newsletter—put out feelers to switch parties to make the race against Sparkman. He could doubtless have beaten him either way. Sparkman, a dull, country-club conservative with a strange reputation as a "southern liberal," has a long record on racial matters not one whit more humane than Wallace's. He said he agreed with Wallace's handling of the Selma march "in principle." He helped write the Southern Manifesto, vowing a last-ditch legal fight against integration, and "gladly" supported a bill by Senator Richard Russell that would have authorized federal funds for shipping southern Negroes into the North. He has propagandized for the Citizens Council; and his vote-and-filibuster record on civil rights legislation is identical with the records of such senators as Talmadge and Eastland. Sparkman's voting record on labor and medical aid is slippery; he has voted both ways on most major social reforms. His activities in Congress have not been free of mud. He was reported to have been the strong arm behind a briefly notorious $3.4-million building loan in Indianapolis back in 1954; his name popped up briefly in the Bobby Baker investigation (after which Sparkman voted against every attempt to expand the investigation), and he wound up with 700 shares in a Washington, D.C., bank in 1964 in what *The Washington Post* called a "deal."

Just where and how Sparkman ever picked up the reputation of being a "southern liberal" is a mystery, but because he rides heavily on his superior reputation as a dignified bigot, Wallace despises him and makes no effort to hide the fact. Throughout most of 1965 Wallace was known to be considering taking Sparkman's seat. But then he suddenly dropped the idea. Why? It has been said that Republican Representative James Martin, who nearly defeated Senator Lister Hill, was induced to drop out of *his* proposed race against Sparkman and make the impossible try for the governorship against Lurleen, after talking to the board of directors of the Chase Manhattan Bank, who did not want Sparkman defeated, because that would put liberal Senator Paul Douglas of Illinois (if he had survived the election, which he didn't) in line for the Senate Banking Committee chairmanship if old Senator Willis Robertson was defeated, as he was. Martin admitted he had met with directors of Chase, but he insisted that "the name of Sparkman was not mentioned at the meeting." Whether Chase's pressures were also responsible for Wallace's backing out is not known, but for some reason throughout Lurleen's campaign George kept denouncing the bank. "We're going to set the Chase Manhattan Bank back on its heels and teach it to keep its money and its mouth out of politics down here." Right on schedule, Sparkman got full support from big business and big banks while banking interests pressured the National Republican Party out of contributing a dime to his Republican opponent. As it turned out, running as Lurleen's prime minister was probably best for Wallace's national ambitions, but being turned aside from defeating Sparkman was a bitter frustration. Sparkman now sits as chairman of the Senate Banking Committee, and though the men at Chase and elsewhere in the world of money have many nice things to say about him, Wallace never mentions him except with contempt.

The quality within Alabama politics that may in the end prove Wallace's downfall is the very rebelliousness which he encourages and which his career is based on. Alabamians are prone to rebel even against rebels. Winston County in northwest Alabama did not like the idea of seceding from the Union, yet it did not see how it could stay in the Union while surrounded by the Confederacy, so instead it seceded from the Confederacy and set up the Free State of Winston (abortively, for the Confederacy crushed it). Throughout Wallace's four years the same spirit was found in a tough and uninhibited group of Alabama senators, a minority group which—using the filibuster with crushing effect—held him in check on many important bills. "Some of us in the senate really love Alabama. I could cry when I think of what Wallace has done to Alabama," chief rebel Bob Gilchrist said at the height of one fight, and the next day proved his point by actually crying as he denounced Wallace on the senate floor. Depending on the issue, there were between nine and twelve senators willing to filibuster until they dropped. (All twelve left the senate at the end of 1966.)

Seventeen days in one thirty-six-day regular session were destroyed in filibuster, while Wallace's pet bills stacked up. At the most intense period, the rebel senators talked back at Wallace for 108 straight hours. Sometimes Wallace would become so enraged by their stalling tactics that he would go on statewide television—at state expense—and denounce the irritants as worthy only of "going North and joining the communists and beatniks."

Just as Wallace used the threat of cutting off state contracts to businessmen and cutting off highway and education funds to some areas in order to pack the Democratic Executive Committee with persons willing to go the unpledged-slate route, he used the same threats to hammer at the state senate when it balked. (The house needed no battering; in four years, it turned down only one Wallace bill, and it was an insignificant one.) But as often as not, on the really controversial bills, he lost. He was turned down on some important patronage bills; he lost his effort to restructure county voter-registrar committees (to make it easier to exclude Negroes); he made two grabs for control of the state colleges, both senior and junior, but lost; and most importantly, he lost his bid to pass a succession bill which would have allowed him to run again for governor (he cut off liquor ads to six of the most influential papers that opposed the bill, he barnstormed the state denouncing the senators who opposed him, and he cut off appropriations to a junior college in the district of one opposition senator; his pressures didn't work).

Getting refused has become a major part of his life. When he invited 1,700 editors of daily newspapers across the country to come to Alabama and be his guests for a week-long tour of the state, fifty showed up, and the tour finally ended in an uproar, several editors accusing Wallace to his face of attempting to brainwash them, and Wallace finally leaving the group in a sulking rage.

On the shore of his almost oceanic success are many incidental defeats that show him to be, notwithstanding his own opinion of himself ("I am the law") and notwithstanding Lurleen's overwhelming victory in 1966, far from politically omnipotent. Aside from the several important efforts to gain more power through the legislature which he lost, he has also met with embarrassing reversals on other occasions.

On January 12, 1963, some of the old last-ditch gang got together in Montgomery to plan a way to undercut President Kennedy the next year. On hand were Wallace, Ross Barnett, Leander Perez, Roy Harris of Georgia, James Gray of Georgia (who ran as one of the leading segregationists in the 1966 gubernatorial campaign) and three or four other, lesser lights. They agreed on the "free elector" plan. Have the electors on the Democratic primary ballot in all the southern states, but have them uncommitted; then run a strong "favorite son" southerner in the fall, and take the electoral votes away from Kennedy. Wallace saw himself as that favorite son of the South. Unhappily for him, only Alabama and Mississippi went through with the plan.

When he went to the Southern Governors Conference in 1965, seeking support for a constitutional amendment that would leave control of the public schools solely in the hands of the states, he was turned down. Meeting with the governors of Arkansas, Louisiana, Mississippi, and Florida in a secret session in New Orleans before the Democratic convention in 1964, he exhorted them to prepare ultimatums for the national confrontation. The support he got from them was, at best, divided. Faubus of Arkansas and Bryant of Florida sidestepped his appeal for solidarity. (He came back complaining that Faubus was "all over the place" and Bryant was nothing but "a pretty boy.") McKeithen of Louisiana, in pained fear of losing the $750-million offshore-oil royalty money, in escrow awaiting federal court decision on whether it belonged to Louisiana, turned white at the suggestion. Again, at the 1966 meeting of southern governors in Miami, Wallace tried to get himself accepted as The Leader against the school guidelines, but he found few governors who wanted to give their share of the potential demagoguing to him.

The half-attained walk-out of the Alabama delegation at Atlantic City in 1964 was, according to Wallace's plans, supposed to be joined by the delegations of North Carolina, South Carolina, Louisiana, and Arkansas. That fell through.

The day before the national convention opened, Wallace, through his henchmen, called a strategy session and invited the delegates from all thirteen southern states to attend. Almost at once it became apparent that the session would be conspicuously ill-attended, and Wallace tried to have it called off. Time was against him, and he had to go through with it. Except for the Alabama delegation, the hall was almost empty. Then Wallace called his unpledged electors together and asked them to resign so that a pro-Johnson group could be named in their place—to be certainly defeated by Goldwater electors. Surprisingly, however, his own hand-picked group refused to quit.

Such auxiliary defeats, which have strangely failed to chip any of the bright enamel from his image, seem to be hermetically sealed off from his public. From the mass of Alabama voters he can get great personal loyalty and support; but like Governor Faubus of Arkansas, he is often unable to transfer that support to issues or subordinates. Four of six former members of the Wallace cabinet were defeated in the 1966 elections.

For a youthful, vigorous politician, Wallace should be content. Instead, he is impatient almost to the point of neurosis. He loathes the confining part of the governorship (which, in fact, he still holds), the office consultations, the paperwork, the necessary patronage chats with back-country supporters. Forever gnawing at his heart are his national ambitions and what Marquis Childs properly calls "an almost Messianic sense of his own mission to free the South of the hated Yankee domination." With some success, the same messianic aura was artificially thrown around Lurleen's service as George's political surrogate. The official inaugural program issued by Wallace reads: "This was the importance of Lurleen Wallace's decision [to enter the governor's race]. At the core of the debate over Mrs. Wallace was the struggle of Western Civilization. With her decision to run for governor, she made a decision to endeavor to keep alive the only inspirational movement begun in the past twenty years in defense of western man's losing war to chaos and communism." Does Wallace really take himself, and his stand-in, that seriously? He does.

When Wallace and his wife Lurleen appeared in the old house chamber in the state capitol on February 24, 1966, to formally announce her candidacy for the governorship, those who witnessed it had varied reactions. Some saw it quaintly as the all-American culmination of a marriage that had begun nearly a quarter century before, she then a sixteen-year-old dime-store clerk, he a truck driver (with an unused law degree in his pocket) who sold old clothes and coat hangers on the side to make ends meet. For her the announcement was recognized as, if nothing else, a beautiful display of will power, overcoming the shyness that in Wallace's 1958 campaign saw her hunching down in their car, hoping nobody would speak to her, unable to respond when they did. But the politicians saw the announcement for what it was: George Wallace's opening of his bid for the presidency on some ticket in 1968.

Next time there would be no Goldwater to foul him up. Wallace had been serious in wanting to get on a dozen or sixteen or thirty-five ballots in 1964. But then, with Goldwater in the running, he saw his friends' interest shifting. Even Georgia's segregationist ex-Governor Marvin Griffin, for months one of Wallace's staunchest supporters, announced he would switch to Goldwater. Wallace got out. He said he had done what he set out to do, "conservatize both parties," but an intimate friend said he quit running "because he couldn't get a single southern governor or congressman to go along with his candidacy." And a powerful enemy of Wallace's said it was "because H. L. Hunt and some of his other money pals told him they were going for Goldwater instead, and for him to get out."

Whatever his reason for quitting the race, he did not quit gracefully. When Goldwater came to Alabama, he was chauffeured around by Wallace's chief muscle man, Colonel Albert Lingo, then head of the state police. But Wallace had a few hours earlier left the state for a "previous engagement" elsewhere. Ironically, Wallace handed Alabama to Goldwater. The unpledged slate of electors—which had been set up to be given to Wallace—pushed Lyndon Johnson's slate off the ballot. Then, with Wallace out of the race, the only meaningful slate remaining was Goldwater's. That the result of this was to leave the Democratic Party in

Alabama a shambles, a demoralized and scattered flock, was of no concern to Wallace. He is, in fact, not one to bother about partisanship: "If the folks are for you, party doesn't matter." At heart he is no longer a "Democrat"—whatever that word means in a region that even today, as for three generations, has mainly one party and one ideology. It would be no wrenching of old loyalties if he were to go to the Republican side. There were strong and lasting rumors that he planned to switch parties in 1964 but—maddeningly for him—he had been upstaged by Strom Thurmond. *He* rated the role of top convert and Wallace was damned if he would come in as the No. 2 switcher. Yet that was more an irritation than a disappointment. Neither major party appeals to him. Robert Kennedy, Lyndon Johnson, Hubert Humphrey are, of course, white devils. But so by his own statement are Romney, Reagan, and Nixon. In classic redneck he philosophizes, "You can put them all in a sack and shake them up and it won't make any difference which comes out first because they are all alike." As for Goldwater, who inspires a special dislike, Wallace believes —with justification—that the Arizonan owes whatever success he had in 1964 to him and that it was a piece of ungrateful doublecross for Goldwater to "come into our state and meddle in our politics," meaning his speaking on behalf of Lurleen's Republican opponent.

This aggressive disenchantment with both major parties by a politician willing to start a third party is something that America has not seen since Henry Wallace's Progressive Party of 1948, and the memory of *that* unhappy episode certainly raises no optimistic predictions for Wallace's future. Boxed in for now, Wallace can only break loose through a third party, and yet, is that a role normal for this super-cocky Lochinvar? Third parties are for Thurmonds and La Follettes, for politicians willing to carry on a suicidal vendetta or for far-out reformers with a program. Wallace has been neither. Third parties are for politicians willing to see their careers decline as their causes are absorbed by one of the two major parties. Wallace is not that way.

And yet, he must be, for he is doing all he can to attract the wild hares of the right who dearly love to think in third-party terms. He has become a participant in the frantic right-wing fantasia.

He is a politician of great persuasive abilities, but he has continued on his present approach to power—his momentum and direction so unchangeable as to seem fated—that he may already be helplessly entangled in a one-issue appeal, which even some of the most dedicated southerners outside of Alabama are tiring of and which, conceivably, Alabamians will eventually tire of also. U.S. Senator Sam Ervin, Jr., of North Carolina, who co-managed the civil rights filibuster with Georgia Senator Richard Russell in 1964, called Wallace "the chief aider and abettor of those who would pass such bad legislation as this civil-rights bill."

Wallace—at heart perhaps what he claims to be, a Populist—is living out the classic story of southern politics. He grew up poor. The mortgage on his family's farm was foreclosed in 1937. Grateful for what the New Deal was doing for rickety Alabamians, Wallace was convinced that Franklin Roosevelt could do no wrong. When he graduated from law school, times were so hard he got a job driving a truck instead of practicing law. Some of his early married life was lived in a renovated chicken coop. As a legislator he did not forget his background. He sponsored a number of progressive bills, and pushed them through. And even into the early 1950's when he was stumping the state for progressive Big Jim Folsom, he damned the rich folks who opposed Big Jim's aims. There was a time when some Alabamians considered him a dangerous radical. Some, indeed, still do.

Then Wallace, like the great but tragic Populist Tom Watson half a century ago, decided he could not really get to the top and stay there by dealing in economic problems and that he would have to bow to what Watson bitterly had called "the inevitable nigger question." Wallace, too, acts as though it were inevitable. Recently a close friend asked him if he did not think that eventually, as Negroes become more widely registered and southern city folk become more adjusted to the law, perhaps he would have to modify his position toward the Negro. No, said Wallace, he could not do that. In fact, he added, the southern white would have to increasingly come to think of bloc vs. bloc, and fight it out at the polls that way. So far, at the state level, he has proved that this can be done.

The way to do it, or at least the way that has always worked for George Wallace, was at no time more sharply set down, almost in textbook crispness, than when he went to the legislature in 1966 to seek support for a bill that would make it illegal for a school board to comply with the U.S. Office of Education guidelines. But there was an unusual show of resistance from ordinarily quiescent sources. Some school boards decided to go ahead and comply with the USOE anyway (Wallace threatened to hold mass meetings around the state to expose the "treachery" of these boards). Many white teachers, professionals not exactly renowned for their courage in political matters, opposed the move. The head of the influential Alabama Educational Association, representing all the white teachers in the state, said his organization would resist Wallace's resistance plan all the way; others siding with the federal plan and against Wallace's legislation were key officials at the state's major universities.

But they were getting no support from the U.S. Justice Department. The November elections were less than three months away and Washington apparently did not want to stir things up.

Seeing that his bluff was working, Wallace pushed it further with fine skill. He called the legislature together in joint session and decked the stage: kleig lights, microphones, statewide television, the works.

Behind him—there in that gleaming white building on Goat Hill over which only the Stars and Bars fly, there where Jefferson Davis had sworn the oath of Presidency to a stillborn empire of the South—was a marble plaque commemorating the signing of the Ordinance of Secession in 1861, and in front of him on the floor and in the petite galleries was a crowd cheering at his every sentence. The sweat of history was there, and Wallace, master showman, made the most of it, trying to create echoes of that 105-year-old confrontation. He started off with a proper tone: ". . . Alabama is taking a historic step as an example . . . which eventually all states must take if we are to save our nation from central tyranny." But then the bumpkin broke through: "That example is, in effect, telling the bureaucrats of power that they can take our federal money—and they know what they can do with it."

They cheered him. They clapped and whistled and stomped the floor. He would not win, of course; nor would the flow of the $70 million which he seemed so heartily to disdain be slowed in the slightest; they all knew that; but the lethargic leviathan in Washington had given him one more opening, and he was using it masterfully for his own private evil, and theirs, and they were behind him solidly there in the capitol of the land of the white muslims.

If national politics has a place for a man with that rigidity, then Governor Wallace, with his proven ability to rally the masses, may have a fine future ahead. But for his type there is no middle ground, and if he has guessed wrong, then he can at best hope to wind up beside that old broken musketeer, Ross Barnett, in Dixie's wax museum.

The Future:
Still Black — and White

Where there is a racially distinct minority whose well-being depends to a degree upon law and to a degree upon the good nature of the majority, the minority will finally be buggered precisely to the degree that the law allows—even when there is considerable good nature at hand. No man can hold out for long against another man's helplessness. Sooner or later one will be seduced and the other will be buggered.

Walker Percy, 1966

Having been dragged into disrepute once again by its leaders, the Deep South is content; those who own and run the region will use the martyrdom of civil rights legislation (passed solely to "harass and hell-hack the South," we are assured by Senator Russell) to keep the same old maestros riding the bandwagon and the same old philosophies wheezing out of its calliope.

Look for no great changes. Most of the men we have been writing about are too young to die soon or too entrenched to raise hopes of dislodging them short of some bonus scandal. And if they succumb either to mortality (which must be closing in on Perez) or to disrepute, others of similar Bourbonic persuasion stand three deep ready to replace them.

302

What will prevent the new and perhaps more subtle (and therefore more successful) wave of segregationists from coming to power?

The answer would have to be one of the following: (1) A change of heart in the region, arising from kinder impulses than it has ever been known to possess. (2) A wise use of black bloc power, to intimidate offensive politicians and encourage the mellower ones. (3) Fear that further rebellion might drive away federal and outside industrial money.

Change of Heart. This is almost too fanciful to pursue, yet it is probably the most commonly recurring theme in any discussion of the South. "Enlightened observers" used to tell us that southerners really *wanted* to integrate but that they had no face-saving way to do so. Federal legislation—so the argument continued—would give them this face-saving mechanism to carry out their deepest desires. Well, of course we now know that the civil rights acts of 1964 and 1965 changed very few hearts. If miracles of the spirit occurred, they were isolated and not regional. And perhaps it was wrong to hope for miracles. Misplaced hopes already were being dragged behind the South like a tangle of scabbards. Since the South of Despair was too visible, the South of Hope had become a favorite discovery for writers. It is what Jonathan Daniels wryly described as "the frayed fantasy . . . the new, new, ever new South." The fantasy has prompted some (retrospectively) amazing statements, such as from Arthur Krock of *The New York Times*, seeing signs that "the day of the party conservative is now ending and . . . southern Democracy is about to join the northern on the left side of the American political scene." *This* he said in *1954*.

Yet supposing that a new South is a possibility, it is still almost certain that anything even nearly deserving the name reconstruction will not be led by reformed southern politicians, not even a reformed southerner who has reached the White House. It is, after all, too easy to get a reputation for repentance in civil rights. Senator Russell Long, who only six years ago was calling federal judges "quislings" and encouraging the people of Louisiana to do away with their public school system rather than admit four Negro girls in starched dresses to the classrooms of New Orleans, is now received far and wide as a changed man. But today he inserts items into the *Congressional Record* denouncing Martin Luther King and other Negro leaders as various kinds of scoundrels, including traitors to their homeland. "You used to be able to get· after niggers as a race,"

Marvin Griffin told me (and Griffin is a scholar of racial slander), "but that don't go over now. Getting after them as individuals is all right." So Russell Long, wise to the code, gets after them as individuals and is hailed as a reformed bigot. Talmadge, too. And Faubus. Should we grant the same conclusion to Leander Perez, who recently had the head of a Louisiana Klan arrested? Heaven forbid that the South's reformation should be woven from such soiled threads.

Black Bloc Power. Through the Civil Rights Act of 1964 the southern Negro was, in a way, spottily, permitted to make the grand discovery of what miserable wayside café food the white folks had been eating all those years, and through the Voting Rights Act of 1965 he is now learning that the ballot is grievously slow in working improvements.

The knowledge of this is unsegregated. Both Negro and white civil rights leaders are now aware they are faced with the problem of pumping enough hope into the unregistered to get them to take time off without pay or walk four or five miles to town or make some similar sacrifices to register and vote, without giving them so much hope that disillusionment will follow their first participation in an election.

This is not easy to do, for the Negro vote has been of sufficient strength long enough in some areas of the South to support the skeptical, yet empirical, prediction that after all the voter leagues have been co-ordinated, and after all the labor unions (pressured from national head-quarters) have as gracefully as possible sat down with their black allies for strategy conferences, and after all the scattered victories at the polls have been toted up (namely, a few legislators who refuse to vote an investigation of the NAACP, a couple of mayors who talk about the interdependency of the races, a dozen congressmen who believe in allowing citizens to vote, three or four U.S. senators who are friendly to Negroes behind closed doors)—about the only political transformation that the Dixie blacks will be able to claim is that on the eve of an election they are sometimes, though surely not always, upgraded to a careful pronunciation of their race.

That's *about* all, but there will be more: a few loads of gravel will be thrown on the road fronting their shotgun shanties; an educated, subdued Negro will be appointed to the Fish and Game Commission here, to the State Commission for Handicapped Children there (but nowhere that the boodle is handed around). Doubtless there will also come a time when state officials sit down with delegations of Negro leaders and agree that more blacks will be hired by the state for office jobs just as soon as *qualified* (a useful bulwark, that) blacks apply. It's a long, long trail awinding through the integrationist's land of dreams.

Let me illustrate this trance: When Victor Schiro ran for mayor of New Orleans, he beat Adrian Duplantier by branding Duplantier as "the Negro bloc's man." But the Negro ward bosses. claim that immediately on taking office and thereafter Schiro courted the Negroes himself, giving them many assists. That's what they claim, but pinning down just what this meant was more difficult. When I was in New Orleans in 1966 there was not one Negro white-collar employe in city hall, not even on the switchboard, where, presumably, their color would not penetrate commerce offensively. Seeking guidance in the matter I went to Schiro's public relations director, who assured me that, yes indeed, the Mayor had done a very great deal for the Negro. Pressed for details, he pointed through the window to a housing development, the construction of which, he said, had found Mayor Schiro "very sympathetic." But wasn't that federal money? "Well, yes," he conceded, "but what the hell, everything is federal money these days." Pressed for other incidents of benevolent leadership, he said that maybe the Mayor's help was too mystical to describe. "It's like an iceberg," he said, "most of it is in the unseen relationship between the Mayor and the Negro leaders to keep down the humbug." Humbug? "Oh, you know, like in Los Angeles." He added, to be sure that I understood: "What the Mayor has done is help develop a state of mind rather than concrete things, see."

The hidden iceberg benefits have been enough to satisfy the old-line Negro political hack, but they will not likely be enough to warm the new voter to continued enthusiastic citizenship. More and more these days the enfranchised Negro is being warned not to expect much, and not to expect that soon.

The sophisticated, friendly white felt a rich optimism immediately after passage of the Voting Rights Act, an optimism neatly expressed by *The New York Times'* reporter Gene Roberts: "By involving the Negro more deeply in southern politics as a participant, the law may remove him from politics as an issue." Ideally this would be true. Given his total vote (which would be no more than between one-fourth and one-fifth the electorate of the South and in no state more than 40 percent of the electorate), and given the wisdom to exercise it with all the delicacy with which a swing vote must be exercised, and given a period of forgetfulness in which the existence of a black bloc would not automatically provoke a white bloc—under those circumstances, race might be removed from politics.

Some reformers saw in the Voter Registration Law the power even to revive a kind of Populism by which the impoverished redneck and his hungry black brother will move arm in arm into a butterfly-and-sunshine future. Only a highly romanticized moment in history would find such a burden of progress laid on such inexperienced and nervous shoulders. Martin Luther King predicted that 900,000 of these faceless ones would be on the rolls within a month after the new law was signed. Then the registration began to dwindle radically, and he changed his prediction to 900,000 new voters within a *year*. And finally he said that, come when they would, these Negro votes would "eventually change the political structure of the South." He was, and is, not alone in thinking so, although it must be added that the grounds for this jubilant prospectus are hard to see.

Just why such great expectations—especially that of "removing race as an issue"—were pinned to the Voter Registration Act is not clear. The previous growth of the Negro vote had not pointed to a Great Day. In 1940 only 5 percent of voting-age Negroes in Dixie were registered, but by 1950 it was up to 20 percent and by 1960 up to 28 percent. By the presidential election of 1964 it had reached 44 percent. Wonderful gains. But the cumulative effect seemed only to be that race was more than ever a central issue, and the white politicians were making it pay off.

The Populist leader Tom Watson more than half a century ago had despaired of getting the Negro out of politics as an issue except by total disenfranchisement. Exclude him, banish him, and perhaps the politicians would forget him and stop using the Negro as an arouser; it hadn't worked out. Could the Voting Rights Act achieve it by swinging to the opposite, democratic extreme of enfranchising even the most debased illiterates? This was the hope and anticipation of most non-Dixie Americans at the time. In that happy hour nobody wanted to be the first to point out that while the Negro's cause is noble, *he* is not: he is merely people, as ready to fumble his political chances as the next race. Earl Long, in that famous Falstaffian shouted argument with the Louisiana legislature, foretold the mystic moment when the notorious segregationist Willie Rainach would wash his feet, look up at the moon, get close to God, and—"When you *do*, you got to recognize that *niggers* is human beings!" It was, as A. J.

Liebling observed, a peach of a civil rights speech; but it should also be
read another way by those who expect great things from civil rights and
voting legislation. Negroes is *human beings,* and therefore subject to feuding, selfish ambitions, splits, venality, fear, disloyalty, stupidity, and
indifference.

The razzle-dazzle of white politics will for a long time keep the poorly
educated Negro off balance and ineffective, assuming he has no native
talent for seeing through campaign lies. The poor white, certainly no more
learned than the Negro in many cases, has dealt with this chicanery for
so long that he should have developed a wise cynicism, but he has not.
On the contrary, he is still only too willing to give substance to spooks.

Memories of the Reconstruction South, when Negro majorities filled
the legislatures of the defeated states, and more recently the chanting of
"black power" by some of the civil rights leaders, have confused contemporary thinking about the black potential. A steady emigration of Negroes
to other regions has made black legislatures an impossibility without the
assistance of white voters. If all eligible Negroes registered and voted in
the eleven southern states of the Old Confederacy, black men could take
over the court houses in about 100 counties, including thirty in Georgia,
twenty-nine in Mississippi, nine in South Carolina, and twelve in Alabama;
they could move into one-third of the seats in Mississippi's legislature,
which would be their best—and most foolhardy—chance at dominating
a statehouse.* They could even elect a congressman from Mississippi. The
shadows thrown by these grotesque improbables have little relation to
reality, yet the fear of bloc "take-over," like the fear of miscegenation,
runs deep among whites, especially in the smaller communities of the
South, even though there is already ample evidence against its likelihood.
In Alabama, where white officials were challenged by Negroes in local
races in '66, the Negroes split and many supported the whites. In one
county where Negro voters outnumbered whites 2 to 1, the incumbent
white sheriff defeated a Negro civil rights worker. Similar splits were
registered in other places, but nowhere more suicidally than in the re-
balloting of local elections in Sunflower County in the spring of 1967. The
black-only Mississippi Freedom Democratic Party had taken local offi-

* One Negro, the first this century, was admitted to the Mississippi legislature
in 1968.

cials to court and, complaining that Negroes had been impeded in their efforts to vote, had had the last election thrown out. Now the Negroes were jubilant. They had the numerical strength to swing their own people onto the local governing boards. And what better place to do it than in Sunflower County, literally the backyard of Senator Eastland's plantation. But when the votes were counted in the re-run, the Negroes had lost again. Their leaders blamed it on intimidation—on the white chief of police lounging by the door through which the Negroes had to pass to vote, and on the crowd of angry white loungers at the rear of the polling place; Negro voters, in short, had to run the traditional Dixie gamut— but these partly justified complaints could not alter the fact that the main reason the blacks failed was simply that they had split.

Sunflower Negroes today, especially their leaders who worked so hard for what they considered a certain victory, are bitter and angry. So are the precinct workers in those other six Mississippi counties where, in the second Democratic primaries of 1967, 22 Negro candidates looked around, saw that black voters predominated, and considered themselves as good as elected. Just to make sure of it, they imported the eloquent black congressman from Detroit, John Conyers, Jr., to whoop it up for them. Not one of them won the Democratic nomination. They claimed total fraud. There may have been some fraud, but there was more disunity. The disunity that cut them down, the disunity that has spoiled so many belligerent black thrusts in Dixie, is nothing new to residents of the upper South, where the Negroes have voted easily for years and have consistently split. A. W. Willis, an extremely talented ward politician and Tennessee legislator, did not even carry all the Negro precincts in his 1967 bid for the mayor's job in Memphis.

Booker T. Washington wrote in his memoirs that when he arrived in Tuskegee, Alabama, to establish his great institute, he received this advice from a fellow townsman: " 'We can't read de newspapers very much, but we knows how to vote, an' we wants you to vote jes' like we votes. We watches de white man, and we keeps watching de white man till we finds out which way de white man's gwine to vote; an' when we finds out which way de white man's gwine to vote, den we votes 'xactly de other way. Den we knows we's right.' "

Washington, who got along with white people all right, didn't like the advice.

Eighty-five years later, cued by the Voter Registration Law, the conversation picked up again, and there are many politicians in the South today who are listening, wondering who will prevail—the "reasonable" Booker T. Washington, with whom he has always been able to do business, or the other Negro, made careless by life in the Bootvilles and the Samtowns of the South, who may be only too delighted to cast his vote from no other impulse than to make it count " 'xactly de other way" than what the dominant whites would desire. Fears of "the bloc" are experienced, however, mainly by the white electorate and the petty politician, the courthouse hack, the sheriff whose biggest favor for the local Negroes is that he allows them to carry on their bootlegging undisturbed. The politician who runs statewide is more curious than concerned; the important politician is not much impressed with the potential "danger" of the Negro vote, although it is good campaigning to *talk* as though he's afraid. Say what you will about the Dixie professional, he does not panic easily. He knows that, like Uncle Earl said, Negroes are human beings. Thus leadership of these emerging have-nots finds them further divided, between those who want all and those willing to settle for a larger portion than they've been getting. When Charles Evers, NAACP leader in Mississippi, went down to the Jackson registrar to sign up—in his words, "not as a Negro but as a man"—members of the Mississippi Freedom Democratic Party sat on the steps outside and hooted at him and sang insulting songs. The FDP wants all; it wants the black belt run by blacks. It does not want Negroes fooling around in support of white parties. As one militant Negro leader expressed his search: "The party of Kennedy is also the party of Eastland. The party of Javits is also the party of Goldwater. Where is our party?" So far the raggedy FDP and SNCC's Black Panther Party are the only organized response, but in some southern cities there are disorganized rumblings of agreement.

Inexperienced, naïve, badly coordinated, southern Negroes—even those who have been out in the world and contended with Dixie politicians on a personal basis—further weaken their political position by often seeming unable to distinguish potential or actual friends from certified enemies. Scarcely a Negro vote went for Lurleen Wallace in 1966 primaries, but across the border in Florida *25 percent* of the Negro vote went to Governor Haydon Burns although he sought renomination in the run-off on a purely racial platform, haranguing Florida whites to "do as

the people of Alabama—beat down the Negro bloc vote." The very fact
that Burns would dare this approach in a state where the Negro vote
totals about 400,000 may demonstrate numbskullery on his part but it
also indicates that the white southern politician does not yet have much
respect for or fear of the Negro in political matters.* The disrespect can
be understood when one out of every four Negroes votes for the man who
abused them. (Burns was defeated, but not by the Negro vote; it was
done by whites who prefer at least a gloss of integrity in their politics.)

At this moment in the South's transition, confusion among the Negro
leadership seems likely not only to continue but to spread. They do not
know which way to turn. The candidates they have to choose between are
often indistinguishably bad. And as often as not it seems that when the
Negroes try to apply touchstones of loyalty and generous persuasion, they
wind up in a senseless snarl.

For example, when then-Governor Carl Sanders talked of opposing
Senator Richard Russell in 1966, he quite normally got support from some
Negro leaders; after all, though not a man of positive progressive action,
Sanders had run a civilized administration. Sanders as against Russell
would certainly seem to be an easy choice for a Negro. But apparently it
wasn't universally easy. Clarence Mitchell, one of the top officials of the
NAACP and head of its Washington office, told me at the time that his
organization might support Russell, not because of Sanders' moderate
defects but because Russell "has an important role as a friend of President
Johnson. It is easier for Johnson to deal with the southern group with
Russell acting as leader than if the bloc leadership were held by, say,

---

* Granted, this does not hold true with some urban areas. Far from being timid
about soliciting Negro support, a Houston politician is considered a sucker if he
doesn't, and openly. When the Houston Council of Organizations, the Negro political coalition, holds a picnic, about 10 percent of the turnout will be white politicians. And, of course, nowhere in America have Negroes demonstrated their ability
to make politicians toe the line better than in Atlanta. It is axiomatic that the
mayor of Atlanta must have their support. Ivan Allen, the chosen one of the
Atlanta establishment, was elected mayor seven years ago over Lester Maddox
by a vote of 65,000 to 36,000; nearly *half* of Allen's votes were Negro, while only
250 Negroes voted for Maddox.

Yet, neither urbanization nor familiarity with the ballot is enough to assure
effective voting. In New Orleans, where the Negro has for years had a decent vote
to barter for improvements, he has been regularly split into about as many factions
as there are white factions in that city, which is famous for having as many warring
camps as medieval Germany.

Senator Strom Thurmond. Russell gives intelligent leadership. For one thing, he knows when he's licked. Russell is essentially a law-and-order man and this is an asset. It's doubtful that we could have gotten the civil rights bill through Congress in 1964 without Senator Russell's help. He was wise enough to know that anything less than the bill that was passed would have brought on a blood bath."

Except for the supposition that Russell could work with Johnson better than Thurmond, this is pure hallucination. There was not a more bitterly determined man in the U.S. Senate opposing the Civil Rights Act of 1964 than Russell. In earlier civil rights fights, it was he who had perfected the three-platoon system of filibustering. Russell is such a stern no-compromise politician that when Georgia's senate, facing the inevitable from the federal courts, unanimously approved an anti-poll-tax amendment, Russell publicly upbraided the action as a "source of humiliation to me." What other southern senator—with the possible exception of Strom— would dare not only to oppose but insult such a large group of politicians back home? The 1960 Civil Rights Bill was allowed to pass *only* after Russell had completely de-clawed it. "If they overcome us, you will find me in the last ditch," he said, and meant. His relationship with President Johnson was never the same after the 1964 civil rights fight, which Russell of all the southern senators took most personally. No other senator resorted to such low tactics—tactics absent from Russell's opposition in previous civil rights fights—which found him charging that the act would "admit the Negro to any bedroom."

To say that Russell knew when he was licked was accurate only in the sense that when the fight was over, he did not go on haranguing it; but until the final vote was taken, he was unshakeable. And yet some very capable Negro leaders find him tolerable.

Negroes are also misled sometimes by the Prodigal Son Mystique. They are not fooled when ex-Governor Griffin attends a Negro night club; but more reputable politicians often do not have to make much more than a gesture to convince them of a change of heart. For fifteen years Herman Talmadge made a career of opposing all civil rights reforms. During his six years as governor he attempted to bar the Negroes from the Democratic primary and to disenfranchise them with stiffer voting requirements; as senator he has always filibustered and voted against civil rights legislation. But for the past four or five years Talmadge has been quietly and

very successfully buttering up the Negro leadership by having them out
to his plantation, where, as the Reverend William Borders, one of the
old-line Atlanta establishment Negro leaders, assured me, "We go right
into the front room and the senator doesn't try to hide the fact that
Negroes are there. He's not the man behind closed doors he is out there
talkin' politics. Behind closed doors he's just as warm and understanding
as he can be and will do any reasonable favors for us, without publicizing
it, of course." The ultimate in this type of confusion was probably reached
in 1966, when it appeared that, sure 'nuff, that wild man Lester Maddox
was going to take the Democratic gubernatorial nomination. Mild hysteria
prevailed among some Georgians. Georgia was going down the sewer!
Among those seeking around for a solution was the Reverend Martin
Luther King, Jr., who finally came up with the idea that Senator Herman
Talmadge must return and run against Maddox. "Senator Talmadge is the
only man," he said, "who can save the state!" Ol' Hummon, the Negroes'
savior?

Negroes must work with the candidates who exist, of course, but if
politicians who have abused Negroes for years and who disdain their
support are publicly *offered* the Negro bloc, the southern power structure
will hardly feel endangered by the new force. So long as Negroes judge
politicians as much by their parlor graciousness and behind-doors warm-
ness as by their voting records and public efforts to lessen tension, there
are not likely to be any sudden or sweeping concessions to the new vote.

And what can the new voter make of such directions from his leaders?
Let him hear enough of these jaunty half-defenses of men he had always
considered to be the enemy and his voting patterns will become so indecisive that he may find himself truly integrated into that great foundation
of the Old Southern Power Structure. Only the wisest Negro leadership
can prevent it.*

---

* Another phenomenon of southern Negro political strategists, less common than
the Prodigal Son Mystique but just as daffy, is the belief that they can win by
losing. A classic statement of this position was made by Charles Evers, Mississippi
field secretary of the NAACP: "I hope Ross Barnett gets in again. We need one
more racist governor. Then the white moderates will see what a mistake it is to
have a governor like [Paul] Johnson who just sits up there and does nothing. Ross
will set back the state another five or six years, and when he does, the Negroes will
consolidate their gains and move forward." It is true that the Ross Barnetts have
been the South's worst enemies and have brought more defeats to the region than

Not long ago a delegation of Negroes showed up in Montgomery to demand that their representatives sit down and talk with them: that's all, they just wanted to talk. The television cameras were there and so were quite a few out-of-state newspapermen, so the Negroes weren't exactly welcomed with open arms by the legislators but neither were they insulted. After the initial jockeying for position and after the first flurries of propaganda and counter-propaganda, emotionalism on both sides was banked. It was at this stage that a couple of Alabama senators came into Governor Wallace's antechamber, and I overheard this exchange:

The Talladaga County senator: "If they ask to see me, I'll see 'em. Not in front of CBS cameras, of course, but I'll *see* 'em. I'll see any citizen of my county."

His colleague: "My granddaddy wouldn't have done it no different."

On the whole, indeed, the black-white political relationship in the Deep South today is no different from what granddaddy would have approved. The politician neither isolates himself from the Negro nor makes a grand production of their meeting. Wallace will meet openly, at his invitation, with Negro educators, and give them autographed photos of himself on adjournment. In few areas of the Deep South does the political script call for a mean attitude toward The Good Darkie. Many a successful Deep South politician has had profitable open alliances with Negro undertakers, Negro teachers, Negro lawyers, Negro bankers, and especially Negro preachers (in every state but Mississippi), for through these leaders the little clots of black votes that have existed for years could be manipulated, although they are not as purchasable as Irish American votes used to be and as Latin American votes still are. When Sheriff Clark, running for re-election, removed the Never button from his lapel (temporarily) and Colonel Lingo, campaigning for public safety commissioner of Birmingham, dropped a dollar in the collection plate at the Negro

all the civil rights organizations put together, but it is political lunacy for the Negro to anticipate that from the re-election of a powerful bad man a better future will emerge. The Negroes of Alabama made much the same predictions to me about Wallace—"everytime he pushes us back one step, we take two steps forward"—but then came Lurleen's victory and the black man was thrown back a thousand steps. From the Negro's point of view the federal government reacts quite well to the demagogue's rococo racism; but at the same time the white bloc reacts to the federal reaction. But inasmuch as the Mississippi Negro isn't about to win anything much anyway, let Evers play out his theory; it is good therapy.

church, these were not actions that broke with the past but rather continued it, treating the Negro voters as an inconsequential mass of childish
mentality. Such has been the traditional evaluation of the Negro in southern politics, and nothing that has happened recently gives promise of
helping the Negro to upgrade his status radically.

Fear of Federal and Industrial Retribution. During 1964, 1965, and
much of 1966, the Deep South was awash with rumors and reports that
unless it promptly changed its racial stance, the federal government
would punish the region by cancelling out military bases and military contracts, and that many reform-minded industrialists of the North and West
would scratch any notion of expanding their plants into the South. This
was the great finger-wagging epoch: If you Rebels don't start acting nice,
the economic boogie man will get you! Southerners enjoy a good spook
story, and they reveled in the fright of this one for a couple of years, and
then they got tired of it and decided to balance the risk against the comfort
of the old ways and see how it added up. They found that, after all the
shrieks and shudderings and ominous wails, there was very little risk.
And so there was very little change in their conduct.

Washington, as the governor of southern morals, has surrendered.
Reforms that could be made by Washington in the farm program to give
Negroes more economic freedom and therefore more courage in voting,
have been indefinitely postponed. The U.S. Agriculture Stabilization and
Conservation Service, which determines who prospers in agriculture, is
still pure white at every policy-making level from the county up. When
Senator Sparkman decided that the appointment of a Negro to the Alabama ASCS might embarrass him politically, Secretary of Agriculture
Orville Freeman delicately deferred the appointment. Because the decision
of who can grow what on how many acres is left strictly up to white
southerners, it is not surprising that white farmers are getting wealthier
and the emigration of broke and hungry Negro farmers to the slums of
the North and West continues. Mississippi lost 40 percent of its tenant
farmers between 1959 and 1964, and since then the rate of exodus has
not diminished. The seeds of ghetto rioting are planted by the U.S. Department of Agriculture on the abandoned Negro farms of the South.

Most Negro farm workers who remain are hungry; some are starving.
Writing in *The New York Times* of February 6, 1966, Gene Roberts told
of eating with a family of eleven on the Mississippi Delta who were sur-

viving on "pork neckbone, water, syrup, and 'flourbread' [an almost taste-less consistency, made without shortening, yeast or eggs]." Some children of the South have never tasted fruit. Commonly field hands have nothing to eat but soybeans and rice and grits. This is a condition consciously enforced on the Negroes by their white neighbors for two reasons: well-fed field hands are not as willing as hungry hands to work a twelve-hour day for $3. Also, with mechanization, field hands are in oversupply; chase them away. And, of course, poorly fed people are lethargic about voting, as about everything else, and this protects the white power structure.

The federal government has known of these conditions for many months. Northern congressmen have regularly made inspection tours of the South and returned to plead with the Secretary of Agriculture to take emergency action to relieve starvation conditions. In the spring of 1967, a Senate anti-poverty subcommittee visited the Mississippi Delta, came back and warned the USDA that there would be between 40,000 and 60,000 Negroes unemployed and hungry in that area by summer and that something must be done; it recommended that the Secretary of Agri-culture use emergency powers he had had for thirty years to distribute federal surplus foods and to give away federal food stamps instead of charging poor people for them. Secretary Freeman—who frequently acknowledges, "I have two bosses, President Johnson and Jamie Whitten" (congressman from Mississippi, chairman of the House Subcommittee for Agriculture Appropriations)—at first refused to budge; then, when the pressure got too much for him, he lowered the cost of the stamps but still refused to give them free to people with absolutely no money; he insists that such people do not exist, but Dixie blacks know better.

Wretched as are Mississippi's conditions, they actually are better than in many areas of the Deep South. Every county in Mississippi has some food program. South Carolina, by contrast, allows the stamp program in only thirteen of forty-six counties and gives away *no* surplus commodi-ties. Alabama has food programs for the poor—but none in the Black Belt counties where the Negroes are thickest. There seems to be everywhere a calculated attempt to drive the unneeded black man out of his native region; and the Department of Agriculture, which is under the domina-tion of congressional committees run by southerners, is doing nothing to prevent it. There has also been a noticeable lack of executive orders for mercy from the White House, which feels it must maintain amiable relations with congressional leaders from the South (who run, for instance, the money committees in both houses as well as the military committees in both houses).

In mid-summer 1967, the editors of *The New York Times Magazine*, lately one of the most aggressive journals in America, assigned me the job of writing up the starvation conditions in the Deep South. Some reporters—such as Gene Roberts of the *Times* and Jim Hyatt of the *Wall Street Journal*—had for months salted their news tories with allusions to starvation conditions, but this was the first time in recent years that a popular magazine with national impact had opened its columns to the topic. Other magazines had talked about "malnutrition" and "hunger," but none had discussed it in the politically taboo terms of actual starvation on a wide scale. The *Times Magazine* report ("It Isn't True That Nobody Starves in America," June 4, 1967) told of families which considered one-course diets and one-meal days commonplace, of children who considered a piece of bread and a glass of Kool-Aid to be nothing short of a banquet, of Negro clans that had to eat their rice or grits off newspapers on the floor because they have no tables, and no utensils but their fingers. The spectator at the starving game was invited to:

> Choose any shanty; only the number of bodies inside will vary. Here is a mother and six children, residents of Washington County, against the river. Four of the children are asleep on the floor. They sleep most of the day as well as all night. Their lips and legs are covered with scabs and open sores. The youngest has a distended stomach and from it the umbilical knot sticks out like a valve from an innertube. Some days they eat nothing. Most days they have one meal, of cornmeal. Washington County quit the commodities program in March and went on food stamps. Left-over commodities are all this family has. Now, it is after 2 p.m., and they have eaten nothing, but the mother says she will cook "a little something" later on. She points to a bag on the floor by the stove; a couple of inches of meal are left of what has lasted them two weeks. When she runs out of cornmeal, she will borrow something from a neighbor. Yes, she nods, the neighbors are in bad shape, too. But she will get something. . . .

A few weeks later, a team of physicians, paid by the Field Foundation and operating on assignment from the Southern Regional Council, came up with their own report on starvation conditions in Mississippi and elsewhere in the South, which they delivered to a Senate subcommittee so effectively that the great wave of indignation set in motion by *The New*

York Times Magazine report reached tidal proportions. Most southern politicians discounted the charges, of course, and Senator John Stennis of Mississippi was among them; but at the same time he said that if there actually was starvation in his land, he wanted to do something about it, and so he pushed legislation through the Senate for a $75,000,000 emergency food-distribution program.

It died in the House. Southern congressmen got the blame, and it is true that many of them did oppose the emergency fund program; but it was killed not so much by their axes as by the chloroform of an indifferent Administration, which—to save money for Vietnam—withheld its support. The national mood had been perfect for reform. Public and congressional enthusiasm had been whipped up to the point that the Administration was offered the best chance it had had in two decades to expand the food-distribution program for impoverished blacks and whites; but it drew back and let the Dixiecrats in Congress have their way.

Likewise federal officials are showing no great enthusiasm for using economic and other pressures to bring quality education to the southern Negro and thereby stimulate both his earning capacities and also his interest in government. Thirteen years after the Brown decision, less than 4 percent of the Negro pupils in Alabama, Mississippi, Georgia, South Carolina, Louisiana and Arkansas are going to integrated schools, and those who attend such schools are abused and beaten on a daily schedule. The South has learned that it can successfully circumvent congressional laws and delay court orders with impunity. There exist today enough court orders, court rulings, and congressional acts to do away with the dual school system three or four times over—but it still remains starkly black and white. The U.S. Office of Education periodically cranks out statistics to show that the integration of southern schools has "doubled" in various spots and that other islands of brotherhood show great gains. One has only to go to the South and look for himself to see the illusionary quality of these statistics. There simply are two school systems in the Deep South, and this condition is maintained in part by the very U.S. Office of Education that is supposed to correct the situation; it is maintained by the misunderstood "guidelines for integration"—guidelines which, so to speak, give diplomatic recognition to the traditional dual system.

Additionally, the Johnson Administration even lends itself as a kind of farm club for the Racist League. Aside from the fact that Administration-approved pork barrel helps keep many of the South's most reactionary politicians in office, some of the segregationist politicians are kept warm by the Administration for future campaigning. When Buford Ellington, a former segregationist governor of Tennessee, left the Office of Emergency Planning to run for office again, President Johnson appointed Farris Bryant, former governor of Florida, to take his place, thus giving Bryant an excellent way to stay politically alive until one of Florida's Senate seats opens, either in 1968 or 1970. Bryant was one of the most enthusiastic segregationists in the South; in his administration, state troopers joined with deputized Klansmen in an effort to crush the civil rights demonstrations in St. Augustine. In his role with the OEP Bryant served as the President's liaison man with the fifty governors—a very strange task to entrust to him, when one recalls that Bryant's days as a state legislator were largely given over to perfecting ways to undercut the federal government; he was Florida's foremost advocate of "interposition" resolutions, the anarchistic gimmickry the South has been trying for the last couple of lifetimes. And when Bryant resigned in 1967, once again President Johnson filled the OEP nest with a Southerner of the very same breed. This time it was Price Daniel, who, as governor of Texas (1957-1962), pushed through some of the meanest anti-Negro laws of that period and, like Bryant, was hot for interposition.

When Senator Talmadge confided to President Johnson that Georgia's moderate governor, Carl Sanders, was contemplating running against Richard Russell in 1966, Johnson is said to have replied angrily, "Well, we can't have that!"* It is not likely that Johnson had anything to do with Sanders' backing out of the race—more probably the young governor simply detected that it was a bad year for nonracists to run in Georgia—but it shows the White House's frame of mind. When racist Haydon Burns was confronted with opposition from liberal Robert King High, Mayor of Miami, in the Florida gubernatorial race in 1966, Vice President Humphrey let it be known that Burns was "a good friend." Mississippi Young Democrats, attempting to plant the seeds of moderation in that state, were rebuffed by both the White House and the Democratic National Committee in its appeal for money. Most southern liberals, that scanty fraternity, assumed that Washington party officials did not want to offend Senator Eastland and other important Mississippi politicians, whose friendship will mean more than a few thousand Negro votes, the

* A remark which passed out of the rumor category when it appeared in Charlie Pou's political column in the Atlanta newspapers.

state being temporarily lost to the National Democrats anyway. This also seems to be the best explanation for the Justice Department's adamant refusal to send a federal voter registrar to Eastland's home county, Sunflower, although the Negroes there never quit begging for one.

From such evidence one might justifiably conclude that the brake is already being applied to whatever emotional momentum was worked up by the 1964-65 civil rights acts, leaving the southern Negro and the southern liberal faced with another "Compromise of 1877," the great sell-out of Rutherford B. Hayes, who in return for the South's electoral votes agreed to pull federal troops out and leave the Negroes to the mercies of the southern bosses.

If this generation of Negroes is to know a new life, it must be *imposed* upon the South. It is all very well to talk of an evolutionary changing of the heart, but that is an evolution which can just as easily take place along rigorously enforced lines. Johnson, who for twenty years before becoming President was renowned for his opposition to the advancement of civil rights, has so far shown little aggressiveness about enforcing civil rights laws in the South. The Equal Employment Opportunity Commission has no power to penalize businessmen for showing discrimination; but it does have the power to collect data and then get help from the Justice Department in prosecuting cases. Of 13,000 complaints of job bias submitted to the EEOC, only two cases have actually been taken to court by the Justice Department. A much more powerful arm against job discrimination is the federal contracting agency of the Department of Labor—that is, it would be powerful if its strength had not withered from disuse. This agency is empowered to cancel federal contracts with any company found to be discriminating against minority-race employees. Although hundreds of such complaints have been made by Negroes working in southern textile and paper mills, not one contract has been cancelled.

Many Negro leaders saw ominous portents also when President Johnson shifted the community relations service from the Department of Commerce to the Department of Justice (the only worse choice would have been the Department of Defense), the governmental arm most at the mercy of Senator Eastland and his judiciary abattoir. The Negroes of the Deep South knew that the brief blaze of federal civil rights sympathy had been snuffed out when a band of their rag-tag black brothers crowded into an abandoned army camp for winter housing near Greenville, Mississippi, distributing leaflets which explained their being there—"We are here because we are cold and hungry and we have no homes"—and were promptly chased out by a storm of U.S. troops, headed by a general and half a dozen colonels, all flown in especially for the eviction. Federal officials said they would do something for this group; but nothing was done. Apparently the feeling in Washington is that enough has already been done for the southern Negro; the White House Civil Rights Conference of 1966 was aimed almost entirely at smothering the ghetto blazes of the North. A Mississippi sharecropper I met at that conference suggested with the mildness that is typical of these stoical, forgotten people, "If the politicians mean to help me, why don't they quit politickin' and *do*." None of the vaunted civil rights laws of the middle 1960's have touched his life. Probably none ever will. Having been evicted from his land by the white owner because he tried to send his children to an integrated school, he now farms five acres which he rents from a friendly black man and tries to raise a family of six children on less than $2,000 a year (which makes him one of the more prosperous blacks in Mississippi, as a matter of fact). There are millions like him in the Deep South. The federal government has worked no miracles for them; it has not even worked a change.

An additional irony of the Deep South's predicament today is that some observers expect salvation of racial sinners to come from the same businessmen–industrialists who were largely responsible for the way things fell apart in the first place. This is a salvation which would depend on turning inside out a region that has never given any indication that it has an inside. The money that once supported the Dixiecrat convention and the slanderous Smathers campaign and the campaign to retire Senator George, the money that once was spent so lavishly to equate unionism with black Communism—some now hopefully see this being spent to control the fury that the same purses loosed.

Those who hope for this are not so simple as to believe the businessmen–industrialists have had a change of heart; they base their hopes simply on the practicalities of the cash-oriented men who do not want to endanger contracts or equipment. Honest cynics observe that it is mostly in those areas where there is a shortage of skilled factory hands that the businessmen–industrialists are pressing for improved education for Negroes. A Negro who cannot read instructions can ruin valuable machinery and waste material; such a Negro is a debit. They will, they have decided, educate him out of the red, and no farther. To the factory owner it is not a moral question but a bookkeeping question. Thus, too, with racism and

Kluxmanship. Frightened now of their thuggish creations, which are certainly out of their control, members of the Mountain Brook Country Club are even more frightened that bad repute will cost them money. What can they do about it? They can apologize like "reasonable" men and hope that in a decade or two the Knights of the Green Forest who operate their lathes and presses will simmer down and that in the meanwhile the federal government will not withhold contracts and that tourists will not go elsewhere. They can, specifically, place ads in northern newspapers on the interminable theme of the New South.

The classic example of this salvation-by-veneer came in the "What we believe and where we stand . . ." advertisement placed in *U.S. News and World Report,* in the national edition of the *Wall Street Journal,* and in twenty-two Alabama daily newspapers early in 1965 by the Alabama State Chamber of Commerce, the Alabama Bankers Association, the hyper-reactionary Associated Industries of Alabama, the Alabama Textile Manufacturers Association, and eighteen local Chambers of Commerce in Alabama.

Nothing like it since has had the same national impact, possibly because this was the first effort of its kind—being a call for moderation by those very organizations which everyone knew had paid for the prior fanaticism—and because it came at a moment when the rest of the nation had run out of patience with the vicious conduct of the Wallace administration and with what appeared to be the indigenous viciousness of the entire Deep South. In the previous two months eighteen Mississippians had been freed of the indictment for the triple murder in Neshoba County*; 770 marchers had been beaten, trompled, shot at and arrested in Selma; Jimmy Lee Jackson, a Negro, was killed in a clash between demonstrators and troopers in Marion, Alabama; and Mrs. Viola Liuzzo was murdered on the highway at the conclusion of the Selma march.

To the outside world it seemed that the South was populated by a mob of murder-happy maniacs, and so long as that impression continued it was not likely to encourage the movement of northern industry into the

---

* Two years later seven of these Mississippians were convicted by a Meridian, Mississippi, jury of violating a Reconstruction-era conspiracy law by taking part in the murders. Was this late attention to justice also tied to the desire for a new image that would pay off in industrial dollars? Ed Lahey of the Chicago Daily News Service commented, "It was probably pure coincidence, but the foreman of the jury in Meridian, an oil exploration man, also is a member of the State Agricultural and Industrial Board, which worries about getting new industry into Mississippi."

South or the equally necessary movement of trained personnel in that direction.

Thus, for the first time in an organized way, the businessmen–industrialists of Alabama decided:

> In light of recent developments in Alabama, we feel
> that the business community has an obligation to speak out
> for what it believes to be right.

To the amazement of the outside world, to the amazement of many Alabamians, the Businessmen's Creed specified the protection of Negroes, the right to register and vote, obedience to the Civil Rights Act of 1964, and "communication between different elements of our society"—meaning, whites should begin talking to blacks.

That may not sound very revolutionary, but it was. A U.S. Supreme Court decision integrating schools and another decision integrating interstate transportation, and three federal civil rights laws had been enunciated in the previous eleven years without the business community of Alabama or any other southern state making the slightest law-abiding response; to the contrary, the response had been in support of the lawless. For good reason, James Free, Washington correspondent for the Birmingham *News,* predicted in a front-page story that "April, 1965, may go down in Alabama history as the month the state rejoined the union."

Not exactly coincidentally, Free took note in the same news story of Alabama's Superintendent of Education being in Washington to talk with the U.S. Department of Education about the threatened loss of more than $50 million to the Alabama school system, and another meeting at the same time attended by Governor Wallace to discuss Alabama's share of $1 billion in federal money to boost the economic development of Appalachia.

It was tin-cup ethics. Big business was active in electing George Wallace governor in 1962, but now that his antics threatened them financially they were rushing to "get right" with Washington—at least to the extent of saying the proper words. One of the principal organizers of the advertisement push was Red Blount of Montgomery, who has become rich as a defense contractor, especially at Cape Kennedy. He is a Republican. Another of the chief instigators was Milton Cummings of Huntsville, the largest independent federally-oriented businessman in that end of the state. He is a "Sparkman liberal." Faced with the larger peril, Republicans and liberal Democrats, businessmen all, forgot their philosophical differences.

Absurdly, some people thought this kind of public rebuking of violence would work a basic social and political revolution in the South. But the cleaning of fingernails and the banning of Klansmen from the country club are not quite enough to constitute a new South. To suppose so would be to assume that the old South approved of nightriders, which was certainly not the case. Murder has generally been considered an undignified outlet for spleen, as are riots and wars and other broad disturbances; society leaders of the South, who would just as soon that it had not taken place because of the subsequent discomfort, sometimes only half mockingly refer to the Civil War as "the late unpleasantness." Looking back on that rich man's war and the poor man's fight, it does now appear a dreadful bother; and besides, it was unprofitable. Confronted with what James J. Kilpatrick calls "the new Occupation," coming after 100 years of subtle rebellion, the economic masters of the South have reached the same conclusion. In 1965 W. Cooper Green, then executive vice president and manager of the Industrial Development Department of Alabama Power Company, said that since he took that post in 1953, "No one to whom we talked ever mentioned integration or the racial situation during most of these years. Now, however, they are asking about unpledged electors, church bombings, the vote for Goldwater, and the voters not having the opportunity to vote for Johnson. We must erase this image."

It may be unfair to observe that he sandwiched church bombings between unpledged electors and a Goldwater landslide, but as a matter of fact it is this vacuous judgment of all elements of the very late unpleasantness that is at the root of the South's present trouble—which is the gentlemanly embarrassment at being caught in perversions. And because embarrassment—and pique at those who stare at its embarrassment —is all that the Deep South feels and only in regard to those abnormalities which give it global notoriety, Dixie has hardly begun to change.

To be sure, there are already some changes. Perhaps, at least, the nation has heard the last of governors who "will go to jail rather than integrate," as so many vowed to do in the late 1950's and early 1960's. Even the most implacable segregationists know they must change their style, if not their opposition, although not all of them are capable of expressing that realization with the humorous fatalism of Marvin Griffin:

"Bein' in jail kind of crimps a governor's style." And there will be no more hilarious–dramatic examples of white registrars who cannot pass the pre-registration tests they were subjecting Negroes to,* because federal legislation has at least freed the Negro of that indignity. And there will of course be new terminology to express the old demagogic ideas, although, as Roy Harris once observed, "Some people *talk* constitution, but they *mean* race"; the white electorate will have no trouble deciphering that.

These changes and others like them that can be expected are, of course, only in apparel. Beneath, there is still the character and the body politic. Long after the pitchmen have become decorous, and after even sheriffs come to look upon the country-lane murders of civil rights workers as unheroic, and after the loud disenfranchisement of black citizens ends, the negative power of this region will continue to shoot up like prickly hedgerows between the races. Laws may make life more endurable for the blacks, but only time will bring the pleasant blandness of equality, for Dixie's mischief is in the blood and must burn itself out.

---

* Registrar: "Well, Rastus, tell me what it means when it says that no state shall grant letters of marque and reprisal."
Rastus: "Why, suh, that means this ol' nigguh ain' goin' vote in Sunflower County!"
(For some reason, that doesn't raise much of a laugh in the South today.)

Index

This book was set on the linotype in Times Roman.
The display faces are monotype Garamont and Jim Crow.
Set by Topel Typographic Corporation, New York, N. Y.
Printed by Noble Printers, Inc., New York, N. Y.
Bound by Publishers Book Bindery, Inc., Long Island City, N. Y.
Designed by Jacqueline Schuman